Psychosocial Peacebuilding

Psychosocial Peacebuilding

A Guide into the Heart of Sustainable Peace

By Katrien Hertog

BLOOMSBURY ACADEMIC
NEW YORK · LONDON · OXFORD · NEW DELHI · SYDNEY

BLOOMSBURY ACADEMIC

Bloomsbury Publishing Inc, 1359 Broadway, New York, NY 10018, USA
Bloomsbury Publishing Plc, 50 Bedford Square, London, WC1B 3DP, UK
Bloomsbury Publishing Ireland, 29 Earlsfort Terrace, Dublin 2, D02 AY28, Ireland

BLOOMSBURY, BLOOMSBURY ACADEMIC and the Diana logo are trademarks of Bloomsbury Publishing Plc

First published in the United States of America 2026

Copyright © Katrien Hertog, 2026

Cover images: ©iStock.com/hadynyah, top right: ©iStock.comJuanmonino, bottom left: © iStock.com/djenkaphoto, bottom right © iStock.com/zabelin" below copyright

All rights reserved. No part of this publication may be: i) reproduced or transmitted in any form, electronic or mechanical, including photocopying, recording or by means of any information storage or retrieval system without prior permission in writing from the publishers; or ii) used or reproduced in any way for the training, development or operation of artificial intelligence (AI) technologies, including generative AI technologies. The rights holders expressly reserve this publication from the text and data mining exception as per Article 4(3) of the Digital Single Market Directive (EU) 2019/790.

Bloomsbury Publishing Inc does not have any control over, or responsibility for, any third-party websites referred to or in this book. All internet addresses given in this book were correct at the time of going to press. The author and publisher regret any inconvenience caused if addresses have changed or sites have ceased to exist, but can accept no responsibility for any such changes.

Library of Congress Cataloging-in-Publication Data

ISBN: HB: 979-8-21636-840-3
PB: 979-8-21636-841-0
ePDF: 979-8-21636-843-4
eBook: 979-8-21636-842-7

Typeset by Deanta Global Publishing Services, Chennai, India

For product safety related questions contact productsafety@bloomsbury.com.

To find out more about our authors and books visit www.bloomsbury.com and sign up for our newsletters.

Peace is not just the absence of conflict and bloodshed;
It is not something that can be bought from the marketplace
or achieved solely by high-level policies.
It's a positive state of one's existence that we all need to nurture within us.
It's inner peace that can bring peace to the family, to the society
and ultimately to the world.

– *Gurudev Sri Sri Ravi Shankar*

Contents

List of Tables xi
List of Figures xii
Exercises xiii
Foreword xiv
Preface xix

Part I Conceptualization of psychosocial peacebuilding 1

1   Peace inside out – Providing the missing link 3

When the human being stood at the sidelines of peacebuilding 3
A human-oriented approach to peacebuilding 7
Psychosocial factors to the centre stage in peacebuilding 9
Definitions and concepts used 17
Key points: Chapter 1 19

2   Psychosocial peacebuilding – What and why? 25

What is psychosocial peacebuilding? 25
Why psychosocial peacebuilding? 28
   Touching humanity and profound transformation 29
   Psychosocial factors interacting with dynamics of conflict, violence and peace 36
Psychosocial peacebuilding frameworks 40
   Socio-psychological repertoire and infrastructure of conflict and peace – Daniel Bar Tal 40
   Peace psychology and positive peacebuilding in action in Kashmir 42
   The integration of MHPSS and peacebuilding: Challenges and opportunities 44
   Spiritual approaches to peace and peacebuilding 51
Key points: Chapter 2 59

3   The integrated psychosocial peacebuilding approach of the International Association for Human Values 67

The International Association for Human Values 67
IAHV's peacebuilding approach 69
IAHV's Theory of Change: From personal transformation to societal peacebuilding impact 69
IAHV's conceptual model of psychosocial peacebuilding 69
   Part one: IAHV model of intrapersonal transformation 70
   Part two: Psychosocial transformation, systems and structures in society 72
   Part three: Psychosocial transformation, relationships and social cohesion 75
   Cross-cutting: Promoting human values for a culture of peace 75
   Sustainable self-empowering transformation of individuals and society 77
Peacebuilding record and impact 77
Methodology: Programmes, SKY and research evidence 80

IAHV programming 80
  SKY technique and research findings 82
  Neuroscience and the autonomous nervous system 85
  SKY as the cornerstone for more peaceful individuals, communities and nations 86
 Strengths of IAHV's psychosocial approach in the current global context 87
 Key points: Chapter 3 88

Part II Application of psychosocial peacebuilding 95

4 IAHV case study: Building peace with war-affected children in Lebanon and Jordan 97

 Peacebuilding impact: Projects from the IAHV Youth Peace Ambassadors 98
 Project methodology 101
 Context analysis and description of target groups 105
  Context analysis Lebanon 2016 105
  Context analysis Jordan 2016 106
  The lives of children in vulnerable refugee and host communities in Tripoli and Jordan 107
 Project results in numbers 109
 The core principles of IAHV's conceptual framework and their concrete case study application 109
 What worked well 119
 Qualitative understanding through stories, case studies and testimonials 123
  Trauma-Relief, Healing, Resilience and Human Values Training (THRH) 123
  Empowering Youth Peace Ambassadors with confidence, skills and knowledge to build peace in their homes, schools and communities 127
  Creating a peaceful and supportive environment with parents and caregivers 131
  Improving stress management, personal resilience and performance capacity for teachers and frontline workers 132
  Training of trainers to facilitate Stress-Relief and Resilience workshops 133
 Lessons learned and challenges 133
 Conclusion: Psychosocial peacebuilding impact 135
 Videos 138
 Key points: Chapter 4 139

5 Inner integration 141

 Our role as peacebuilders 144
 IAHV's training for peacebuilders: Psychosocial well-being, knowledge and skills for increased peacebuilding impact 148
 Stress, trauma and self-care 149
  Stress 149
  Raising energy levels 152
  Trauma 153
 IAHV's personal transformation model: 7 levels of existence 161
  Body 161
  Breath 162

Mind 165
  Intellect 169
  Memory 171
  Ego 173
  Self 176
  On emotions 178
Restoring inner peace 180
  Inner Empowerment through ownership and responsibility 181
  Non-violence in feelings, thoughts, words and actions 182
  Resilience 184
Case study: 'In every culprit there is a victim crying for help': Trauma, adverse childhood experiences and criminality – IAHV's approach to offender rehabilitation 184
  Adverse childhood experiences, trauma and criminality: Survival mechanisms that become life-threatening 185
  Rehabilitation process through the IAHV/Art of Living Prison Program 191
  Breaking the cycles of violence through a transformative human-oriented approach to rehabilitation 195
Case study on the Healing, Resilience and Empowerment workshop: The trauma- and stress-relief intervention of IAHV and the Art of Living 195
Key points: Chapter 5 201

6 Weaving a peaceful social fabric – Interpersonal and intergroup peacebuilding 209

The socio-psychological repertoire, infrastructure and culture of conflict and peace – generation, escalation and resolution of interpersonal and intergroup conflicts 209
  The challenge of conflict 210
  How do we respond to conflict? Interpersonal conflict and conflict styles 210
  Intergroup conflict 213
  Reconciliation as a psychosocial process 226
Case study: Reconciliation between Dioula and Guéré tribes in Ivory Coast 230
From inner peace to social peace: Culture of conflict and culture of peace 233
Key points: Chapter 6 235

7 Creating peace-supporting systems and structures and addressing global challenges 237

Psychosocial dimensions in the security sector 242
  Radicalization and violent extremism 243
  IAHV approach and methodology in the Prevention and Countering of Violent Extremism (PCVE) 244
  The psychosocial dimensions of the reintegration of ex-combatants 248
  IAHV programmes and training to prevent and counter violent extremism and break cycles of violence 249
  Examples of IAHV and Art of Living Implementation in the security sector and in 20+ conflict- and war zones 252
  Case study: Reintegrating gang members in the ghettos of Curundu, Panama City (2008) 256

      Case study: Reduced PTSD symptoms in US war veterans 257
      Case study: Militant groups (ULFA and UPLA) in Assam, India 259
      Case study: Naxalites, India (2002–Present): From bullets to ballots 263
      Case study: The upper-caste Ranvir Sena – Left-wing Maoist conflict in Bihar, India 264
      Case study in the Philippines: Addressing the psychosocial gaps in government-led interventions to prevent and counter violent extremism in Mindanao 265
  Political systems and good governance 266
      Case study on village councils in India 268
      Case study on the Kurdistan Parliament in Iraq 269
  Economy and sustainable development 270
      Case study: Women empowerment in Iraq 271
      Case study: Healing the farmer 272
      Case study: TLEX 273
  Justice 274
  Education 275
      Case study: SKY Schools 278
      Case study: Tribal and slum schools 281
      Case study: SKY Campus Happiness 282
  Health sector 282
      Case study: Holistic support throughout the Covid-19 pandemic 284
  The global challenge of climate change 285
  Peacebuilding leadership 288
  Challenges and conclusion 290
  Key points: Chapter 7 291

8   The psychosocial peacebuilding project cycle 299
  Psychosocial factors throughout the project cycle 299
      Analysis and assessment 299
      Future vision, intended overall impact and project objectives 304
      Strategy 305
      Theory of change and checking assumptions 306
      Activities 308
      Monitoring and evaluation 308
  Synergies for optimal impact 309

Conclusion 311
  Building capacity for psychosocial peacebuilding and transforming organizations 311

Afterword: The peace that emanates from consciousness: Gurudev Sri Sri Ravi Shankar's mission of integrated peace 315

Bibliography 321
Index 325
About the author 328

Tables

1.1 Definitions and Concepts Used 17
2.1 Definition of Psychosocial Peacebuilding (PSPB) 26
2.2 Overview of Negative and Positive Impacts of Different Forms of Violence on Psychosocial Factors at Individual and Social Levels 36
2.3 Overview of Negative and Positive Impacts of Different Psychosocial Factors on Violence and Peace 37
3.1 IAHV and Art of Living Comprehensive Contributions to the 17 UN Sustainable Development Goals 68
3.2 IAHV Theory of Change 70
3.3 Universal Human Values According to IAHV's Model 75
3.4 Overview of Strengths of IAHV's Approach 88
4.1 IAHV Project Results in Numbers 109
5.1 IAHV Model of 7 Levels of Existence 161
5.2 Wisdom Keys That Are Shared in IAHV's Programs 171
6.1 The 4 Main Steps in Non-violent Communication 213
6.2 Characteristics of Cultures of War and Cultures of Peace 234
7.1 Psychosocial Drivers of Violent Extremism Addressed in IAHV's PCVE Approach 245
7.2 Intrapersonal and Interpersonal Factors Addressed in IAHV's PCVE Approach 246
7.3 Important Psychosocial Factors for the Reintegration of Ex-combatants 248
8.1 Psychosocial Changes in a Peacebuilding Strategy 305
8.2 Assumptions in Theories of Change Related to Psychosocial Factors 307
8.3 Synergies of Psychosocial Interventions for Increased Peacebuilding Impact 309

Figures

2.1 Overview of bio-psycho-social factors in peacebuilding 28
3.1 IAHV model of intrapersonal transformation 71
3.2 IAHV model of mutual interaction between the individual and the different aspects of society 73
3.3 IAHV model of interrelationships and social cohesion 74
3.4 IAHV model of interrelationships and social cohesion 74
5.1 Blind men describing an elephant 166
6.1 Conflict styles 211
8.1 Overview of bio-psycho-social factors in peacebuilding 300
8.2 Project cycle 301
8.3 Psychosocial actor mapping 302
8.4 Psychosocial conflict – peace tree: Example of domestic violence 303

Exercises

Exercise 1:	Peacebuilding Qualities 147
Exercise 2:	Impact of Stress 151
Exercise 3:	Energy Levels 153
Exercise 4:	Mind 168
Exercise 5:	Intellect 170
Exercise 6:	Acceptance 170
Exercise 7:	Memory 173
Exercise 8:	Connectedness 174
Exercise 9:	The Self 178
Exercise 10:	Positive and Negative Qualities 178
Exercise 11:	Responsibility and Blame 182
Exercise 12:	Psychosocial Actor Mapping 303
Exercise 13:	Psychosocial Theory of Change 308

Foreword

The hidden dimensions of war – and the path to transformative peacebuilding

For far too long, across decades and geographies, the deep psychosocial dimensions of conflict and peacebuilding have received too little attention. High-level negotiations and post-war recovery efforts have rightly focused on governance, security and infrastructure. But what is often missing is an equally robust focus on the more invisible dynamics that shape the lives of individuals and communities – the emotions, identities, worldviews, values, relationships and social narratives that influence both the escalation of violence and the building of peace. These psychosocial factors are not merely consequences of war – they are also powerful drivers of conflict or, potentially, resources for peace.

In the world's most fragile and violence-affected settings – from Israel-Palestine to Ukraine, Sudan, Ethiopia, Myanmar and elsewhere – people carry the weight of humiliation, fear, distrust and grief. Communities fracture under the strain of dehumanization and the erosion of safety. Even when the guns fall silent, conflicts remain in the minds and hearts of people. And yet, I have also seen something else: the remarkable potential of psychosocial resources – resilience, empathy, shared meaning, values of dignity and non-violence – to transform conflict and strengthen peace. This is the core insight of Psychosocial Peacebuilding (PSPB): that sustainable peace and violence and war prevention must attend not only to visible structures but to the inner lives and social connections of those affected by conflict, building peace and surviving war.

Today's global context makes this more urgent than ever. Armed conflicts are at a historic high. In 2023, the world witnessed fifty-nine active armed conflicts – the most since the end of the Second World War. Over 123 million people have been forcibly displaced due to conflict and persecution, a number that continues to grow. These crises affect not only physical safety and livelihoods but also the psychosocial foundations of societies: trust, identity, belonging, emotional well-being and intergroup relations. Left unaddressed, these dimensions can contribute to cycles of violence that replicate across generations. Addressed constructively, they can become the cornerstone of violence prevention, resilience and peacebuilding.

Over the last few years, an increasingly shared understanding has developed that mental well-being, trauma, neurological pathways, narratives, stereotypes, anger and frustration, grief and depression, greed and identity, among others, play a central role in generating, driving and resolving factors of conflict, violence and peace. Integral, human, psychosocial aspects, as well as structural aspects, are interdependent, interacting and mutually reinforcing components for peacebuilding. Integral aspects are part of the process of shaping structures in a peace-supporting manner, while political, economic, security and judicial institutions and structures, in their turn, can foster peace-supportive mindsets, attitudes, behaviours, relations and climates.

Nowadays, the majority of international agencies, NGOs, research departments and donors increasingly understand the importance of the psychosocial dimensions of peacebuilding. The pertinent questions which remain, however, are: 'how do we do it?'. How do we *actually* integrate psychosocial healing and strength into peacebuilding in practical, effective ways? What approaches work on the ground, in cultures and communities scarred by violence? How can we ensure that this newfound priority is not just a passing trend but becomes a standard, well-funded component of how the world responds to conflict?

Dr Katrien Hertog, the author of *Psychosocial Peacebuilding*, is one of the true pioneers in this field. For over twenty years, she has been devoted to bridging the worlds of peacebuilding and psychosocial factors. I have had the privilege of knowing Katrien and witnessing some of her work firsthand. I've seen her working with local peacebuilders and trauma survivors in places like the Middle East and South Asia, helping to design programmes that teach stress-relief and resilience skills to former fighters, war widows and young people. I've also seen her in policy forums, articulating why donors should invest in psychosocial support as part of peace and development programmes. Often, she was a lone voice – or one of very few – advocating for this comprehensive approach. It is not an exaggeration to say that Katrien was ahead of the curve. Now, as more and more of the world begins to engage with these ideas, her experience and insights are more valuable than ever.

A groundbreaking guidebook for a new field

It is against this backdrop that Dr Katrien Hertog's book, *Psychosocial Peacebuilding: A Guide into the Heart of Sustainable Peace*, makes a truly landmark contribution. This book is the culmination of decades of learning, practice and research in a newly developing field – and it delivers a much-needed comprehensive resource for all of us committed to building peace. As I read through the chapters, I found myself nodding in recognition at some points and learning something entirely new at others. It is no small feat to produce a work that is simultaneously practical and profound, but this guidebook achieves exactly that.

This book offers a comprehensive, evidence-based framework for understanding and addressing the broad range of psychosocial factors that shape conflict dynamics and peacebuilding outcomes. It emphasizes how psychosocial dynamics are embedded in every aspect of peacebuilding – from dialogue and reconciliation to education, governance and prevention. It looks at how conflict affects psychosocial realities, and how those realities, in turn, influence the trajectory of peace or violence.

One of the book's major contributions is that it provides a comprehensive conceptual framework for psychosocial peacebuilding. Katrien maps out, in clear and accessible language, the *full spectrum* of psychological and social factors that play into peace and conflict. She examines how conflict affects individuals on the inside – their emotions, memories, identities – and also how it affects relationships between people and groups, and even the wider societal structures that can either perpetuate cycles of violence or support lasting peace. In essence, this framework connects the intrapersonal, interpersonal and structural dimensions of peacebuilding. Rather than treating 'psychosocial issues' as a vague add-on, the book lays out a structured way to understand these issues as integral to the peace process. This kind of holistic thinking is invaluable. By offering a unifying framework, *Psychosocial Peacebuilding* gives us a lens to make sense of complex, interwoven factors that often have been considered in isolation.

The book provides a clear overview of bio-psycho-social factors that cut across these levels, including emotions, cognition, beliefs, identity, relationships, behaviour patterns, social norms, cultural narratives and more. It shows how these factors are not limited to victims – they affect perpetrators, bystanders, peacebuilders and policymakers alike. Crucially, it demonstrates that transformative peacebuilding must engage these psychosocial dimensions – not only as sources of harm, but as potential sources of resilience, insight and transformation.

This is not just a book of theory – it is grounded in real-world practice and filled with lived experience. Dr Hertog masterfully integrates theoretical insights with practical guidance, case studies, and even exercises that readers can use. The pages come alive with examples: initiatives that have successfully fostered healing in war-torn societies, personal stories from survivors and peacebuilders, and clear 'how-to' advice for designing and implementing psychosocial interventions. One chapter, for instance, might introduce a key concept from psychology or peace studies, and the next chapter will show how that concept was applied in a workshop for former combatants in Africa or a peace education programme in Asia. The result is that the book speaks equally to the mind and the heart. It has the scientific credibility of being evidence-based – drawing on research in psychology, neuroscience and conflict studies – and the practical relevance that comes from real examples and tools developed over years of fieldwork. For academics and students, this book offers rigorous concepts and a foundation for further research. For practitioners on the ground, it serves as an invaluable toolbox – a source of ideas, techniques and guidance that can be directly applied to their work. And for anyone – including those who have personally endured conflict – the book offers understanding and exercises that can be part of an empowering journey.

As Director of the Peacebuilding Programs at the International Association for Human Values (IAHV), Dr Hertog builds on a theory of change that places intrapersonal transformation, including the inner world of the peacebuilder, as central to broader societal change. IAHV's experience shows that when individuals align their physical, emotional, cognitive, relational and existential dimensions, they become agents of peace not only in what they do, but in how they are. This internal grounding supports deeper interpersonal connections, greater community resilience and more coherent and ethical structural change.

Another remarkable aspect of this guidebook is how thorough and well-rounded it is. *Psychosocial Peacebuilding* strikes a balance by covering the 'what, why, how, and who.' It explains *what* psychosocial peacebuilding entails and *why* it is crucial for sustainable peace. It then delves into *how* to actually do this work, step by step. And importantly, it highlights *who* can play a role: showing that this is a collaborative effort that involves peacebuilders, mental health professionals, educators, community leaders, policymakers and conflict-affected people themselves. The guidance is presented in a clear, user-friendly manner, making the content accessible to a broad range of readers. Whether you are a seasoned expert or new to these concepts, the book meets you where you are and enriches your understanding.

In my view, this work is a foundational text for an emerging field. Just as earlier generations of peacebuilders had seminal books that defined concepts like conflict transformation or human security, *Psychosocial Peacebuilding* is poised to become a key reference for anyone interested in integrating the psychosocial dimensions of peace work. It lays down a marker that says: *here is the state of the art in this field, here is how far we've come, and here is a vision for where we can go*. Future practitioners and scholars will build on this foundation – and thanks to Katrien's foresight, they will not have to start from scratch. She has given us a common vocabulary and conceptual touchstone, as well as a compendium of lessons learned from around the world. In doing so, she has also validated the experiences of countless local peacebuilders and psychosocial workers who have been toiling in relative obscurity. This book shines a light on their efforts and demonstrates that their approach is not only deeply human but also effective.

Moving forward with hope and action

Reading this book leaves one not only informed but also deeply moved and inspired. It is a call to action for all of us. The insights in these pages carry profound implications for policymakers, practitioners and everyday people everywhere who are affected by conflict or care about building peace. As someone who has worked in peacebuilding and dealing with the impacts of violence and war for nearly thirty years, I can see the relevance of Katrien's message to *every* level of engagement.

- To policymakers and leaders, the message is clear: prioritize the psychosocial dimension of peacebuilding – not as an afterthought, but as a foundation. This book equips decision-makers with arguments and data to advocate for resources in this area. I hope government officials and international agencies take these lessons to heart and turn them into concrete initiatives. It is the need of the hour to complement existing peacebuilding efforts with an equally massive investment in the psychosocial factors of peacebuilding.

- To local peacebuilders and humanitarian workers on the ground, this foreword carries my deepest respect for your work and a heartfelt encouragement to integrate the approaches detailed in this book. Many of us in the field in recent years have been doing psychosocial peacebuilding, perhaps under different names. Know that your intuition about more integrated approaches to peacebuilding is backed by global research and practice. The practical exercises and case studies here can spark new ideas and improve the effectiveness of what you do.

- To academics and researchers: here is a rich field ripe for further exploration. Dr Hertog's work provides a solid scientific grounding, weaving together insights from psychology, neuroscience, conflict resolution and sociology. It opens up many questions that future research can delve into, such as the layered and dynamic relationships between psyche, society and peace. I hope you will be inspired to deepen the evidence base, critically evaluate what works and innovate new methodologies. The credibility of this field will grow with each rigorous study and thoughtful analysis – and those, in turn, will influence policy and practice.

- And to those directly affected by conflict and war – survivors, refugees, ex-combatants, families who have lost loved ones – this book is, above all, *for you*. It recognizes the suffering you have endured and insists that the world must do more to support true healing and recovery. It also affirms that trauma is not destiny. With the right support, individuals and communities *can* recover and transform their pain into strength. The case studies in these chapters include stories of people who have found resilience and even a renewed sense of purpose through psychosocial programmes. I hope this can also be helpful to those dealing with their own experiences.

The journey towards consistently integrating psychosocial factors into peacebuilding is still just beginning, but this book gives us a clear roadmap. It shows that it is not just human and *right*; it is also *strategic*. It makes peacebuilding more effective and peace more sustainable. Imagine what our world could look like if every peace process, every post-war recovery and every reconciliation effort made the psychosocial dimensions a top priority. We would likely see stronger communities, fewer relapses into violence and generations freed from inheriting their parents' nightmares. We would likely see more peace. This is the future that *Psychosocial Peacebuilding* invites us to create. It is a vision in which peace is truly built not just in documents and conferences, but in the lived experience of people spreading trust, safety and hope.

Dr Katrien Hertog's book is a visionary, yet deeply practical, guide for turning that promise into reality. As you turn the pages ahead, you will encounter challenges to conventional thinking, uplifting examples of human resilience, and actionable guidance that can inform your own role in peacebuilding – whatever that may be. May you, the reader, be as moved and enlightened by this journey as I have been. And more than that, may you be inspired to join us in action. The human foundations of peace are lived realities that can be nurtured, supported, and strengthened through thoughtful, comprehensive psychosocial peacebuilding.

For anyone working in the field – or aspiring to – this book offers a profound resource. It is timely, essential, and full of hope. And perhaps most importantly, it reminds us that the true promise of peace lies in the cultivation of conditions that allow human beings to flourish – together.

Kai Brand-Jacobsen, Peace worker

Preface

Peace I leave with you; my peace I give to you.

It is not as the world gives that I give to you. (Jn 14:27)

We were cycling endless roads between vast expanses of water towards a never-changing horizon, blown left and right by strong winds. It was 1999, and I was cycling home to Belgium with two friends from Groningen, in the north of the Netherlands. I had been studying there for several months to finish my MA degree in Eastern European Languages and Cultures. At one of our stops on the 6-day journey, I bought a newspaper to find out what was happening in Kosovo. Thousands of people there were fleeing killings and violence was escalating. That day I read that NATO had decided to bomb Serbia and Kosovo to bring an end to the conflict. I could not believe it! How could it be, in this day and age, that humanity was not able to find another, better solution to resolve conflict than to resort to such 'barbarous' means? That was the moment and the place, on the side of that road in an undefined Dutch village, that I dedicated my life to peacebuilding, rather than to Russian language and literature, however much I loved those.

I applied for a master's in peace research at Bradford University in the United Kingdom, which was at the time one of the most prestigious places to study peacebuilding. We explored many topics, such as conflict analysis, human rights, international relations, regional security, peace philosophy and others. However, I was left with the feeling that something crucial was missing. We did not really look into the experience of the human beings going through violence and conflict and the central role that they can play to reverse these. Somehow, **I was looking for something, a switch, deeper within human existence, that could transform violence into sustainable peace.**

Since I was left partially unsatisfied, I embarked on a PhD to explore the deeper layers of peacebuilding. In a post 9/11 era, when most academics in the field were analysing the role of religion as a cause of violence, I analysed the potential of religion to contribute to peacebuilding. I developed a comprehensive theoretical model that highlighted the specific added value that could be offered by religion within a broader framework of sustainable peacebuilding. Based on a case study on the role of the Russian Orthodox Church and Islam in the Russian-Chechen conflict, I developed a detailed screening model to permit the analysis of religion in a context of conflict in order to define their resources and obstacles to realize their peacebuilding potential. Although the publication of my research became one of the reference books in the newly developed field of 'religious peacebuilding',[1] I would not pursue this promising new academic subfield. Instead, I pursued my concluding remarks on spirituality versus religion to further explore the possibilities of deeper peacebuilding.

In the second year of my PhD, a close friend from Russia told me about the Art of Living course. I was never really interested in yoga, but I somehow felt this course was going to be different and touch upon something more. I decided to attend this course in Bad Antogast in the Black Forest, where the European Centre of the Art of Living Foundation is located. The breathing practices and the knowledge shared in the course had a strong positive effect on me, much more so than any of the physical yoga exercises I had come across before. It was especially my first experience of the Sudarshan Kriya (SKY) breathing technique that I will never forget: I felt a peace I never imagined even existed in this world! This was a very deep, existential revelation for me. I could not help but think about the words I remembered from the Bible that there exists 'a peace not from this world'. Though I wasn't aware of feeling stressed when I started the course, I noticed I felt much lighter and happier afterwards and somehow filled with a new energy.

Our teacher shared that the Art of Living Foundation and its partner organization the International Association for Human Values (IAHV) also give programmes in prisons and in conflict zones. Following my own experience of Sudarshan Kriya, that was the moment I realized: this is what is needed, we need to bring these techniques into peacebuilding! I had found the switch I was looking for: a shift that goes to the core of human existence and transforms violence, aggression, stress and trauma into inner peace, cooperation, wholeness and non-violence. From then onwards, I would continue working on my PhD while at the same time deepening my Art of Living journey, convinced that this approach could help to make peacebuilding transformative on a deeper level.

My training ground in prisons: Breaking cycles of violence through personal transformation

Following my first Art of Living course, I quickly proceeded to several advanced programmes and soon became an Art of Living trainer. In 2006, I joined the then 25,000+ teachers and many more volunteers in 156 countries who were engaged in all sectors of society to uplift human values and create a more stress-free, violence-free society. Inspired to apply the Art of Living techniques to reduce suffering, break cycles of violence and build peace, I was wondering where to start. At that time, I was living in Belgium. Interested to work at the core of violence and peace dynamics, I decided that teaching these courses in prisons would be the most meaningful.

As an organically growing movement rather than a well-established organization, Art of Living did not have designated staff or strategies to organize an entry into the Belgian prison system. However, as I have experienced regularly since: when the mind is calm and the intention is pure, nature cooperates. One day, when I shared at the end of an Art of Living course about the social work we could do in Belgium, one of the participants mentioned that he teaches gymnastics in a prison. He suggested he could introduce me to the prison director. As it turned out, this prison was the highest security prison in Belgium, and the director was very open-minded and progressive in his approach to rehabilitation.

A few months later I found myself walking through dozens of prison doors and long corridors to reach a room, halfway under the ground, where twenty prisoners with mostly life sentences were waiting. I was struck seeing people so broken, so depleted of life energy, so withered away after more than ten years of prison. At the same time, I was struck by their codes of honour, gratitude, authenticity, interest to learn, and the easiness with which connection was established between us. It was not only the first but also one of the most powerful and touching courses in my Prison Programme career. The experience of witnessing such profound personal transformations, of seeing sparkles light up in eyes which were devoid of life before, of authentic self-reflection and growth and of humanization in sometimes inhuman conditions, left a deep impact on me. This stayed with me as an inspiration throughout the following ten years, during which I taught dozens of Prison Programmes across Europe.

Prisons in Europe have been one of my major training and learning grounds. I saw human beings curtailed in often inhuman systems, the failure of existing rehabilitation efforts and the resulting impact on society in the form of vicious cycles of violence, high recidivism numbers, ever-expanding security infrastructure and technology, and huge economic and social costs. **Attention and funding for effective rehabilitation often got sacrificed in the light of chronic staff shortages, structural problems, moral support for punitive approaches, a generally repressive climate, risk assessment and short-term security demands**. All too often, the offending human is not the focus in criminal justice, but 'the criminal case', which is evaluated by technical means according to fixed criteria set by specialists, and consequently referred to standard programming. I witnessed the frustration, anger and helplessness that the prison climate and regulations can evoke among prisoners, the despair and suicidal tendencies, the prisoner's dilemma of negating oneself in order to be approved by the system and changing expert diagnoses on individual cases that can completely overturn people's lives and hopes. Existing rehabilitation efforts, such as education, vocational training, sports, arts, counselling and de-addiction programmes, are supportive in many ways, but did not always reach deeper layers of offenders' inner lives. They also did not always provide real human connection, which is considered an important desistance factor. As a Prison Programme trainer, I experienced that authentic, human connection is one of the most fruitful foundations for any rehabilitation efforts. Many well-wishing, competent and skilled volunteers and staff inside the prison system establish such foundations on a daily basis, but there is comparatively little humanness and connection embedded in the system as such. Systematic research has consistently shown that **human-oriented, positive and empowering approaches are more effective in reducing recidivism and promoting long-term behavioural change than punitive approaches aimed at correcting what is wrong**.[2] The effect of empowering offenders to make positive changes in their lives is constructive and significant, while sanctions are in some instances even counterproductive. However, there is still a big gap between the research evidence and implementation in most correctional facilities.

The human-oriented, empowering, rehabilitative approach is also the foundation of the IAHV/Art of Living Prison Programme, a now internationally renowned rehabilitation training. The

Programme transforms the mindsets, attitudes and behaviour of offenders, thus aiming to break the cycle of violence in our societies at the root and reducing reoffending. Since its start in 1992, the Art of Living Prison Programme has benefited more than 800,000 prisoners and staff in more than sixty countries. Through advanced breathing techniques, physical exercise, knowledge and skills training, offenders become more aware of themselves, are able to let go of negative emotions, accumulated stress and destructive behaviour, and are empowered to take responsibility for their lives. By calming the mind and reducing the impact of stress, also anger, depression, violence, and dysfunctional behaviour are reduced. Offenders become more able and willing to strive for improvement, and become more receptive to other forms of rehabilitation. They are empowered for their life outside while they are in prison and prepared with essential life skills to handle stressful situations, live up to their highest potential and contribute in a positive way to society.[3]

> Experience testimonials of participants of the Art of Living Prison Programme I facilitated in Thameside prison, London, 2014.
>
> - *If we continue doing what we learned in this course, I am sure no one from this group will come back to prison.*
> - *In my whole prison career, I have never done a course twice, but this one I will do again.*
> - *The most positive life-changing thing I have ever done in my life, in or out of prison.*
> - *This is the only programme in the prison that we cannot manipulate*

I recall a severely traumatized mercenary who had been fighting eight wars during five decades. He suffered so severely from post-traumatic stress that he could no longer stay in one room with anyone. The risk that at any time he might lose control over his emotions and attack someone with a knife was all too real. He had been addicted to metal cleaning liquid for three years, suffered from serious flashbacks and could no longer sleep. After doing the 8-day Prison Programme in a London prison, he could sleep again, had his emotions fully back under control and could come out of solitary confinement. He was stunned: 'This is the most powerful thing I have ever done in my life!'

I have trained offenders of all possible crimes, with life sentences, on parole or on remand, with the widest range of personalities and diagnosed disorders, in century-old and hyper-modern prison settings. The programmes were organized thanks to visionary, pragmatic, proactive and caring staff and management who recognized the need for a more human transformative rehabilitation programme and often worked through many obstacles within the system to make it happen. Some of them were inspired by their own personal experience of participating in the programme, which greatly benefited their stress levels, performance, energy levels and relationships.

Supported by hundreds of personal testimonials and very positive evaluative statistics on physical, psychological and social indicators collected from Prison Programmes in Belgium, I approached ministries, federal and regional prison authorities, politicians, criminology departments, journalists, NGOs, prison associations, researchers, ex-prisoners, victim associations and foundations. The pilot study results seemed convincing enough to consider supporting, scaling up and structurally integrating a deeply human, transformative rehabilitation programme that could help in addressing some of the biggest challenges within the Belgian prison system, such as suicide, overpopulation, staff burnout, violence, drugs, recidivism and psychological harm. However, the doors did not open.

The quest for deeply human and strategic peacebuilding

When it became clear after a few years of intensive volunteer work that neither the Belgian prison system nor the time were ready yet to take on the Prison Programme, I decided to move on and accepted a job as a peacebuilding trainer with one of the bigger peacebuilding organizations in London. With my aspiration for deeply impactful and human-oriented peacebuilding, it turned out to be challenging to work in an organization which had a very clear analytical and strategic approach but seemed to lack human connection in its programming and operation.

Earlier, I had worked in Brussels at the headquarters of one of the largest religiously inspired peace organizations around the world. This dynamic peace movement, which started in the visionary minds of French and German citizens during the Second World War, has a strong focus on the human and relational dimension of peacebuilding. After the war, the movement remained inspired by faith and motivated by a deep mission for peace, bringing hope and restoring relationships in conflicts around the world through a very human, connected approach. However, I found their approach lacked an analytical and strategic dimension that could facilitate a more lasting impact on conflict and violence dynamics.

Having worked for these and other peacebuilding organizations, as well as with dozens of their partner organizations and agencies, I concluded that **the peacebuilding field needed an approach that was simultaneously deeply human AND strategic in its aim, in order to have a truly profound impact on the dynamics of conflict and violence.**

Following my PhD, I spoke at various conferences, academic gatherings, international institutions and NGOs on the 'soft, integral' aspects of peacebuilding. However, there was not much response at the time. I considered myself very fortunate though that my academic and practitioner's quest for deeply transformative peacebuilding coincided with my discovery of the Art of Living courses. It reassured me that my quest was not unrealistic, that such approaches did exist, and that it would be possible to reshape our understanding and way of practising peacebuilding.

IAHV's innovative psychosocial peacebuilding approach

Supported by my personal experience, the experiences of participants affected by conflict and violence, and my background in peacebuilding research and practice, I decided to develop IAHV's Peacebuilding approach, articulate its specific added value, and scale it up to be integrated into international peacebuilding efforts.

The International Association for Human Values is an international NGO, registered in 1997 in Geneva, with around twenty-five branches worldwide. Its mission is to build a sustainable and inclusive peace by promoting the development of human values in both the individual and societies on a global scale. Integrating the Art of Living techniques, IAHV offers an innovative and comprehensive psychosocial approach to peacebuilding. Since the Art of Living Foundation was established in 1981, its methods to release acute, episodic and chronic stresses have benefited millions of people in 185 countries, and have been successfully integrated in trauma-relief, disaster responses, education, health, prisoner rehabilitation and other sectors. Providing an effective link between inner and outer peace through a profoundly human-centred approach, it offers a model to scale up personal transformation to peacebuilding impact.

> **IAHV peacebuilding mission**
>
> IAHV Peacebuilding Programmes effectively transform the mindsets, attitudes, well-being and behaviour of individuals and communities engaged in or affected by conflict and violence. Cooperating with other organizations in a holistic approach, IAHV lays a strong psychosocial foundation in which other peace and development efforts can take root. Supplying this missing link in peacebuilding, IAHV turns personal transformation into greater peacebuilding impact.

Over the years, IAHV's human-centred peacebuilding approach has become better known and recognized: its model to prevent and transform violent extremism has been included in the RAN collection – the Radicalisation Awareness Network set up by the EU that collects best practice approaches across Europe. The new global guidelines developed by IASC on the Integration of MHPSS and Peacebuilding include an IAHV case study as a best practice example of an integrated approach.[4] IAHV's Model of Integrated Psychosocial Peacebuilding has been described in detail and published in the journal *Interventions*.[5] The established international *Journal of Peacebuilding & Development* has published a briefing on IAHV's Peacebuilding approach and its specific training for peacebuilders: 'Towards Integrated Peacebuilding: Comprehensively Integrating Psychosocial Factors in Peacebuilding Trainings and Programmes for Increased Impact'.[6] More than one hundred independent studies have been published in peer-reviewed journals confirming a comprehensive range of psychological and physiological benefits of IAHV's methodology, with direct relevance for emotion regulation, decreased violence and conflict, reduced depression and PTSD, and improved social connectedness.[7] Stanford, Harvard, Yale and over one hundred forty other university campuses in the United States have integrated the Art of Living programmes for students on their campuses. The Art of Living workshop is required training across the entire judicial system in Panama and offered to the police force in Brazil.[8] Santos, the former president of Colombia, confirmed the effectiveness of the personal intervention by Gurudev Sri Sri Ravi Shankar, founder of Art of Living and IAHV, in facilitating a breakthrough with FARC leadership during a critical phase of the peace negotiation process.[9] Gurudev Sri Sri Ravi Shankar has been nominated several times for the Nobel Peace Prize and has received numerous awards and honorary doctorates worldwide in recognition of his contributions to uplift communities, resolve conflicts and reduce stress and violence in society.[10]

Becoming the peace you want to see in the world

Since 2003, I have been practising the Art of Living breathing techniques and meditation daily. More than anything, this practice and the advanced programmes have opened up ever new dimensions of existence which I had not been aware of before. They have deepened, broadened and uplifted my experience of life, something I am very grateful for. I feel connection with many more people in the world. I can also much better accommodate challenging people and situations through a sense of expansion of my inner space. Being able to look at life from a broader perspective and to process major upheavals in my own life, I am much less shaken by disturbing events. With increased resources of enthusiasm, dynamism and energy, I am able to start up and manage many initiatives and projects simultaneously. My mind has become more silent, clear and focused, and my ability to perceive, analyse, filter, grasp and express has improved. Rather than being caught up and boiling with anger and frustration at the injustices and imperfections of the world, I am better able to observe, to turn them into constructive action where I can, or to surrender, where I cannot.

If it wasn't for the practice of these techniques, I would definitely have been a more insensitive, impatient and intolerant 'peacebuilder'. **The quality and impact of our work are to a great extent defined by who we are as 'peacebuilders' and how we engage with communities and the people we work and interact with on the ground.** This includes nurturing and strengthening on a deeper level those core aspects within ourselves that support the development of peacebuilding qualities and skills which are essential for transformative and effective practice, such as active listening, compassion and empathy, holding multiple realities, patience and endurance, balancing simplicity and complexity, sensitive facilitation, tranquillity, discernment and integrity. Rather than operating as technocrats, peacebuilders can develop their full potential, both as a human being and a professional, for truly transformative and effective peacebuilding. However, mainstream curricula and training programmes for peacebuilders rarely go beyond skills training or cognitive levels and do not bring about the deep personal transformation which is required for ourselves to become 'the peace we want to see in the world'.

Even more convincing than my personal experience has been the life-changing transformation I have witnessed in participants of the IAHV programmes I have been conducting, whether Palestinians in Hebron, Chechen refugees in Belgium, mothers of Russian recruits sent to Chechnya, orphans in Lebanon, vulnerable youth in Jordan, refugees from Syria, Afghanistan, Ukraine and Iraq, healthcare workers in the pandemic, youth delinquents, prisoners, university students, peace workers, UN and international agencies personnel, NGO staff, lawyers, journalists, members of parliament, mothers of ISIS fighters or war widows.

I recall a woman from Chechnya who had been forced by Russian soldiers to look on when her house was set on fire with her family members captured inside. They were destined to be burnt alive. As a refugee in Belgium, she would talk about this traumatic experience every day for a period of three years. However, after doing the IAHV trauma-relief programme, she stopped talking continuously about it. For the first time, a glimpse of a life, which was not the past, resurfaced in her.

I recall a female staff member of a security organization who was at the scene of the Brussels airport terror attack on 22 March 2016. One year after the attack, she was still at home, unable to drive, sleep or socialize, let alone go back to the airport and work. Her psychologist prescribed medication, but these drugs made her feel so hyper that she intentionally bumped into the car of her ex-husband. When she started feeling suicidal, she stopped the medication. Therapies did not work either. She seemed to have totally lost her ability to live, until she participated in a 4-day IAHV trauma-relief programme. For the first time in one year, she found some rest, could get some sleep and regained hope that there was a way out of being locked up in trauma for the rest of her life.

I recall the mother of a boy in Antwerp who had left his home to go and fight in Syria. Two years later she was informed that he had died there. As a mother of a foreign fighter, it was difficult for her to mourn and to express her grief and loss, since society sees her mostly as 'a terrorist mother'. However, in addition to the grief about losing their children, these mothers are also often suffering from self-blame, guilt and anger. After doing a 4-day IAHV Healing and Resilience programme in Molenbeek (Brussels), this mother was able to forgive herself and to forgive her son. She felt freed from the burden in her chest and able to take proper care of her other children again.

For me, peace starts with bringing healing to those who have been at the receiving end of violence, whose eyes have seen the unimaginable, whose bodies have been violated, whose psyche has been crushed and whose souls seem broken. It is to bring freedom to those who are trapped in the vicious cycle of violence, the prison of their wounds and the grip of their anger, despair and frustration. It is to see people in our societies smile again from the heart, a smile that is both resilient to life's challenges and an expression of deep joy and inner peace. Facilitating IAHV programmes for people involved in or affected by conflict and violence touches upon the humanity inside each one of us. It restores and revives life there where it was suppressed.

Being able to facilitate transformation in deeply wounded people has been the most gratifying experience in my life. When I step out of a prison or leave a trauma-relief programme, I often catch myself thinking, 'This is the best job in the world.''

Towards integrated psychosocial peacebuilding

My own personal journey, my professional career and the articulation of IAHV's integrated approach, as well as the simultaneous evolution of the peacebuilding field and the experience of colleague scholar-practitioners, have come together in the development of a distinct new field of psychosocial peacebuilding. They have provided conceptualization for this new field, built up valuable pioneering expertise and were rooted in constant practice on the ground. This also illustrates how we as peacebuilders are intrinsically interconnected with the context in which we are working, and are in turn affected by and influencing this context. **Psychosocial peacebuilding brings the human being back to the centre of peacebuilding, making it human-centred inside out.**

This book

Essentially, this book is about humanizing the peacebuilding field. It is a call to refocus and bring the human being and their lived experience back to the centre of peacebuilding, after having been sidelined by the liberal peacebuilding model for a few decades**.** No matter which side of a conflict they are on, people are affecting and are being affected by those conflicts and peace dynamics and carry a great potential to influence these. Research and policy should be rooted in a deep understanding of the essential human factors at the heart of each situation and embrace the great potential for peacebuilding impact through individual transformation.

This book is an introduction to human-centred psychosocial peacebuilding. Exploring the 'what, why, how and who' of psychosocial peacebuilding, it offers both a conceptual framework as well as a practical implementation approach, including case studies, examples, lived stories, scientific evidence, guidance and exercises. It is set in the current peacebuilding context and largely based on the integrated peacebuilding approach of IAHV which forms the core of the model presented.

There are many publications that deal with psychosocial factors in peacebuilding, but most of them

(1) highlight only selected aspects of psychosocial peacebuilding, such as trauma,[11] forgiveness, trust,[12] reconciliation, local wisdom, inner peace,[13] traditional practices,[14] relationships,[15] resilience,[16] neuroscience[17] and so on;

(2) collect descriptive case studies within a limited framework, such as restorative justice,[18] mindfulness,[19] or specific countries and contexts[20]; or

(3) describe practical approaches without broad applicability.

To my knowledge, there is no previous scholarly or practitioner's publication offering a comprehensive, practical framework and guide to psychosocial peacebuilding.

This book, on the other hand,

(1) works with a much wider range of psychosocial factors;

(2) provides a comprehensive framework in which descriptive case studies are embedded and

(3) has broad applicability.

This book is aimed at professional practitioners, decision-makers, students and academics working in or on conflict. As a practical handbook, it aims to encourage students and practitioners new to the field to get a basic understanding of how integrated peacebuilding can work. More experienced practitioners and organizations may find a new angle or ideas to enrich their work, broaden or deepen their approach, or gain confidence to proceed on the pioneering path they have started. I hope that anyone interested in strengthening their impact in peacebuilding, integrating psychosocial factors and well-being into their work or simply making peacebuilding more human-centred, will find something helpful and inspiring in this guidebook.

This book has been informed by my experience as a researcher and practitioner of peacebuilding in Europe, Asia, the Middle East and Africa, my global activities in advocacy and networking, the many organizations and individuals I have interacted with from the grassroots to the top levels, and my Western educational background. It does not aim to offer an overall account, classification or evaluation of psychosocial peacebuilding approaches already implemented across the world. While I have broad cross-cultural experience and while IAHV's approach is universal in its humanness, the conceptualization, angle and language in this book are nevertheless informed by my Western background. Lastly, this book is not a direct guide on specifically integrating MHPSS and Peacebuilding but describes an already integrated approach.

Chapter 1 outlines recent developments in the peacebuilding field and in the wider world which have opened the field to the human and psychosocial factors and gradually prepared the ground for the emergence of psychosocial peacebuilding as an innovative distinct approach for sustainable peace. While mainstream peacebuilding policy and practice have long been centred around more technical, system-oriented and structural approaches, recent developments in the thinking of peacebuilding, including in peace psychology, peace education, neuroscience, conflict resolution and local peacebuilding, have confirmed the importance of the more human, integral aspects of peacebuilding.

Psychosocial approaches were until recently mostly implemented by grassroots organizations, but nowadays there is an increasingly shared understanding in peacebuilding and development sectors that human factors play a central role in generating, driving and resolving conflict, violence and peace. Integral human psychosocial aspects, as well as structural aspects, are interdependent, mutually reinforcing components for peacebuilding.

This chapter also includes a clarification of the definitions and concepts used throughout the book.

Chapter 2 describes the what and why of psychosocial peacebuilding (PSPB). It starts by providing a definition and conceptual framework of PSPB, including an overview of bio-psychosocial factors. This is followed by an outline of the important reasons for its operationalization, highlighting why PSPB is viewed as the core of sustainable peace. With illustrations drawn from IAHV and Art of Living experiences across diverse global contexts, I explore the profound humanness in psychosocial peacebuilding practice, which facilitates authentic and impactful transformation that is especially relevant to people's lives and circumstances. An overview of how psychosocial factors interact with the dynamics of conflict, violence and peace illustrates a vicious cycle. The last part of the chapter offers several conceptual frameworks and examples of psychosocial peacebuilding as it is implemented in practice, including spiritual approaches. In view of the emerging global discourse and efforts towards integrating Mental Health, Psychosocial Support and Peacebuilding, the chapter concludes with a critical and constructive perspective from the lens of integrated psychosocial peacebuilding on these efforts towards integration.

Chapter 3 starts with a short description of the International Association for Human Values (IAHV) and its psychosocial peacebuilding approach, before describing in detail the underlying theory of change and the conceptual framework. The framework focuses on intrapersonal transformation as the cornerstone and foundation for peacebuilding, while at the same time addressing structural change, engaging with behavioural and relational dimensions of peacebuilding and strengthening underlying human and peace-promoting values. An overview of IAHV implemented projects related to conflict, war, violence and trauma provides examples of how this model produces peacebuilding impact in a variety of settings, at different stages and with different groups involved in peacebuilding processes. How IAHV programmes work in practice is further clarified through a sample list of IAHV programmes and a presentation of the SKY technique, a cornerstone in IAHV programming. The unique added value of IAHV programmes is explained as combining emotion regulation and cognitive peacebuilding strategies with physiological techniques (regulated breathing techniques) that prime the physiology for peace. An overview of published research on the physiological and psychological changes ascribed to the SKY technique, such as reduction in PTSD, depression and anxiety and improved well-being, underpins the scientific basis for IAHV's peacebuilding approach. The chapter concludes with a summary of the particular strengths of IAHV's psychosocial peacebuilding approach in the current global context.

The second part of the book is practice-oriented and deals with the question 'How to do it?' The following practical chapters in the book are accompanied by exercises, reflective questions, application examples, templates and figures to encourage and support readers to engage with the content in an applied way. Readers can use these materials for themselves, their organization, their projects and the context in which they work to check, enrich or develop their current way of working.

Chapter 4 presents a case study of an integrated psychosocial peacebuilding project as it was developed and implemented by IAHV. The aim of the project was to facilitate the transformation of people affected by violence, conflict, stress and trauma into healed, resilient and empowered actors of change who have the well-being, confidence and skills to address the very driving factors of violence that caused them and others harm in the first place. This project in the Middle East aimed to enhance the well-being, resilience and psychological reintegration of children impacted by armed conflict and violence and reduce violent behaviour risk. Target groups were empowered with the knowledge, skills and tools to improve their own physical, mental and emotional well-being and to design, organize and implement effective actions to improve the safety, well-being and resilience of (other) children and to prevent radicalization. This case study, rich with experiences, testimonials and stories from the project participants, illustrates how all integrated components of IAHV's conceptual framework work in practice and come to life in a real case scenario, creating profound and sustainable peacebuilding impact on personal, interpersonal and societal levels. We also identify the project's strengths and key drivers of success and highlight areas for improvement and obstacles encountered in the implementation and the context.

Chapter 5 dives into the intrapersonal dimension of psychosocial peacebuilding. It starts with an opening reflection as to who we aspire to be as peacebuilders and how we understand our role. How we respond to these questions has a direct impact on how we understand and implement psychosocial peacebuilding. IAHV's Training on Psychosocial Wellbeing, Knowledge and Skills exemplifies such a holistic approach, acknowledging peacebuilders as integral parts of the peacebuilding processes and the environments in which they operate.

This chapter on the intrapersonal dimension aims to enrich our understanding of ourselves and the people we are working with. It is structured in line with the seven different levels of a human's existence as per IAHV's model: body, breath, mind, intellect, memory, ego and self. We describe basic characteristics of these different layers to gain increased knowledge on how they function, both under excessive stress and in favourable conditions, along the scale between the restoration of well-being and optimal functioning. We also explore the human potential for empowerment, inner peace and active non-violence. The importance of the breath as a practical tool to manage stress, prevent burnout, release trauma, strengthen resilience and optimize overall well-being and potential is developed further. We explore in more detail the varied ways in which trauma affects the capacity for peace-oriented behaviours, both in theory and through the illustration of an applied IAHV case study on trauma, adverse childhood experiences and criminality. Two case studies present firstly IAHV's effective approach to offender rehabilitation, as implemented with hard-core criminals in Denmark, followed by an examination of IAHV's trauma-relief work for war-affected communities and refugees around the world. The chapter is supported with references to existing theories, evidence and insights from the fields of peace psychology, neuroscience, behavioural science and others.

Chapter 6 explores the practical dimension of interpersonal and intergroup peacebuilding. We will unpack some of the core psychosocial dynamics of interpersonal and social conflict that are at play during the transition from conflict to entrenched conflict infrastructure and eventually to a culture of war. These psychosocial factors can be addressed and transformed at every stage, in the generation, escalation and resolution of interpersonal and intergroup conflicts. Thus, conflicting relationships can be transformed into peaceful ones, social connections can be restored and social cohesion can serve as prevention for social breakdown. The analysis and suggested interventions in this chapter are informed by IAHV's model of relational peacebuilding and Bar Tal's socio-psychological framework, and supported by other existing theories, evidence and insights on social identity and psychodynamics. A practical IAHV case study on reconciliation between warring tribes in Ivory Coast illustrates how the transformation of values, emotions, beliefs, attitudes and behaviour of conflicting groups can transform cultures of conflict and war into cultures of peace.

Chapter 7 highlights the important role of psychosocial factors in creating and operating peace-supporting structures and systems in society. Since well-being, mindsets, values, beliefs, attitudes, emotions, memories, social and economic conditions, relationships and other factors all influence how people interact with social systems and are affected by them, the psychosocial dimension in the systems and structures in our society cannot be overestimated. Peace-enhancing systems, in turn, exert a positive influence on individual and community well-being as well as on intrapersonal and interpersonal psychosocial dynamics. While the intrapersonal and interpersonal psychosocial factors at the core of social transformation have been described in previous chapters, this chapter explores how psychosocial factors relate to different sectors of peacebuilding, such as security, governance, economy, development, justice, education, health and others. We elaborate on some of the crucial psychosocial factors to be taken into account to envision, create and operate peace-enhancing systems and structures in these different peacebuilding sectors, illustrated with practical examples of the Art of Living and IAHV. The psychosocial approach of reintegrating ex-combatants and transforming violent extremism is extensively developed and supported by case studies on gangs in Panama, US war veterans and non-state armed groups in India. The transformative potential of psychosocial approaches in other peacebuilding sectors is illustrated by practical case studies on SKY Schools, burnout prevention for Covid-19 healthcare personnel, training in resilience and organic farming for suicidal farmers and others.

Chapter 8 focuses on the very practical question of how we can integrate the psychosocial dimension in projects and programmes for increased peacebuilding impact. With reference to the overview of psychosocial factors presented in Chapter 2, this chapter looks into identifying the psychosocial factors contributing to and inhibiting peace in programming contexts, and into the design and integration of effective psychosocial peacebuilding interventions. It offers tools and tips to integrate psychosocial factors in conflict analysis and needs assessment, in the formulation of goals and objectives, in strategy design, activity development and monitoring and evaluation. Throughout the process, attention is paid to revisiting common theories of change and uncovering peacebuilding assumptions related to psychosocial factors. The short practical overview in this chapter aims to increase the confidence and skills of practitioners to implement psychosocial peacebuilding in practice.

The Way Forward focuses on the future development of the field of psychosocial peacebuilding. It pays attention to the importance of transforming and readying organizations and outlines important aspects of capacity building for future peacebuilders.

The Epilogue concludes the book by opening up another dimension of peace, the serene energy that emanates from consciousness, as embodied and demonstrated by the founder of IAHV and the Art of Living, Gurudev Sri Sri Ravi Shankar.

I am grateful

To Gurudev Sri Sri Ravi Shankar, for revealing depths of inner peace I did not know existed and for showing me such a profound way to build peace in this world. Thanks to Him, my peacebuilding journey has far transcended my imagination of how I would be able to contribute to world peace when I decided to do so that day on the side of the road in the Netherlands.

To my parents, for their unconditional support throughout my life, including for my, at times, unconventional choices.

To all people who were part of the journey of writing this book, through conversations (countless), proofreading (Sue), design (Hannes), or providing quiet writing space in Wales and the Black Forest.

To all peacebuilders around the world, who, through their daily acts, relieve suffering, uplift people, unite communities, prevent atrocities, restore justice and make this world a better place to live for all.

Notes

1. Hertog, K. 2010. *The Complex Reality of Religious Peacebuilding: Conceptual Contributions and Critical Analysis*. Rowman & Littlefield.
2. Lipsey, M. W., & Cullen, F. T. 2007. 'The effectiveness of correctional rehabilitation: A review of systematic reviews'. *Annual Review of Law and Social Science* 3, pp. 297–320; McGuire, J. 1995. *What Works: Reducing Reoffending – Guidelines from Research and Practice*. Wiley & Sons Ltd.
3. See IAHV and Art of Living Prison Programme website, www.prisonsmart.eu (Consulted 24 Sept 2024).
4. Inter-Agency Standing Committee (IASC). 2024. 'IASC guidance integrating MHPSS and peacebuilding: A mapping and recommendations for practitioners'. https://interagency standingcommittee.org/iasc-reference-group-mental-health-and-psychosocial-support -emergency-settings/iasc-guidance-integrating-mhpss-and-peacebuilding-mapping-and -recommendations-practitioners (consulted 24 Sept 2024).

5   Hertog, K. 2017. 'The intrinsic interlinkage between peacebuilding and mental health and psychosocial support: The International Association for Human Values model of integrated psychosocial peacebuilding'. *Intervention* 15:3, pp. 278–92.

6   Hertog, K. 2019. 'Towards integrated peacebuilding: Comprehensively integrating psychosocial factors in peacebuilding trainings and programmes for increased impact'. *Journal of Peacebuilding & Development* 14:3, pp. 333–9. https://doi.org/10.1177/1542316619862766.

7   IAHV and Art of Living Research website. www.aolresearch.org / www.iahv-research.org. (consulted 1 Nov 2024).

8   IAHV and Art of Living. 2021. *India Impact Report 2018–2020*. https://www.artofliving.org/sites/www.artofliving.org/files/wysiwyg_imageupload/India-Impact-Report-2021.pdf (consulted 1 Nov 2024).

9   Art of Living. 2016. 'Gurudev Sri Sri Ravi Shankar helps end half century old civil war'. https://www.youtube.com/watch?v=74gWGKa5YHY (consulted 1 Nov 2024).

10 Gurudev Sri Sri Ravi Shankar, Honors and Awards. https://www.srisriravishankar.org/life/honors-awards/ (consulted 1 Nov 2024).

11 Funk, J., et al. 2020. *Healing and Peacebuilding after War: Transforming Trauma in Bosnia and Herzegovina*. Routledge.

12 Alon, I., & Bar-Tal, D. (Eds.). 2016. *The Role of Trust in Conflict Resolution: The Israeli-Palestinian Case and Beyond*. Springer Cham; Kelman, H. C. 2005. 'Building trust among enemies: The central challenge for international conflict resolution'. *International Journal of Intercultural Relations* 29:6, pp. 639–50. https://doi.org/10.1016/j.ijintrel.2005.07.011.

13 Sims, G. K., Nelson, L. L., & Puopolo, M. R. 2014. *Personal Peacefulness*. Springer NY.

14 Hoffman, L. 2022. *The Answers are There: Building Peace from the Inside Out*.

15 Allen, S. 2022. *Interactive Peacemaking: A People-Centered Approach*. Routledge.

16 Korostelina, K. 2022. *Neighborhood Resilience and Urban Conflict: The Four Loops Model*. Routledge.

17 Fitzduff, M. 2021. *Our Brains at War: The Neuroscience of Conflict and Peacebuilding*. OUP.

18 Velez, G., & Gavrielides, T. 2022. *Restorative Justice: Promoting Peace and Wellbeing*. Springer Cham.

19 Njoku, M. G., Jason, L. A., & Johnson, R. B. (Eds.). 2019. *The Psychology of Peace Promotion: Global Perspectives on Personal Peace, Children and Adolescents, and Social Justice*. Springer Cham.

20 Sharvit, K., & Halperin, E. (Eds.). 2016. *A Social Psychology Perspective on The Israeli-Palestinian Conflict*. Springer Cham; Palmary, I., Hamber, B., & Núñez, L. (Eds.). 2015. *Healing and Change in the City of Gold: Case Studies of Coping and Support in Johannesburg*. Springer Cham; Sacipa-Rodriguez, S., & Montero, M. 2014. *Psychosocial Approaches to Peacebuilding in Colombia*. Springer Cham; Carpenter, A. 2014. *Community Resilience to Sectarian Violence in Baghdad*. Springer MY.

PART I

Conceptualization of psychosocial peacebuilding

1 Peace inside out – Providing the missing link

If we want to know the origins of conflict we must enter its humanity.
We must get to know the human beings who are within a conflict,
whether they are victim, villain or, indeed, both.
We must retrace the story of their anger and travel into the pain that lies within it.
We must hear their sense of justice and discover the integrity that lies beneath it.[1]

Brendan McAllister

Peace started to be studied as a specific field of Western scholarly enquiry following the end of the Second World War. The second devastating world war of the twentieth century, followed by the start of the Cold War and the threat of nuclear destruction, prompted serious interest in the causes of war and its prevention. University courses, research projects, publications and conferences dedicated to the understanding of violence and peace emerged, especially in the Western world. Since its initial focus on war causation and prevention, the peacebuilding field has broadened and diversified immensely. It has grown into a vast and multidisciplinary field and gained greater prominence in response to other dynamics of conflict and violence during the twentieth and twenty-first centuries, such as terrorism, nuclear arms races, ethnic conflicts, failed states, climate change, school shootings, migration and large-scale international peace-support interventions. While the peacebuilding field has been closely linked to the fields of international relations, security, development, conflict transformation and philosophy, it has also become increasingly interlinked with other critical fields such as climate, migration, technology, psychology, anthropology, sports, education and social justice. It has also broadened culturally, socially and conceptually.

This chapter outlines some of the recent developments in the peacebuilding field and in our current world, which have opened up the field to the human and psychosocial factors and gradually prepared the ground for the emergence of psychosocial peacebuilding as an innovative, distinct approach for sustainable peace.

When the human being stood at the sidelines of peacebuilding

When I embarked on my research into the deeper layers of peacebuilding at the beginning of this century, the **'softer', more human approaches to peacebuilding were not taken very**

seriously in theory and policies. They seemed to be perceived more as an optional addendum to the hard core of peacebuilding, which focused on the development of structures and systems that support peace, such as economic development, security, democratic institutions, rule of law and human rights. The assumption seemed to be that once functioning economic, political, security and justice systems were in place, peace would follow. Softer, more human-oriented approaches to peacebuilding seemed secondary, undefined, unstructured and difficult to grasp and measure.

Mainstream peacebuilding has been dominated for a long time by the **liberal peacebuilding model**, which is characterized by a Western-oriented, prescriptive, top-down, managerial approach to state-building, peacebuilding and societal transformation. Influenced by a sense of Western hegemony, it rarely engaged meaningfully with the people or communities it was supposed to benefit. Focusing on the state as the central constituent actor in conflict and peace, people were largely left out from the analyses and design of interventions. Local experiences, identities, self-agency, norms, ownership, knowledge, perspectives and opinions were rarely integrated in peacebuilding interventions. Emotions were seen as 'changing and unreliable' and relegated to the subjective realm of individuals, not of interest to the planned changes on macro-levels. An assumed thinking/feeling divide, long present in the field of international relations, functioned as a central organizing principle of intervention strategy. There seemed to be an underlying belief that emotionality was a lack of proper restraint and considered to be a root cause of conflict and chaos, whereas the management of emotions and their subordination to reason are a precondition for a peaceful world governed by law and democracy.[2] Liberal institutions were widely perceived as able to channel and hence manage these negative tendencies and therefore efficient in addressing conflict. Briefly put: 'In order to build a sustainable liberal peace, the fewer emotions the better.'[3]

Even though the dominant peacebuilding paradigm was focused mostly on structures and systems, attention on the experience and role of the human being and psychosocial factors was already very present in certain existing subfields of peacebuilding. This attention was especially present in reconciliation, trauma-relief, peace education, non-violence, creating cultures of peace and the more interpersonal field of conflict resolution.

For example, the pioneering peacebuilding scholar Johan Galtung already emphasized the importance of social reconstruction, rehabilitation and reconciliation as essential elements that make a peace process durable and sustainable.[4] Post-violence peacebuilding was often discussed with reference to psychosocial factors such as trust- and confidence-building measures, mutual reassurance and positive incentives aiming to induce cooperation and positive attitudes. The understanding and practice of post-war reconciliation is focused on restoring relationships, healing wounds and trauma, changing mindsets and attitudes, handling emotions, commitment, revisiting identities and other psychosocial factors at the individual and social levels, in combination with attention on truth, justice and structural changes.

Active non-violence, which is a peacebuilding strategy practised for centuries and in itself a specialized field of study and practice, involves deep personal transformation, self-reflection, connecting with 'the other', empathy and inner strength as a foundation for the transformation of conflict and violence.

Cultures of peace are aimed at strengthening values, attitudes, perceptions, feelings and actions that nurture peace. The concept of a culture of peace was elevated to global attention when in 1998, the General Assembly of the United Nations declared an 'International Decade for a Culture of Peace and Nonviolence for the Children of the World'. Peace education is recognized as an important way to promote and strengthen cultures of peace around the world, among both children and adults.[5]

In the process of conflict resolution, attention is paid to confidence-building measures, dialogue, the breaking down of stereotypes, the building of relationships and the sociopolitical capacity for coexistence, while addressing the actual issues in the conflict itself.

However, while these fields have been part of peacebuilding practice and scholarship over decades, they seem to be considered less important than the 'hard core' of peacebuilding, if significant at all.

Towards the end of the Cold War in the 1990s and the increased outbreak of **ethnic conflicts**,[6] such as in the Balkans, Nagorno-Karabakh, Chechnya, Rwanda, Darfur and Iraq, peacebuilding scholars and practitioners started highlighting the important role of psychosocial factors. They argued that contemporary conflicts, in contrast with the classic inter-state conflicts over boundaries, territory, hostile regimes or resources, were much more driven by human needs and fears related to identity, security, recognition, autonomy, self-esteem and a sense of justice.[7] In 1997, prominent peacebuilding scholar and practitioner John Paul Lederach mentioned: 'Often psychological, socio-psychological and even cultural features drive and sustain a conflict more than substantive issues. Needs, fears, perceptions, emotions, and subjective experiences, which can be wholly independent of the originating issues, are critical to the dynamic that drives contemporary conflicts.'[8] These features can create a cycle of violence and counterviolence based on the principle of reciprocal causation, in which the response mechanisms actually become the cause for perpetuating the conflict rather than the substantive issues. Joseph Montville, peacebuilding scholar and promoter of citizen-led Track 2 diplomacy, argued that contemporary ethnic and sectarian conflicts have always been resistant to traditional diplomacy and negotiating processes because of the high state of rage, the sense of injustice, basic distrust and continual fear that often rages among individuals and groups, haunted by their memories.[9] Also Johnston and Sampson stated that ethnic and nationalistic conflicts were peculiarly resistant to diplomatic compromise. Instead, they required different approaches that key into deep-rooted human relationships and greater insight into the human dimensions of conflict and its resolution.[10] Sampson pointed out that in internal conflicts, where antagonists live in close proximity, 'it is necessary to move beyond conflict management to reconciliation and healing [. . .] in order to restore the torn fabric of human relationships and community.'[11] In his study of intractable conflicts, Daniel Bar Tal stated that almost all these conflicts 'are accompanied by intense socio-psychological forces, which make them especially difficult to resolve.'[12]

Because of the nature of contemporary conflicts, Lederach argued that the emotive, perceptual, social-psychological and spiritual dimensions should be made core, not peripheral, concerns of conflict transformation: 'The immediacy of hatred and prejudice, of racism and xenophobia, as primary factors and motivators of conflict means that its transformation must be rooted in social-psychological and spiritual dimensions that traditionally have been seen as either irrelevant or outside the competency of international diplomacy.'[13] Since needs, fears, emotions, frustrations and other psychological elements permeated contemporary conflict, they also needed to be integrated in genuine conflict transformation and peacebuilding.

References to psychosocial aspects of peacebuilding could already be found in theories and reflections of several scholars and practitioners, who integrated psychosocial factors in their models and practice. Hugh Miall, Oliver Ramsbotham and Tom Woodhouse spoke of the psychosocial deficit after war, which requires measures to overcome distrust, managing the conflicting priorities of peace and justice, healing psychological wounds, and long-term reconciliation.[14] Lewis Rasmussen spoke of the need to expand the focus on 'hard-nosed' geopolitics with attention on the realm of "geosocial politics", that is the conscious conduct of politics in the service of relationships, in which relationship building and reconciliation take centre stage.[15] John Burton's 'whole person' approach and human needs theory emphasized that human beings are not just actors with economic or political interests, but complex beings who also have deeper, intangible needs such as identity and recognition, and that these psychological and social needs also need to be addressed in order to resolve conflicts.[16] Working on the interlinkage between psychoanalysis and political psychology, Vamik Volkan developed the psychodynamic approach, analysing how deep-seated emotional and psychological factors, such as trauma and identity, influence conflicts between groups.[17] Psychodynamic theory has become one of the important lenses through which we can better understand the interdependence between internal and external conflicts. In his discussion of rehabilitation and reconciliation, Ho Won Jeong reflected on the concerns of the populations that have been victimized by violence and on the attitudinal and motivational changes that are needed to deconstruct a violent system.[18] In her analysis on the causes of intrastate conflict, Anne-Marie Gardner paid a great deal of attention to perceptions, private incentives and the feelings of insecurity and fear.[19] Underpinning the essential need for social-psychological processes to deal with violent conflict, Ronald Fisher defined the goal of conflict resolution as including changes in the thinking, feelings and behaviour of participants: 'It is generally hoped that misperceptions will be corrected, attitudes will be improved, positive emotions towards the other side will be rekindled or developed, and that a cooperative orientation will begin to re-emerge or be established.'[20] In his socio-psychological analysis of international peace, Herbert Kelman focused on understanding the psychological underpinning of conflict, such as perceptions, identity factors, emotional responses and mutual fears, and addressing these through interactive problem-solving workshops that humanize the opponent and develop mutual understanding.[21] Baruch Bush developed the concept and practice of transformative person-centred mediation, which emphasizes the empowerment of the parties involved in a conflict and their ability to recognize each other's perspectives, as such transforming their interactions and their capacity to resolve conflict issues.[22] Reychler paid attention to 'sentimental' walls, multiple loyalties, expectations of an attractive future, reconciliation and social capital as elements constituting an integrative climate conducive to sustainable peacebuilding.[23] According to Abdul Aziz Said and Nathan Funk, conflict resolution refers to the affirmation of identity, the restoration of meaning, social reintegration, restoration and redemption, existential security, personal transcendence, and transformation.[24] Adam Curle distinguished the inner and outer, the private and public, or the yin and yang dimensions of peacemaking, where the former refers to the psychological atmosphere, attitudes and feelings.[25] Gopin spoke about 'healing the heart of conflict' and 'deep peacemaking.'[26]

There was a distinct school within peacebuilding that emphasized the central role of individuals, communities and relationships in peacebuilding and that came to be known as the **people-centred approach**. This approach sees people as the real means and end to making peace sustainable. It has been represented by excellent scholar-practitioners in the field such as John Paul Lederach, Marc Gopin, Susan Allen Nan, and organizations such as CDA Collaborative Learning. As peacebuilding scholar and practitioner Susan Allen summarizes in her book on Interactive Peacemaking: 'While institutions and governance structures surely influence war and peace, individuals are essential drivers of peacemaking. People make peace. Many individual people make choices that add up to war or peace. . . . Only three things [that] matter in peacemaking: people, people, and people.'[27] However, until the 1990s, this school had mostly remained on the margins of peacebuilding, often implemented in the form of community peacebuilding by individuals or grassroot non-governmental organizations on a local scale.

Major peace agreements, respective policy decisions and the majority of funds for peacebuilding at national and international levels had all been centred around more technical, system-oriented, structural approaches to peacebuilding. The human being had been on the sidelines of peacebuilding for a long time.

A human-oriented approach to peacebuilding

Nowadays there is an increasingly shared understanding in the peacebuilding and development sectors that **people play a central role in generating, driving and resolving factors of conflict, violence and peace.** There is a general realization that mental well-being, trauma, neurological pathways, narratives, stereotypes, identities, greed, anger, frustration, grief and depression, among others, are strong influencing factors which can undermine peace and development plans. Intervening agencies, international peace missions, NGOs, policymakers and practitioners have learned by experience, for example, that vocational training for youth to increase employment opportunities and improve livelihoods is hampered when the youth feel too depressed to take part, do not have hope for any improvement, or are too worried to be able to focus on learning. Restorative justice practice remains superficial when it does not engage deeply with healing processes, truth-telling, introspection and relationships. Demobilization and disarmament processes can be disrupted when basic trust between groups is not restored and combatant identities not transformed. Structurally reforming the security sector, equipping armies and training police forces can turn out to be counterproductive when mindsets, loyalties and value systems remain unchanged.

The human being who lives in fear of violence, in the midst of violence, or who lived through violent conflict, is **crucial to conflict and peace dynamics**. A **human-oriented approach to peacebuilding** focuses our lens on the broken lives of individuals who are traumatized, raped or tortured, who have lost close family members and homes, who are paralyzed by fear, or uprooted from their daily lives as they know them. It focuses on shattered communities in need of reconciliation. It focuses on the mindset of a leader, whose thinking pattern is challenged by a personal encounter; on the inner conviction of a man who chose to confront violence with compassion; on the belief of young people in conflict regions that they can shape a different future; on nurturing social climates of isolation and radicalization into mutual understanding and cooperation.

Daniel Bar Tal, expert on the social psychology of intergroup conflict, states that there are many aspects to intergroup conflict, such as historical, political, economic, sociological and cultural, but 'first of all there is a need to recognise that it is human beings who initiate conflict, take part in them, manage them and sometimes peacefully resolve them. Human beings perceive, evaluate, infer and act. These human psychological behaviours are integral parts of conflicts' interactions as **human beings are the only actors on the conflict stage**.'[28] 'Even in large-scale international, interethnic and intrasocietal conflicts, people (leaders and other society members) are the ones who perceive and evaluate situations as a conflict', and act accordingly.[29]

Social psychology has a long tradition of studying human conflict behaviour and provides some of the core knowledge to understand the dynamics of conflict and peacemaking. A basic tenet of social psychology is that how people think and feel is important to understand why they act the way they do.[30] The social-psychological approach tries to reveal the thoughts, feelings and behaviours that are underlying the evolution and maintenance of the conflict as well as later its eventual resolution and reconciliation. Thus, peacebuilding must be initiated in human minds first. As it is said and heard often nowadays, **no outer peace without inner peace**. For any outer peace to be sustainable, peace needs to be internalized and socially supported as well.

The international community can spend billions to uphold peace-enhancing structures and systems in conflict-affected countries, only to see these 'peace frameworks' collapse the moment this structural support is withdrawn because a strong **psychosocial foundation towards peace** has been missing. Large-scale state-building projects have failed partially because of misperceptions, misunderstandings and misrepresentations among the actors involved.[31] Emotions of exclusion, frustration, alienation and anger among the target populations regularly turned out to be counterproductive to the goals set by ambitious peacebuilding mandates.

One can only speculate how Afghanistan would look today if half the resources spent by the international community over the last twenty years had been focused on effectively engaging with psychosocial factors of trauma, identity, frustration, hopelessness, resilience, values, grief, grievances and more. In Rwanda and Bosnia-Herzegovina, where the scale and severity of atrocities committed affected every citizen directly or indirectly, it became particularly clear that attention to systemic and structural restoration needed to be complemented with profound psychosocial transformation. Perpetrators and victims living next door to each other in a small country posed an immediate challenge to the possibilities of peaceful coexistence and a risk of perpetually repeating cycles of violence with interchanging roles. As a representative of an African MHPSS/Peacebuilding organization shared: 'We have not appreciated the depth of the woundedness of society. This interferes and hinders the peacebuilding and governance investments that we bring to rebuild our communities.'[32] In Israel-Palestine, core conflict issues around security, territory, water, structural inequality, representation and human rights have been deeply exacerbated, escalated and entrenched in a vicious cycle by psychosocial dynamics related to identities, grievances, loss, trauma, frustration, radicalization, beliefs, narratives, deep existential fears and more. Also closer at home, at the domestic level, anger, depression, trauma and high stress can lead to various forms of conflict, violence and abuse within a family, despite good socio-economic circumstances.

It is now clear that emotional, psychological, socio-psychological and existential-spiritual issues are an integral part of peacebuilding and development.

Integrated peacebuilding

Both integral, human, psychosocial aspects and structural aspects are interdependent, interacting and mutually reinforcing components for peacebuilding. Integral aspects lay a strong and healthy psychosocial foundation and are needed to shape and operationalize structures in a peace-supporting manner, while political, economic, security and judicial institutions and structures can foster peace-supportive mindsets, attitudes, well-being, behaviours, relationships and climates.

Therefore, it is the need of the hour to complement existing peacebuilding efforts with an equally massive investment in the (often) intangible psychosocial factors of peacebuilding.

Psychosocial factors to the centre stage in peacebuilding

There is now a much clearer understanding of the need for effective psychosocial approaches to peacebuilding as well as much more openness to ways of peacebuilding

beyond the mainstream Western approaches. This is reflected in **ongoing developments in different fields of peacebuilding**.

During the last twenty years, **peace psychology** has further developed and expanded as a distinct field with its own concepts, perspectives, knowledge expertise and methods.[33] While the focus of peace psychologists during the Cold War was mostly on the prevention of the annihilation of humanity, it evolved into researching the various psychological dimensions of conflict, war, violence and peace, including direct, structural and cultural violence. Developed within the field of psychology, it places human psychology at the centre of violence prevention, conflict resolution and peacebuilding. From a deep understanding that today's global challenges need psychologically informed theory and practice, human well-being and harmonious relationships are at the core of its endeavour.[34] Peace Psychology researchers and practitioners highlight the importance of inner peace as the prerequisite for social peace.[35] They focus, for example, on mindful awareness, emotion regulation, cognitive reappraisal, empathy and compassion, all of which help individuals to recognize and navigate opportunities for peacebuilding.[36]

The attention on specifically the role of **emotions and affect** has greatly developed across the fields of political psychology, international relations, peace psychology and conflict transformation. While emotions were previously disregarded as unhelpful and subordinate to reason, they are now proactively engaged in conflict transformation theory, research and practice based on the understanding that conflict is emotionally defined and therefore working with emotions is necessary for conflict transformation. The focus on emotions is broad and includes the fostering of peace-enhancing emotions, the transforming of peace-inhibiting emotions, emotional intelligence, the leveraging of individual emotions into the public sphere, the role of emotions in decision-making, emotional worldviews and much more.[37] The Center for Compassion and Altruism Research and Education at Stanford University School of Medicine conducts scientific studies specifically on compassion and altruistic behaviour in collaboration with neuroscientists, behavioural scientists, geneticists and biomedical researchers.

Peace Psychology has close roots and links to the study of human conflict behaviour in the field of **social psychology**. Very early on, social psychologists studied prejudice, perceptions, social identity, group formation, competition and cooperation, and developed simulations to understand human behaviour in conflict. They have shown that intractable conflicts are often seen as zero-sum, irresolvable, and even existential—threatening goals, needs, or values that a group considers essential for its survival. Such conflicts seep into the minds and daily lives of those who endure them, demanding enormous psychological resources simply to cope with them, let alone to transform them.

Insights from behavioural science, drawing on neuroscience, psychology, sociology, economy and other disciplines, also show that as human beings, we do not always follow rational courses of action. Behavioural science investigates why we as human beings make the decisions we make and behave the way we do. Behavioural insights related to peacebuilding focus, for example, on cognitive bias, emotional regulation, group identity, trust mechanisms, stereotypes and decision-making under stress. Because of the specifics of human behaviour, behavioural scientists argue for the integration of more human-centred approaches to policies and projects.

The last two decades have also seen a surge in interest in **locally led and traditional peacebuilding practices.**[38] Intervening actors have experienced that working without involving local communities or solely with national elites does not make peace sustainable. Engagement with local communities is needed to embed projects within a context, tailor them to local needs and cultural expectations and build on pre-existing local peace systems and knowledge. The emancipatory approach has consistently focused on the strength and agency of all people, challenging the focus on international actors and on the state actor as being dominant, and critically reviewing mainstream Western understandings of power, agency and legitimacy.

While this so-called 'local turn' in peacebuilding acknowledges and engages local agency and capacity, the voice and presence of local peacemakers from the local to the global scene have also become stronger. Local and traditional approaches to peacebuilding are geographically, culturally and socially close to people's lives; hence, they naturally pay more attention to psychosocial factors and integrate relevant contextual factors in their peace work.

The need for increased attention on emotions, attitudes, identities and relationships in peacebuilding also contributed to the increasing development of 'creative' peace methods. These are often implemented at the grassroots level through different forms of art, sport, theatre, storytelling, memory work, music, audio-visual initiatives and other digital and artificial intelligence projects.

Relationships, perceptions, emotions and identity are also at the core of the concept of **'every day peace'** in conflict and war zones. 'Every day peace' acknowledges that individuals decide to engage, avoid or resist conflictual tendencies in their daily interactions. Thus, they may maintain cooperation with enemy others, even in the midst of war or when tensions dominate intergroup relations in the larger societal context.

While the field of modern peace studies and peacebuilding has been dominated by Western concepts and rationality, the last decade saw a huge surge in the acknowledgement and appreciation of **other cultural approaches to peace and peacebuilding**. Across time and place, peace has been understood in many different ways: as a state of mind, a process, a value system, a social concept, an experience, an absence of war, an institutional or constitutional framework and more. This recent cultural and social opening in the field broadened the understanding of peace and peacebuilding from the more rational and moral concepts of modern peace thinking to include also spiritual, relational and energetic dimensions of peace. These dimensions are still present in many cultures around the world and often form the core of the experience of individual and social peace.[39]

The inclusion of varied peace and peacebuilding concepts and practices in the peacebuilding field as a whole is facilitated by the recent idea of **hybrid peace**. This suggests that there exist multiple 'peaces' across societies, cultures and states around the world at the same time. The aim of the peacebuilding field here is to enable coexistence among different entities practising different forms of peace.[40] Embracing the diversity and complexity of human life and organization, the concept of hybrid peace entails much more openness to and appreciation of varied psychosocial factors of human existence. With the previously dominant liberal peacebuilding model being criticized by many actors and from a varied range of angles, space has opened up for more inclusive and comprehensive approaches to peacebuilding.

In the subfield of religious peacebuilding, which analyses the potential of religions to contribute to peace and peacebuilding, psychosocial factors also play a central role, since it looks at beliefs, value systems, ethics, identities, spiritual experiences, meaning systems and other deeply human factors embedded in different traditions.[41]

Also, the field of peace education, which has developed over decades and is now well recognized in both formal and informal educational settings, aims to empower children and adults with understanding, skills and attitudes to handle conflicts non-violently and create more peaceful coexistence.

Restorative justice is another exponentially growing field within peacebuilding that looks intensely into psychosocial factors. It is a people-centred approach to justice that aims to repair harm, support survivors, restore relationships and rehabilitate perpetrators of crime and violence.[42]

Human security has emerged as a prominent paradigm in considering security at the human level, thus complementing the earlier overwhelming focus on national security. This people-centred approach to security includes psychosocial factors of strengthening local resilience, enhancing social cohesion, the aspiration towards freedom from fear and want and adherence to respect for human rights and dignity.

Interest in the neuroscience for peacebuilding has also developed greatly in recent years thanks to new scientific discoveries opening up new research possibilities. The nexus between neuroscience and peacebuilding looks at how experiences of violence, stress and trauma affect the brain and body and therefore our emotions and behaviour. It also looks at how the intricate functioning of the human nervous system can inform peacebuilding processes, such as supporting dialogue, fostering reconciliation, preventing violence and addressing fundamental causes of injustice and societal divisions.[43] Neuroscience explores the neurobiological underpinnings of key processes, such as existential fears, 'us versus them' thinking, empathy, dehumanization and trauma. It informs our understanding about the important role of the human brain and body in defining our attitudes, emotions, behaviours, decisions and actions or reactions. The growing body of neuroscientific research and the increasing understanding are a fundamental contribution to the peacebuilding field. Its insights can help resolve some persistent challenges related to conflict transformation, reconciliation and sustainable peacebuilding. Neuroscience also explains that the nervous system of any intervenor or peacebuilder influences the environment she works in and that it is therefore important to become aware of this and learn how to handle it best.

Psychosocial factors also come to the fore in systems thinking, an approach that connects human individuals and communities with the systems in which they live and operate. Systems thinking has also become part of mainstream peacebuilding theory and practice, locating the individual in a web of relationships and social, political, economic and other systems. Comprising the different levels, the personal, psychological and inter-relational aspects are intrinsically included in these paradigms.

Against the background of these developments in the peacebuilding field, **several scholars, practitioners and institutions have focused explicitly on the integrated approach of psychosocial peacebuilding.**

For example, the American Psychological Association (APA), the leading professional organization representing psychologists in the United States, established the division of Peace Psychology in 1990. In 1995, APA's Peace Psychology division launched the journal *Peace and Conflict: Journal of Peace Psychology*, which has been publishing quarterly issues ever since, including new theories, reflections and hundreds of case studies from around the world. Daniel Christie, the former president of the APA Peace Psychology Division and editor of *Peace and Conflict*, also edited Springer's Book Series on Peace Psychology, which has published entire specialized volumes on the intersection between peace, conflict, violence and psychology since 2008. In 2001, Christie, together with Wagner and Winter, also published the reference book 'Peace, Conflict, and Violence: Peace Psychology for the 21st Century', collecting research and case studies from around the world linking psychology with direct violence, structural violence, peacemaking and peacebuilding.

In 2011, the social psychologist Daniel Bar Tal published the important key work 'Intergroup Conflicts and Their Resolution: A Social Psychological Perspective'. This was followed in 2013 by 'Intractable Conflicts: Socio-Psychological Foundations and Dynamics', which applies a social-psychological lens to various aspects of intractable conflicts, such as identity, memory, perceptions, ideologies, emotions, negotiation, reconciliation and peacemaking.[44] Through his study of intractable conflicts over several decades, Bar Tal developed an elaborate framework to understand the socio-psychological foundations and dynamics that lead to societal involvement in intractable conflicts and to elucidate those that can facilitate peacemaking. In a comprehensive model, he distinguishes the psychological challenges that arise in order to cope with intractable conflict, the socio-psychological repertoire that emerges to meet these challenges, how this repertoire gets solidified as a dominant socio-psychological infrastructure over time, and eventually evolves into a culture of conflict. Such culture, in turn, becomes the major inhibiting factor to the resolution of the conflict. Bar-Tal also explains how peacemaking entails the challenging process of replacing this negative socio-psychological repertoire with a peace-promoting one. Apart from providing an in-depth comprehensive framework of psychosocial factors involved in intergroup and intractable conflicts, Bar Tal made a major contribution to peacebuilding excellence by highlighting the psychosocial repertoire as a crucial, if not the most crucial dimension in conflict and peacebuilding, while at the same time articulating his framework in a clear and digestible format.

In 2015, Brandon Hamber together with Elizabeth Gallagher, published another key volume, *Psychosocial Perspectives on Peacebuilding*, a collection of varied case studies from around the world describing how psychosocial interventions are part of and interact with the context.[45]

Hamber is also one of the leading experts developing a more comprehensive approach within the UN that integrates mental health and psychosocial support into restorative justice.

In 2012, Deutsch and Coleman made an important contribution with their work on the psychological components of sustainable peace in which they examined the components of various psychological theories that contribute to the promotion of peace.[46] Rather than concentrating solely on conflict prevention and violence reduction, they examined the underlying psychological conditions that enhance the likelihood of enduring, cooperative peace.

Another important source of information for the study of psychosocial dimensions of conflict, violence and peace is *Intervention*,[47] *the Journal of Mental Health & Psychosocial Support in Conflict Affected Areas*. This is published twice a year and hosted by ARQ International. Intervention has focused on publishing articles related to mental health, psychosocial support and peacebuilding for individuals working in conflict-affected areas or with refugees from armed conflict.

Attention to psychosocial factors in peacebuilding has also increased due to rising awareness of certain developments in our world.

Firstly, there is the increased use and the spreading of forms of violence which are deliberately perpetrated with the aim of destroying life and ways of life beyond the obvious 'battlefield'.[48] Such **violence, intended to break people and societies, is especially characterized by deep psychosocial impacts**. It includes using rape as a weapon of war, eliminating cultures, rewriting history, transforming education into brainwashing, persecution of intellectuals, infiltrating social fabrics, misinformation campaigns, undermining values, destroying essential civil infrastructure, and so on.

The mere **scale of violence and displacement around the world** also calls for new approaches and solutions. In 2022, fifty-six states experienced armed conflict and more of these conflicts have become intractable. Millions of people were affected by floods, heatwaves and drought. The UN reported a tragic record of over 100 million forcibly displaced people, including 48 million internally displaced persons, 26.6 million refugees and 35 million children.[49] In 2023, the Global Peace Index recorded fifty-two major conflicts, the highest number since the Second World War. Ninety-seven countries deteriorated in their levels of peacefulness and ninety-two countries were involved in conflicts beyond their borders. This was more than in any year since the inception of the Global Peace Index in 2008.[50] The global economic impact of violence increased to 19.1 trillion US dollars in 2023, or 2,380 US dollars per person, representing 13.5 per cent of the global GDP. The state of our world clearly calls for new and innovative approaches to violence prevention and sustainable peacebuilding. Given WHO's estimate that one in five people who live in a war zone will likely develop a mental disorder,[51] the importance of Mental Health and Psychosocial Support (MHPSS) in humanitarian, peacebuilding and development settings is increasingly evident.

In addition, global challenges around mental and physical health, climate change, migration, economic and financial crises have raised questions about the underpinning **social-ecological models** that facilitate these crises, and the values and attitudes that these models entail. In light of these multiple crises and pressures on people, core psychosocial concepts such as **resilience, agility and mindfulness** have become mainstream thought in many sectors around the world.

Illustrative of this rising awareness of psychosocial factors was the focus of the trend-setting 2015 World Development Report of the World Bank on Mind, Society, and Behaviour, recognizing the impact of the human mind and decision-making on development outcomes.[52]

Well-being and peacebuilding are also at the core of the Sustainable Development Goals, especially SDG 3 (Good Health and Well-being) and SDG 16 (Peace, Justice and Strong Institutions), which connect the goals of individual and societal well-being, stability and sustainable development.

The **importance of mental health** as a strong foundation for the overall well-being and thriving of individuals and the sustaining of peaceful relationships and well-functioning societies has also gained more prominence, especially following the Covid-19 pandemic. The impact of heightened psychological distress due to Covid-related challenges has become clear across all sectors. These challenges include isolation, unemployment, poverty, domestic tension, financial stress, the lonely death of family members, health concerns, discrimination, injustice and divisive policies, to name just a few. UN Women (the United Nations Organization for the Empowerment of Women) spoke about the shadow pandemic of increased domestic and gender-based violence since the outbreak of Covid-19. Many women were trapped with their abusers and isolated from social contact and support networks due to lockdowns, mobility restrictions and increased economic precariousness. These factors further limited women's ability to leave abusive situations.[53] In November 2021, the World Health Organization (WHO) reported that the Covid-19 pandemic had a severe impact on the mental health and well-being of people around the world, including a 27.6 per cent increase in cases of major depressive disorder and a 25.6 per cent increase in cases of anxiety disorders worldwide.[54] 'This is a wake-up call to all countries to pay more attention to mental health and do a better job of supporting their populations' mental health,' said Dr Tedros Adhanom Ghebreyesus, WHO Director-General.[55] It prompted WHO Member States to scale up mental health services and psychosocial support as an integral component of universal health coverage. The WHO has predicted that by 2030, depression will be the leading cause of the disease burden globally.[56] The economic impact of mental health conditions such as depression and anxiety is estimated to cost the global economy $1 trillion annually in lost productivity according to a 2016 joint study by WHO and the World Bank.[57] The cost of mental health issues, including burnout, is expected to rise to 16 trillion dollars by 2030.[58]

As part of this new awareness, **global efforts are now also under way to bridge the fields of Mental Health, Psychosocial Support (MHPSS) and Peacebuilding**. From the local to the global level, individuals, organizations and institutions are identifying best practices, developing models, writing frameworks and guidelines, issuing policy statements, collecting data, organizing discussions and much more in the field of research, policy and practice. In his July 2020 Report on Peacebuilding and Sustaining Peace, the UN Secretary-General explicitly referred to the need for MHPSS in Peacebuilding: 'The further development of the integration of mental health and psychosocial support into peacebuilding is envisaged with a view to increasing the resilience and agency of people and communities.' In 2022–4, UNDP and the International Agency Standing Committee published global guidelines on the integration of Mental Health, Psychosocial Support and Peacebuilding, including examples of best practices from the grassroots and community levels. As one practitioner shared, however: 'The needed approach is much broader than just bringing MHPSS and peacebuilding together ... the high levels of violence and conflict all over the world urgently require an improved understanding of how cycles of violence work.'[59]

In the ongoing discussions and developments described above, much attention is paid to the **deficit** of well-being and to the impact of weak or negative psychosocial factors in undermining peacebuilding and thriving societies. Similarly, mainstream peacebuilding (with the exception of peace psychology and conflict resolution) largely focuses on the role and transformation of negative and destructive emotions rather than on the positive impact of peace-enhancing emotions, as productive and constitutive elements of identity and community building.[60] In discussions on peacebuilding and related psychosocial factors, there is in particular a great emphasis on trauma. While attention to trauma is crucial, the theme is often framed in a pathologizing and disempowering approach. All too often, populations in war and conflict zones are seen as 'vulnerable damaged victims requiring third party support for self-empowerment'.[61] Trauma is also perceived as 'potentially conflict producing', without necessarily taking into account the structural and cultural violence that is at the root of the traumatizing events in the first place. There is also a risk of responding with a medicalized or narrow healthcare approach that does not capture the broader impacts of armed conflict, and does not pay attention to the resources, cultural specificities, resiliences or other factors affecting the well-being of populations in conflict settings.[62] In addition, 'an approach to addressing trauma requires a different question, moving beyond "what happened to you" to "what's right with you", and viewing those exposed to trauma as agents in the creation of their own well-being rather than victims of traumatic events.'[63]

Indeed, well-being and psychosocial factors are also a great **resource for peacebuilding**, too often overlooked. Psychosocial factors can be as life-giving to a peacebuilding process as they can be detrimental. They can be a resource and a skill which can be learned and applied.

It is in this comprehensive understanding of the interaction of psychosocial factors with the dynamics of conflict, violence and peace that this book on **psychosocial peacebuilding** is situated. It explores:

(1) **how psychosocial factors can influence conflict and peacebuilding dynamics both positively and negatively, and**

(2) **how psychosocial factors themselves are impacted positively or negatively by conflict and peace dynamics.**

Nowadays, the majority of peacebuilding organizations and individuals, international agencies, NGOs, research departments and donors seem to understand the importance of psychosocial dimensions in peacebuilding. The pertinent question which remains, however, is: '**How to do it**?'

While examples, approaches and applications across several disciplines are many, psychosocial peacebuilding as an integrated field is still relatively new. Research, conceptualization and a solid evidence base for psychosocial peacebuilding still seem to be lagging behind the experience and knowledge available on the ground. As a specific paradigm, it still needs more conceptualization and operationalization. This is the gap that this book aims to start addressing, illustrated by the integrated psychosocial peacebuilding model of the International Association for Human Values. IAHV's model presents a conceptual framework for psychosocial peacebuilding that uses evidence-based practices and is successfully implemented around the globe in a variety of settings, with huge potential for upscaling and multiplication.

Definitions and concepts used

The overall framework for this book is a comprehensive, holistic view on peacebuilding. The concepts of conflict, violence and peacebuilding have been intensely explored and revised over the last decades and developed into truly multifaceted and multi-layered phenomena. In this book, we use these more comprehensive understandings and definitions (Table 1.1).

It is this holistic view that forms the basis for this book on psychosocial peacebuilding.

Table 1.1 *Definitions and Concepts Used*

Violence
Violence is not limited to direct, physical and psychological violence, which is most visible in the forms of aggression, physical attacks, torture, killing, maiming, rape, manipulation, humiliation, threat, bullying and physical, verbal and sexual abuse. We also consider structural violence as the violence embedded in structures and systems which limit people's quality and length of life, such as social discrimination, political oppression and economic exploitation. In addition, we need to consider cultural, ecological, criminal and other forms of violence. Therefore, when we talk about peacebuilding, it is in relation to the prevention, management and resolution of all these forms of violence.
Conflict
Conflict is inherent in life and a natural part of human interactions. It is usually described in terms of perceived incompatibility of goals and interests of two or more parties. There is a general negative connotation to conflict. However, being part of human life, it also constitutes a means towards positive change, transformation and progress. Rather, the way conflict is handled, and especially the use of violence, greatly impacts whether they manifest constructively or destructively. Here conflict is considered across the different stages of conflict management from proactive prevention to ultimate transformation or reconciliation, and involving a wide range of factors such as causes, consequences, fault lines, dynamics, actors, stakeholders, interests, values and more. In this book, the focus is on interpersonal and intergroup conflicts of different scales, from a basic domestic level to conflict involving whole societies.

(Continued)

Table 1.1 *Continued*

Peace

The time that peace was understood mainly as the absence of war and violence is long over. Peace scholar and practitioner Johan Galtung introduced the concept of positive peace as the attitudes, institutions and structures that create and sustain peaceful societies. Since then, the idea of what sustainable peace entails has continued to be developed into a multifaceted, positive aspiration. Sustainable peace is a situation characterized not only by the absence of physical violence but also by:

- the elimination of unacceptable political, economic and cultural forms of discrimination;
- the operation of peace-enhancing political, economic, legal, educational, health, information and security structures and systems;
- a high level of internal and external legitimacy or support;
- self-sustainability;
- effective communication, consultation and negotiation systems in order to resolve conflicts in a non-violent way and constructively transform them;
- a positive social climate characterized by peaceful coexistence and social cohesion, supported by peace-supporting values of inclusiveness, respect for life, cooperation and solidarity;
- mental and emotional well-being of individuals and communities. [64]

Peacebuilding

The concept of peacebuilding has also been significantly refined and developed, resulting in more diversified approaches, elaborated knowledge and a wider range of peacebuilding methods. Peacebuilding no longer refers to post-settlement interventions aimed at preventing a relapse into violence,[65] but has evolved into an integrative, holistic concept, both in theory and in practice.[66] Currently, peacebuilding refers to a wide range of activities carried out by many actors in different spheres and at different levels over a period of time. Countless small and large activities contribute to a peacebuilding process: activities aiming to enhance public security, generate economic recovery, facilitate social healing, promote democratic institutions, build sustainable relationships or install mechanisms to resolve conflicts in a non-violent way.[67] Peacebuilding activities can be geared towards long-term change, addressing the principal political, economic, social and ethnic root causes of conflict, ensuring that the drivers for the adoption of destructive strategies fall away. Other activities can focus on short-term goals, such as management of humanitarian crises, establishing ceasefires, negotiating settlements, dealing with refugee issues or providing temporary essential government functions. Actors involved in a peacebuilding process can be state and non-state actors, individuals and communities, religious and secular actors or theoreticians and practitioners. They can come from the local or grassroots level, the middle-range or the top level, or they can be interacting and networking through all levels. Peacebuilding relates to the individual as well as to community, society, state, international and global systems. As a process, peacebuilding encompasses the prevention of violence up to the reconstruction of society post violence. It is a dynamic but not necessarily linear process. In the words of Lederach, peacebuilding is 'a comprehensive concept that encompasses, generates and sustains the full array of processes, approaches and stages needed to transform conflict towards more sustainable, peaceful relationships. The term thus involves a wide range of activities and functions that both precede and follow formal peace accords.'[68]

Psychosocial

Psychosocial refers to the interrelationship between one's inner world (thoughts, emotions, ...) and the outer reality: How one's thoughts and feelings are influenced by the surrounding world and how they in turn influence the surrounding world. As human beings, we are continuously perceiving, experiencing and interpreting our environment as well as expressing our inner world and acting in that environment, in a dynamic, continuously changing process.

Key points: Chapter 1

The peacebuilding field needs an approach that is simultaneously deeply human and strategic in its aim.

The emotional, psychological, socio-psychological and existential-spiritual issues are an integral part of peacebuilding and development.

Both integral, human, psychosocial aspects, as well as structural aspects are interdependent, interacting and mutually reinforcing components for peacebuilding. Integral aspects lay a strong and healthy psychosocial foundation and are needed to shape and operationalize structures in a peace-supporting manner, while political, economic, security and judicial institutions and structures can foster peace-supportive mindsets, attitudes, well-being, behaviours, relationships and climates.

Therefore, it is the need of the hour to complement existing peacebuilding efforts with an equally massive investment of focus and resources into the (often) intangible psychosocial factors of peacebuilding.

Attention on the experience and role of the human being and psychosocial factors was already very present in certain existing subfields of peacebuilding such as reconciliation, trauma-relief, peace education, non-violence, creating cultures of peace and the more interpersonal field of conflict resolution.

Now there is a much clearer understanding of the need for effective psychosocial approaches to peacebuilding and development due to:

- Developments in disciplines such as peace psychology, social psychology, neuroscience, peace education, restorative justice, local and traditional peacebuilding, religious peacebuilding, systems thinking and others.
- Global developments: increased psychologically destructive violence, the scale of violence and displacement around the world, increased attention on mental health, the Covid-19 impact and others.

Psychosocial factors can be as life-giving to a peacebuilding process as they can be detrimental. They can be a resource and a skill which can be learned and applied.

Nowadays, the majority of peacebuilding organizations and individuals seem to understand the importance of psychosocial dimensions in peacebuilding. The pertinent question which remains, however, is: 'How to do it?'

Notes

1. Brendan, McAllister, Director of Mediation Northern Ireland, cited in United Religions Initiative. 2004. *Interfaith Peacebuilding Guide*. s.l., p. 286.
2. Travouillon, K. 2021. 'Emotions and post-liberal peacebuilding'. In Jeong, H. W. (Ed.), *Transitions to Peace. Between Norms and Practice* (1st ed., Vol. 1, pp. 51–70). Rowman & Littlefield Publishers Inc., pp. 53–4.

3   Travouillon, K. 2021, p. 56.

4   Johan Galtung as cited in Jeong, H. W. 2005. *Peacebuilding in Postconflict Societies*. London: Lynne Rienner, p. 1.

5   See also UNESCO. 1996. 'From a culture of violence to a culture of peace'. Peace and Conflict Issues Series. Paris: UNESCO Publishing; Mayor, F. 1995. 'How psychology can contribute to a culture of peace'. *Peace and Conflict: Journal of Peace Psychology* 1:1, pp. 3–9. https://doi.org/10.1207/s15327949pac0101_2.

6   Between 1985 and 1994, there were 160 recorded cases of ethnic violent conflicts, which accounted for 67 per cent of all observed cases of political violence. Marshall referenced in Bar Tal. 2013, p. 12.

7   Kelman, H. C. 1997. 'Social-psychological dimensions of international conflict'. In Zartman, W., & Rasmussen, J. L. (Eds.), *Peacemaking in International Conflict: Methods and Techniques*. Washington: USIP Press, p. 195; Johnston, D., & Sampson, C. (Eds.). 1994. *Religion: The Missing Dimension of Statecraft*. New York: Oxford University Press, p. 3.

8   Lederach, J. P. 1997. *Building Peace: Sustainable Reconciliation in Divided Societies*. Washington: USIP Press, pp. 14, 18.

9   Montville, J. 2001. 'Justice and the burdens of history'. In Abu-Nimer, M. (Ed.), *Reconciliation, Justice and Coexistence: Theory and Practice*. Oxford: Lexington Books, p. 132; Johnston, D., & Sampson, C. 1994, p. 3.

10 Johnston, D., & Sampson, C. 1994, p. 7.

11 Sampson, C. 1997. 'Religion and peacebuilding'. In Zartman, W., & Rasmussen, J. L. (Eds.), *Peacemaking in International Conflict: Methods and Techniques*. Washington: USIP Press, p. 275.

12 Bar Tal, D. 2013. *Intractable Conflicts: Socio-Psychological Foundations and Dynamics*. Cambridge University Press.

13 Lederach, J. P. 1997, p. 29.

14 Miall, H., Ramsbotham, O., & Woodhouse, T. 1999. *Contemporary Conflict Resolution*. Cambridge: Polity Press, p. 203.

15 Rasmussen, L. 2001. 'Negotiating a revolution: Toward integrating relationship building and reconciliation into official peace negotiations'. In Abu-Nimer, M. (Ed.), *Reconciliation, Justice and Coexistence: Theory and Practice*. Oxford: Lexington Books, pp. 101–27.

16 Burton, J. 1990. *Conflict: Human Needs Theory*. Houndmills: Macmillan Press Ltd.

17 Volkan, V. D. 1988. *The Need to Have Enemies and Allies: From Clinical Practice to International Relationships*. Northvale, NJ: Jason Aronson; Volkan, V. D. 2006. *Killing in the Name of Identity: A Study of Bloody Conflicts*. Charlottesville, VA: Pitchstone Publishing; Volkan, V. D. 2020. *Large-Group Psychology: Racism, Societal Divisions, Narcissistic Leaders and Who We Are Now*. UK: Phoenix.

18 Jeong, H. W. 2005, pp. xi, 21.

19 Gardner referred to in Reychler, L., & Langer, A. 2006. *Researching Peace Building Architecture*. Cahiers Internationale Betrekkingen en Vredesonderzoek Vol. 75. Leuven, Belgium: Center for Peace Research and Strategic Studies, pp. 8–9.

20 Fisher, R. J. 2001. 'Social-psychological processes in interactive conflict analysis and reconciliation'. In Abu-Nimer, M. (Ed.), *Reconciliation, Justice and Coexistence: Theory and Practice*. Oxford: Lexington Books, pp. 31, 42.

21 Kelman, H. C. 1990. 'Interactive problem-solving: A social-psychological approach to conflict resolution'. In Burton, J., & Dukes, F. (Eds.), *Conflict: Readings in Management and Resolution*. The Conflict Series. London: Palgrave Macmillan, pp. 201–45. https://doi.org/10.1007/978-1-349-21003-9_11; Kelman, H. C. 'A social-psychological approach to conflict analysis and resolution'. In Sandole, D., Byrne, S., Sandole-Staroste, I., & Senehi, J. (Eds.), *Handbook of Conflict Analysis and Resolution*. London and New York: Routledge [Taylor & Francis], 2008, pp. 170–83.

22 Bush, R. A. B., & Folger, J. P. 1994. *The Promise of Mediation: Responding to Conflict Through Empowerment and Recognition*. San Francisco: Jossey-Bass.

23 Reychler, L., & Langer, A. 2006, pp. 36–7.

24 Said, A. A., & Funk, N. 2002. 'The role of faith in cross-cultural conflict resolution'. *Peace and Conflict Studies* 9:1, p. 2.

25 See Curle, A. 1981. *True Justice: Quaker Peace Makers and Peace Making*. London: Quaker Home Service, p. 45.

26 See Gopin, M. 2004. *Healing the Heart of Conflict: 8 Crucial Steps to Making Peace with Yourself and Others*. s.l.: Rodale.

27 Allen, S. H. 2022. *Interactive Peacemaking: A People-Centered Approach*. Routledge. https://doi.org/10.4324/9781003189008, p. 5 and p. 60.

28 Bar Tal, D. 2011. *Intergroup Conflicts and Their Resolution: A Social Psychological Perspective*. New York: Psychology Press, intro.

29 Bar Tal, D. 2013, p. 24.

30 Bar Tal, D. 2011, intro.

31 Richmond, O. as cited in Travouillon, K. 2021, p. 57.

32 UNDP. 2022. 'Integrating mental health and psychosocial support into peacebuilding: Research findings: Summary report'. NY: UNDP, p. 54. https://www.undp.org/sites/g/files/zskgke326/files/2022-05/UNDP-Integrating-Mental-Health-and-Psychosocial-Support-into-Peacebuilding-Summary-Report-V2.pdf.

33 See, for example, American Psychological Association. *Peace and Conflict: Journal of Peace Psychology*.

34 See, for example, the Peace Psychology Book Series. Springer. https://www.springer.com/series/7298.

35 Blumberg, H. H., Hare, A. P., & Costin, A. 2006. *Peace Psychology: A Comprehensive Introduction*. New York: Cambridge University Press; Kool, V. K. 2008. *The Psychology of Nonviolence and Aggression*. New York: Palgrave Macmillan.

36 Njoku, M. G., Jason, L. A., & Johnson, R. B. (Eds.). 2019. *The Psychology of Peace Promotion: Global Perspectives on Personal Peace, Children and Adolescents, and Social Justice*. Springer Cham.

37 See, for example, Travouillon, K. 2021. 'Emotions and post-liberal peacebuilding'. In Ho-Won Jeong (Ed.), *Transitions to Peace. Between Norms and Practice*. Rowman & Littlefield Publishers Inc; Payne, K. 2015. 'Fighting on: Emotions and conflict termination'. *Cambridge Review of International Relations* 28:3, pp. 480–97. https://doi.org/10.1080/09557571.2014.888539; Baele, S. J., Sterck, O. C., & Meur, E. 2016. 'Theorizing and measuring emotions in conflict: The case of the 2011 Palestinian statehood bid'. *Journal of Conflict Resolution* 60:4, pp. 718–47. https://doi.org/10.1177/0022002714550083; Bar-Tal, D., Halperin, E., & de Rivera, J. 2007. 'Collective emotions in conflict situations: Societal implications'. *Journal of Social Issues* 63, pp. 441–60; Bleiker, R., & Hutchison, E. 2008. 'Fear no more: Emotions and world politics'. *Review of International Studies* 34, pp. 115–35; Halperin, E., Russell, A., Dweck, C., & Gross, J. 2011. 'Anger, hatred, and the quest for peace: Anger can be constructive in the absence of hatred'. *Journal of Conflict Resolution* 55:2, pp. 274–91; Halperin, E., Sharvit, K., & Gross, J. 2011. 'Emotion and emotion regulation in intergroup conflict: An appraisal-based framework'. In Bar Tal, D. *Intergroup Conflicts and Their Resolution. A Social Psychological Perspective*. New York: Psychology Press, p. 249; Jameson, J. K., Bodtker, A. M., Dennis, M. P., & Jordan, W. J. 2009. 'Exploring the role of emotion in conflict transformation'. *Conflict Resolution Quarterly* 27:2, pp. 167–92. https://doi.org/10.1002/CRQ.254.

38 See, for example, Mathews, D. 2001. *War Prevention Works: 50 Stories of People Resolving Conflict*. Oxford Research Group; Ginty, R. Mac, & Richmond, O. P. 2013. 'The local turn in peace building: A critical agenda for peace'. *Third World Quarterly* 34:5, pp. 763–83. https://doi.org/10.1080/01436597.2013.800750; Since 2005, the London-based NGO 'Peace Direct' is one of the leading organizations supporting local people to prevent war and build peace: www.peacedirect.org; The online resource 'Insight on Conflict' aims to map local peacebuilding initiatives around the world: www.peaceinsight.org.

39 See, for example, Dietrich, W. (Ed.). 2011. *The Palgrave International Handbook of Peacebuilding: A Cultural Perspective*. Palgrave Macmillan.

40 Ginty, R. Mac. 2011. *International Peacebuilding and Local Resistance: Hybrid Forms of Peace*. Basingstoke: Palgrave Macmillan.

41 See, for example, Hertog, K. 2010. *The Complex Reality of Religious Peacebuilding: Conceptual Contributions and Critical Analysis*. Rowman & Littlefield, p. 146; Abu-Nimer, M. 2003. *Nonviolence and Peacebuilding in Islam: Theory and Practice*. Gainesville, FL: University Press of Florida; Appleby, R. S. 2000. *The Ambivalence of the Sacred: Religion, Violence and Reconciliation*. New York–Oxford: Rowman & Littlefield Publishers; Gopin, M. 2000. *Between Eden and Armageddon: Essays on the Future of Religion, Violence and Peacemaking*. New York: Oxford University Press.

42 See, for example, Velez, G., & Gavrielides, T. 2022. *Restorative Justice: Promoting Peace and Wellbeing*. Springer Cham; Zehr, H. 1990. *Changing Lenses: A New Focus for Crime and Justice*. Scottdale, PA: Herald Press; Van Ness, D. W., & Heetderks Strong, K. 2014. *Restoring Justice: An Introduction to Restorative Justice*. New York: Routledge.

43 See, for example, Fitzduff, M. 2021. *Our Brains at War: The Neuroscience of Conflict and Peacebuilding*. OUP; Rausch, C. (Ed.). 2021. *Exploring the Neurobiological Dimensions of Violent Conflict and the Peacebuilding Potential of Neuroscientific Discoveries*. Arlington, VA: Mary Hoch Center for Reconciliation; https://www.neuropeace.org/volumes of the Neuroscience and

Peacebuilding Initiative; and organizations such as Beyond Conflict, El-Hibri Foundation and the Rewiring the Brain project of the Alliance for Peacebuilding.

44 Bar Tal, D. 2011. *Intergroup Conflicts and Their Resolution: A Social Psychological Perspective*. New York: Psychology Press; Bar Tal, D. 2013. *Intractable Conflicts: Socio-Psychological Foundations and Dynamics*. Cambridge University Press.

45 Hamber, B., & Gallagher, E. 2015. *Psychosocial Perspectives on Peacebuilding*. Springer.

46 Coleman, P. T., & Deutsch, M. (Eds.). 2012. *Psychological Components of Sustainable Peace*. Springer Science. https://doi.org/10.1007/978-1-4614-3555-6_1.

47 Intervention Journal: https://interventionjournal.org/aboutus.asp.

48 Bracken, P. J., & Petty, C. 1998. *Rethinking the Trauma of War*. London: Free Association Books, p. 3.

49 *SIPRI Yearbook 2023*, https://www.sipri.org/yearbook/2023, Summary p. 2; UNHCR. 2021. 'Refugee data finder'. https://www.unhcr.org/refugee-statistics/; UN News. 2022. *UNHCR: A Record 100 million People Forcibly Displaced Worldwide*. https://news.un.org/en/story/2022/05/1118772.

50 Institute for Economics and Peace. 'Global peace index briefing 2024'. https://www.visionofhumanity.org/wp-content/uploads/2024/06/GPI-2024-briefing-web.pdf.

51 Charlson, F., van Ommeren, et al. 2019. 'New WHO prevalence estimates of mental disorders in conflict settings: A systematic review and meta-analysis'. *Lancet* 394, pp. 240–8.

52 World Bank. *World Development Report 2015: Mind, Society, Behavior*. https://www.worldbank.org/en/publication/wdr2015 (consulted 24 Sept 2024).

53 UN Women. Nov 2021. 'Measuring the shadow pandemic: Violence against women during COVID-19'. https://data.unwomen.org/publications/vaw-rga (consulted 24 Sept 2024).

54 WHO. March 2022. 'Mental health and Covid-19: Early evidence of the pandemic's impact'. Scientific Brief.

55 WHO. March 2022. 'COVID-19 pandemic triggers 25 per cent increase in prevalence of anxiety and depression worldwide'. https://www.who.int/news/item/02-03-2022-covid-19-pandemic-triggers-25-increase-in-prevalence-of-anxiety-and-depression-worldwide.

56 WHO Report. 1 Dec 2011. 'Global burden of mental disorders'. https://apps.who.int/gb/ebwha/pdf_files/EB130/B130_9-en.pdf.

57 WHO. 'Mental health in the workplace'. https://www.who.int/news-room/commentaries/detail/mental-health-in-the-workplace (consulted 24 Aug 2024).

58 World Economic Forum. 10 Oct 2019. 'What causes us to burn out at work?' https://www.weforum.org/agenda/2019/10/burnout-mental-health-pandemic/ (consulted 24 Aug 2024).

59 UNDP. 2022, p. 54.

60 Travouillon, K. 2021, p. 62.

61 Humphrey, C. H., Pupavac cited in Travouillon, K. 2021, p. 62.

62 Hamber, B. 'The nexus between peacebuilding and mental health and psychosocial support'. Paper presented at the UN Peacebuilding Commission Expert-level Meeting, 3 December 2021.

63 UNDP. 2022, p. 54.
64 Hertog, K. 2010, p. 144.
65 'Peacebuilding' has entered the mainstream lexicon since the Secretary-General of the United Nations, Boutros Boutros-Ghali, presented his 'Agenda for Peace' in 1992. At that time, he distinguished peacebuilding from preventive diplomacy, peacekeeping, and peacemaking, as the actions in the post-settlement phase 'to identify and support structures which will tend to strengthen and solidify peace in order to avoid a relapse into conflict' and 'to build bonds of peaceful mutual benefit among nations formerly at war.' (Hertog, K. 2010, p. 145)
66 Hertog, K. 2010, p. 146.
67 Idem, p. 147.
68 Idem, p. 148.

2 Psychosocial peacebuilding – What and why?

With Psychosocial Peacebuilding we can:
Master the art and soul of building peace
Develop our fullest potential as a peacebuilder
And create the strongest cornerstone for global peace.

In Chapter 1, we have described how different disciplines and developments have converged in the understanding that psychosocial factors are important for peacebuilding. In this chapter, we want to consolidate the understanding of what PSPB is and why we consider it to be the core of sustainable peace.

We have seen that aspects of psychosocial peacebuilding have been implemented for decades around the world, but the number of articles and books published explicitly on psychosocial peacebuilding is still limited. The description, definitions and concepts on psychosocial peacebuilding outlined below are based on the author's research, personal experience and insights, and her professional work with IAHV and its implementation of a comprehensive psychosocial approach to peacebuilding, over more than two decades (Table 2.1).

What is psychosocial peacebuilding?

- In all stages, levels and sectors of peacebuilding **it is the human being who shapes, undergoes, experiences and responds to the dynamics of conflict and violence experienced**. As human beings we have our mindsets, attitudes, states of mental and physical well-being, emotions, traumas and wounds, behavioural patterns, sense of identities, perceptions, cognitive thinking patterns, values, expectations, desires, assumptions, motivations, intentions, concerns, taboos, principles, norms, beliefs, loyalties, worldviews, memories and so on. With these complex sets of internal dynamics, we are affecting and being affected by what happens around us. Neglecting this central dimension and powerful driving force in peacebuilding dynamics would indeed be short-sighted.

- These psychosocial factors **permeate the lives of people on all sides of conflict, whether victims/survivors, perpetrators, third parties or observers**. For example, common psychosocial experiences among survivors of violent conflict are psychological wounds, post-traumatic growth, perceptions of threat, the need for dignity and honour,

Table 2.1 *Definition of Psychosocial Peacebuilding (PSPB)*

PSPB is an approach to peacebuilding that integrates the full range of psychosocial factors at every stage, level and sector of peacebuilding. Therefore, we need to look at

(1) **how psychosocial factors can influence conflict and peacebuilding dynamics both positively and negatively;**

AND

(2) **how psychosocial factors themselves are impacted positively or negatively by conflict and peace dynamics.**

We need to apply this lens:

(1) **at all stages of peacebuilding processes:**
   a. **prevention and mitigation**
   b. **open conflict**
   c. **rehabilitation and reconstruction**

(2) **at all levels of peacebuilding:**
   a. **individual**
   b. **family – relationships**
   c. **community – grassroots**
   d. **national**
   e. **global**

(3) **in all sectors of peacebuilding, such as:**
   a. **security, terrorism and violent extremism**
   b. **justice, restorative justice, human rights**
   c. **politics**
   d. **social cohesion, social capital**
   e. **education**
   f. **economy, development and livelihood**
   g. **well-being, healthcare**
   h. **climate change**

4) **throughout the project cycle:**
   a. **analysis and assessment**
   b. **project design**
   c. **project implementation**
   d. **monitoring, evaluation and learning**
   e. **capacity building**
   f. **advocacy and policy development**

resistance to entering into a common future and existential meaning. With regard to perpetrators, psychosocial factors can include belief in defending the 'truth', concern about saving face, deep war fatigue, indifference and dehumanization. On the side of third parties or observers, they can manifest as assumptions, bias, moralizing, taboos, indifference and cultural arrogance.

- Psychosocial peacebuilding is an approach to peacebuilding that puts the human being back at the centre of peacebuilding, after it has been sidelined for several decades by the prevailing liberal peacebuilding model. **Psychosocial peacebuilding effectively addresses the psychosocial consequences of conflict and violence and enhances the psychosocial resources for peacebuilding.** Thus, it engages with deep core driving factors of conflict, violence and peace: transforming aggression, depression, trauma, division and greed, and strengthening well-being, agency, hope, connectedness and humanness. While conflicts, contexts and manifestations of related experiences differ, there seem to be **similar underlying psychosocial factors, processes and experiences at play at the human level**. Working at these deeply human levels, **psychosocial peacebuilding strengthens a strong psychosocial foundation in individuals and communities, which can then serve as the cornerstone and driving force for effective structural and systemic change, and for sustainable peace in the long term.**

- Psychosocial peacebuilding can be strengthened in all sectors of our society. For example, in the health sector it could bring about the enhancement of the holistic well-being of people rather than simply treating symptoms, which may limit people's opportunities to fulfil their potential in the long-term. In the education sector, formal education, often currently focused on the absorption of information, could be complemented by inner training on life skills, values and connection, which would promote resilience and self-confidence in children and youth to become active, contributing citizens in today's society.

- PSPB is a holistic approach that integrates mental health (MH), psychosocial support (PSS) and peacebuilding (PB). More than mainstream mental health or psychosocial support, however, psychosocial peacebuilding works with the complete human being and its full potential,[1] strengthening peacebuilding potential and creating maximum possible excellence at every stage and level.

- Attention to psychosocial factors has been very present in post-conflict settings, especially for trauma-relief, but they are equally important throughout all stages of conflict.

- When planning an intervention in a conflict context, psychosocial factors should be included in the initial conflict analysis or needs assessment, and related indicators should be evaluated in the impact assessment.

- The comprehensive integration of psychosocial factors into peacebuilding also includes peacebuilders themselves. Intervenors are not acting in an outside world that is separate and independent from them. According to the psychosocial peacebuilding paradigm, **deeply transformative psychosocial peacebuilding is rooted in the inner world of peacebuilders.** Many people can learn and transmit skills, conduct analyses, come up with solutions and develop peacebuilding plans and projects. However, on the basis of my experience and in the words of IAHV and Art of Living founder Gurudev Sri Sri Ravi Shankar, transformation for other people on a deeper level happens more through the being and presence of the peacebuilder than through actions and words: 'Only those who have peace can spread peace. Only those who have love can spread love. Only those who feel connected can create connection.' The inner world of peacebuilders and inner peace itself are indeed central and essential components of optimal peacebuilding processes (Figure 2.1).[2]

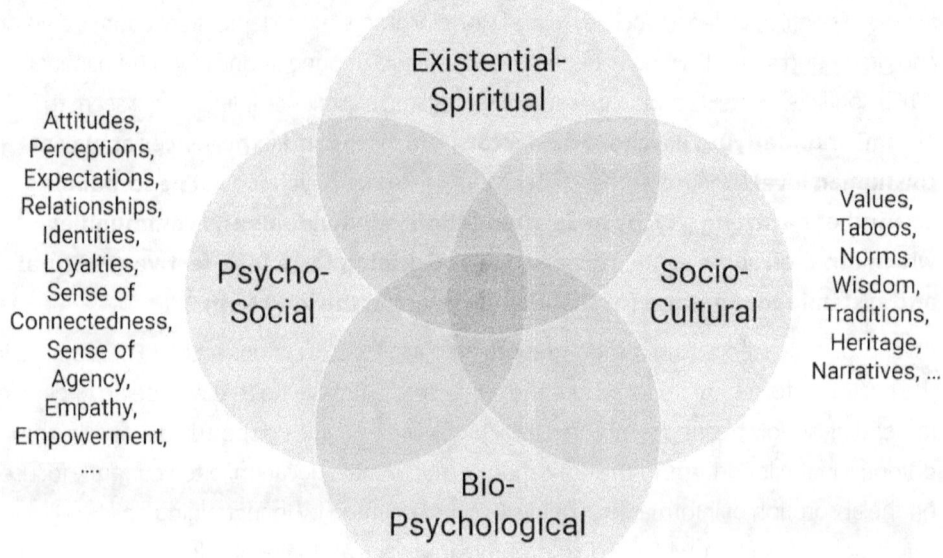

Figure 2.1 *Overview of bio-psycho-social factors in peacebuilding (Katrien Hertog). Note: This overview has been developed and presented by the author based on her academic and practitioner experience in this field for twenty years, in order to illustrate the range of bio-psycho-social factors in peacebuilding, without aiming to be comprehensive.*

Why psychosocial peacebuilding?

In this section, I want to present insights as to why I consider PSPB to be the core of sustainable peace. I will do so from both a deeply personal perspective as well as a scholarly one.

In my view, PSPB works comprehensively, for example:

To break the cycles of war in protracted conflicts at a fundamental level, to break the cycles of intergenerational trauma and empower interest groups to achieve their goals non-violently.

To inculcate human values into the system from childhood education through to governmental operations as a healthy buffer against discrimination, oppression, human rights abuses, violent extremism and terrorism.

To resolve long frozen conflicts, shift mindsets from divided pasts to shared futures, and expand ethnic and religious identities to embrace our fundamental common human identity.

To give vulnerable groups intrinsic self-esteem, well-being, energy and self-confidence to change their life circumstances.

To heal the lives of those who feel broken, who have lost trust in people and lost meaning in life.

To strengthen the well-being and resilience of people working for peace and development, and to fine-tune their skills to be empathetic, courageous and skilled agents of change.

To give young people hope, a purpose, a team and a sense of belonging.

To ultimately create a more peaceful, prosperous world for everyone.

Touching humanity and profound transformation

Psychosocial peacebuilding touches upon the core of humanity, without evading the challenging, difficult, complicated aspects of our human nature and experience, including the deepest wounds we carry, fundamental identities passed down through generations, storms of emotions, questions about the meaning of life, unforgivable atrocities, long-time interpersonal conflicts or the cherished values we adhere to. This approach touches, embraces and transforms our thoughts, emotions, sense of being and relations. **Psychosocial peacebuilding practice facilitates transformations at the deepest levels that are profound, meaningful and relevant to our lives and circumstances.**

To illustrate this, I share here some deeply human stories of transformation towards inner and outer peace: from a peacebuilder in India, a traumatized girl from Syria and rebel fighters in Colombia. These are based on the accounts of Art of Living/IAHV trainers who were involved in these respective peace initiatives.

Compassion full circle: Opening the hearts of those who killed my husband (India)

One evening, a mob of agitated men entered the house of Ritu and her husband Sandeep, mayor of a village in Champaran in India, while they were having dinner. The villagers had requested Sandeep to become their mayor because of his integrity, good work and popularity. Sandeep and Ritu had worked intensively for the development and welfare of the village. However, certain sections among the local population were not pleased with this and had started to agitate, manipulate innocent minds and create trouble.

The mob brutally attacked both of them. They held Ritu and beat her into unconsciousness. When she regained consciousness, she saw her husband lying immobile, in a pile of blood, and in an eerie silence. He was dead. Since then, that silence enveloped and permeated her whole being. Stupefied, she would not speak for months. Life was going on; her children needed to be taken care of. Her family tried everything to get her out of the stupor, but nothing worked. They didn't know what else to do.

One day a distant relative visited Ritu. She had lost her son and had found it impossible to come out of bereavement until she attended the Art of Living workshop. Since then, life had changed for her. Ritu's parents decided to enrol Ritu for that workshop. Initially feeling restless and disturbed in the sessions, Ritu changed as soon as she started breathing with the Sudarshan Kriya technique. Something shifted. She no longer felt like herself anymore, but instead felt the enormity of life and the vastness of her own being. Words were too finite to contain her experience of infinity. When she opened her eyes after the Kriya, her life had changed completely. A wave of life had hit her and she felt completely renewed, in fact born again.

> They asked me how I felt and held out the microphone for me to speak. I stood up with my legs still shaky and grabbed the microphone with my hands, that were still tingling with the life force surging through them. I took a deep breath and held the mic near my lips. It was after eight long, silent, painful months that I uttered my name. The sound echoed in my entire being. I couldn't say anything more.

The course catapulted Ritu back into life. She was smiling again, engaging again in the world, feeling dynamic, open to hope, joy and the possibilities that life had to offer. Ritu decided to dedicate every second of her life to the service of humanity. She took back the full responsibility for her ageing parents and growing children, as well as for promoting, organizing and later also teaching the Art of Living courses.

Sandeep's memory was still there, as a void that could never be filled, but Gurudev Sri Sri Ravi Shankar's breathing techniques, meditations and knowledge gave her the resolve to draw strength from that void. When she first met Gurudev Sri Sri Ravi Shankar, she was able to leave behind whatever agony, anger or anxiety she was still experiencing. It all seemed to flow out and leave her in His presence; she felt serene from inside, an instrument of His peace.

> I had seen the brutal face of violence. I had been through it and seen it turn my life upside down in a matter of minutes. Had it not been for Sudarshan Kriya and Sri Sri's knowledge, violence would have robbed my entire life and along with it, the precious future of my children. I didn't want to see one more soul suffer at the hands of violence.

Ritu started teaching the Art of Living course in prisons. One day, Gurudev Sri Sri Ravi Shankar asked her to go and teach in Motihari prison in Bihar. She organized the course, travelled there, and on the first day of the course welcomed the inmates who had registered. One of them approached her.

She related the experience thus:

> He had a quizzical expression on his face. He looked at me with deeply intrigued eyes. In a husky voice he asked, 'what are you doing here?' I folded my hands in a namaste and said with a smile, 'I am the Art of Living instructor. I will be conducting your workshop.' He stared unblinkingly into my eyes, 'How can you?' I felt a little puzzled with his query. Nevertheless, keeping my smile intact, I asked, 'Why can't I?' He replied: 'Don't you remember me?' 'Have we met before?' I asked. 'I killed your husband.' Silence fell between us. I could hear the footsteps of the participants walking in the background. I looked at Sri Sri's picture kept on the table and closed my eyes. I took a deep breath and a flurry of images hit me. That scene from years ago, that had taken Sandeep away from me, played in front of my eyes. I could recall all of their faces. I opened my eyes and they fell on a woman standing behind this man. She was the same girl who had tightly held on to my arms as I had screamed for help that night. I lifted my eyes; I could see many of them. They were all staring at me. That guy who had held the blood-stained big knife that night now stood near the window staring at me. My husband's murderers were standing in front of me. I closed my eyes and took another deep breath.

In that moment of introspection, Ritu observed she did not feel any resentment or anger towards them; rather, compassion and the wish to help them come out of a life of violence and embrace a peaceful life. Both Ritu and the inmates were amazed at her response. They started the course. After some initial suspicion, the inmates got into it. At the end of the six days, they had experienced deep transformation and had tears of remorse and gratitude in their eyes.

> My life had come a full circle with that workshop. Sri Sri had prepared me for this day and made me stand in front of my worst fear. I realized that I had found my peace within me and I was ready to become an instrument of peace in the world.

(as recorded by Ritu)

A divorced mother at the age of sixteen: Healing a young life from trauma (Syria)

One day, during an IAHV Healing, Resilience and Empowerment training for mothers in one of the suburbs of Tripoli, Lebanon, a very young Syrian girl came in, carrying a baby and accompanied by an elderly lady and another young woman. When I saw the young girl, I thought she was just accompanying her mother and would wait for her outside, but she came in. So I went to talk to her to introduce her to IAHV's youth programme, which seemed more suitable for her age, as the current workshop was exclusively for mothers. The girl looked at me with much agony and said: 'But I am a mother, this is my baby!!!' Since trauma is an everyday reality for many women in Tripoli, I didn't know what else to say; I just nodded to her.

The girl was sixteen years of age, although she looked so tiny sitting there. I had hardly taken her to be more than twelve or thirteen. I noticed that she wasn't communicating with the other two women she came with. Later I learned from the elder lady that she was her mother and that the young girl refused to talk to her as she held her responsible for what happened.

The first two days of the training were intense for her. She kept quiet the whole time and did not interact with anyone. On the last day, after the powerful IAHV trauma-relief techniques, she came to me and said: 'Now I am ready to talk to you privately.'

Then she shared her story, how at the age of fourteen, her parents had gotten her married to a relative, fearing that she might get raped during the war. She shared how traumatizing it was for her that he physically abused her as she was not able to get pregnant immediately. Then she did get pregnant but lost the baby, which made him even more determined to continue trying for a child. After a very hard time suffering much ill health, she fell pregnant and had her baby. However, the husband immediately wanted yet another child. She was unable to do that as she had become too weak. He abused her again. Then, when nothing worked, he decided to divorce her.

She was scarcely able to speak when, filled with sorrow, she shared how she could not talk to anyone about what had happened. Especially not to her mother, who had insisted on marrying her off at such a young age (albeit thinking that she was protecting her). At that time, their lives were entirely woven around the narrative of war. They were a living testament to its brutality. Even before she could start comprehending life, it had left her as a divorced mother at sixteen. She had suppressed her emotions and was wading through life like a lifeless doll. This was the only means of protest available to her until she came to the training and was able to open up and share her pain and dreams.

Now, by the end of the training, the girl had found the strength to stand up for herself and her baby. She spoke out with conviction when she declared that she was a divorced mother at just sixteen. She wanted to send out a strong message to all parents not to do the same thing to their daughters.

(as narrated by Manal Karrara, IAHV and Art of Living trainer from Egypt)

Infusing non-violence into a fifty-year-old war: Rescuing a peace agreement through humanization

The fifty-year civil war in Colombia is often referred to as one of the longest wars on the planet. Fought over issues of land ownership, discrimination, social inequities and injustice, the government and a range of armed groups engaged in armed conflict for decades. This created a legacy of violence, drug production and trafficking, environmental destruction, landmines and the social normalization of violence. Since 1985, around 8 million people had been victimized by forms of violence, such as massacres, forced displacements, disappearances, torture, threats, assassinations, kidnappings, illegal recruitment (including children), sexual violence, attacks on civilian property, expropriation and extortion and use of antipersonnel mines, among others.

In 2012, peace talks started between the Government and one of the main armed groups, the Revolutionary Armed Forces of Colombia – People's Army (FARC-EP), which concluded in the signing of a peace agreement in 2016. The peace negotiations faced many hurdles, however, and were at risk of total breakdown in 2015. That was when Gurudev Sri Sri Ravi Shankar met the

Colombian president Juan Manuel Santos to receive the Simon Bolivar Order of Merit, the highest civilian award offered by the Colombian Congress for the Art of Living work done in Colombia. During that meeting, Santos shared his concern that the negotiations were going badly and that he saw military force as the only remaining option. In response, Gurudev Sri Sri Ravi Shankar shared his willingness to support the peace process and got approval from Santos to meet the FARC leadership in Cuba. He recognized that the FARC guerrillas, too, were suffering from insomnia, anxiety and trauma due to the conditions of the Colombian jungle and the unending war.

(The following excerpt is recorded by Francesco Moreno Ocampo, Art of Living teacher in Latin America, involved in the peace initiatives in Colombia)[3]

In Havana, Sri Sri met sixty-two high-ranking members of the FARC, including its leadership Iván Márquez, alias Pablo Catatumbo, alias Ricardo Tellez, alias Marco León Calarcá and other members. During the main meeting that lasted for more than two hours, Sri Sri spoke to the FARC leaders about the importance of following the Gandhian principle of non-violence. He gave examples of other armed groups who had decided to fight for their causes within the political arena. The FARC members shared their reasons for starting the war and their desire for social justice in Colombia. It touched me deeply when Sri Sri said: 'In this conflict, everybody is a victim'.

During this meeting, I witnessed that much more than words were exchanged. 'We convey more through our presence than through our words' is one of Gurudev Sri Sri Ravi Shankar's most notable statements. There was understanding, empathy and love - in the broader sense of the word. One of the FARC members said: 'Master, this spiritual knowledge is what we have needed. Please don´t leave us. You can consider us as your followers'. At the end of the meeting, alias Pastor Alape (a high-ranking commander of the FARC) stood up and shook Sri Sri´s hand saying: 'I was once told that one could only touch wooden or stone saints, but now I´m touching a real saint.' When I saw the faces and attitudes of the FARC leaders who were meeting this world-renowned humanitarian leader for the first time, I realized that there is innocence in the deepest essence of every human being; and I was a privileged witness to this transformation.

I also realized for myself that there are no bad people. Ignorance, lack of education, lack of love and trauma can lead people to destructive behaviours. Pablo Catatumbo told us how he signed up for the FARC in the seventies: He was nineteen years old when walking with two friends behind a demonstration. He was shouting about how bad the police were, without realizing they were walking in front of the police station. One of the policemen heard him, beat him and took him to jail. He was then beaten by five other policemen. When Catatumbo saw that the same was done to a shoe shiner who was thrown into jail after him, he decided to enter the guerilla group.

Afterwards, most of the FARC members attended the event held at the personal residence of the Indian ambassador to Cuba. For the first time, perhaps in their lives, the FARC leaders meditated and received deep spiritual wisdom from someone who has dedicated his life to serving humanity. Gurudev Sri Sri Ravi Shankar's words resonated visibly with the audience, especially with those who had spent the last three years negotiating peace. The last meeting of the day ended with a press conference and a hopeful statement from alias Iván Márquez: 'We hope that Colombia embraces the Gandhian principle of non-violence'. Although Sri Sri's visit came to an end, I felt it was only the beginning.

A few weeks after our trip to Cuba, guerrilla leaders in Colombia destroyed an electrical tower and the water supply in an oil well. The patience of the government and the Colombian people was fading away. The three years of the peace process were coming to an abrupt end. Immediately, Sri Sri sent a clear message to Iván Márquez: if there is no clear action towards peace from the FARC, the Colombian government will have the moral authority to attack and there will be thousands of casualties. But if the FARC is willing to take a bold step towards peace, the Art of Living Foundation will support that initiative and there will be hope. The day after this message was conveyed, Iván Márquez declared a unilateral ceasefire. It was July 2015. The peace process was revitalized!

The meetings with both government representatives and the FARC leaders continued and progressed after the ceasefire. Invited by the Art of Living Foundation, my father (who was the first prosecutor of the International Criminal Court) and I travelled to Havana to share his insights regarding various international justice issues concerning the peace process and the options of transitional justice. The FARC members were discussing how to apply the Gandhian principle of non-violence in a post-agreement scenario in Colombia. They then also participated in the Art of Living programme and learned the breathing techniques and meditation. I gave them books by Gurudev Sri Sri Ravi Shankar which they eagerly received. They experienced all the benefits that these tools bring: peace of mind, increased energy, focus and well-being. 'With the help of Gurudev, we have placed our spirit to achieve reconciliation and coexistence of a big and benevolent country, whose destiny can't be that of the war. The teachings of The Art of Living are essential to achieve a stable and long-lasting peace', said Iván Márquez. They were so impressed with all these results in such a short period of time, that they asked for help on another very sensitive issue.

One of the worst phases of the guerrilla war was during 2002 in the region of 'Valle del Cauca' in Colombia. Some members of Congress there were evacuated by the army because there were signs of an upcoming attack by the FARC guerrilla. After all the congressmen boarded the buses, one of the soldiers tore off his insignia to reveal the FARC symbol underneath, saying, 'We are FARC commanders, and you are our prisoners.' This was one of the most infamous cases of the Colombian war. For five years, twelve congressmen were held hostage in the jungle. Although there were attempts to reach a 'humanitarian agreement', no real progress was made. According to the testimony of the FARC commanders, a FARC battalion that did not recognize the camp where the deputies were held hostage opened fire. The FARC soldiers, in turn, thought that the Colombian army was trying to rescue the congressmen, so they executed all the hostages. Only one of the prisoners, who was in a different camp at that time, survived.

Part of Art of Living's work had been to support the families of these congressmen (brothers, sisters, wives, sons and daughters). Now, as part of a reconciliation process, we facilitated a meeting between the families and the commanders of the FARC who were responsible. In August 2016, the family members of the twelve congressmen flew with the Art of Living Foundation to

Havana, Cuba, to meet the commanders of the FARC. I was with them, witnessing their fear, hatred and resentment. Many of them couldn't sleep that night. The breathing and meditation helped them a lot, however. I vividly remember the day the families met with the FARC commanders. It was heart-breaking. The family members were waiting in the hall of an attractive government building in Havana, Cuba. The FARC commanders were waiting outside, visibly nervous. Iván Márquez, the leader of the FARC peace delegation, was the first one to enter the hall. He started greeting and shaking hands with each of the family members. Some of them didn´t reciprocate the greetings. After Márquez, the other commanders came in and started to greet the family members one by one. Some of the relatives started to cry; others shouted 'Why?' 'Why?' It was an extremely stressful situation. After everyone was seated, each of the family members had the time to express the suffering, pain and hatred they had been holding on to for so many years. The FARC commanders listened in deep silence. Then the FARC leaders expressed their regret. 'The congressmen were our responsibility. I´m ashamed of what happened', said Pablo Catatumbo. We even did a joint prayer for the deceased souls, while holding hands together. After this, the environment totally changed. It felt like new people had entered the room. People could now look into each other's eyes and talk normally. It was amazing to see how people can be transformed, to be able to see humanity in the eyes of somebody you have hated for years. This was a life-changing moment for the families as well as for me. If these family members could drop hatred towards the FARC leaders, I didn't have any reason to hate anybody. Since that moment, I promised myself that I would let go of hatred in my life.

In June 2016, the Colombian Government and the FARC announced a bilateral and final ceasefire thus putting an end to armed clashes. On several occasions, President Santos and the FARC leaders, including Iván Márquez, have thanked Gurudev Sri Sri Ravi Shankar and The Art of Living for supporting the Colombian peace initiative so effectively.[4] The official signing of the Peace Agreement in September 2016 was attended by Gurudev Sri Sri Ravi Shankar. However, supported by only 49.78 per cent of the population, it was not endorsed in the subsequent referendum. In subsequent years, Gurudev Sri Sri Ravi Shankar continued to support the peace process throughout all the challenges. He met with President Juan Santos, Joshua Mittroti, director of the Colombian agency for reintegration, Henry Acosta, Colombian peace process mediator and Alvaro Uribe, former Colombian president and the leader of the opposition, with whom he discussed the approach and role of the opposition parties to take the peace process forward.[5]

Gurudev Sri Sri Ravi Shankar observed that 'when one is in victim consciousness, it is hard to understand the benefits of forgiveness. One can only think of revenge and punishment.'[6] During his keynote address at a reconciliation meeting in Cali in December 2016, he emphasized the importance of reintegrating the FARC guerrillas into the mainstream: 'The tendency in the civil society is to take revenge – we need to bridge this trust deficit. That's why we started the forgiveness process. Without such a process, the common people will continue to treat the former guerrillas differently. They need to know that FARC people are also victims.'[7]

Psychosocial factors interacting with dynamics of conflict, violence and peace

It is understood that **psychosocial factors and the dynamics of conflict, violence and peace continuously interact in a vicious cycle**. Only for reasons of clarification do we provide below a breakdown of the seemingly linear impact of violence on psychosocial factors and of psychosocial factors on dynamics of violence and peace.

(1) The Impact of Violence on Psychosocial Factors

Violence and aggression have an impact on the psychosocial well-being and capacity of people to thrive. We consider the direct impact of armed conflict and physical violence, as well as the impact of related problems often accompanying situations of war and armed conflict. These include poverty, multiple losses, family separation, gender-based violence (GBV), disability, inability to meet basic needs, ongoing insecurity, displacement, loss of livelihoods, interrupted education, unemployment, environmental degradation, corruption and more. Also, the impact of longer-term structural, cultural and ecological violence can be considered here, such as discrimination, injustice, marginalization, lack of opportunities, lack of access to basic services, disappearance of livelihoods, and more. We also consider the effects of direct interpersonal violence, including psychological, physical and sexual abuse, threats and bullying, as well as criminal and gang violence (Table 2.2).

Table 2.2 *Overview of Negative and Positive Impacts of Different Forms of Violence on Psychosocial Factors at Individual and Social Levels (examples)*

NEGATIVE IMPACT *Individual level*: mental disorders such as post-traumatic stress disorder (PTSD), anxiety and depression, intense emotions of loss / grief / anger / frustration / helplessness / despair / resentment / hatred / revenge / guilt, psychosomatic symptoms, hypervigilance, sleeping problems, black-white thinking, loss of self-esteem, loss of sense of agency, limited perception, narrow mindsets, singular identities, loss of basic trust, violent masculinities / submissive femininities, sense of alienation and isolation, loss of moral compass.
Inter-relational / Family / Society level: lack of belonging and connectedness, community fraction, erosion of human values, changed values of radicalization and polarization, divisive and destructive narratives, disregard for wisdom, stigma, cultures of war and violence, normalization of violence and aggression.
POSITIVE IMPACT *Individual level*: resilience, intense emotions of courage / compassion / gratitude / love / forgiveness / hope / empathy, sense of agency, skills development, inner strength, discernment, empowerment, strengthened faith, post-traumatic growth.
Inter-relational / Family / Society level: connectedness, community cohesion, human values, solidarity, strengthened ethics and norms, cohesive and uplifting narratives, respect for wisdom.

(2) The Impact of Psychosocial Factors on Violence and Peace

The psychosocial factors mentioned above influence in their turn the dynamics of conflict, violence and peace (Table 2.3).

Table 2.3 *Overview of Negative and Positive Impacts of Different Psychosocial Factors on Violence and Peace (examples)*

NEGATIVE IMPACT (violence-inducing) institutional distrust, revolution, human rights abuses, economic breakdown, reduced functionality, inertia, political instability, social isolation, lack of access to basic services, violence, aggression, substance abuse, suicide, a culture of violence, exploitation, bullying, recruitment into gangs or armed groups, ongoing cycles of violence.
POSITIVE IMPACT (peace-strengthening) Restoration, rehabilitation, integration, renewal, positive action, inclusivity, innovation, reconstruction, active citizenship, institutional reform, addressing grievances, restorative justice, strengthened social capital for development and peace.

We can distinguish two tendencies which are at work at both the individual and group levels: either internalizing psychosocial factors of anger, frustration, depression, pain and intolerance, leading to addictions, depression and suicidal tendencies, or externalizing them, leading to aggression, violence and wars.

(3) Vicious Circles and Intergenerational Impact

Various forms of violence and related negative psychosocial factors interact with each other and, when not positively addressed, generate cycles of increasing violence and deteriorating psychosocial well-being.

- This is observed in children who have become victims of recruitment by armed groups and later turn into ruthless perpetrators. When they in turn want to demobilize and reintegrate into society, they often face resistance, stigma and non-acceptance from their communities of origin.[8]
- Experiences of abuse, when not healed, may lead to depression, suicide and substance abuse, or to abusive behaviour by the erstwhile survivor of abuse.
- Systems of discrimination, oppression and exclusion can create anger, grievances and frustration which in turn can lead to social and political violence by those who feel oppressed or excluded.
- People suffering from depression, PTSD, anxiety or other mental health problems due to violence or war-related experiences may later not engage in or support peace processes or reconstruction initiatives.[9]

These and similar dynamics sustain vicious circles of violence both within families and the international arena. There is ample evidence from psychology, sociology and peace research that unaddressed harm contributes to cycles of retribution and violence.[10] They deeply impact the quality of life of individuals, undermine community cohesion, and pose challenges to global aspirations for development, peace, health, education and environmental care.

This is most evident in the cycle of **transgenerational trauma**, where the trauma experienced by one generation has lasting impacts on behaviours and norms in subsequent generations. Trauma is transmitted across generations through narratives, communication, behavioural patterns, social transmission, mental modules as well as epigenetic modulation. Trauma and the related experiences of deep-running emotion, entrenched identities, memories, victim and perpetrator legacies, social division and distrust may become part of the collective narrative and social identity. Trauma narratives can be passed on within families and communities, turning victim cultures into perpetrator cultures. Children may grow up in cultures of war and violence with strong psychosocial driving forces that may at times erupt again into renewed cycles of violence and war. These harmful psychological and social effects can undermine any peacebuilding initiatives and processes.

Recent research has found that trauma symptoms can be heritable. Epigenetics is a branch in biology that studies changes in gene expression that do not involve alterations in the DNA structure. It has identified the mechanism through which symptoms induced by trauma can be inherited. Exposure to trauma can change the activity of DNA, increasing the expression of certain genes while suppressing the expression of others.[11] These changes are then transmitted to the offspring and lead to specific traits in them: 'Transgenerational epigenetic inheritance [of trauma symptoms] refers to transmitted changes across several generations, including depressive-like behaviour, altered responses to stressful environments, more risk-taking behaviours and impaired social abilities.'[12] For example, studies on animals have shown that inducing interruptions of maternal care or inducing high stresses or fearful stimuli among the parents diminished social interactions among the offspring, transmitted depression and resulted in changes in the hormones responsible for stress regulation and social bonding.[13] Some studies show such effects of trauma across several generations. For example, chronic stress induced by disrupting social hierarchy in adult mice alters social behaviours across three generations.[14] Studies on humans give many indications of the same mechanism. For example, studies on the offspring of genocide survivors show increased psychiatric illnesses, anxiety, depression and PTSD.[15] Children of individuals who developed PTSD after forced displacement developed avoidance mechanisms to stimuli related to displacement. Combat trauma among parents may be inherited as behavioural dysfunctions among their offspring in the form of violence and hostility which have a similar duration and intensity as the combat trauma of the parents.

The insight that the effects of trauma are heritable and can affect the mental and physical well-being of exposed people, their children and grandchildren, has huge implications for society.[16] Given the number of individuals who have been traumatized, this constitutes a huge challenge to peace in the world.

A clear example of transgenerational cycles of violence is the history of the Israeli-Palestinian conflict, which is permeated with deeply traumatizing events, during which victims have become perpetrators and vice versa. On the Israeli side, the centuries-old antisemitism which culminated in the Holocaust of the Second World War, during which an estimated 6 million Jews were killed, has left unspeakable wounds on the Israeli population for generations. On the Palestinian side, the Nakba, or catastrophe, in 1948, during which the majority of the Palestinian population was exiled and displaced, followed by decades of occupation, apartheid and loss, has had an irreversible impact on generations of Palestinians. Decades of conflict, war, terrorism and life under a constant state of emergency have impacted well-being, narratives, memories, identities, beliefs and behaviour on both sides. There followed the recent escalation in October 2023, in which Hamas killed more than one thousand Israelis and took hundreds hostage, after which the Israeli army waged a devastating war on Gaza, killing tens of thousands of people and depriving hundreds of thousands of basic needs. This is not only one more consequence of the cycle of historical trauma, but is in itself another traumatizing event that will also leave its mark for generations to come.

Among the effects of transgenerational trauma, we can identify on the Palestinian side:

- Feelings of anger and aggression;
- Sense of victimhood, lack of agency, defeat, depression, apathy, lack of self-confidence, alienation of the issues and Palestinian society, numbness;
- Survivors' guilt;
- Destruction of social fabric, distrust of others, competition, erosion of human values, corruption;
- Perpetuation of violence and oppression in homes, schools, communities and society.

Since transgenerational, historical trauma is collective, its treatment must also have collective dimensions in addition to individual ones. Breaking transgenerational cycles of trauma is a long, complex and multifaceted process, including components such as

- awareness raising around transgenerational trauma and its effects, reshaping and recontextualizing trauma-related narratives,
- positive transformation of the collective memory, critical awareness of history,
- accompaniment and social support networks, strengthening cultural, local and spiritual resources,
- open communication and intergenerational dialogue,
- the restoration of a resilient positive identity, strengthening a sense of agency and empowerment,
- advocacy and action to remove the root causes of traumatization,
- recognizing woundedness, facilitating shared spaces for healing, engaging in community-based healing approaches such as storytelling and collective mourning,

- transforming patterns of trauma transmission within families,
- and more.

We can create a strong psychosocial foundation for sustainable peacebuilding when these harmful vicious circles are interrupted, negative psychosocial impacts are positively transformed, psychosocial resources positively strengthened, and root causes of war and violence addressed. This restored foundation includes resilience against violence and war as well as long-term violence prevention. The resulting tremendous savings in human, social and financial costs could then be invested in positive development and peace.

(4) Methods and Processes for Transformation

Processes to transform psychosocial factors of peacebuilding are very varied and include, among others, healing, empowerment, trust-building initiatives, dialogue, the changing of attitudes, truth-telling, humanizing the other, expressing respect, fostering a sense of belonging, reformulating identities, breaking down stereotypes, dealing with emotions, negotiating expectations, relationship building, regaining hope and inculcating positive values.

(5) The Impact for Sustainable Peace

Though scientific evidence is still limited, **there is an increasing understanding that a non-integrated approach causes harm and continuous violence and that an integrated approach leads to more effective and sustainable peacebuilding outcomes.**

PSPB precisely addresses this challenge in peacebuilding by working in an integrated manner with all psychosocial factors involved in conflict, violence and peace dynamics. Both as a conceptual model and practical approach implemented on the ground, evidence-based PSPB has been shown to increase peacebuilding impact.

Psychosocial peacebuilding frameworks
Socio-psychological repertoire and infrastructure of conflict and peace – Daniel Bar Tal

The social psychologist Daniel Bar Tal is one of the few scholars who have developed a comprehensive framework for the socio-psychological foundations present in intractable conflicts, based on his in-depth study over decades of the Israeli-Palestinian conflict.[17] With this framework, which sheds light **on the 'psyche' of society members involved in intractable conflicts as individuals and collectives,** he aims to promote **a better understanding of intractable conflicts, their resolution and their prevention.**

To start with, he distinguishes *three psychological challenges* that emerge when coping with intractable conflict:

(1) Psychological needs for safety, mastery over destiny, and for positive identity;

(2) The need to learn to cope with stress, fears and other negative psychological phenomena;

(3) The need to develop psychological conditions to win over rivalry.

In order to meet these challenges, societies in intractable conflict develop a socio-psychological repertoire that includes shared beliefs, attitudes, motivations and emotions.

Such a *socio-psychological repertoire has three elements*:

(1) Collective memories: shared representations of the past and a socially constructed narrative concerning the history of the conflict;

(2) An ethos of conflict: societal beliefs about the conflict, its justification and goals, risks and safety, the positive collective self-image, collective victimization, delegitimization of the opponent, patriotism, leadership and more;

(3) A collective emotional orientation: dominating emotions, especially fear, anger, hatred and a sense of humiliation and injustice.

These three elements of the socio-psychological repertoire have the following *functions*:

(1) Providing a meaningful and coherent picture of the conflict to society members;

(2) Justifying the actions of the in-group against the enemy, including violence;

(3) Preparing one's own society to face violence from the enemy and difficult life conditions;

(4) Motivating for solidarity, mobilization and action;

(5) Creating a sense of differentiation and superiority.

With time, this repertoire turns into a *socio-psychological infrastructure* and penetrates into institutions and communication channels. It can evolve into a *culture of conflict*, when the tangible and intangible elements of the psychosocial infrastructure are integrated into its basic political, social and educational context as a dominant repertoire. Providing meaning to the experience of prolonged conflict, this new culture of conflict is present in the public discourse, mass communication, cultural products, educational materials, thus encompassing collective life. These developments, in turn, can also lead to the formation of new social identities.

Through this solidified socio-psychological infrastructure and culture of conflict, beliefs become rigid and new information is perceived in selective, biased and distorted ways. This restricted prism defines perception, interpretation and action, and becomes in itself an obstacle to peaceful resolution. It closes minds and prevents them from seeing alternatives. At this stage, it is not the disagreements over the goals that are crucial in the conflict analysis, but the social-psychological repertoire that includes hostility, hatred, fear, resentment, anger, delegitimization and mistrust. Whereas the repertoire initially fulfilled important functions, with time it itself becomes the main motivating and justifying factor in the conflict, perpetuating it. It serves as a major factor in its continuation and is a major barrier to its resolution, through its exclusion of empathy, of responsibility for one's own actions, its justifications for harming the opponent, and other elements. The negative actions taken by each side reinforce the negative psychosocial infrastructure in a vicious circle.

This psychosocial infrastructure can change over time and its hold on society members can differ and include the possibility of internal disagreements. However, according to Bar Tal, the study of intractable conflicts shows that it is much easier to mobilize people on a path of violent conflict than on a path of peace making. He sees a variety of combined reasons for this:

- Human beings are more perceptive to threats and risks to secure their survival and preserve their life and safety than to peaceful signs. These threats and risks require immediate action and response.
- Fear is activated without effort and cognitive control, while hope, which is essential for societal peacemaking, requires some cognitive processing. People may be programmed with specific responses to fear from the past, such as defence or aggression, while hope requires conceiving new behaviours towards a new desired goal.
- People are more perceptive to negative information about potential harm than to positive information about opportunities for peace.
- Psychology of terror management has shown that the threat of death can create constant terror and the belief in the need to defend oneself against it.

In order to move towards peace, a new repertoire needs to be formed and disseminated among society, including the need to solve the conflict peacefully and to humanize the opponent. However, the psychological roots of conflict are not easily eliminated. When a threat, real or imagined, is perceived, the whole bio-psycho-social system is activated. Moving towards peace requires the cessation of the activation of this old system as well as its replacement with a new system with new beliefs and behaviours.

Peace psychology and positive peacebuilding in action in Kashmir[18]

'Our concept of peace is very much driven from the intersection of mental health and inner peace at different levels', writes Ufra Mir, the founder of the grassroots organization Paigaam. She emphasizes that **the link between psychosocial well-being and social peace** is indeed very clear on the ground and is underwritten throughout her work and discourses.[19] Ufra grew up as an adolescent in the violent context of Kashmir, where bloodshed, human rights violations and violence were the norm. She had to deal with their brutal consequences on a daily basis. Paigaam started as a health-peace initiative for youth in Kashmir and evolved into an international non-profit, non-governmental organization which worked with youth and adults on the values, principles and best practices of positive peacebuilding. Based on the foundation of peace psychology, the approach is centred around positive peacebuilding with holistic well-being, mental health, self-transformation, changemaking, inner peace and empowerment forming the core. This approach not only helps people to survive in a violent context and to facilitate a degree of healing, but also fosters their development through skills training related to conflict transformation, leadership, justice and human rights advocacy. These core principles help people build a more peaceful, cohesive, empathetic, just and resilient world and support them in a realistic way to make steps to transform a culture of violence into a culture of peace.

This integrated approach is rooted in the understanding that inner integration and intrapersonal transformation are an essential element of peacebuilding work, while being mindful of structural and cultural violence: 'It starts with us first. We can only first change ourselves and with that, through our responses, thinking, and dialogue, we allow ripples of sustainable transformation to take place. None of this is possible without constant conscious reflection and the decision to learn, unlearn and empathize, every single day.'

From the intrapersonal dimension evolves the interpersonal dimension and the sense of connectedness and responsibility for our shared world.

> 'It's important that we all do something for the common good with authenticity, courage and resilience; keeping our skills, talents, interests and values in mind. Taking personal accountability for our actions and collaborating with others, is a very practical and important approach to doing anything useful in the world today. When we all can acknowledge and accept our differences, and feel united in diversity, that's when magic happens and we together are able to create a space for a more just, peaceful and inclusive world to unfold and sustain in front of our eyes. Changing systems, behaviours and attitudes is not easy, but doable. I believe with empathy, imagination and critical thinking, we all can make it happen, again, everywhere.' (Ufra Mir)

The vision is to 'create a new, kinder, inclusive world together that has space for differences, vulnerabilities and creativity.' Ufra Mir's action in this world is rooted in a broader vision of life 'that we are "nothing" in the bigger scheme of things, a speck of dust in the multiverses; but the moment we decide or choose to meaningfully contribute through our existence, we become something.'

This example of an integrated conceptualization and implementation of peace psychology is an empowering, empathetic, sustainable, transformative and multidimensional approach, aiming to strengthen peace and healing at different levels in order to make a positive difference in the wider society.

The integration of MHPSS and peacebuilding: Challenges and opportunities

This section examines how the conceptual frameworks and practical implementation experience of psychosocial peacebuilding relate to the current efforts towards integrating Mental Health and Psychosocial Support (MHPSS) and Peacebuilding, highlighting some of the tendencies and differences between both approaches.[20] It identifies a range of challenges often present in efforts for integration, as well as insights gained from frameworks and experience in the field of psychosocial peacebuilding which could address these. This section is informed by my active participation in global discussions and working groups on integration over the last four years.

Integration of MHPSS and peacebuilding

For several years a specific global discourse has developed to address one of the missing links in peacebuilding, namely the integration of Mental Health and Psychosocial Support in Peacebuilding. Its spearhead is the awareness in development, peacebuilding and humanitarian settings, from the local to the global level, that previous practice did not work or even did harm.

MHPSS is defined by the Inter-Agency Standing Committee (IASC) Reference Group on MHPSS in Emergency Settings as a composite term used 'to describe any type of local or outside support that aims to protect or promote psychosocial well-being and/or prevent or treat mental health conditions'.[21] The MH component of MHPSS is, in a limited sense, mostly focused on preventing and treating mental health conditions at the individual level. In a broader sense, MHPSS interventions encompass the addressing of needs at the individual level, restoring relationships at the family, communal and societal levels, as well as addressing the wider social issues in communities that impact mental health and well-being.[22]

In 2007, the IASC MHPSS Reference Group developed standard reference guidelines on MHPSS in Emergencies 'to enable humanitarian actors to plan, establish and coordinate a set of minimum multi-sectoral responses to protect and improve people's mental health and psychosocial well-being in the midst of an emergency'.[23] More than a decade later, in 2019, the IASC MHPSS Reference Group convened a special Thematic Working Group on MHPSS and Peacebuilding to bring MHPSS and peacebuilding expertise together in order to develop a more integrated approach. The important role of MHPSS in achieving and sustaining peace was emphasized in the UN Peacebuilding Architecture Review and the Sustainable Peace Agenda. In July 2020, the UN Secretary-General highlighted in his Report on Peacebuilding and Sustaining Peace that 'The further development of the integration of mental health and psychosocial support into peacebuilding is envisaged with a view to increasing the resilience and agency of people and communities.'[24]

To articulate and support this new understanding, UNDP and the IASC MHPSS Reference Group took the initiative to develop and publish global guidelines and knowledge products on the topic. This resulted in

(1) UNDP's Report and Guidance Note on integrating MHPSS into peacebuilding (2022);[25]

(2) IASC's report 'Integrating MHPSS and Peacebuilding: A Mapping and Recommendations for Practitioners' (2024), based on mapping exercises and global consultations with representatives of the peacebuilding and MHPSS sectors. The report aims to offer a framework for integration, describing the rationale, practitioners' understandings, commonalities and differences, facilitators and challenges, conceptualizations of integration, specificities for certain subgroups, and examples of best practice from the grassroots and community level, resulting in a list of recommendations for improved practice.

In recent years, also an increasing number of individuals, organizations and governments are identifying best practices, developing models, writing frameworks and guidelines, issuing policy statements, collecting data, organizing discussions and much more on MHPSS and Peacebuilding. They have been instrumental in creating more awareness, knowledge and experience in the field of policy, research and practice.

Recent attention and efforts to more effectively integrate MHPSS and Peacebuilding programming stem from the realization that an integrated approach would improve outcomes for the interrelated objectives of sustainable peace and well-being, and that separation not only undermines outcomes but can also do harm.[26] As written in the IASC Guidelines: 'Peace cannot take root if conflict-affected people suffer from deep psychological and social impacts of war, armed conflict, and destructive, inter-communal or inter-group conflict, which can impede peacebuilding and animate ongoing hostilities. Conversely, without peace, there are significant limits on people's mental health and psychosocial well-being. Fear, insecurity, and ongoing violence impose enormous stresses, damage mental health and psychosocial well-being, and shatter social cohesion.'[27] It is understood and supported by 'growing evidence . . . that more strategic efforts to capitalise upon these intersectoral synergies can create an impact that is significantly greater than what each sector can achieve through siloed efforts.'[28]

While it has been widely acknowledged that trauma and wounds from the past can inhibit peacebuilding and development efforts, there is also now increasingly more awareness and attention for other psychosocial factors involved, such as identity, emotions or narratives, and, in return, for the impact of social conflict and violence on one's mental and emotional well-being.

In general, grassroots organizations have more often implemented approaches that integrate elements of both fields, probably because in their work on the ground the link between psychosocial well-being and social peace is very clear.

On the macro-level, and especially in the West, however, both professional fields have been working largely in silos, having developed their own frameworks, theories, assessments, terminology, methods, staff training and interventions. The MHPSS field had a tendency to focus more on the level of individuals, on mental disorders and treatments based in Western psychology and psychiatry, while peacebuilding also has a focus on society, context and local practices, and works with a broad variety of groups.

Integration efforts intentionally focus on bringing together both of these fields, or components of them. They therefore span a wide range of topics, such as looking at commonalities, differences, integration levels, facilitators and challenges, gaps and priorities, and a wide range of initiatives, such as mapping, consultations, donor awareness raising, organizing co-learning processes, knowledge management, monitoring and evaluation, research and more.

The current spectrum of integration of MHPSS and Peacebuilding programming ranges from total separation to occasional ad hoc inclusion, complementary integration in a rather parallel fashion, and fully integrated approaches.

Total separation refers to MHPSS and Peacebuilding approaches that operate separately and do not include any elements of the other approach, due to lack of awareness, knowledge or capacity, for example.

Ad hoc inclusion refers to programmes which sometimes and occasionally include an element of the other approach, but without an integrated methodology or framework and no theory of change which outlines how elements of both approaches are necessary to achieve the project goals. For example, in a peacebuilding project psychologists and psychiatrists may deal with mental health problems of individual survivors and perpetrators of violence, without paying attention to the influence of mental well-being on conflict and violence and vice versa. Or a peacebuilding project for strengthening social cohesion might also include staff care. However, this may arise more from concerns about burnout than from an integrated conceptualization of how the mental health and psychosocial well-being of staff are an integral aspect of the peacebuilding process towards social cohesion.[29]

MHPSS and Peacebuilding approaches can also be implemented in a complementary way, where both MHPSS and Peacebuilding activities are carried out on the basis of an understanding of the importance of both aspects to achieve the project goals, while not necessarily being conceptually or operationally interlinked.

Fully integrated approaches are based on an integrated conceptual framework in which MHPSS and Peacebuilding are inextricably interlinked. Consequently, this understanding is applied at all stages of the project cycle, from assessment to design, implementation and impact evaluation. The theory of change clearly integrates both approaches as interlinked components necessary to achieve the project goals and includes indicators for all components.

The fully integrated approach of MHPSS and Peacebuilding, though still distinct, comes closest to the intrinsically integrated approach of psychosocial peacebuilding.

In current discussions on integration, comparatively little attention is paid to already integrated approaches, their models, concepts, methodologies, wisdom and practicality. Instead, the overwhelming focus remains on how to integrate ways of working that are not already integrated. Presentations, working seminars, policy statements and reports mention the importance of learning from grassroots organizations and from what already exists, but the knowledge and experience of such individuals and organizations already implementing integrated approaches are still poorly acknowledged, presented and used. One example of such an intrinsically integrated approach is psychosocial peacebuilding, as explained above.

The union of optimal health and positive peace

Whether discussing approaches that are already integrated, or efforts undertaken towards such integration, it is important to understand that the ultimate aspirations of MHPSS and Peacebuilding, as reflected in their more visionary definitions, converge in a unified vision of positive peace with optimal health. Positive peace is defined as a state that builds on well-being, positive relationships, peace-supporting systems and conflict resolution mechanisms which enable the prevention of violence. This contrasts with concepts of negative peace, which is understood as simply the absence of violence. Similarly, optimal health is not just the absence of illness, but 'a state of complete physical, mental, and social well-being in which every individual realizes his or her own potential, can cope with the normal stresses of life, can work productively and fruitfully, and is able to make a contribution to her or his community', according to the definition of the World Health Organization.[30] Therefore, it could be said that an optimum state of health in its broader understanding correlates very closely, if not fully, with a state of positive peace and vice versa.

The relation of PSPB to Integration efforts: Tendencies, differences, challenges and opportunities

Below we will look into some tendencies and differences between psychosocial peacebuilding and the Integration frameworks and efforts. We will focus on mainstream trends and tendencies in both fields, acknowledging that the fields of PSPB and Integration, as well as individuals and organizations working in these, are far from homogeneous and there are meaningful exceptions to the main tendencies described here below.

(1) In a way, psychosocial peacebuilding is both related and unrelated to the newly developing paradigm of Integrating MHPSS and Peacebuilding. It is related in the sense that it covers mental health, well-being, psychosocial support and peacebuilding. However, it is unrelated in the sense that it transcends the discussion to integrate both fields, since psychosocial peacebuilding is an approach that is intrinsically integrated to begin with.

(2) The approach of psychosocial peacebuilding transcends the 'mere' integration of MHPSS and PB. PSPB works with people's minds and mindsets in general, not just with mental health issues, and integrates a wide range of psychosocial factors (see Figure 2.1), not just those related to psychosocial support. More than providing mainstream mental health or psychosocial support, PSPB works with the whole of the human being and its full potential. It works in a paradigm of optimal, holistic health and positive peace, rather than one limited to mental well-being. Focusing on trauma and the wounds of conflict, integration efforts seem to be mainly directed at deficiency rather than empowerment or strengthening existing peacebuilding potential. PSPB instead focuses on optimal mental well-being as a cornerstone and resource for peace, the lack of which undermines the potential for peace. PSPB strengthens peacebuilding potential and creates maximum possible excellence at every stage of a peacebuilding process, including prevention.

(3) Many of the discussions on the integration of MHPSS in Peacebuilding focus on post-conflict recovery, while PSPB consistently focuses on all stages of peacebuilding processes, from prevention to rehabilitation. It aims to facilitate optimal peacebuilding potential at every level and throughout the process. PSPB works on a continuum and on the different layers of peacebuilding, violence prevention, conflict and violence. Throughout, it lays a strong, healthy psychosocial foundation for sustainable peacebuilding for all involved.

(4) The integrated field of PSPB does not face several of the challenges that are often mentioned as an obstacle to integration and mutual understanding between MHPSS and Peacebuilding, such as:

- *The reported traditional disconnect between the different respective focuses on micro-level individualized action (MHPSS) and macro-level group efforts (Peacebuilding), or on the individual versus the collective.*

    The core of psychosocial peacebuilding is the inherent recognition of the mutual interaction between micro- and macro-levels and internal and external factors. Already integrated approaches have successfully bridged these conceptual barriers. For example, through initiatives of IAHV and Art of Living, peace agreements have been signed between authorities and non-state armed groups after an intense process where they worked together on personal transformation, grievances, structural violence issues and trust. PSPB recognizes that just as individuals make up a society, individual mindsets and attitudes create the social climate. 'Sometimes we lose sight of a simple truth about systems: They are made up of people. If most collective impact efforts fall short of supporting people to change in fundamentally consciousness-altering ways, then, the system they are a part of will not significantly change either.'[31]

- *The distinct and highly specialized terminology in both fields and poor interdisciplinary understanding.*

    PSPB uses less specialized jargon and more accessible psychosocial methods rooted in the reality of people's lives and circumstances, which are more easily understandable for target groups and practitioners in both fields.

- *Targeting challenges, where it is broadly understood that the focus of MHPSS is on people with mental health problems*

    PSPB strengthens the mental well-being of all people on a wide spectrum from mental disturbance towards optimal mental functioning and excellence.

- *The stigma related to mental health problems.*

    The inclusive community approach of PSPB significantly reduces the risk of people feeling stigmatized and then not engaging with community initiatives around peace and well-being.

- *Caution against a 'one size fits all' approach, the need for a lot of attention on context and the need to adapt.* The IASC report presents five country studies, concluding that *the contextual diversity of the country case studies cautions against using a 'one size fits all' approach.*[32]

    This is certainly a valid concern on one level. However, at another, profoundly human level, there are fundamental common factors within humanity, beyond context, which are similar and unite. This has been shown, for example, by IAHV, which has effectively operated in four out of five of these case study countries using its one, very similar approach. Successfully working with these actors at a deeply human level, it showed its approach to be universal and applicable across contexts. Contextual adaptation in IAHV's implementation of psychosocial peacebuilding is present at a surface level, but not fundamental for its efficacy.

- *Consideration that the integration of MHPSS and peacebuilding cannot be achieved overnight.*

    The long-term focus of integration efforts seems to overlook the fact that every day integrated approaches are already being implemented on the ground. Moreover, the need for them is urgent and widespread given the scale of distress, violence, war and trauma present in the world today, and they should not be unnecessarily postponed.

- *Integration discussions mention the need for bi-directional integration of Peacebuilding into MHPSS and MHPSS into Peacebuilding. The first of these focuses seems largely limited to looking at the societal factors that affect MHPSS, such as conflict, strife, social cohesion, violence, trust, dialogue, truth-telling and so on.*

    PSPB applies a broader perspective, not just consideration of the impact of social factors on one's mental health but also the impact of these on one's whole internal state of being, as well as their constant mutual interaction, in a comprehensive way. (See Chapter 3)

- *Concerns about peacebuilding having a political focus, versus the neutral stance and duty of impartiality of MHPSS work in relation to different conflict groups.*

    PSPB actors work with everyone on all sides of a conflict, grounded in a deep understanding of human nature and in universal human values, transcending the divisions within the conflict, as do humanitarian organizations.

- *There is reference to the scarcity of materials for operationalizing the linkage of the two areas, the need for knowledge of the other sector, and for theories and conceptual frameworks that embody the importance of both MHPSS and peacebuilding.*

    PSPB is rooted in already integrated conceptual frameworks which can be used and applied immediately.

(5) Discussions on integration rightly emphasize the crucial importance of staff training in order to facilitate integrated approaches. However, the focus seems to be on training staff in stress resilience, trauma-relief and methods of preserving empathy. PSPB, on the other hand, trains staff to develop their full potential as a peacebuilder. From the understanding that peacebuilders are not separate from the context in which they work and that as human beings they are equally subjected to interactive psychosocial dynamics, PSPB works with peacebuilders in a fully integrated way. PSPB also builds their knowledge and capacity to effectively design and implement fully integrated psychosocial peacebuilding programmes.

(6) PSPB does not normally engage with cases of mental illness which require specialist treatment, as MHPSS services do. Empowering the general population affected by conflict, violence, stress and trauma with tools to improve and strengthen their own well-being, however, could free human and financial resources to invest more in specialized treatment needed for severe mental disorders.

Way forward: Strengthen what is

As explained above, psychosocial peacebuilding approaches already embody, conceptually and practically, the goals of current efforts to integrate MHPSS and Peacebuilding. PSPB already intrinsically addresses some of the challenges these efforts face. This section **proposes that more attention and effort be directed at strengthening and developing what already exists and is integrated, rather than focusing efforts on the invention of something new, or the merging of currently widely disparate approaches. Bringing together the current separate extremes of both the MHPSS and Peacebuilding fields is a considerable undertaking involving bridging cultures, methodologies, approaches, strategies, staff training and more. This is predictably a long-term and resource-intensive endeavour. Faster and better results may be achieved in the shorter term, through the highlighting, strengthening, sharing and supporting of already integrated or closely collaborative approaches, with their shared understanding and range of good practices.**

Elements of, or comprehensive approaches to, psychosocial peacebuilding have been practised by grassroots organizations, have been at the core of the work of some of the prominent peacebuilding scholars and practitioners, and have been part since several decades of conflict transformation, restorative justice, creating cultures of peace, trauma-relief, peace education and peace psychology, to name just a few peacebuilding subfields. It seems, however, that researchers and policymakers involved in integrating MHPSS and Peacebuilding are not always aware that such expertise and experience already exist, including in the various fields of peacebuilding. This is also illustrated by the case of the UNDP Global Guidance Note,[33] which lacks a comprehensive peacebuilding framework, does not unpack peacebuilding terms, and offers as innovative guidelines a set of principles which are already widely known in the peacebuilding field. A 2017 report on the Integration of MHPSS and Peacebuilding stated: 'the recognition that MHPSS and

PB [peacebuilding] should be integrated with one another in order for both disciplines to jointly achieve sustainable social transformation goals in post-conflict societies is relatively new [. . .] this is not yet practiced in a way that is fully integrative from the outset and that is holistic at a systemic level'.[34] Even in 2020 Huser mentioned that 'those doing inter-disciplinary research widely agree that effective integration is not yet being practiced in a meaningful manner'.[35]

While speakers and reports speak about the importance of acknowledging and supporting the *'extensive, highly promising work on integrating MHPSS and peacebuilding by grassroots organisations'*,[36] it still seems that much more use could be made of existing integrated approaches in the respective discussions, reports and guidelines.

Much remains to be done to translate verbal support into concrete leverage of the vast experience, evidence and knowledge that already exists. Currently, the attention given to already integrated approaches such as psychosocial peacebuilding is very little compared to that given to the efforts to integrate ways of working that are still a long way apart.

However, while advocating for engagement with the vast resource of knowledge and experience of grassroots organizations, it is also important to **support and invest in the methods and practice of reliable impact measurement.** The integration of MHPSS and Peacebuilding is becoming the latest hot topic, and, as with all 'fashionable topics' in the peacebuilding field, it may well develop into the next 'cross-cutting' good practice, following earlier trends such as gender-, trauma- and conflict-sensitivity. Many organizations may be claiming to do MHPSS/Peacebuilding integrated projects, but few may be equipped with the knowledge, expertise and effective methods to do so in a positive, impactful way.

Last but not least: The importance of integrating internally

In IAHV's philosophy and experience, integrated peacebuilding approaches will have a deeper and more sustained impact if they are also integrated internally within ourselves as peacebuilders, within our teams and our target groups, as well as within our implementation practice and the design of our programmes. The way we as peacebuilders connect and integrate within ourselves will affect the quality and impact of our integrated peacebuilding work in the world. Already, the integration of MHPSS and Peacebuilding is predominantly talked of and discussed as an external exercise. As with any cross-cutting topic, despite its crucial importance, there is a real risk that integrated projects will become reduced to a technical exercise or tick-box practice, due to lack of understanding or training.

Spiritual approaches to peace and peacebuilding

Spiritual approaches to peace and peacebuilding have existed throughout millennia and have also been studied more recently in the field of peacebuilding.[37] **Some of the predominant characteristics of spiritual approaches are the emphasis on inner peace as the foundation for world peace and the interconnectedness of all life.**

Spiritual approaches to peacebuilding are not simply about resolving conflicts on the surface. **They address the inner dimensions of thoughts, emotions, and existential experience that give rise to violence and therefore need to be addressed to reestablish inner and outer peace. Spiritual principles, practices and values have the capacity to address these depths of human existence and the inner lives, minds and hearts of people.** Therefore, they are a powerful resource for personal and social transformation. This perspective maintains that peace emerges from spirituality, and that by nurturing our inner life, we tap into a universal source of love and interconnectedness. **Spiritual peacebuilding is about practical ways in which spiritual changes become the foundation for peace.**

Spiritual approaches to peacebuilding are permeated by psychosocial factors, both in their philosophies and social applications, but also in the personal practice of spiritually inspired peacebuilders.

Spirituality and religion

Spiritual leaders often differentiate between the spiritual essence of religious traditions and their more formal, institutionalized expressions. While the latter typically manifests in the form of rituals, symbols and organized practices, spiritual peacebuilding emphasizes the deeper, transformative core that underpins these traditions. While the differences in the outer manifestations of religion can easily create divisiveness and strife, spirituality unifies and transcends distinctions of race, nationality, religion, gender, or social background. There is a widely shared understanding that conflicts often arise because excessive emphasis is placed on religious affiliation and identity. In contrast, spiritual peacebuilding draws on shared human values that exist at the heart of every tradition, surpass sectarian boundaries and promotes well-being universally. Such reservoir of deeply embedded prosocial values can form the basis of an effective alternative to violence, profound conflict transformation, and deeply grounded non-violent action.[38]

Inner peace – World peace

All over the world, spiritual leaders have stressed the need for inner peace in order to reduce violence and conflict in the world and to spread social peace. By nurturing inner peace and fostering personal transformation, individuals can cultivate such qualities as compassion, empathy and mindfulness that, in turn, radiate outward and heal communities. This holistic perspective recognizes that every intolerant attitude or violent act has their roots in negative inner experiences like anger, hatred, jealousy, frustration and despair, and that overcoming these internal challenges is essential for creating a just and peaceful society. Cultivating inner peace enables individuals to break free from destructive cycles and orient themselves towards love, forgiveness, and reconciliation. As the Dalai Lama said: 'We must generate a good and kind heart, for without this, we can achieve neither universal happiness nor world peace.'[39] His words encapsulate the notion that inner transformation is not merely a personal indulgence but a critical prerequisite for social peace. Thus, internal change is the key to changing violent interpersonal behaviour and to lay the groundwork for a more harmonious collective existence.

According to spiritual approaches, individuals are able to alter their sense of self, the world, and fellow human beings, to develop personally and to discover inner peace.[40] This inner transformation can be pursued through a variety of spiritual practices that help individuals reconnect with their authentic nature and dissolve unhelpful patterns. Such practices include meditation, breathing exercises, fasting, celebration, prayer, silence, service, yoga, knowledge, self-reflection and so on. Spiritual practices can nurture important peace-promoting values and qualities, such as a belief in the transformative power of love, positive involvement in the world, faith in the face of seemingly impassable obstacles, a predisposition towards healing and reconciliation, the ability to suspend judgement, the inner strength to adhere to non-violence and an experience of oneness in which contradiction dissolves.[41] By replacing negative emotions with a spirit of generosity, compassion and clarity, practitioners gradually build an inner reservoir of peace that can transform interpersonal relationships and, ultimately, the broader society.

It is particularly within spiritual approaches that one can find an approach to peacebuilding which makes action for peace conditional to being peace. Being peace and doing peace have to go hand in hand in order to make an effective contribution to peacebuilding. Being peace refers to a state of calm, the connection with one's inner self and a sense of being part of something larger.[42] At its deepest level, spirituality is a transformative path that works through shifts in consciousness.

Many spiritual approaches adhere to a broad outlook on life and the world and uphold an awareness about the infinity of time and space, the different layers of existence, the limitations and possibilities of human life, and the fundamental interdependence of the whole of creation. Such a broad awareness sheds a different light on the causes, purposes, and significance of our daily conflicts on earth.

From a sense of being part of something universal and of a shared humanity, a natural tendency emerges to take responsibility for society and the planet and strive towards peaceful coexistence through compassion, skillful conflict transformation and reconciliation. This broader identification brings freedom from the limiting boundaries of narrow identifications and fosters respect for the diversity on this planet.

Spiritual peacebuilding is centred on the belief that the inner life of each individual plays a pivotal role in either perpetuating or transforming conflict. Even more, the inner life of one individual can be the starting point for processes of social change that transform the fate of thousands or millions of people, as well as of society as a whole. Powerful examples include Jesus Christ, Mahatma Gandhi, Martin Luther King, Maha Ghosananda, the Dalai Lama, Ghaffar Khan, and Gurudev Sri Sri Ravi Shankar, who have inspired and guided masses towards more just and peaceful coexistence. Rooted in a deep spirituality, they stand up against the odds to transcend situations of destruction, violence, war, and injustice. Touched, but not shaken by external circumstances, such powerful personalities are able to advance their vision of a more peaceful and just world.[43]

Examples of spiritual peacebuilding

Different models of spiritual peacebuilding have been developed and implemented by individuals and communities around the world, such as Swami Agnivesh, Thich Nhat Hanh, McConnell, the Quakers, the United Religions Initiative, the Mennonites, Desmond Tutu, the Sulha movement, Thomas Merton, the Moral Rearmament Movement and the Sarvodaya Shramadana Movement.

In his classification of approaches to conflict transformation, Appleby, a scholar in religious peacebuilding, described the spiritual and contemplative approaches as models that see the commitment to peacebuilding as an end in itself, as a spirituality rather than as a strategy or a technical process. He notes that for communities with this mentality, conflict transformation is a way of life, the outcomes of which are left to the divine or a higher power.[44]

Swami Agnivesh, who was also a social activist in India, distinguished between a secular model of conflict resolution, which tries to resolve conflicts without necessarily honouring the otherness of the other, and the spiritual model, which aims at the transformation of oneself to be able to coexist creatively with what is different.[45] He explained that spirituality is not limited to resolving conflicts from time to time but that it seeks instead to transcend the very logic of conflict. Spiritual conflict resolution attends to the spirit of negativity, which lies at the basis of conflicts, and fosters instead a culture of positivity and love. Swami Agnivesh argued that a paradigm shift is needed from power to love: The surface, where conflict and restlessness belong, can be controlled and manipulated by power. However, power is powerless in the depths beneath the surface, where spirituality belongs and where only the power of love works. Love condemns the wrongs, but saves the wrongdoer. In order to secure peace, therefore, Agnivesh said a shift is needed from the surface to the depths of human existence.

Other examples include Desmond Tutu's Ubuntu Philosophy, rooted in African spirituality, which emphasizes interconnectedness and shared humanity as the foundation for reconciliation.[46]

Transformative mediation is an approach to mediation that focuses on respecting and listening to the other, on mutual recognition and self-empowerment, seeing the conflict as an opportunity for moral and relational transformation.[47]

In his book *Healing the Heart of Conflict*, Gopin has designed a series of eight steps for conflict resolution which start from the inner workings of the individual.[48]

Also for United Religions Initiative, peacebuilding starts from individual self-examination and the grounding in a personal spiritual path: 'Prejudices cannot be undermined through discussion or even prayer, but by working on our emotional reactions. The dialogue with our self before the dialogue with others is more important than the dialogue itself.'[49]

Spiritual ecological approaches to peacebuilding emphasize harmony with nature as a foundation for peace, acknowledging that human peace and the health of our planet are deeply interconnected.[50] In this view, the conflicts we witness in societies are mirrored by the disharmony between humanity and nature. Sustainable peace requires a profound transformation in how individuals relate to themselves, each other, and the earth, and the restoration of balance on all fronts. According to this view, awareness of being part of an interdependent whole can lead to a profound shift in values, moving away from exploitative or competitive attitudes towards a more cooperative and caring engagement with people and the environment. Inner transformation and cultivating a sense of interconnectedness can bring both personal well-being and healing of social and ecological crises. Ecological spiritual peacebuilding approaches are about nurturing a thriving, interconnected world where both human and natural communities can flourish.

Buddhist peacebuilding

Some very interesting contributions to peacebuilding have come from a Buddhist perspective, such as those of Thich Nhat Hanh and John Mc-Connell. Thich Nhat Hanh is very well-known in the West as a spokesman of socially engaged Buddhism and a teacher on peace and non-violence from a Buddhist perspective.[51] He consistently emphasized that individual serenity should not be sought in isolation from the world, but that inner change and social change are inseparable, and that inner peace serves as the empowerment for outer action.

Mindful Mediation, a handbook for Buddhist peacemakers by McConnell,[52] is a very detailed, in-depth, and at the same time practical description of spiritual peacebuilding based on Buddhist psychology, insights, and wisdom. McConnell presents a Buddhist psychology of conflict founded on deep insight into the mental, emotional, and spiritual dynamics of conflict, including relevant Buddhist teachings, practical examples and an overview of required skills and ways to enhance them. Applying the central Buddhist teachings of the middle path and the four noble truths to conflict, he posits: (1) conflict is a part of the human condition; (2) there are psychological roots and inner dynamics to a conflict; (3) peace can emerge from conflict; (4) and peace is a way of life which can be attained by following the eightfold path of Buddhism. *Mindful Mediation* illustrates in a practical way how spiritual changes can become the foundation for peacemaking.

Generally, Buddhist peacebuilding is grounded in the belief that everything is fundamentally interconnected. The interdependence of all existence implies that the suffering of others is like one's own and the violence committed by others is like the violence committed by oneself. But it also implies that one's inner peace and peace of mind contribute to outer peace. While traditional Buddhist interpretations often seem to promote personal transformation at the expense of social concern, socially engaged Buddhism emphasizes the mutual enrichment of outer action and inner peace, in the understanding that meaningful peace work starts from the inner state of 'being peace'. The understanding that everything is interrelated and that the origin and transformation of conflict lie in the hearts and minds of people implies a fundamental personal responsibility for everyone.

More specifically, the Buddhist understanding of conflict teaches that the fundamental root of all conflict lies in an egocentric understanding of the world.[53] An ego-centred view does not really reflect reality as it is but distorts understanding, feelings and relationships. Such perceived separation from existence leads to a sense of insecurity. This in turn results in a need to defend and strengthen one's self-image, in susceptibility to greed, hatred and delusion, and in increased conflict behaviour. It is through the practice of mindfulness that one can become aware of this insecure self-image, its origin and dynamics. By increasing awareness of oneself and existence, the egocentric picture loosens up, defensiveness and other mental habits are transformed into self-awareness and self-management and agency replaces the passive undergoing of reactive patterns. Negative emotions of greed, hatred, and delusion can transform into generosity, compassion, and insight. As such, psycho-spiritual processes can overcome habitual ways of coping with conflict and lay the basis for peaceful ways of resolving conflict.

The Buddhist practice of meditation, therefore, includes raising awareness among the conflicting parties about the underlying dynamics of conflict, the processes by which it is sustained, and providing insights and tools to overcome these. It focuses on the underlying conditions of conflict rather than just treating the symptoms and offers psycho-spiritual ways of overcoming these conditions. Mindfulness is seen as the spiritual foundation of wholesome change. Peacebuilding is not a series of techniques, but relates directly to the self-awareness with which one lives every day. One could say that addressing 'spiritual ignorance is a central component of Buddhist peacebuilding'.[54] The spirituality of the peacemaker him or herself, including the qualities of mindful stillness, loving kindness for all living creatures and selflessness in action, is considered an important practical resource for this approach.

An example of applied Buddhist peacebuilding is the Sarvodaya Shramadana Movement in Sri Lanka. Situating much of the causes of Sri Lanka's political conflict and tensions in alienation, ill will and mutual fear, the movement aims to deal with the causes of the conflict on a socio-psychological level by focusing among others on reestablishing a value system; constructive activity; transforming the war consciousness; anchoring non-violence and compassion in people's hearts and minds; meditation; emotional healing; as well as tackling the immediate problems through relief, rehabilitation, reconstruction, and reconciliation programmes.[55] The Sarvodaya Shramadana Movement translates Buddhist principles into actions that promote self-reliance, participatory democracy and sustainable development, tackling issues of poverty, marginalization and injustice. Integrating economic, social and spiritual dimensions, the example of the Sarvodaya Shramadana Movement demonstrates that spiritual values, when actively applied in community contexts, can lead to significant social empowerment and development.[56] Critics have argued, however, whether these ideals can adequately address structural inequalities, economic disparities and deep-seated political divisions in Sri Lanka. The Sarvodaya Shramadana Movement is an inspiring model of spiritually grounded, community-led development, but they comment that it lacks the structural power to address national-level injustices, struggles with economic sustainability and faces challenges in truly bridging ethnic and religious divides.

Mennonite peacebuilding

Mennonites have developed a distinctive approach to conflict transformation and peacebuilding that centres on relationships.[57] Guided by a holistic vision, they aim to address both the consequences and roots of conflict while creating spaces for conciliation grounded in deep respect for human dignity and cultural sensitivity. Both conflict and reconciliation are seen as embedded in relationships and therefore, relationships are crucial for long-term peacebuilding and healing. As John Paul Lederach puts it: 'We resolve issues, but we reconcile people.'

For the Mennonites, building relationships is not only strategic but also has an inherent moral value since it is seen as a celebration of the opportunity to meet the other in relation. Their peacebuilding practice is characterized by a deep respect for the otherness of the other, rooted in respect for human sacredness, and permeated with conscious identity affirmation and cultural sensitivity.

Committed to grassroots engagement, Mennonites support local initiatives and empower community peacebuilders, choosing to remain in the background themselves. Their peace work is not about imposing solutions, but about 'walking with' those who make peace a reality. Inspired by the example of Jesus, they stand with the defenceless, seek justice, and witness in solidarity.

Their peacebuilding practice emphasizes humility, deep listening, learning, patience, care, service, self-awareness, and a willingness to confront internal as well as external sources of conflict.[58] It transcends technical methods, evolving into a way of being.

Mennonite peacebuilding distinguishes itself from the general instrumentalist and consequentialist thinking in the field of conflict resolution also by keeping a long-term perspective. Since Mennonites understand their peace work as a testimony to God, it diminishes their need for immediate outcomes and relativize their sense of final responsibility for the outcomes and results.

Mennonite John Paul Lederach is one of the most renowned peacebuilding scholars and practitioners today. He insists that effective peacebuilding is not simply about managing disputes or implementing technical steps, but about engaging deeply with the underlying social and emotional dynamics that fuel conflict and, in the process, re-envision relationships, identities, and communities. Lederach has introduced the psychosocial concepts of truth, justice, mercy, forgiveness and hope as the central spiritual concerns of reconciliation. In his book, *Moral Imagination: The Art and Soul of Building Peace*, Lederach argues that space should be given to the moral imagination in human affairs, so as to invoke, set free, and sustain innovative responses to the roots of violence, while rising above them.[59] This also involves a spiritual capacity to envision and sustain constructive relationships even amidst conflict. Peacemakers must understand the transformative potential hidden in every conflict situation and explore creative solutions. Peacebuilding is, therefore, both an art and a science, and requires humility and self-reflection, recognition of interdependence and empathy, courage to venture into unknown and often uncomfortable territory, and a willingness and capacity to open space for innovation and envisioning of new possibilities. These qualities and skills can be fostered through spiritual practice.

While certain groups of Mennonites have been criticized for fuelling division, discrimination and injustice, Mennonites have made lasting contributions to peacebuilding theory and practice.

Quaker peacebuilding

Just like the Mennonites, the Quakers have developed a specific kind of peacebuilding, which is rooted in their belief that God is present in everyone.[60] Fundamental to their understanding of peacebuilding is the conviction that the source of violence can only be eliminated by evoking the true identity of people, which is founded in God. This central belief provides them with a deep respect for every human being involved in conflict and a deep commitment to relieve the suffering resulting from conflict. From this vision follows a consistent attention to the human elements involved in peace work, whether it concerns establishing communication, fostering deep listening, building trust among conflicting parties, facilitating growth of awareness, or fostering positive attitudes towards opponents. Quakers integrate both the inner and the outer, the private and the public, the spiritual and the practical realities of peacemaking. In practice, Quaker peacebuilding is mainly characterized by advocacy, or 'speaking truth to power', empowering the weaker parties in conflict, opening and maintaining channels of communication between conflicting parties, facilitating dialogue, mediation, and conciliation.

In their work as facilitators and shuttle diplomats, they actively work to nurture an environment where reconciliation and healing can occur by reducing suspicions, fears, and misperceptions. Conciliation is defined by peacebuilding scholar and Quaker Adam Curle as 'activities aimed at bringing about an alteration of perception that will lead to an alteration of attitude and eventually to an alteration of behavior.'[61] In accordance with their belief, Quaker peacemaking follows the principles of acknowledging God in all, listening and attention, non-judgement, earning acceptance among conflict parties and friendly impartiality. They are well known for their practice of emphatic listening and the special role they assign to stillness as an essential preliminary to peacemaking. For Curle, awareness is 'the root of all change and therefore the source of peace.'[62] Quakers often operate behind the scenes and in silence. They have been well known in particular for their access to decision-making levels on the basis of the trust they gained through humanitarian service or relationship building activities.

Ken Wilber's Integral Theory

Ken Wilber's Integral Theory offers a multidimensional approach to human development, conflict, spirituality, and peacebuilding by integrating spiritual, psychological, cultural and systemic dimensions.[63] His model maps reality into four quadrants: individual interior (emotions and spirituality), individual exterior (behaviours and biology), collective interior (cultural values and worldviews) and collective exterior (social systems and institutions).

Central to this framework is the idea that personal transformation, focusing on the spiritual and consciousness dimensions of human experience, is foundational to effective peacebuilding. Practices fostering self-awareness, healing, inner growth and spiritual enrichment help individuals move beyond self-centred and self-interested (egocentric) or group-bound (ethnocentric) perspectives towards a more inclusive, world-centric, or even integral consciousness that recognizes the interconnectedness of everything. By fostering higher levels of consciousness, individuals become better equipped to empathize with others, reconcile differences and engage in transformative dialogue that addresses the deeper roots of conflict. Wilber distinguishes between regressive, dogmatic or tribalistic ideologies, on one hand, and integrative spiritual insights that unify communities, facilitate reconciliation, and are grounded in universal values as well as authentic inner transformation, on the other hand.

Despite its promise, Integral Theory faces criticism for its complexity, limited empirical validation, perceived elitism and insufficient engagement with structural and political realities. Still, Wilber maintains that elevating human consciousness and integrating inner experience with systemic change is vital for breaking cycles of violence and creating transformative change.

Spiritual peacebuilding

Spiritual peacebuilding contends that lasting peace in the world begins from within the individual and offers a comprehensive and transformative approach to resolving conflict by addressing the deepest roots of violence within the human heart and mind. Fundamentally, it calls for a shift from merely managing conflict to transforming the very consciousness that gives rise to it. When individuals embark on a journey of inner transformation, they not only free themselves from negative patterns but also contribute to a broader culture of peace and understanding. By cultivating inner qualities such as compassion and self-awareness, individuals are better equipped to engage constructively with others, break down entrenched barriers, and build bridges of trust and empathy. Inner qualities such as empathy, love, and compassion have the power to influence broader social, political, and economic dynamics. This holistic approach challenges the conventional, often reductionist, models of conflict resolution that rely solely on negotiations, policy changes, or power balances. Spiritual peacebuilding emphasizes how cultivating a culture of peace within individuals can create ripple effects that contribute to broader societal transformation.

Key points: Chapter 2

Psychosocial peacebuilding looks at:

(1) how psychosocial factors can influence conflict and peacebuilding dynamics both positively and negatively and
(2) how psychosocial factors themselves are impacted positively or negatively by conflict and peace dynamics.

We need to apply this lens

(1) At all stages of peacebuilding
(2) At all levels of peacebuilding
(3) In all sectors of peacebuilding
(4) Throughout the project cycle

- Psychosocial factors permeate the lives of people on all sides of conflict, whether victims/survivors, perpetrators, third parties or observers.
- Psychosocial peacebuilding effectively addresses the psychosocial consequences of conflict and violence and enhances the psychosocial resources for peacebuilding.
- Psychosocial peacebuilding strengthens a strong psychosocial foundation in individuals and communities, which can then serve as the cornerstone and driving force for effective structural and systemic change, and for sustainable peace in the long term.
- While conflicts, contexts and manifestations of related experiences differ, there seem to be similar underlying psychosocial factors, processes and experiences at play at the human level. See *Overview of Bio-Psycho-Social Factors in Peacebuilding* (Figure 2.1).
- Deeply transformative psychosocial peacebuilding is rooted in the inner world of peacebuilders.

Why psychosocial peacebuilding?

(1) Touching Humanity and Profound Transformation: psychosocial peacebuilding practice touches upon the core of humanity and facilitates transformations at the deepest levels that are profound, meaningful and relevant to our lives and circumstances.

(2) Psychosocial factors are interacting with dynamics of conflict, violence and peace in a vicious cycle.

- Various forms of violence and related negative psychosocial factors interact with each other and, when not positively addressed, generate cycles of increasing violence and deteriorating psychosocial well-being.
- The insight that the effects of trauma are heritable and can affect the mental and physical health and well-being of exposed people, their children and grandchildren, has huge implications for society.
- We can create a strong psychosocial foundation for sustainable peacebuilding when these harmful vicious circles are interrupted, negative psychosocial impacts are positively transformed, psychosocial resources positively strengthened, and root causes of war and violence addressed.
- There is an increasing understanding that a non-integrated approach causes harm and continuous violence and that an integrated approach leads to more effective and sustainable peacebuilding outcomes.

Psychosocial peacebuilding frameworks

(1) Socio-psychological repertoire and infrastructure of conflict and peace – Daniel Bar-Tal: analysing the 'psyche' of society members involved in intractable conflicts as individuals and collectives, he aims to promote a better understanding of intractable conflicts, their resolution and their prevention.

(2) Peace Psychology and Positive Peacebuilding in action in Kashmir

(3) The Integration of MHPSS and Peacebuilding: challenges and opportunities: Psychosocial peacebuilding approaches already embody, conceptually and practically, the goals of current efforts to integrate MHPSS and Peacebuilding, and already intrinsically address some of

the challenges these efforts face. More attention and effort should be directed at strengthening and developing what already exists and is integrated, rather than focusing efforts on the invention of something new, or the merging of currently widely disparate approaches.

(4) Spiritual Approaches to Peacebuilding:

- Some of the predominant characteristics of spiritual approaches are the emphasis on inner peace as the foundation for world peace and the interconnectedness of all life.
- Spiritual approaches address the inner dimensions of thoughts, emotions, and existential experience that give rise to violence and therefore need to be addressed to reestablish inner and outer peace. Spiritual principles, practices and values have the capacity to address these depths of human existence and the inner lives, minds and hearts of people.
- Spiritual peacebuilding is about practical ways in which spiritual changes become the foundation for peace.
- Spiritual approaches to peacebuilding are permeated by psychosocial factors, both in their philosophies and social applications, but also in the personal practice of spiritually inspired peacebuilders.

Recommended reading: Chapter 2

Bar Tal, D. 2013. *Intractable Conflicts: Socio-Psychological Foundations and Dynamics*. Cambridge: Cambridge University Press.

Deutsch, M. 2012. *The Psychological Components of Sustainable Peace*. New York; London: Springer.

Gopin, M. 2000. *Between Eden and Armageddon: Essays on the Future of Religion, Violence and Peacemaking*. New York: Oxford University Press.

Gopin, M. 2004. *Healing the Heart of Conflict: 8 Crucial Steps to Making Peace with Yourself and Others*. s.l.: Rodale.

Hamber, B., & Gallagher, E. 2015. *Psychosocial Perspectives on Peacebuilding*. New York: Springer.

Hertog, K. 2024. 'Integrating mental health and psychosocial support (MHPSS) and peacebuilding: A critical and constructive perspective from the integrated field of psychosocial peacebuilding'. *Peace and Conflict: Journal of Peace Psychology*. https://doi.org/10.1037/pac0000773.

Inter-Agency Standing Committee (IASC). 2024. 'IASC guidance integrating MHPSS and peacebuilding: A mapping and recommendations for practitioners'. https://interagencystandingcommittee.org/iasc-reference-group-mental-health-and-psychosocial-support-emergency-settings/iasc-guidance-integrating-mhpss-and-peacebuilding-mapping-and-recommendations-practitioners.

Lederach, J. P. 2005. *The Moral Imagination: The Art and Soul of Building Peace*. New York: Oxford University Press.

McConnell, J. A. 1995. *Mindful Mediation: A Handbook for Buddhist Peacemakers*. Thailand: Buddhist Research Institute & Mahachula Buddhist University.

Notes

1. See Chapter 2.
2. See Chapter 4.
3. See also https://l.artofliving.org/peaceincolombia-en (consulted 24 Sept 2024).
4. https://www.srisriravishankar.org/work/peace-initiatives/colombia-farc-relaunches-political-party-calls-miracle/; https://www.srisriravishankar.org/work/peace-initiatives/peace-initiatives/ (consulted 24 Sept 2024).
5. https://www.srisriravishankar.org/work/peace-initiatives/sri-sri-meets-top-colombian-leaders/ (consulted 24 Sept 2024).
6. https://www.srisriravishankar.org/work/peace-initiatives/referendum-colombia-farc-peace-agreement/ (consulted 24 Sept 2024).
7. https://www.srisriravishankar.org/work/peace-initiatives/sri-sri-meets-top-colombian-leaders/ (consulted 24 Sept 2024).
8. Betancourt, T. S., et al. 2010. 'Past horrors, present struggles: The role of stigma in the association between war experiences and psychosocial adjustment among former child soldiers in Sierra Leone'. *Social Science & Medicine* 70, pp. 17–26; Denov, M., & Marchand, I. 2014. '"One cannot take away the stain": Rejection and stigma among former child soldiers in Colombia'. *Peace and Conflict: Journal of Peace Psychology* 20:3, pp. 227–40; Tonheim, M. 2012. '"Who will comfort me?" Stigmatization of girls formerly associated with armed forces and groups in eastern Congo'. *The International Journal of Human Rights* 12:2, pp. 278–97; Wessells, M. G. 2006. *Child Soldiers: From Violence to Protection*. Cambridge, MA: Harvard University Press.
9. Vinck, P., Pham, P. N., Stover, E., & Weinstein, H. M. 2007. 'Exposure to war crimes and implications for peace building in northern Uganda'. *JAMA* 298:5, pp. 543–54.
10. Staub, E. 2011. *Overcoming Evil: Genocide, Violent Conflict, and Terrorism*. Oxford University Press. https://doi.org/10.1093/acprof:oso/9780195382044.001.0001; Bloomfield, D., Barnes, T., & Huyse, L. (Eds.). 2003. *Reconciliation after Violent Conflict: A Handbook*. International IDEA; Felitti, V. J., et al. 1998. 'Relationship of childhood abuse and household dysfunction to many of the leading causes of death in adults: The Adverse Childhood Experiences (ACE) Study'. *American Journal of Preventive Medicine* 14:4, pp. 245–58; Widom, C. S. 1989. 'Child abuse, neglect, and adult behavior: Research design and findings on criminality, violence, and child abuse'. *American Journal of Orthopsychiatry* 59:3, pp. 355–67.
11. Rausch, C. (ed.) May 2021, p. 7.
12. Idem, p. 10.
13. Idem, p. 9.
14. Ibidem.
15. Idem, p. 11.
16. Idem, p. 13.

17 This section is based on Bar Tal, D. 2011. *Intergroup Conflicts and Their Resolution: A Social Psychological Perspective*. New York: Psychology Press, intro.

18 The concepts and reflections mentioned below are mainly from Ufra Mir's thought processes and work between 2005 and 2012. Her reflections have evolved since then, and she may or may not agree with everything she believed in back then.

19 See https://www.uwc.org/impact/one-alums-work-as-the-first-peace-psychologist-in-kashmir and the website of Paigaam: http://www.paigaampeace.org/founder-ceo.html (consulted 16 July 2024).

20 This section is largely based on Hertog, K. 2024. 'Integrating mental health and psychosocial support (MHPSS) and peacebuilding: A critical and constructive perspective from the integrated field of psychosocial peacebuilding'. *Peace and Conflict: Journal of Peace Psychology*. https://doi.org/10.1037/pac0000773.

21 IASC. 2007. Guidelines on Mental Health and Psychosocial Support in Emergency Settings. p. 1.

22 IASC. 2007.

23 IASC. 2007, p. iii.

24 IASC. 2024, p. 11.

25 UNDP. 2022. 'Integrating mental health and psychosocial support into peacebuilding: Guidance note'. https://www.undp.org/publications/integrating-mental-health-and-psychosocial-support-peacebuilding.

26 IASC. 2024, p. 24.

27 IASC. 2024, p. 20.

28 Huser, K. s.a. 'Integrating mental health & psycho-social support in peace-building programming: Conceptual framework for Norwegian church aid'. s.l., p. 4.

29 IASC. 2024, p. 75.

30 World Health Organization. 17 June 2022. 'Mental health fact sheet'. https://www.who.int/data/gho/data/major-themes/health-and-wellbeing#:~:text=Mental%20health%20is%20a%20state,to%20his%20or%20her%20community.

31 Milligan, K., et al. 18 Jan 2022. 'The relational work of systems change'. In *Stanford Social Innovation Review*. https://ssir.org/articles/entry/the_relational_work_of_systems_change.

32 IASC. 2024, p. 10.

33 See Hertog, K. 2024. 'Integrating mental health and psychosocial support (MHPSS) and peacebuilding: A critical and constructive perspective from the integrated field of psychosocial peacebuilding'. *Peace and Conflict: Journal of Peace Psychology*. https://doi.org/10.1037/pac0000773.

34 Institute for Justice and Reconciliation and the War Trauma Foundation. 2017. 'Peacebuilding and mental health and psychosocial support: A review of current theory and practice', p. 32.

35 Huser, K. 2020, p. 8.

36 IASC. 2024, p. 46.

37 This section is largely based on Hertog, K. 2010.
38 Gopin, Marc. 2000. *Between Eden and Armageddon: Essays on the Future of Religion, Violence and Peacemaking*. New York: Oxford University Press.
39 http://www.dalailama.com/page.62.htm cited in Hertog, K. 2010, p. 35.
40 Carmody, Denise L., & Carmody, John T. 1988. *Peace and Justice in the Scriptures of the World Religions*. New York: Paulist Press, p. 174.
41 United Religions Initiative and Galtung referred to in Hertog, K. 2010, p. 79.
42 Louise Diamond as cited from *The Peace Book: 108 Simple Ways to Create a More Peaceful World* in URI, 2004, p. 281.
43 Hertog, K. 2010, p. 72.
44 Appleby, 2000, referred to in Hertog, K. 2010, pp. 87–8.
45 See Hertog, K. 2010, pp. 36–7.
46 Tutu, D. 1999. *No Future Without Forgiveness*. New York: Doubleday.
47 Bush, R. A. B., & Folger, J. P. 2004. *The Promise of Mediation: The Transformative Approach to Conflict*. Jossey-Bass.
48 Gopin, M. 2004. *Healing the Heart of Conflict: 8 Crucial Steps to Making Peace With Yourself and Others*. s.l.: Rodale.
49 United Religions Initiative. 2004. *Interfaith Peacebuilding Guide*. s.l.
50 Esbjörn-Hargens, S., & Zimmerman, M. E. (Eds.). 2009. *Integral Ecology: Uniting Multiple Perspectives on the Natural World*. Boston, MA: Integral Books; Capra, F. 1996. *The Web of Life: A New Scientific Understanding of Living Systems*. New York: Anchor Books; Berry, T. 1999. *The Dream of the Earth*. San Francisco, CA: Sierra Club Books.
51 Thich Nhat Hanh. 1987. *Being Peace*. Berkeley: Parallax Press; Thich Nath Hanh. 1992. *Touching Peace*. Berkeley: Parallax Press; Thich Nath Hanh. 1993. *Love in Action: Writings on Nonviolent Social Change*. Berkeley: Parallax Press.
52 McConnell, John A. 1995. *Mindful Mediation: A Handbook for Buddhist Peacemakers*. Thailand: Buddhist Research Institute & Mahachula Buddhist University. Also, the publication Kenneth Kraft, ed. 1992. *Inner Peace, World Peace*. Albany: State University of New York Press, contains some interesting reflections on the practical daily implications of the many Buddhist teachings and resources on non-violence and their relevance in concrete situations.
53 Hertog, K. 2010, p. 94.
54 McConnell cited in Hertog, K. 2010, p. 95.
55 See URI. 2004, pp. 143–7.
56 Bond, P. D. R. 2004. *Buddhism at Work: Community Development, Social Empowerment and the Sarvodaya Movement*. Bloomfield, CT: Kumarian Press.
57 Lederach, J. P., & Sampson, C. (Ed.). 2000. *From the Ground Up: Mennonite Contributions to International Peacebuilding*. New York: Oxford University Press; Hertog, K. 2010, p. 91.
58 Hertog, K. 2010, p. 92.

59 Lederach, J. P. 2005. *The Moral Imagination: The Art and Soul of Building Peace*. Oxford University Press.

60 This section is mostly based on Curle, A. 1981. *True Justice: Quaker Peace Makers and Peace Making*. London: Quaker Home Service; and Hertog, K. 2010, pp. 92–3.

61 Curle cited in Hertog, K. 2010, p. 93.

62 Curle, A. 1981, p. 44, cited in Hertog, K. 2010, p. 38.

63 Wilber, K. 2000. *Integral Psychology: Consciousness, Spirit, Psychology, Therapy*. Shambhala; Wilber, K. 2006. *Integral Spirituality: A Startling New Role for Religion in the Modern and Postmodern World*. Shambhala.

3 The integrated psychosocial peacebuilding approach of the International Association for Human Values

For the past 40 years, The Art of Living [and IAHV] has led millions to find deep peace and silence within while expanding their vision to serve society through dynamic action to create a violence-free and stress-free world.

—*Gurudev Sri Sri Ravi Shankar*[1]

In the previous chapter, we have defined and conceptualized PSPB and explored different existing frameworks. In this chapter, we want to present **the PSPB framework of IAHV, which is not only a comprehensive conceptual framework but also an integrated approach rooted in evidence-based practices that is actually implemented around the world in a variety of contexts and target groups, in both conflict and peace settings.**

The International Association for Human Values

The International Association for Human Values (IAHV) is a largely volunteer-based, non-profit, non-governmental organization (NGO) established in 1997 in Geneva by Gurudev Sri Sri Ravi Shankar and other global leaders. With approximately twenty-five branches worldwide, its mission is to **foster sustainable and inclusive peace by promoting the development of human values in both the individual and societies.**

Human values, such as a sense of connectedness, respect for all life, non-violence, cooperation, friendship, integrity, an eco-friendly attitude, compassion, responsibility and service to society, form the foundation of a culture and practice of peace. They are shared across religions, cultures and nationalities. However, they are often not lived or expressed fully due to stress and other inhibiting factors.

IAHV's programmes aim to reduce stress and trauma to create conditions that allow innate human values to emerge, be practised and be expressed. These programmes are designed to enhance clarity of mind, facilitate attitudinal and behavioural shifts, and develop resilient, responsible and inspired leaders and communities.

IAHV works in cooperation with the Art of Living Foundation and employs Art of Living's methods that have been shown to alleviate acute, episodic and chronic stress. Over the last forty-five years, these researched and evidence-based methods have benefited millions of people across 185 countries and have been successfully integrated in trauma-relief, disaster response, educational initiatives, healthcare, prisoner rehabilitation and other sectors with significant social impact.

The programmes offered by IAHV address the root causes of several major global challenges, including conflict and war, recidivism and prisoner rehabilitation, mental health issues such as depression, climate change, greed and corruption, radicalization and polarization.

Through an integrated vision of life and a broad range of projects, IAHV and the Art of Living Foundation contribute to each of the 17 UN Sustainable Development Goals (Table 3.1).

IAHV's human-centred approach facilitates collaboration across various sectors and populations. This includes partnerships with international organizations (such as the UN, EU and World Bank), governments, managers and CEO's, social and community workers, women's groups, religious leaders, refugees, victims of violence, children and youth, terrorists, militants and prisoners, thereby bridging religious, ethnic and social divides.

Gurudev Sri Sri Ravi Shankar, the founder, is recognized as a prominent spiritual and humanitarian leader whose programmes have reached an estimated 600 million people. His initiatives are designed to empower and transform individuals, enabling them to address challenges at global, national, community, and individual levels.

Table 3.1 *IAHV and Art of Living Comprehensive Contributions to the 17 UN Sustainable Development Goals*

IAHV and Art of Living comprehensive contributions to the **17 UN Sustainable Development Goals**[2] include: • peacebuilding initiatives,   • skill development to alleviate poverty,   • humanitarian and trauma-relief efforts in disaster areas,   • the provision of holistic education encompassing mental health and life skills,   • social and economic empowerment of women,   • youth leadership empowerment,   • strengthening resilience and agility in the corporate sector,   • ensuring access to clean drinking water,   • organizing health awareness camps for vulnerable populations,   • river rejuvenation projects aimed at water access and rural community preservation,   • the delivery of clean energy solutions to disadvantaged communities,   • protection of the girl child,   • bringing stakeholders together to address shared social challenges,   • training in natural farming,   • and planting trees, among others.

IAHV's peacebuilding approach

The International Association for Human Values (IAHV) employs an innovative and comprehensive psychosocial approach to peacebuilding. Its peacebuilding programmes are designed to transform the mindsets, attitudes, well-being and behaviours of individuals and communities involved in or affected by conflict and violence, including perpetrators, impacted communities and intervening parties.

IAHV's programmes utilize an integrated set of processes and tools aimed at facilitating physical, mental, emotional and existential change, thereby positively transforming both internal and external psychosocial factors. Recognizing that no peace can become self-sustainable if it is not internalized and socially supported by the people involved, **IAHV prioritizes the development of a fertile psychosocial foundation within individuals and communities through a profoundly human-centred approach across conflict lines. Such profound, healthy psychosocial foundation is intended to reinforce other peacebuilding and development initiatives, thereby enhancing overall impact.**

By establishing a clear linkage between inner and outer peace, IAHV provides a model **to scale up personal transformation to achieve substantial peacebuilding impact**. The efficacy of IAHV's peacebuilding approach is supported by well-documented evidence, as outlined in the following sections.

IAHV's Theory of Change: From personal transformation to societal peacebuilding impact

IAHV's Theory of Change posits that individual and community transformation leads to broader societal peacebuilding impact. The model is based on several key assumptions (Table 3.2).

Overall, the theory suggests that personal transformation, when scaled collectively, forms the cornerstone of sustainable societal peace.

IAHV's conceptual model of psychosocial peacebuilding

(The below description of IAHV's Conceptual Model is largely based on the article published in Interventions[3])

IAHV focuses on intrapersonal transformation as the cornerstone and foundation for peacebuilding, while at the same time addressing structural change, engaging with behavioural and relational dimensions of peacebuilding and strengthening underlying human and peace-promoting values.

Table 3.2 *IAHV Theory of Change*

IAHV Theory of Change and Its Key Assumptions

- When individuals and communities have access to techniques and tools that enhance mental, emotional, physical, and social well-being, and when these methods are self-empowering, accessible, easy to use, cost-effective, and applicable across cultures, a significant proportion of these populations will integrate them into their lives.
- When individuals and communities use evidence-based techniques and tools that strengthen their physiology for peace, reduce symptoms of depression, anxiety, PTSD and stress, and bring improved clarity, focus, calm and optimism, the negative impact of adverse experiences will reduce, overall well-being will improve, and attitudes, behaviour and relationships will be positively affected.
- When individuals and communities are empowered to process their negatively impacting experiences, wounds and responses to trauma, the likelihood of self-harm or harm to others is reduced. When individuals and communities become resilient, they can withstand and recover more quickly from such negative impacts and better resist violent and divisive tendencies.
- When individuals and communities are non-violently empowered, they can act as agents of positive change in society, transforming negative impacts and improving both overall well-being and peacebuilding outcomes.
- A collective of healed, resilient, empowered, and trained individuals and communities constitutes a strong psychosocial foundation for any society to prevent or overcome the effects of conflict and violence, to strengthen peacebuilding and development efforts, to address root causes, and to create peace-enhancing systems. Thus, overall impact will be increased, and peace becomes more self-sustainable.
- Finally, when peacebuilding practitioners enhance their personal well-being and develop key peacebuilding qualities, their professional performance is optimized, contributing to more effective interventions in the field.

Profound and holistic intrapersonal transformation of all people involved in, or affected by conflict and violence, is the essential cornerstone of peacebuilding. It positively affects communities and context, where simultaneous efforts are undertaken to transform driving forces of direct, cultural and structural violence. **The transformation of structures into peace-promoting systems, along with the promotion of peace-enhancing values within society, alongside the transformation of individual and collective mindsets, attitudes and behaviours towards peace, mutually interact and reinforce each other as components of sustainable peace.**

Part one: IAHV model of intrapersonal transformation

On the personal level, IAHV programmes transform the mindsets, attitudes, behaviour and well-being of individuals and communities involved in or affected by conflict and violence. IAHV uses a holistic approach to personal transformation that addresses the entire human system from the physical to deeply existential layers, transcending the strictly cognitive (Figure 3.1). It addresses the individual's system from a holistic perspective, transforming physical, emotional, mental, attitudinal, behavioural, relational and existential aspects:

Figure 3.1 *IAHV model of intrapersonal transformation.*

- **Physical**: It achieves stress release and deep relaxation (reduction of the stress hormone cortisol), improved functioning of the neurobiological stress response system, increased energy levels, and improved physical health and well-being.
- **Emotional**: It releases negative emotions (anger, frustration, depression, hatred, revenge, ...) and brings increased ability to connect to people and a deeper sense of community, increased capacity to handle overwhelming emotions (emotional resilience and regulation), self-confidence, experience of more positive and life-supporting emotions, improved sense of well-being, healing of emotional wounds, and a sense of empowerment.
- **Mental**: It releases negative impressions and trauma, and brings increased peace of mind, improved capacity to handle challenging situations, insights into the functioning of the mind, self-knowledge, practical wisdom to look at life in a constructive way, a sense of empowerment, a more positive and contented mindset, broadened and refined perception, decreased worry and tension, more collected judgement and decision-making, the opening up of narrow-minded concepts, and improved discernment.
- **Attitudes**: It fosters more tolerant attitudes, increased ability to embrace differences, an increased ability for empathy and compassion and a better understanding.
- **Identity/ego**: It broadens narrow identities, develops multiple identities, develops shared identity with humanity, transforms self-centredness into self-awareness and self-management, and transcends destructive and unhelpful ego-positions.
- **Behavioural**: It generates less harmful behaviour towards self or others, increased responsibility for oneself and surroundings, behaviour becomes more oriented towards the well-being of oneself and others, with improved communication and problem-solving skills, and increased ability to act instead of react.

- **Existential**: It brings enhanced processing of meaning, the seeing of life in a broader perspective, reflection on the purpose of life, and the experience of being part of something larger, restoring fundamental trust.

Stress in the body, mind or emotions, including anger, fear, hatred, greed, fanaticism, frustration, trauma or depression, negatively influences our perception, interpretation, decision-making and behaviour. We become negatively biased in how we perceive situations, react instead of act, engage in destructive instead of constructive behaviour, act upon negative emotional impulses instead of reason, and narrow our sense of possibilities. Many of us have not learned, either at home or at school, how to deal constructively with negative emotions, challenging situations and internal or external conflict.

When individuals are enabled with IAHV's techniques to release stress and negative emotions, calm their worries and tensions in the mind, and thus become positively established in themselves, this becomes reflected in their behaviour, relationships and outlook towards the world. Building on restored mental and emotional well-being, IAHV programmes then apply a set of pedagogical methods and strategies (processes, knowledge, discussions, games, practical tools, self-reflection) to strengthen self-confidence, explore a broadened and shared self-identity, inculcate human values, improve non-violent conflict resolution, address issues of trust, fear, suspicion and hatred, reduce resentment, build connectedness and reinforce healthy attitudes and skills for peaceful coexistence.

On a behavioural level this can then lead to a diminished need for negative coping strategies, improved communication and life skills for handling challenging situations, and increased inclination to take responsibility. It reduces the inclination towards harmful behaviour towards oneself or others, which in turn can manifest in reduced frequency and severity of violent incidents, criminal activity, substance abuse, aggression or recruitment into armed groups. Similarly, individuals can feel more resilient in the face of peer pressure, overwhelming emotions, discriminatory behaviour, intimidation, or recruitment.

On the existential level, IAHV's Peacebuilding approach can elicit and restore a sense of meaning in life, provide a way out of deep disappointment and despair, re-establish a connection within oneself and with existence and restore fundamental trust. It can broaden the outlook and perspective on life and life events and give a personal experience of being part of something larger.

IAHV programmes are deeply empowering, life affirming and truly holistic. They restore peace at every level of human existence, well beyond the cognitive.

Part two: Psychosocial transformation, systems and structures in society

As social beings, we find ourselves, through all seven dimensions of our existence, in constant and mutual interaction with different aspects of society (Figure 3.2). This interaction with society

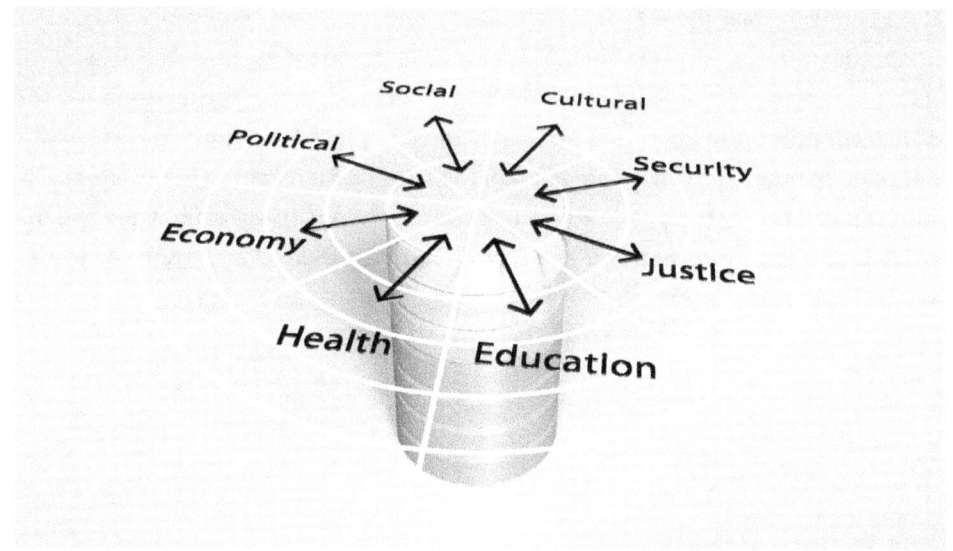

Figure 3.2 *IAHV model of mutual interaction between the individual and different aspects of society.*

involves the development and modification of our perceptions, interpretations, analyses, feelings, memories, sense of self, behaviour and relationships.

Negative societal inputs, such as injustice, discrimination, violence, poverty or lack of health care, can cause or exacerbate inner turmoil, stress, tension, illness or frustration. A supportive environment, on the other hand, one that provides security, justice, fulfilment of basic needs, health care, education and a sense of dignity, can strengthen health, inner well-being and positivity.

Different IAHV initiatives foster the development of human, effective and just systems in all sectors of society. These include inclusive leadership, transparent governance, ethical business, humane prison rehabilitation and holistic education. IAHV and Art of Living, in partnership with other organizations, promote longer-term structural change through a wide variety of initiatives. These include, for example, the organization of Transformational Leadership in Excellence Programmes on the political and corporate leadership levels, as well as global awareness raising and networking symposia on acute social topics such as peacemaking, ethics in business and sports, artificial intelligence, the girl child, interreligious understanding and climate issues.

Similarly, when our inner world is disturbed, our impact in society is more likely to be neutral or negative in terms of disengagement, frustration, anger, disappointment, radicalization, disrespect, violence or depression. Individuals who are well established in themselves, healed and empowered, are more likely to bring a positive contribution to different aspects of society and to play a peace enhancing role in their communities and institutions. The development of peaceful, healthy and prosperous societies correlates to the positive inner empowerment of its individuals. Focusing on the individual as the basis for social and political transformation is how IAHV aims to turn personal transformation into peacebuilding impact.

The outer, structural aspects of peacebuilding and the inner, psychological factors are interdependent, interacting and mutually reinforcing components of peacebuilding. IAHV works on the transformation of both the inner and outer world. The **cornerstone for social and peacebuilding impact** is the **strong emphasis placed on inner transformation: Dependant on how a person is able to align the seven dimensions of her existence, that person can still be centred, connected and contribute positively even when the outer world is in chaos, or alternatively can feel disturbed, stressed and angry inside even when the outer world is peaceful.**

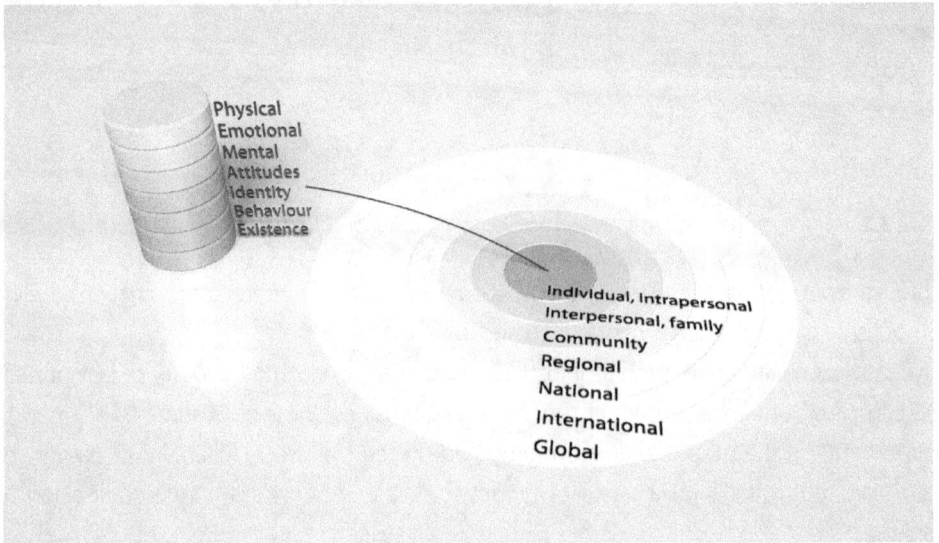

Figure 3.3 *IAHV model of interrelationships and social cohesion.*

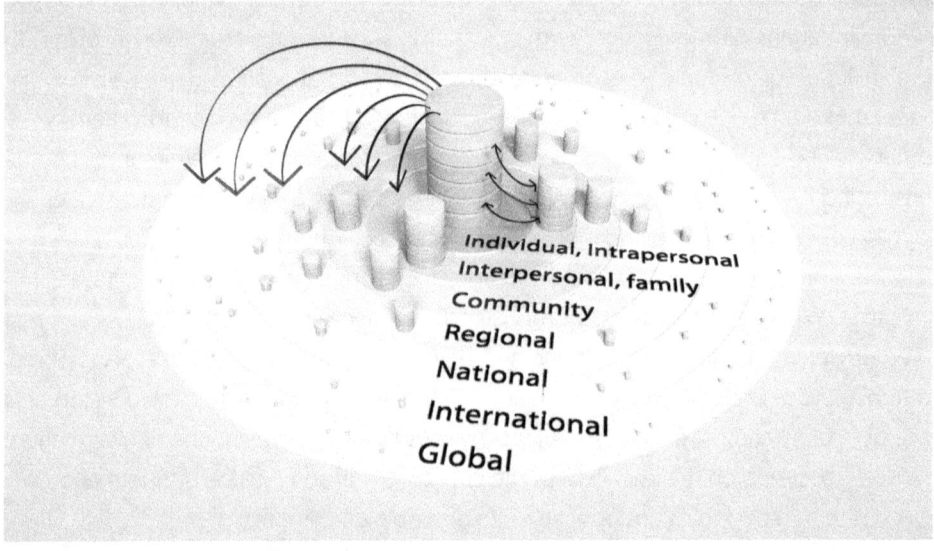

Figure 3.4 *IAHV model of interrelationships and social cohesion.*

Part three: Psychosocial transformation, relationships and social cohesion

As social beings, we also find ourselves, through all seven dimensions of our existence, in constant and mutual interaction with other people and our environments. How one feels inside has a direct impact on the level and extent to which one feels connected to the people around: family members, neighbours, communities and the nation, but also to the world at large, the environment and the universe. When individuals are stressed and tense, they can feel more isolated and disconnected from themselves, others and their environment. **When individuals feel connected within themselves, they are more likely to develop stronger connections interpersonally and within communities, creating inclusive relationships and greater community resilience to conflict or contributing to the restoration of the social fabric after conflict.**

Cross-cutting: Promoting human values for a culture of peace

In order to build a sustainable peace, it is crucial to nourish human values as the foundation. Many of the world's challenges and the resulting war and violence are triggered by greed, aggression, hunger for power, intolerance or selfishness. Such values and attitudes permeate cultures, politics, media and socio-economic life and can come to be considered normal, appropriate, or even laudable. Values, in turn, influence attitudes, mindsets and behaviours. As Gopin states: 'It takes a great many human relationships to fail and a great many interpersonal values to be violated in order to bring war to full consciousness and acceptance.'[4]

IAHV's mission is to **promote positive human values in all sectors of society as the core of a culture and practice of peace** (Table 3.3). According to IAHV, human values are 'those

Table 3.3 *Universal Human Values According to IAHV's Model*

Universal Human Values – IAHV
1. A deep caring for all life, which is the fundamental basis for all the other human values;
2. Non-violence, which arises spontaneously from an awareness of the sacredness of all life;
3. Compassion, characterized by the desire to eliminate suffering and misery for all life;
4. Friendliness and cooperation, which blossom with the awareness that we belong to one human family;
5. Generosity and sharing, qualities that grow with the awareness that true prosperity is the result of giving, not of hoarding;
6. A sense of belonging and oneness with all life;
7. An eco-friendly attitude and caring for the planet, arising from the understanding that the earth is our mother, to be revered and cared for;
8. Service to society, rooted in the awareness that we are here to contribute something of value to society, not so much to get something for ourselves;
9. A sense of commitment and responsibility, ultimately extending to all of society and all life; a foundation for true empowerment;
10. Peace and contentment, part of our deepest nature, to be nurtured and encouraged, bringing peace to our surroundings and ultimately throughout the entire world;
11. Enthusiasm, to be supported and nurtured as life itself;
12. Integrity, honesty and sincerity, honoured by all spiritual traditions and forming the foundation of social order and justice.

attributes and qualities that are the very heart of humanity, representing the highest expression of the human spirit.'[5]

IAHV works from the premise that these values are shared across cultures, religions and nationalities, though often not lived or expressed due to stresses, lack of awareness and other factors. If such values can be instilled in individuals and communities as well as in social, cultural and political life, we can lay a psychosocial foundation to positively impact the way individuals and communities think and interact at every level of society. In this regard, Gurudev Sri Sri Ravi Shankar often calls upon the youth to re-instil a sense of pride in being non-violent, compassionate, helpful and friendly. He emphasizes the importance of creating new role models who exemplify these qualities.

It is not sufficient to declare human values; they also need to be internalized and nurtured. Participation in the stress-relief and personal development programmes of the Art of Living creates the sense of well-being, calm and resilience in which human values can blossom. It is important to strengthen a foundation inside individuals in which human values are anchored, since history has shown abundantly how the behaviour of otherwise peaceful people radically changes under the conditions of fear and anger. It is in extraordinary situations of violence, war and genocide that the difference becomes visible in the behaviour of people who have internalized values of non-violent resistance, inner strength, love, empathy and compassion, and those who do not adhere to such values or adhere to them only in words.[6] Through practices such as meditation, prayer, surrender, practising awareness, breathing, silence, singing or fasting, one can discover these values in oneself, nourish them and internalize them. The blossoming of human values internally inspires people to contribute to a more peaceful and prosperous world and at the same time provides a fundamental layer for the prevention of violence.

To this end, Gurudev Sri Sri Ravi Shankar formally proposed a Universal Declaration of Human Values to the United Nations,[7] envisioning that **the incorporation of human values into all aspects of life will ultimately lead to a more peaceful, just and sustainable world**. Socio-economic development must be built on aforementioned human values to be sustainable. Human values are also a clear basis from which to ensure respect for human rights: 'For human rights to flourish, human values must be nurtured, just as the roots of a tree must be watered for the fruit to grow. Rekindling human values throughout the world is essential to achieving universal human rights, peace and security on the planet, and harmonious coexistence among different peoples and cultures.'[8]

The activities and projects of IAHV and the Art of Living are rooted in these human values and many initiatives are undertaken to actively nurture and promote them, transform cultural and societal norms, and change behaviours. These include the organization of large world culture festivals to promote peaceful coexistence and understanding, the honouring of traditional cultures, action campaigns against injustice and for the environment, value-based education initiatives, holistic approaches to health and education, the empowerment of marginalized groups in society, campaigns for peace and non-violence, reconciliation initiatives, among many others.

Sustainable self-empowering transformation of individuals and society

As such, **IAHV's psychosocial approach and techniques bring about changes in the individual, the communities and the context itself, restoring peace within and between individuals, communities and society**. The core of IAHV's approach is to empower individuals and communities to become self-reliant and to create the change they want to see themselves. IAHV **empowers individuals and communities by providing knowledge, skills and tools to improve their own physical, mental and emotional well-being**. They are also empowered **to develop and implement their own initiatives that address local community needs and priorities that they themselves identify**. Thus, individuals and communities are directly empowered to overcome responses to trauma and build local resilience, thus creating **self-sustaining change** and reducing dependency on external support. This inherently self-sustainable approach strengthens local resources and focuses on existing capacity instead of deficit. It **brings about individual transformation and structural change at every level of society, from grassroots to global leadership**. Thus, the IAHV Psychosocial Peacebuilding approach works for prevention, intervention, transformation and rehabilitation, and can be applied at all stages of a peacebuilding process.

Peacebuilding record and impact

This approach has been implemented with considerable success in numerous conflict zones worldwide.

IAHV and its partner, the Art of Living Foundation, have worked extensively on issues of conflict, war, refugee displacement, trauma, violence, rehabilitation, sustainable development, and youth and women's empowerment in a diverse array of contexts, including India, the United States, Kosovo, Sri Lanka, Ivory Coast, South Africa, Colombia, Mexico, Lebanon, Jordan, Iraq, the Caucasus, the Philippines, Ukraine, Russia, Denmark, Afghanistan, among others.

Empirical evidence demonstrates the impact of these programmes across various domains, including

- Reduction of stress and trauma among approximately 700,000 trauma-affected beneficiaries worldwide, with interventions implemented in regions such as Iraq, Israel-Palestine, Kashmir, India, the United States, the Balkans, Sri Lanka, the Northern Caucasus, Ukraine, Syria, Lebanon, Colombia and Afghanistan, as well as following terrorist attacks (e.g. Brussels Airport 2016, Taj Hotel Mumbai 2008, New York 2001).
- Disarmament, Demobilization, and Reintegration (DDR) initiatives have resulted in more than 7,400 combatants from non-state armed groups renouncing violence. This includes militants and rebels associated with groups such as the Kashmiri militants, Naxalite terrorists, FARC

rebels, Kosovo Liberation Army veterans, LTTE members in Sri Lanka, militants in Assam, and Maoists in Nepal.
- A breakthrough in the peace process in Colombia was achieved in June 2015 when the leadership of the FARC declared a unilateral ceasefire and adopted Gandhian principles of non-violence.
- Rehabilitation programmes have been implemented in prisons worldwide, reaching approximately 800,000 prisoners and staff, with some initiatives in the United States reporting a 61 per cent reduction in recidivism.
- Rehabilitation and reintegration initiatives have also been applied to gangs in Panama, Mexico and Denmark.
- Programmes focusing on healing, resilience and prevention of extremism have benefited 18,000 war-affected children in Lebanon and Jordan (under an EU project), with 100 at-risk youth trained as Peace Ambassadors who subsequently led fifteen peacebuilding projects addressing key drivers of violence.
- Interventions in the United States have reduced symptoms of post-traumatic stress disorder (PTSD) in approximately 2,500 veterans from the Iraq, Afghanistan and Vietnam wars.
- Ongoing trauma-relief and women's empowerment initiatives have been sustained in Iraq since 2004.
- Efforts in Ivory Coast have facilitated reconciliation between the Deula and Guere tribes following ethnic violence.
- Reconciliation processes in Kashmir have addressed the grievances of 140 families affected by the loss of militants and soldiers.
- Violence prevention measures in three villages in Assam were effectively implemented amidst widespread regional conflict.
- During the Covid-19 pandemic (2020–2), resilience training was provided to more than 50,000 healthcare workers.
- The resolution of a centuries-old conflict in Ayodhya, India, between Hindus and Muslims has contributed to ending a history of recurring wars and extensive casualties.
- Comprehensive sustainable development interventions in rural India have impacted 50,000 villages, including the training of 100,000 youth leaders for social change, the instruction of 2 million farmers in organic farming practices, the provision of free holistic education to 120,000 children, the skill development of 300,000 villagers for improved livelihoods, the revival of 47 riverine ecosystems, and progress in gender equality, poverty reduction, conflict mitigation, and the reduction of substance abuse and corruption.

These outcomes indicate that the integration of evidence-based psychosocial interventions can produce measurable improvements in both individual well-being and broader societal peacebuilding outcomes.

Data on Violence Reduction:

- A 61 per cent reduction in recidivism has been observed among participants in IAHV's Prison Programme. Specifically, recidivism rates for graduates at the Indianapolis Reentry Education Facility (IREF) during the period from 2009 to 2015 were recorded at 14.6 per cent, which represents a 61 per cent reduction relative to the state average. These findings show that SKY Breath Meditation[9] may be an effective component of rehabilitation efforts.[10]

- Multiple studies conducted in at-risk schools in the United States have documented reductions in aggression, bullying, anger, violent incidents, disciplinary measures and suspensions following implementation of IAHV's SKY programme. These positive behavioural changes are correlated with improvements in social-emotional learning skills, including emotional regulation, self-awareness, self-management, resilience, relational skills and responsible decision-making.[11]

    For instance, a study at a high school in Milwaukee reported that after the SKY programme, 43 per cent of students exhibited decreased anger, 31 per cent demonstrated reduced bullying behaviours and 47 per cent showed diminished aggression and fighting. Additionally, the study noted a 58 per cent increase in caring and cooperative behaviours. These outcomes contributed to a 60 per cent decrease in disciplinary infractions. Similar outcomes have been observed across various schools in the United States.

    At Eastside High School in Newark, data indicated that the proportion of students meeting adequate yearly performance standards increased from 20 per cent to 90 per cent. The number of students on the honour roll increased from 100 to 800, while formal disciplinary actions decreased by 90 per cent. At Dodd Middle School in New York, suspensions dropped by 44 per cent and formal disciplinary actions declined by 64 per cent over a two-year period during which the SKY programme was implemented. In a California school, implementation of SKY was associated with a 38 per cent reduction in violent incidents, a 28 per cent decrease in disruptive behaviour, a 45 per cent reduction in drug and alcohol use and a 45 per cent decrease in suspension hours over two years.

    In Wetaskiwin, Alberta, Canada – a community with high youth homicide rates attributed to gang violence – 66 per cent of students reported a decrease in perceived stress; there was a 26 per cent reduction in substance use, a 22 per cent increase in healthy coping strategies and a complete (100 per cent) reduction in reported violent behaviour.

    These findings collectively indicate that the SKY programme is associated with significant reductions in violent and disruptive behaviours, as well as improvements in academic performance and social-emotional skills in at-risk educational settings.

- In 2001, a study conducted by the Lancaster Violence Alternative Programme in Los Angeles County examined the effects of SKY Breath Meditation on violent youth offenders aged thirteen to eighteen, all of whom had prior convictions for serious violent crimes, including murder and rape. The study found that, after completing the SKY programme, participants experienced a 38 per cent reduction in physical altercations, a 23 per cent reduction in disciplinary removals and a 21 per cent decrease in facility incident reports.[12]

- A study involving 219 surrendered ULFA militants from Assam found that participants exhibited a marked decrease in aggression and significant improvements in quality of life and life satisfaction within forty days of participating in the programme. These changes facilitated their rehabilitation and reintegration into society.[13]
- Research on the SKY Resilience Programme, conducted with over 3,000 officers from the Bahia Military Police in Brazil, demonstrated a 60 per cent reduction in the use of force and a 70 per cent reduction in community complaints, indicating substantial improvements in police-community relations.[14]
- According to prison officials, trauma-relief interventions conducted by IAHV and the Art of Living in Kosovo following the 1998–9 conflict contributed to an 85 per cent reduction in suicides in Kosovo prisons, underscoring the programme's impact on mental health and crisis management.[15]

Methodology: Programmes, SKY and research evidence
IAHV programming

IAHV's programming is grounded in its overarching conceptual framework, with practical **implementation tailored to the specific needs, contexts, and target groups.** The duration and content of these initiatives vary accordingly. Examples of IAHV programmes include:

- One-hour stress and trauma-relief workshops for populations affected by disasters or experiencing high levels of stress.
- Six-hour stress-relief and resilience workshops designed for children impacted by conflict.
- Nine-hour stress management and professional excellence training sessions for service providers, first responders, and frontline personnel.
- Twelve-hour in-depth trauma-relief training for refugees.
- Twenty-hour rehabilitation and reintegration training for veterans and former combatants.
- Five-day youth empowerment programmes.
- Ten-day youth leadership training.

Core techniques and modules are combined and adapted to the specific needs of each target group, resulting in a diverse array of programmes. These include, where feasible, follow-up sessions, mentoring, advanced programmes, training of trainers and projects focused on addressing social issues.

The following is a non-exhaustive list of target groups for IAHV/Art of Living programmes:

- The general public;
- Youth (ages 8–12 and 13–18);
- Young adults and students (ages 18–35);
- Professionals in humanitarian aid, development, and peacebuilding;
- Health professionals and service providers;
- School teachers and administrators;
- Law enforcement personnel, including police and prison staff;
- Incarcerated populations, gang members and at-risk youth vulnerable to criminalization and radicalization;
- Refugees, displaced persons, and host communities;
- Corporate sector employees;
- Decision-makers and government officials;
- Individuals traumatized by natural or man-made disasters;
- War veterans and ex-combatants;
- Women, including war widows and rural women;
- Others as identified by contextual needs.

Programme participants are taught to engage in daily practices and, where feasible, are supported by regular follow-up sessions designed to sustain and enhance the benefits of the intervention.

IAHV programmes integrate widely recognized and commonly used methods, such as life skills training, physical exercise, relaxation techniques, group facilitation, personal reflection, safe space creation, storytelling, artistic activities, games and cognitive approaches, in conjunction with IAHV's own specific techniques.

The distinctive aspect of IAHV's peacebuilding approach lies in its combination of emotional regulation and cognitive peacebuilding strategies with physiological techniques, specifically, regulated breathing practices that prime the body for a state of peace.

This unique approach is characterized by:

1. The integration of evidence-based breathing techniques, particularly the SKY technique, which has demonstrated multiple benefits.
2. The holistic incorporation of all the above components into one comprehensive approach.
3. The facilitation of the programmes by certified trainers who routinely practise and integrate these tools and techniques in their daily lives.

SKY technique and research findings

Core techniques employed in IAHV and Art of Living programmes are **Sudarshan Kriya and accompanying breathing practices, collectively referred to as SKY**, which include gentle stretching exercises (yoga postures), specific breathing techniques and cognitive strategies for coping with and evaluating stress. The central component of SKY is Sudarshan Kriya, which employs distinct rhythmic breathing patterns designed to reduce stress, support the functioning of various bodily systems, modulate intense emotional states and restore mental tranquillity, thereby promoting an integrated mind-body balance. SKY is implemented worldwide as a well-established method for stress management and health promotion, with its health benefits supported by contemporary medical research. Furthermore, subjective reports from a large number of practitioners indicating enhanced health, vitality, well-being, and peace of mind, corroborate these research findings.

Published research shows that SKY practice significantly reduces stress, depression, anxiety and post-traumatic stress disorder (PTSD), and significantly increases well-being, both mentally and physically.[16] Research has shown that the effects of SKY extend even to the molecular level and can alter gene expression within the DNA, which may be a reason for the wide range of beneficial effects of SKY on different levels of physiology.[17] To date, over **120 independent studies conducted on four continents and published in peer-reviewed journals** have demonstrated a comprehensive range of benefits from SKY practice for physical and mental health, a selection of which is summarized below:

- **Reduced biochemical markers of stress**: SKY practice has been shown to reduce cortisol (the stress hormone), corticotrophin, blood lactate, ACTH and plasma malondialdehyde (MDA).[18] For example, blood lactate levels, a biochemical measure of stress that increases under extended psychological stress, were four times lower in police cadets who learned SKY than in those who did not. This suggests a greatly increased resilience to stress in SKY practitioners.[19] This 2003 study concluded that 'SKY is an effective method to release stress and enhance resilience against stress'.[20] The stress levels in our lives are a very important but often overlooked determinant of wellness. The field of psychoneuroimmunology has shown that our thoughts, emotions and stress levels interact with the endocrine system, which releases specific hormones promoting or undermining our state of wellness, and vice versa. Chronic stress can break down the smooth interactions of our mind-body complex and negatively affect every aspect of our health and well-being.[21] Regular practice of SKY develops progressively greater levels of both relaxation and resilience to stress.[22] For example, regular SKY practitioners had significantly lower blood cortisol levels at baseline than beginning practitioners, indicating that they experienced less physiological stress under the demands of daily living.[23]

- **Reduction of burnout**: A 2022 randomized clinical trial showed that physicians who regularly practised SKY throughout a 2-month period experienced improvements in wellness such as reduced stress, anxiety, depression, work exhaustion, personal disengagement, insomnia and physician burnout, and increased professional fulfilment. This data suggests that SKY may be an effective, practical and safe strategy to increase wellness and mitigate burnout in physicians.[24]

- **Relief of clinical depression** 68–73 per cent (mild, moderate and severe): Several independent studies have shown that SKY practitioners experience a 68–73 per cent success rate in the treatment of clinical depression, regardless of severity.[25] Relief from depression, determined by psychiatric evaluation and standard psychiatric measures, was experienced within a few weeks. At the three-month follow-ups, patients remained stable and in remission. Published studies further suggest that SKY normalizes patients' brainwave patterns and is as effective as standard anti-depressant drug regimens. Yet it is safe, free of unwanted side effects, cost-effective, and self-empowering. According to a 2000 study, 'SKY was statistically as effective as the conventional treatments for depression studied and may be more effective for preventing relapse.'[26] A study by the Department of Neurosciences in Fatebenefratelli Hospital in Milan among patients with clinical depression and/or anxiety who had not achieved adequate response after six months of standard pharmacotherapy showed that SKY significantly reduced anxiety and depression and the improvement was sustained after six months: 98 per cent of those with clinical anxiety and 80 per cent of those with clinical depression achieved remission. These findings suggest that SKY can be considered as a self-empowering, cost-effective adjunct to other options, or in specific cases an alternative method, for treating anxiety disorders and melancholic depression.[27]

- **Relief of anxiety**: Independent studies have also shown significant reductions in both clinical and non-clinical anxiety. For example, an open trial of patients with Generalized Anxiety Disorder who had not responded to prescription medication showed a 73 per cent response rate (HAM-A) after four weeks' practice of SKY.[28]

- **Reduced rates of PTS**: Rapid and significant reductions in PTSD symptoms among war veterans were found in 4–6 weeks and were sustained at six months and one year.[29] An 8-h IAHV workshop for tsunami displaced persons living in refugee camps resulted in a 65 per cent drop scores on the PTSD checklist (PCL-17) and an 85 per cent drop scores on the Beck Depression Inventory (BDI), remaining stable through twenty-four weeks.[30]

- **Reduced impulsivity**: The results of a UCLA study among US high school students showed that SKY significantly reduced impulsivity, a trait that can lead to risky health behaviours, such as violence and substance abuse. This finding suggests that SKY can promote mental health in adolescents, potentially protecting them from harmful coping behaviours.[31]

- **Improved emotional regulation:** The same study also found that SKY substantially improves students' ability to emotionally regulate, enhance self-awareness, improve interpersonal relationships and agency.[32] The effect of reappraisal of strong emotional reactions persisted longer in SKY participants than in a control group who only used cognitive reappraisal, indicating that SKY can help regulate the emotional response and thus promote psychological wellness.[33]

- **Reduced aggression:** A 2020 study on former ULFA militants who participated in a 40-day yoga with SKY programme showed a significant decline in the overall level of aggression as well as specifically in physical aggression (hitting others, tendencies to threaten, get into fights, break things in anger, respond to provocation with violence), verbal aggression (frequent disagreements, arguments, inability to have a calm discussion, getting annoyed, and saying hurtful things), anger and hostility.[34]

- **Increased levels of optimism, joviality (e.g. joy, happiness, energy), serenity, life satisfaction and quality of life**[35]

    A Research Triangle Institute study documented significant improvements in positive affect including increased happiness, energy, joy, creativity and serenity, and decreased sadness and fatigue when tested one month post SKY workshop.[36] A University of Wisconsin study demonstrated significant improvements in life satisfaction and social connectedness, as well as significant declines in depression and perceived stress both one week and one month after learning SKY. This suggests that within a short time span greater levels of emotional well-being and life satisfaction are associated with regular practice of SKY.[37]

    A comparative research study at Yale University evaluated the impact of three well-being interventions in university students: (1) SKY, (2) Mindfulness-Based Stress Reduction and (3) Foundations of Emotional Intelligence (a wellness programme that teaches techniques to improve emotional awareness and regulation).[38] Of the three programmes, participants in the SKY programme had the most significant benefits, including improvements in mental health, social connectedness, positive emotions and mindfulness. They also showed the greatest decrease in their stress levels and depression. The Emotional Intelligence programme improved one factor: mindfulness. The Mindfulness-Based Stress Reduction, surprisingly, showed no significant impact. This study suggests that the SKY programme significantly increases wellness in university students and is more effective compared with the other two wellness programmes.

- **Enhanced brain and autonomous nervous system function, including increased mental focus, heightened awareness, recovery from stressful stimuli.**[39] SKY practitioners have demonstrated significantly greater mental alertness (EEG Beta wave activity) in the left frontal, occipital, and midline regions of the brain than a control group of physicians and medical researchers, whose profession requires development and daily use of these very skills.[40] Another study found an increase in EEG alpha activity, with interspersed persistence of beta activity, indicating a state of relaxation co-existing with heightened alertness.[41] In a post-course assessment of eighteen SKY schools across the United States in 2017, 76–85 per cent of the 7,333 students surveyed showed significant improvement in six focus areas: mood and feelings, calm state of mind, focus and concentration, anger and frustration, ability to sleep, stress and worry.[42]

- **Changes in DNA expression**: Several studies have found that SKY actually has an influence on the expression of DNA. It creates distinct effects at the molecular level and changes in gene expression profiles, supporting positive expressions and suppressing negative ones.[43]

- In addition, other studies demonstrate a range of **physical health benefits** through SKY practice, such as an enhanced immune system, cardiovascular and respiratory function.[44] There seems to be increasing evidence that through the stimulation of the vagal nerve that the SKY practice provides, many conditions associated with impaired vagal activity can be addressed, to the benefit of overall physical health.[45]

These research findings confirm the subjective reports of hundreds of thousands of practitioners that SKY significantly improves mental, emotional and physical well-being. More studies should be conducted on the specific effects and workings of SKY.

Neuroscience and the autonomous nervous system

There is a physiology that promotes peace, and one that thwarts it. The autonomic nervous system (ANS) is active in every organ and system in the body, and it functions independently of our own will or cognitive faculties. It has two primary branches: the sympathetic nervous system which is activated under stress (the 'fight or flight' response), and the peaceful parasympathetic nervous system which is activated when we are relaxed and rested ('rest and digest' response). These two systems complement each other: as one increases, the other decreases. Homeostatic balance in the autonomic nervous system (ANS) is the balance between the peaceful parasympathetic and the stressful or more activated fight or flight sympathetic nervous system. **In this state of homeostasis, the newer parts of our brain, the prefrontal cortex, dominate. These higher brain centres are capable of creating peaceful solutions using executive function, emotion regulation, problem solving and peacebuilding strategies. In situations of conflict, high stress and emotional intensity, the sympathetic nervous system automatically dominates, reverting brain function to more reactive, primitive brain centres (limbic system). Instinctive reactions are predominant, and peacebuilding capabilities deteriorate.**

The 'window of tolerance' indicates the range in which the sympathetic and parasympathetic nervous systems naturally flow up and down in daily life without adverse effects. This range can be limited under the influence of adverse or highly stressful experiences in life, and it can be expanded with practice and favourable circumstances. In extreme stress or trauma, however, the sympathetic and parasympathetic nervous systems may become overactivated resulting in a hyperactivated state (overly responsive) or hypoactivated state (underly responsive).

ANS function is automatic, and out of our control: we cannot slow down or speed up our blood circulation or digestion. However, there is one exception: respiration. Our breath is part of the ANS and continues automatically, but we can change the way we breathe. Thus **ANS**

homeostasis can be restored via breath-based techniques. SKY regulated breathing technology is validated to be a potent tool for reducing sympathetic drive and simultaneously increasing parasympathetic drive, restoring a more balanced, optimal state of homeostasis. This benefits the entire mind/body complex. It stabilizes the higher brain function, even when under duress, shifts thoughts through physiological change, and brings the brain back to optimal conditions so that it can apply the cognitive tools needed.[46] SKY increases activation in the prefrontal cortex, strengthening the neural processes underlying emotional regulation.[47] Emotion regulation strategies can be better applied when autonomic nervous system balance is restored through SKY. It fortifies individuals to utilize peacebuilding skills even when challenged and to persist in difficult times. **Providing tools to strengthen the ANS homeostasis is the most fundamental human-oriented approach to strengthen peacebuilding and reduce violence**.

IAHV's peacebuilding approach is unique in that it employs evidence-based physiological techniques to prime the body for peace, alongside emotion regulation and cognitive peacebuilding strategies.

SKY as the cornerstone for more peaceful individuals, communities and nations

The research findings so far indicate that SKY practice confers important benefits for people affected by conflict, violence, war or trauma. Evidence suggests that SKY is an effective tool for establishing both a physiological foundation conducive to peaceful strategies and behaviour as well as a psychological state characterized by positive mental and emotional well-being. By strengthening the overall mind-body system, SKY practice appears to empower individuals from inside, regardless of their experiences on the war/peace spectrum.

PTSD, depression and anxiety are among the most prevalent consequences of exposure to war, violence and trauma. The empirical studies have demonstrated that SKY practice is particularly helpful in relieving trauma and helping individuals overcome adverse emotional experiences, as evidenced by its robust effects on symptoms of PTSD, anxiety and depression. These outcomes may also benefit individuals experiencing despair or suicidal tendencies.

Strong emotions often have a significant impact on overall well-being, surpassing the impact of cognitive processes and abilities. Difficulty regulating emotional responses to violence, traumatic events, war, displacement, loss and other events plays a critical role in our overall well-being and influences our attitudes towards others, events and the world as a whole. It also affects behaviour, which is more likely to be reactive, destructive, aggressive, isolationist, radicalized or discriminatory. In this context, SKY offers accessible, self-empowering techniques to attenuate intense emotional reactions and enhance emotional well-being.

Physiological assessments reveal that SKY practice induces a state of relaxed awareness, or aware relaxation, as indicated by changes in brain wave patterns and reductions in blood cortisol and lactate levels. This state of calm can be especially beneficial for service providers, peacebuilders, and humanitarian personnel, enabling them to maintain focus and composure even amidst emergency and chaotic situations. In particular, improvements in prefrontal cortex functioning associated with SKY practice can allow people physiologically to think before they act in times of distress.

Overall, the documented physiological, mental, and emotional transformations resulting from regular SKY practice suggest that realistic opportunities exist to break cycles of violence, beginning at the individual level.

Strengths of IAHV's psychosocial approach in the current global context

In the context of chronic emergencies and societal breakdown, humanitarian and development organizations frequently encounter constraints in providing appropriate psychosocial programmes at the scale required in today's world. More people than ever are refugees or displaced, depression and mental health issues are a rising global phenomenon, and local healthcare systems are under pressure. War, climate change, poverty and economic crises are directly and indirectly causing widespread distress across the globe. Standard psycho-pharmacological, psychotherapeutic and one-on-one interventions are costly for mass deployment. The prescription of psycho-pharmaca and the largely cognitive approach used in psychotherapy often prove ineffective and culturally unsuitable.

Given these challenges, there is a pressing need for innovative, scalable, and cost-effective approaches that address acute psychological and psychosomatic needs while also mitigating long-term negative consequences.

In this regard, and in addition to the importance and need for psychosocial peacebuilding outlined earlier, psychosocial approaches such as those offered by IAHV possess distinctive advantages which can be engaged in conjunction with, and complementary to, the mainstream MHPSS approaches and helpful local practices.

IAHV's programmes are grounded in evidence-based practices that are accessible, inclusive, scalable and cost-effective. The techniques employed are characterized by their simplicity and robust impact, while also being non-invasive and free of undesirable side effects. Importantly, these practices do not foster dependency on external support and have the potential to reduce overall healthcare costs. The interventions yield significant and effective outcomes, are straightforward to learn and integrate into daily life, and are applicable across diverse cultural contexts

without risk of stigmatization. Moreover, they can be administered to large groups while still facilitating a deeply personal and transformational experience, thereby alleviating the demand on often limited psychological and psychiatric resources in complex emergency scenarios (Table 3.4).

Table 3.4 *Overview of Strengths of IAHV's Approach*

The strengths of IAHV's approach can be summarized as follows:
- Evidence-based (measurable improvements in physiological and psychological indicators);
- Effective (facilitation of intrapersonal transformation and peacebuilding impact);
- Easily accessible (easily learned and used by a wide range of individuals, free from stigmatization);
- Cost-effective (reduced reliance on expensive healthcare resources, such as psychologists, psychiatrists and medications);
- Inclusive (Its human-centred approach is applicable across diverse cultural, social and demographic groups, regardless of nationality, age or gender);
- Ownership and empowerment (populations acquire tools they can practice independently to improve their own well-being, no long-term dependency created);
- Innovative (Introduction of novel methods that distinguish it from traditional interventions);
- Globally active (widespread volunteer network in 180 countries);
- Scalable and multipliable (ability to reach large groups in single interventions, training of trainers for local capacity building).

Key points: Chapter 3

The psychosocial peacebuilding framework of IAHV is not only a comprehensive conceptual framework but also an integrated approach rooted in evidence-based practices and implemented around the world in a variety of contexts and target groups, in both conflict and peace settings.

Mission and approach

IAHV's peacebuilding programmes are designed to transform the mindsets, attitudes, well-being, and behaviours of individuals and communities involved in or affected by conflict and violence, including perpetrators, impacted communities and intervening parties.

IAHV prioritizes the development of a fertile psychosocial foundation within individuals and communities through a profoundly human-centred approach across conflict lines. Such profound, healthy psychosocial foundation is intended to reinforce other peacebuilding and development initiatives, thereby enhancing overall impact.

IAHV's Theory of Change posits that individual and community transformation leads to broader societal peacebuilding impact.

IAHV focuses on intrapersonal transformation as the cornerstone and foundation for peacebuilding, while at the same time addressing structural change, engaging with behavioural and relational dimensions of peacebuilding, and strengthening underlying human and peace-promoting values.

The transformation of structures into peace-promoting systems, along with the promotion of peace-enhancing values within society, alongside the transformation of individual and collective mindsets, attitudes and behaviours towards peace, mutually interact and reinforce each other as components of sustainable peace.

Intrapersonal, interpersonal and structural transformation

IAHV uses a holistic approach to personal transformation that engages the individual's entire system, transforming physical, emotional, mental, attitudinal, behavioural, relational and existential aspects. IAHV programmes restore peace at every level of human existence, well beyond the cognitive.

Dependant on how a person is able to align the seven dimensions of her existence, that person can still be centred, connected and contribute positively even when the outer world is in chaos, or alternatively can feel disturbed, stressed and angry inside even when the outer world is peaceful.

When individuals feel connected within themselves, they are more likely to develop stronger connections interpersonally and within communities, creating inclusive relationships and greater community resilience to conflict or contributing to the restoration of the social fabric after conflict.

IAHV's psychosocial approach and techniques bring about changes in the individual, the communities and the context itself, restoring peace within and between individuals, communities and society.

In addition, IAHV's mission is to promote positive human values in all sectors of society as the core of a culture and practice of peace.

Programmes and methodology

Core techniques and modules are combined and adapted to the specific needs of each target group, resulting in a diverse array of programmes. These include, where feasible, follow-up sessions, mentoring, advanced programmes, training of trainers and projects focused on addressing social issues.

The distinctive aspect of IAHV's peacebuilding approach lies in its combination of emotional regulation and cognitive peacebuilding strategies with physiological techniques, specifically, regulated breathing practices that prime the body for a state of peace.

Evidence

Published research shows that SKY practice significantly reduces stress, depression, anxiety and post-traumatic stress disorder (PTSD), and significantly increases well-being, both mentally and physically.

SKY regulated breathing technology is validated to be a potent tool for reducing sympathetic drive and simultaneously increasing parasympathetic drive, restoring a more balanced, optimal state of homeostasis and strengthening peacebuilding capacities in the brain and nervous system in times of duress. Providing tools to strengthen the ANS homeostasis is the most fundamental human-oriented approach to strengthen peacebuilding and reduce violence.

The documented physiological, mental and emotional transformations resulting from regular SKY practice suggest that realistic opportunities exist to break cycles of violence, beginning at the individual level.

Application

There is a pressing need for innovative, scalable and cost-effective approaches that address acute psychological and psychosomatic needs while also mitigating long-term negative consequences.

Strengths of IAHV's psychosocial approach: Evidence-based, Effective, Easily accessible, Cost-effective, Inclusive, Ownership and empowerment, Innovative, Globally active, Scalable and multipliable.

Recommended reading: Chapter 3

Art of Living. 2021. *Impact Report 2018–2020*. https://www.artofliving.org/sites/www.artofliving.org/files/wysiwyg_imageupload/India-Impact-Report-2021.pdf.

Hertog, K. 2017. 'The intrinsic interlinkage between peacebuilding and mental health and psychosocial support: The International Association for Human Values model of integrated psychosocial peacebuilding'. *Intervention* 15:3, pp. 278–92.

Neuroscience and Peacebuilding Initiative. 2015. https://www.neuropeace.org/volumes.

Seppälä, E. M., et al. 2014. 'Breathing-based meditation decreases posttraumatic stress disorder symptoms in US military veterans: A randomized controlled longitudinal study'. *Journal of Traumatic Stress* 27:4, pp. 397–405.

Seppälä, E. M., Bradley, C., Moeller, J., Harouni, L., Nandamudi, D., & Brackett, M. A. 2020. 'Promoting mental health and psychological thriving in university students: A randomized controlled trial of three well-being interventions'. *Front Psychiatry* 11, pp. 590. https://doi.org/ 10.3389/fpsyt.2020.00590.

Notes

1 IAHV and Art of Living. 2021. 'India impact report 2018–2020'. https://www.artofliving.org/sites/www.artofliving.org/files/wysiwyg_imageupload/India-Impact-Report-2021.pdf., p. 4. (consulted 1 Nov 2024).

2 United Nations General Assembly (2015). "Transforming our world: the 2030 Agenda for Sustainable Development." Resolution A/RES/70/1, https://digitallibrary.un.org/record/3923923?v=pdf (consulted 24 Sept 2024).

3   Hertog, K. 2017. 'The intrinsic interlinkage between peacebuilding and mental health and psychosocial support: The International Association for Human Values model of integrated psychosocial peacebuilding'. *Intervention* 15:3, pp. 278–92.

4   Gopin, 2000, p. 86.

5   www.iahv.org, https://uploads-ssl.webflow.com/60b0461ace7a9afaeb3f142f/60bb478d3288c5f9186cf225_Universal-Declaration-of-Human-Values.pdf.

6   Gopin, 2000, p. 57.

7   www.iahv.org, https://uploads-ssl.webflow.com/60b0461ace7a9afaeb3f142f/60bb478d3288c5f9186cf225_Universal-Declaration-of-Human-Values.pdf.

8   www.iahv.org, https://uploads-ssl.webflow.com/60b0461ace7a9afaeb3f142f/60bb478d3288c5f9186cf225_Universal-Declaration-of-Human-Values.pdf.

9   See the explanation of the SKY methodology, the core of Art of Living and IAHV programming, later in this Chapter.

10 IAHV and Art of Living. Service Projects Worldwide. https://issuu.com/aolrc/docs/aolf_service_initiatives_overview (consulted 24 Sept 2024).

11 The below data are from the 'SKY Schools Impact Report 2021', pp. 2–3. www.skyschools.org.

12 IAHV and Art of Living. Service Projects Worldwide. https://issuu.com/aolrc/docs/aolf_service_initiatives_overview (consulted 24 Sept 2024).

13 Kanchibhotla, D., Kulkarni, S., & Singh, S. 2020. 'Effectiveness of a comprehensive yoga program on convicted extremist offenders'. *International Journal of Yoga* Jan–Apr 13:1, pp. 50–4. https://doi.org/10.4103/ijoy.IJOY_79_18. PMCID: PMC6937884. https://pubmed.ncbi.nlm.nih.gov/32030021/.

14 https://skyresilience.org/research/ (consulted 24 Sept 2024).

15 Testimonial by prison officials. See also Art of Living. 2007. 'Rebuilding war Torn Kosovo: Art of living report'.

16 See www.aolresearch.org and www.iahv-research.org.

17 Sharma, H., et al. 2008. 'Gene expression profiling in practitioners of Sudarshan Kriya'. *Journal of Psychosomatic Research* 64:2, pp. 213–18; Qu, S., et al. 2013. 'Rapid gene expression changes in peripheral blood lymphocytes upon practice of a comprehensive yoga program'. *PLoS One* 8:4, p. e61910. https://doi.org/10.1371/journal.pone.0061910.

18 Vedamurthachar, A., et al. 2006. 'Antidepressant efficacy and hormonal effects of Sudarshana Kriya Yoga (SKY) in alcohol dependent individuals'. *Journal of Affective Disorders* 94:1, pp. 249–53; Kumar, N., et al. 2013. 'Randomized controlled trial in advance stage breast cancer patients for the effectiveness on stress marker and pain through Sudarshan Kriya and Pranayam'. *Indian Journal of Palliative Care* 19:3, p. 180; Mulla, Z. R., & Vedamuthachar. 2014. 'Impact of a Sudarshan Kriya-based occupational stress management intervention on physiological and psychological outcomes'. *Management and Labour Studies* 39:4, pp. 381–95; Sharma, H., et al. 2003. 'Sudarshan Kriya practitioners exhibit better antioxidant status and lower blood lactate levels'. *Biological Psychology* 63:3, pp. 281–91; Agte, V. V., Jahagirdar, M. U., & Tarwadi, K. V. 2011. 'The effects of

Sudarshan Kriya Yoga on some physiological and biochemical parameters in mild hypertensive patients'. *Indian Journal of Physiology and Pharmacology* 55:2, pp. 183–7; Kjellgren, A., et al. 2007. 'Wellness through a comprehensive yogic breathing program – a controlled pilot trial'. *BMC Complementary and Alternative Medicine* 7, p. 43; Agte, V. V., & Chiplonkar, S. A. 2008. 'Sudarshan kriya yoga for Improving antioxidant status and reducing anxiety in adults'. *Alternative & Complementary Therapies* 14:2, pp. 96–100; Kharya, C., et al. 2014. 'Effect of controlled breathing exercises on the psychological status and the cardiac autonomic tone: Sudarshan Kriya and Prana-Yoga'. *Indian Journal of Physiology and Pharmacology* 58:3, pp. 210–20; Subramanian, S., et al. 2012. 'Role of sudarshan kriya and pranayam on lipid profile and blood cell parameters during exam stress: A randomized controlled trial'. *International Journal of Yoga* 5:1, p. 21.

19 Sharma, H., Sen, S., Singh, A., Bhardwaj, N. K., Kochupillai, V., & Singh, N. 2003. 'Sudarshan Kriya practitioners exhibit better antioxidant status and lower blood lactate levels'. *Biological Psychology* 63:3, pp. 281–91. https://doi.org/10.1016/S0301-0511(03)00071-1.

20 Sharma, H., Sen, S., Singh, A., Bhardwaj, N. K., Kochupillai, V., & Singh, N. 2003.

21 IAHV and Art of Living Research. 'Science of breath'. http://www.aolresearch.org/2021/Science_of_Breath_Brochure_2022.pdf.

22 Ibidem.

23 Vedamurthachar, A., et al. 2006.

24 Korkmaz, A., Bernhardsen, G. P., Cirit, B., et al. 2024. 'Sudarshan Kriya yoga breathing and a meditation program for burnout among physicians: A randomized clinical trial'. *JAMA Network Open* 7:1, p. e2353978. https://doi.org/10.1001/jamanetworkopen.2023.53978.

25 Vedamurthachar, A., et al. 2006; Kjellgren, A., et al. 2007, p. 43; Kharya, C., et al. 2014.

26 Janakiramaiah, N., et al. 2000. 'Antidepressant efficacy of Sudarshan Kriya Yoga (SKY) in melancholia: A randomized comparison with electroconvulsive therapy (ECT) and imipramine'. *Journal of Affective Disorders* 57:1–3, pp. 255–9.

27 Sharma, A., Barrett, M. S., Cucchiara, A. J., Gooneratne, N. S., & Thase, M. E. 2017. 'A breathing-based meditation intervention for patients with major depressive disorder following inadequate response to antidepressants: A randomized pilot study'. *Journal of Clinical Psychiatry* 78:1, pp. e59–e63. https://doi.org/10.4088/JCP.16m10819; Toschi-Dias, E., Tobaldini, E., Solbiati, M., Costantino, G., Sanlorenzo, R., Doria, S., & Montano, N. 2017. 'Sudarshan Kriya Yoga improves cardiac autonomic control in patients with anxiety-depression disorders'. *Journal of Affective Disorders* 214, pp. 74–80. https://doi.org/10.1016/j.jad.2017.03.017.

28 Katzman, M. A., et al. 2012. 'A multicomponent yoga-based, breath intervention program as an adjunctive treatment in patients suffering from Generalized Anxiety Disorder with or without comorbidities'. *International Journal of Yoga* 5:1, p. 57.

29 Seppälä, E. M., et al. 2014; Martin, A. 2013. 'Multi-component yoga breath program for Vietnam veteran post traumatic stress disorder: Randomized controlled trial'. *Journal of Traumatic Stress Disorders & Treatment* 2:3, pp. 1–10. https://doi.org/10.4172/2324-8947.1000108.

30 Descillo, T., et al. 2010.

31. Ghahremani, D. G., et al. 2013; Kochupillai, V., et al. 2005. 'Effect of rhythmic breathing (Sudarshan Kriya and Pranayam) on immune functions and tobacco addiction'. *Annals of the New York Academy of Sciences* 1056:1, pp. 242–52.

32. Ibidem.

33. Gootjes, L., Franken, I. H., & Van Strien, J. W. 2011. 'Cognitive emotion regulation in yogic meditative practitioners'. *Journal of Psychophysiology* 25:2, pp. 87–94; Goldstein, M. R., et al. 2016. 'Improvements in well-being and vagal tone following a yogic breathing-based life skills workshop in young adults: Two open-trial pilot studies'. *International Journal of Yoga* 9:1, pp. 20.

34. Kanchibhotla, D., Kulkarni, S., & Singh, S. 2020. 'Effectiveness of a comprehensive yoga program on convicted extremist offenders'. *International Journal of Yoga* Jan–Apr 13:1, pp. 50–4. https://doi.org/10.4103/ijoy.IJOY_79_18. PMCID: PMC6937884. https://pubmed.ncbi.nlm.nih.gov/32030021/.

35. Goldstein, M. R., et al. 2016. 'Improvements in well-being and vagal tone following a yogic breathing-based life skills workshop in young adults: Two open-trial pilot studies'. *International Journal of Yoga* 9:1, pp. 20; Jyotsna, V. P., et al. 2012. 'Comprehensive yogic breathing program improves quality of life in patients with diabetes'. *Indian Journal of Endocrinology and Metabolism* 16:3, p. 423; Warner, A., & Hall, K. 2012. 'Psychological and spiritual well-being of women with breast cancer participating in the art of living program'. In Hicks, N. L., & Warren, R. E. (Eds.), *Psychology of Cancer*. Nova Science Publishers, Inc; Kjellgren, A., et al. 2007. 'Wellness through a comprehensive yogic breathing program – A controlled pilot trial'. *BMC Complementary & Alternative Medicine* 7, p. 43; Sureka, P., et al. 2014. 'Effect of Sudarshan Kriya on male prisoners with non-psychotic psychiatric disorders: A randomized control trial'. *Asian Journal of Psychiatry* 12, pp. 43–9.

36. IAHV and Art of Living Research. 'Science of breath'. http://www.aolresearch.org/2021/Science_of_Breath_Brochure_2022.pdf.

37. Ibidem.

38. Seppälä, E. M., Bradley, C., Moeller, J., Harouni, L., Nandamudi, D., & Brackett, M. A. 2020. 'Promoting mental health and psychological thriving in university students: A randomized controlled trial of three well-being interventions'. *Frontiers in Psychiatry* 11, p. 590. https://doi.org/10.3389/fpsyt.2020.00590.

39. Murthy, P. N. V., et al. 1998. 'P300 amplitude and antidepressant response to Sudarshan Kriya Yoga (SKY)'. *Journal of Affective Disorders* 50:1, pp. 45–8; Bhatia, M., et al. 2003. 'Electrophysiologic evaluation of Sudarshan Kriya: An EEG, BAER, P300 study'. *Indian Journal of Physiology and Pharmacology* 47:2, pp. 157–63.

40. Bhatia, M., et al. 2003.

41. IAHV and Art of Living Research. 'Science of breath'. http://www.aolresearch.org/2021/Science_of_Breath_Brochure_2022.pdf.

42. SKY Schools Impact Report. 2021, pp. 2–3. www.skyschools.org.

43. Bhaskar, L., Kharya, C., Debnath, et al. 2023. 'Effects of Sudarshan KriyaYoga and advanced meditation program on genetic expression of pro-inflammatory and antioxidants genes'.

Cureus 15:7, p. e41377. https://doi.org/10.7759/cureus.41377. PMCID: PMC10400732; Ayyildiz, D., & Arga, K. Y. 2017. 'Hypothesis: Are there molecular signatures of yoga practice in peripheral blood mononuclear cells?'. *OMICS* 21, pp. 426–8; Qu, S., Olafsrud, S. M., Meza-Zepeda, L. A., & Saatcioglu, F. 2013. 'Rapid gene expression changes in peripheral blood lymphocytes upon practice of a comprehensive yoga program'. *PLoS One* 8:4, p. e61910. https://doi.org/10.1371/journal.pone.0061910.

44   See www.aolresearch.org.

45   Brown, R. P., & Gerbarg, P. L. 2005. 'Sudarshan Kriya yogic breathing in the treatment of stress, anxiety, and depression: Part I-neurophysiologic model'. *Journal of Alternative and Complementary Medicine* Feb 11:1, pp. 189–201. https://doi.org/10.1089/acm.2005.11.189; Goldstein, M. R., et al. 2016, pp. 20.

46   http://www.aolresearch.org/2021/Science_of_Breath_Brochure_2022.pdf.

47   Ghahremani, D. G., et al. 2013; Kochupillai, V., et al. 2005.

PART II

Application of psychosocial peacebuilding

The second part of this book aims to invite and support readers to engage with psychosocial peacebuilding in an applied way. More concretely, it provides **a more practical guide on how to develop and implement an integrated psychosocial peacebuilding approach**. The practical chapters in the book are accompanied by exercises, reflective questions, application examples, templates and figures. Unravelling different aspects of psychosocial peacebuilding in practice, readers can use these more practice-oriented chapters to check, enrich or develop their current way of working, for themselves, their organization and projects, and in the context in which they find themselves. Depending on one's motivation, interest or need, one can focus on specific parts or on the whole practical guidance outlined below.

When we want to embark on an integrated psychosocial peacebuilding approach, the psychosocial factors involved may seem like a Pandora's box: a varied range of multiple, complex, irrational and entangled dynamics which are difficult to get a grip on, identify or measure. One may wonder where to start or how to disentangle the complex inner and social world of human beings. We may think that psychosocial topics relate to deep and often unexplored spaces of our human existence which are the prerogative field of professionally trained psychologists and psychotherapists. Especially if we are not comfortable facing and managing our own deeper emotional and mental patterns and wounds, we may prefer to stay at a safe distance from the 'unknown'. Practitioners' lack of proper exposure and training on how to work with these issues often means they are neglected in peacebuilding programmes.

However, IAHV offers a very practical, methodological approach which is outlined in the following chapters. First of all, we present a practical case study of a psychosocial peacebuilding project as it was implemented for and with war-affected children at risk of violence and radicalization in Lebanon and Jordan. In the next chapter, we take a deeper look inside ourselves in order to gain a better understanding of the different aspects of our existence, and hence also of the people we are working with. Unpacking the link between inner and outer peace, we zoom in on the role of personal transformation. We then move on towards the psychosocial dimensions of intergroup and interpersonal peacebuilding as well as the psychosocial dimensions in the different sectors of peacebuilding. Throughout these chapters we variably address peacebuilders as well as people involved in or affected by conflict and violence. Finally, we offer a set of concrete, practical steps to design integrated psychosocial peacebuilding projects.

4 IAHV case study
Building peace with war-affected children in Lebanon and Jordan

I was alive before just because I had to, but now I live because I have a goal: I want to leave my print on the society and spread peace.

—Rama, IAHV Youth Peace Ambassador

I always wanted to bring peace into society, but I didn't know how. Now that I have found peace in myself, I know how I can spread peace in society.

—IAHV Youth Peace Ambassador

I looked inside myself and found a light, a small, faint, far light. You gave me your hand and walked with me on a path I didn't know anything about. I was even scared of it at one time, yet I walked onto it. I breathed, loved, shared, healed and, most importantly, I got to know myself and my breath.

I kept walking on the path till I got to know the light: it was peace, inner peace. It took you less than a month to teach me the unknown, you introduced to us life and its values and gave us knowledge we never got at school. You believed in us, trusted us and constantly encouraged us to be better.

Thanks isn't enough to express my gratitude and appreciation for you.

Just know very well that, come what may, we, your students, the peace ambassadors, will always make you proud.

—Jana Hazeem, IAHV Youth Peace Ambassador

Chapter 3 presented the conceptual framework for IAHV's Psychosocial Peacebuilding approach, offering a theoretical and evidence-based model.

In this chapter, I will show **how the different components of IAHV's conceptual framework come to life in a real case scenario and how the conceptual model is operationalized on the ground.**

The practical application is an integrated psychosocial peacebuilding project developed and implemented by IAHV with funding from the European Commission: *Healing, Nonviolent*

Empowerment and Preventing Extremism for Children impacted by armed conflict in Jordan and Lebanon through a comprehensive, innovative, sustainable psychosocial approach (2016–2019).[1]

The aim of the project was to facilitate the transformation of children and adults affected by violence, conflict, stress and trauma, into healed, resilient and empowered actors of change who have the well-being, confidence and skills to address the very driving factors of violence that caused them and others harm in the first place.

The project engaged with a wide range of psychosocial factors to lay a strong foundation for peace and **illustrates how IAHV's Theory of Change 'Peacebuilding Impact through Personal Transformation' works in practice.**

In this case study, I describe the context, methodology, the concrete application of the conceptual components, participants' experiences, sub-case studies and peacebuilding impact.

We also look in more detail into

(1) What worked well and why: Identifying the project's strengths and key drivers of success.
(2) Weaknesses and challenges: Highlighting areas for improvement and obstacles encountered in the implementation and the context.

Peacebuilding impact: Projects from the IAHV Youth Peace Ambassadors

In 2019, political, social and economic unrest was unraveling in Lebanon. Strong emotions of anger and despair were engulfing people; violent clashes occurred, and the risk of a renewed civil war hung in the air. At a time when most people in Tripoli stayed indoors, IAHV's newly trained Youth Peace Ambassadors went out into the streets, among people of all social and political factions, to spread their **strong message of shared humanity, non-violence and positivity**.

> *'Don't underestimate the power of words, because it can be stronger than a bullet.'*
> *'You won't understand until you start listening.'*
> *'Grudge is a poison that kills the person holding it.'*
> *'Bullying is a form of violence that comes from a form of weakness.'*

These were some of the messages the youth propounded amidst a social climate of frustration, resentment, blame, aggression, violence and hatred. They had brainstormed these powerful slogans and integrated them into a lively **dabke flashmob**. Dabke is a traditional dance in which people hold hands; thus, it was a symbol for them of overcoming bullying and promoting friendship and togetherness.

After several weeks of practising the dance, the Youth Peace Ambassadors were ready to perform it across Tripoli, but it was then, in October 2019, that the Lebanon protests broke out. Noticing the high level of bullying that took place in the protests, they realized their message was more relevant than ever. The Peace Ambassadors performed the dabke flashmob several times in the midst of the street protests which gathered tens of thousands of people. The lively dancing youth from different backgrounds and ages, the unifying song and dance, their powerful messages and the unusual spectacle of it all, attracted a lot of attention, including from mainstream media. Their performances were streamed live on TV and the youth could explain their messages in several interviews.

In addition, they also toured around Tripoli to bring their message to different audiences in the farthest corners of the city. The youth were very well received in the different neighbourhoods, which are characterized by distinct social, religious and economic compositions. Their performance and messages were recorded by hundreds of people who shared it across social media.

In order to reach even more people, the Peace Ambassadors launched a social media campaign called Hebo Ba3ed (Love each other), which reached 70,000 views a few days after it was launched.

This peace project was born from the lived experiences of the youth in Tripoli: the experience of being bullied, but also of seeing the detrimental effect of bullying around them, leading to depression and suicides among their peers. They were also ready to honestly recognize the bully inside themselves. After they jointly discussed and analysed the violence in their lives during the IAVH Youth Leadership Peacebuilding Training, they had decided to launch an **anti-bullying campaign** to counter this widespread phenomenon in society and promote friendliness and togetherness instead.

Materials:
Video Anti-bullying campaign: https://www.youtube.com/watch?v=ifxG8walmCc&t=3s
Video Anti-bullying campaign – Dabke Flashmobs in Tripoli: https://www.youtube.com/watch?v=z9lVLH3O2pzg
Social media campaign: https://www.facebook.com/heboba3ed/

A group of teenage girls in Tripoli focused on their lived experience of **early marriage** and the violence embedded and stemming from this widespread practice: being denied a say in one's own future, being deprived of education and working opportunities, and sometimes being subjected to psychological, physical and sexual forms of violence. In the Youth Leadership Peacebuilding Training, this group of girls discussed and intimately shared their own experiences with each other. They then decided to raise awareness about the misery early marriage causes in society and to bring more informed understanding about it from different angles. Together, they wrote a script for a theatre play which they called 'What is behind the letter?'. Over a period of several months during which they worked together with a lot of inspiration and commitment, supported by a theatre producer, they refined the script, practised the roles, designed the stage and promoted their performance. They performed four times, including one time live on Al Arabi TV for the broader Middle East, followed by interactive discussions with the audience.

> **From the letter:**
> *'I would have become a journalist to inform people about what many girls my age have been suffering, like me. Or maybe a teacher who spreads awareness. Or an engineer who builds. It doesn't matter what I would have been, I am sure I would have made you proud by it, definitely more than through this marriage. I might have met my knight in shining armor while studying or while working. I would have lived the sweetest love story and got married. Like that, I would have made you proud twice: once because I did what I wanted, and at the same time I also did what you wanted.'*

Viewers of the play said that they were deeply touched because the play so vividly depicted their lived experiences, struggles and questions. The aim of the play was not to accuse one party or the other but to raise awareness about the different points of view and the effects these have on all people involved. Some viewers testified that they had changed their opinion after watching the play.

> *'I affected my father, a very important person in my life. He was pro early marriage. However, when he saw the play he said: "Now I know why you were always against this idea." He changed his opinion and now sees it is wrong.'* (Youth Peace Ambassador, affected by early marriage)

In Jordan, a group of Syrian Youth Peace Ambassadors took the initiative to improve **relations between Jordanians and Syrians** in their community. Until then, these were characterized by distancing, stereotypes, resentment and youth clashes around the football field. During the Youth Leadership Peacebuilding Training, the youth envisioned paving a way for peace in their community in Menshieh. In order to create cohesion between Jordanian and Syrian youth and develop sportsmanship among them, Syrian boys organized peaceful football matches with mixed teams and the integration of human values and conflict resolution skills. They not only created fun activities for the other boys of their community but also mobilized their entire community to come together and support the teams. The football tournament created social cohesion among Syrian and Jordanian community members, young and old.

At the same time, a group of creative girls organized music and art classes centred around the idea of peace and promoted a safe space where Syrian refugee children could occupy their time constructively, develop their creativity and confidence, and avoid isolation and violent habits and tendencies. The classes brought many children and youth together and created new friendships. During the final project celebration in the community of Menshieh, the girls showcased the artwork made during the classes and several of the music students showed their new skills in a live performance of dance and songs on the topic of peace, human values and togetherness.

Rana was one of the Peace Ambassadors who organized the Peace through Music & Art project. She organized the project activities and classes so well that a UNICEF Centre (called Makani in Arabic, meaning 'My Space') in Mafraq offered her a job. Rana became an employed peace builder, coordinating music and art programmes to foster peace in her Makani.

> 'IAHV programmes have had a huge impact in Menshieh, on personal lives, work, homes and the community as a whole. You have changed the mentality of this community. It created brotherhood among the communities here. The violence among the children has reduced. They smile more, are more relaxed and more motivated. Now there is friendliness without fighting. First through the football matches, this project created familiarity, what was needed. The local community came together because of this project. Syrians started coming to our community centre. We convinced the parents to allow their children to develop their talents in music and art. It created bridges of trust.' (Mayor of Menshieh, Mafraq, Jordan)

In **Zaatari, the biggest refugee camp in the Middle East** at the time, it became clear to the youth that the **high levels of stress** were leading to increased tension and conflict as well as to harmful and negative coping mechanisms among the 80,000+ refugee population. During the Youth Leadership Peacebuilding Training, a group of young Syrian men decided to promote positive coping strategies in the camp to release stress. For this, they envisioned the production and screening of an awareness-raising movie and the implementation of IAHV Stress-Relief and Resilience workshops conducted by the youth themselves. They wrote an engaging script, excelled in their video filming and editing skills and screened their film to hundreds of refugees in partnership with local NGOs in the camp. The film presents the harmful effects of negative coping mechanisms and presents alternative ones to deal with stress, while the accompanying workshops taught the residents to release stress in a practical way and created a more connected community. The Peace Ambassadors from Zaatari camp graduated from the IAHV Training of Trainers programme so that they could organize and deliver the workshops themselves to the children in the refugee camp. They were so successful in delivering impactful trainings to over 5,000 children in Zaatari that the parents of the children requested workshops as well. Therefore, the Peace Ambassadors participated in another Training of Trainers to also support the adults within their community. This group continued to apply their newly gained skills and knowledge through an ongoing initiative within the camp to strengthen and spread well-being and peacebuilding objectives on a sustained basis.

Project methodology

The peacebuilding projects of the Youth Peace Ambassadors were part of a larger Psychosocial Peacebuilding Project providing Healing, Resilience and Nonviolent Empowerment for war-affected children in Lebanon and Jordan.

The aim of the project was to **enhance the well-being, resilience and psychological reintegration of children impacted by armed conflict and violence and reduce violent behaviour risk**. Children, caregivers and teachers were empowered with the **knowledge, skills and tools to improve their own physical, mental and emotional well-being** without becoming dependent on external support. By facilitating healing, stress- and trauma-relief, IAHV's approach takes away a major driving force of violence, crime and destructive behaviour, while it restores a strong and healthy psychosocial foundation in individuals and communities for stable and cohesive families, successful education, social and economic empowerment, social cohesion and reconciliation, rehabilitation and reintegration of fighters and prevention and transformation of violence and extremism.

In addition to addressing the psychosocial consequences of stress, conflict, violence and war on an individual level, the project also empowered local youth and adults to address the driving factors of these in their homes, schools and communities. The participants were empowered to **design, organize and implement effective actions to improve the safety, well-being and resilience of children and prevent and transform radicalization in their communities**.

Through a community-based approach, **families and caregivers** of the children also improved their coping and stress management capacity to create healthy and unified families as a support basis for children. Training for **teachers, frontline workers and service providers** improved their well-being and resilience in order to better support the well-being of the children they worked with.

Through physical, emotional, mental and social empowerment programming, the local communities strengthened their acting capacity and ownership to support vulnerable children and prevent violence and tendencies of extremism in their communities.

In addition, IAHV also sensitized and engaged with wider stakeholders in the community on the crucial factors that affect the well-being of children, and on the preventative and rehabilitative support required for children affected by armed conflict.

The project supported and empowered different target groups through a range of activities, facilitating profound personal transformation leading to interpersonal harmony and social peacebuilding impact.

The most widespread activity in this project was the Stress-Relief and Resilience (SRR) workshop, a low-threshold workshop to release acute and basic stress and fears, address reactivity and violence, improve sleep and provide relief. SRR is a basic 1- or 1.5-hour workshop conducted over two or three days which can easily be implemented in all conditions and for all kinds of groups. The workshop contains physical exercises, deep relaxation, short and effective breathing techniques, cognitive input on human values, emotions and energy, and games. Through SRR, 16,249 Syrian, Jordanian and Lebanese children affected by trauma, conflict and violence received basic training in stress-relief and resilience tools.

Children who really needed this kind of programme and who were interested in them, were invited to join the **more intensive Trauma-Relief, Healing, Resilience and Human Values Trainings (THRH - an adaptation of the Art of Living YES course)**. THRH is a more profound, four-day training which includes practising the SKY breathing technique, more elaborate physical exercises, relaxation and breathing techniques, games and exercises on human values and teamwork, cognitive input related to conflict resolution and friendships, and practical skills to deal with emotions and to improve focus of mind. THRH provides deeper trauma-relief and healing, strengthened resilience, better emotional regulation, improved learning capacity, strengthened connectedness, human values, and positive self-esteem and outlook.

Some of the Social-Emotional Learning Skills of the training include:

- Social Connection and Healthy Relationships: a sense of improved connection with self, peers, parents and teachers, including safety and communication.
- Self-Awareness and Social Awareness: an understanding of one's emotions and actions and their impact on oneself and the environment.
- Stress Management: Managing stress and emotions in healthy ways.
- Self-Motivation and Goal Setting: Sense of purpose and direction. Sense of self-worth and future possibility.
- Responsible Action: sense of discipline and ownership to be able to skillfully respond to life's challenges and feel a greater sense of self-agency.

The trainings were organized for 636 children most at risk of self-harm, suicide, aggression or recruitment. Apart from physical and mental health improvements, THRH addresses on a fundamental level the range of emotional, cognitive, behavioural and social problems often experienced by youth.

One hundred sixty-seven graduates from the THRH training enrolled in the **Youth Anti-Violence and Peace Ambassadors Program (YAVAP - an adaptation of the Art of Living YLTP).** YAVAP is a seven-day intense training programme which combines personal empowerment with social empowerment and peacebuilding skills training. YAVAP strengthens the techniques and knowledge of the THRH training and brings in new modules. Participants deepened their practice of powerful stress and trauma-relief techniques, learned new social and emotional skills to deal with other people and challenging situations, trained in teamwork and effective communication. They also learned and engaged with different forms of art, such as theatre, musical, flash mobs, dance, songs and rap, movies, silent tableaus, graffiti and social campaigns, which helped them to explore their selves and give expression to their inner world. As preparation for their peacebuilding roles, they were supported to analyse their living contexts for the causes and drivers of violence at home, in their schools and camps, to distil effective intervention strategies, and to design peacebuilding projects to reduce the violence in their lives and the lives of other children.

Building on the improved mental, emotional, physical and social well-being of the youth, YAVAP empowered them with confidence, knowledge and skills to become effective change agents in society.

Syrian, Lebanese and Jordanian boys and girls aged 15–18, who had all graduated from THRH trainings in different areas, mingled together, ate, played and celebrated together, and became a strongly bonded group.

In order to support the well-being of children, teachers and frontline workers who take care of children on a daily basis in difficult circumstances also need to be supported in maintaining their own well-being. Four hundred seventy-seven staff benefited from IAHV's short and effective **Professional Care (PC - an adaptation of the Art of Living Part 1 course) training to prevent burnout and improve stress management, personal resilience, well-being and performance capacity.** The Professional Care Training is given over three days x three hours and includes the SKY breathing technique, reflective processes, cognitive input on stress, mind, breath and emotions, skills to deal with challenging situations and conflicts, physical exercises, relaxation and group discussions.

In order to strengthen a more supportive environment for the children, IAHV also worked intensely with **parents, families and caregivers** to enable them to release stress, anxiety and worry, and to increase their coping capacity and sense of empowerment. The short and effective **Healing, Resilience and Empowerment (HRE) trainings** strengthened awareness, well-being and resilience to improve the quality of life and strengthen capacity to support their families. The four- to nine-hour programmes are a combination of the SRR and PC programmes mentioned earlier.

Participants of the THRH, YAVAP, PC and HRE trainings were supported after their completion of the programmes through **regular follow-up sessions** in which they practised and deepened the techniques learned, revised the knowledge, brainstormed new activities and initiatives, and bonded more with each other in a peer support group that felt like a strongly bonded family.

The project team also created various **social opportunities** for participants in the project to meet and bond across age, nationality, religion, gender and social backgrounds, such as picnics, walks and film evenings.

In order to strengthen new local capacity for trauma-relief, resilience and non-violent empowerment of youth, ninety-nine staff and volunteers among the project participants and partnering organizations were trained to become trainers of the SSR and HRE workshops. The intense **training of trainers** consisted of a four-day advanced training programme, a three-day practical training programme and a supervision period. The advanced training programme was aimed to deeply strengthen the well-being and resilience of the participants on a personal level. Besides the regular practice of breathing techniques, physical exercises and relaxation, it also included wisdom series and guided meditations by Gurudev Sri Sri Ravi Shankar, which deeply relax the mind-body system and remove unwanted impressions from the consciousness. The practice of silence over a couple of days allowed the participants to engage in finer introspection, conserve energy and deeply rejuvenate themselves. The practical training programme trained the participants in delivering the various components of the SRR and HRE workshops and provided them with insights on group management, trauma symptoms and treatments, active listening and other useful skills in training delivery. Following the training, participants first assisted senior IAHV trainers in the implementation of the workshops and were later mentored and supervised while delivering the workshops themselves.

Context analysis and description of target groups

In order to make sure IAHV's project would benefit the children most at risk and least supported, IAHV consulted key stakeholders in Amman and the refugee camps in Jordan, as well as in Tripoli, Lebanon. Together with representatives of the ministries, municipalities, local and international NGOs, UN agencies and others, we analysed the driving factors of violence in children's lives which needed to be addressed, and looked into which services were already provided and where the gaps existed.

The location, target groups, objectives and activities of the project were defined through a psychosocial conflict and peace analysis and a related needs assessment. The analysis was conducted through various methods, including focus groups and key informant interviews with representatives of the target groups and other stakeholders; joint participatory analysis processes; baseline surveys; and the consultation of existing primary and secondary sources. The analysis looked at the types of conflict, violence and distress that children were experiencing at the time, the direct and indirect actors that were involved in this and their relative influence, the specific psychosocial driving forces and consequences of social peace and conflict, the local culture of psychosocial well-being, the positive local practices of resilience and support, the existing gaps in support provision and the existing opportunities and positive dynamics, among others. Below are some important aspects of this analysis:

Context analysis Lebanon 2016

In 2016, Lebanon hosted 1.5 million refugees from Syria, while the total vulnerable refugee and host population inside Lebanon was estimated at approximately 3 million. An estimated 1.4 million children were deprived and growing up at risk, more than half of the displaced Syrian children were out of school, one fifth of displaced Syrian girls were subject to early marriage, and youth unemployment was high. In Lebanon's northern city of Tripoli, with its mixed history of peaceful coexistence as well as conflict, wars and extremism, there was a high prevalence of urban poverty, social marginalization and unemployment due to low levels of education, high school drop-outs, lack of investment and services, high turnover of refugees and migrants, regional political instability, war, and the economic crisis that Lebanon as a whole was experiencing. Prior to the war in Syria, more than half of Tripoli's residents lived under the poverty line. Tens of thousands of Syrian refugees moved into these already vulnerable and impoverished neighbourhoods, exacerbating the existing lack of resources, social services and employment, impacting on social cohesion and increasing mutual resentment which could spark violence and inter-neighbourhood clashes. The focus of refugee assistance in Akkar in the north and Bekaa in the east meant the refugee population in Tripoli was largely overlooked.

The war in Syria and related pro- and anti- Syrian government positions exacerbated long-standing conflict between the mostly Alawite neighbourhood of Jabal Mohsen and the mostly Sunni Bab al-Tabbaneh, resulting in regular deadly clashes. Manifestations of intolerance and extremism were on the rise.

Children out of school were mostly engaged in informal employment, child care, household chores and begging. Both refugee and Lebanese youth at risk, marginalized or disadvantaged, were increasingly drawn towards drugs, crime and militant Islam. The sense of marginalization, local and global injustice, grievances, human rights violations, arrests and detention of family and peers, and rising sectarian tensions were driving youth into the arms of extremist groups, where their concerns were articulated, their voice seemed heard and a path of action was proscribed. Various Islamic militant groups were actively attracting youth in Tripoli to join their ranks in combatant and non-combatant roles. An estimated 400–1000 youth left to join radical groups abroad and in Syria.

Context analysis Jordan 2016

In 2015, 110,000 Syrian refugee children were studying in government schools. Because of the widespread violence, bullying and harassment between Jordanian and Syrian students in between the shifts, many Syrian students stopped going to school, citing discrimination and harassment as a main reason. Some of the major refugee camps were experiencing an escalation of violence on their school campuses, often leading to the intervention of the riot police, youth sent to hospital and classes being shut down.

Half of Syrian child refugees suffered from nightmares, sleeping disorders and other forms of psychological distress, such as clinically significant levels of anxiety, PTS symptoms and displacement stress. A key protection concern was the active recruitment of children under eighteen by numerous armed groups for combat and non-combat roles, which put the children at great risk of psychological distress, death or injury.

The 2014 IASC mapping in Jordan emphasized the need to develop effective strategies to integrate Mental Health and Psychosocial Support in educational/school settings, to build capacity of additional mental health staff due to a gap in human resources, and to provide self-care, stress management and psychosocial support for frontline workers and caregivers of children, which was not provided in most of the organizations. Almost half of Jordan service providers felt tired and overwhelmed, without much space for self-care.

The lives of children in vulnerable refugee and host communities in Tripoli and Jordan

From 2016 till 2019, the International Association for Human Values (IAHV) worked with some of the most vulnerable and least supported children and adults in Lebanon and Jordan affected by war, violence and stress. Ongoing vicious cycles of poor mental, emotional and physical well-being and of direct, structural and cultural violence were playing out throughout homes, schools, camps and neighbourhoods in Jordan and Lebanon, affecting children, parents, families, teachers and the broader society as a whole.

Many children were suffering from depression, mental/physical/emotional stress, trauma/PTS, anxiety, frustration, sense of disconnect, feelings of loss, anger and aggression, nightmares, sadness, constant worry, sleeping problems, issues of self-esteem, self-mutilation, isolation, lack of purpose or a sense of humiliation. Major challenges affecting vulnerable refugee and host community children included tensions between refugee and host communities, family tension and domestic violence, bullying, intimidation, child abuse, harassment, school dropout, child labour, early marriage, early pregnancies, drugs, crime, safety concerns, lack of educational and employment opportunities, marginalization, discrimination, grievances, human rights violations and arrests of family members and peers.

During the consultations and analysis, stakeholders expressed that IAHV programmes were needed on a big scale, but especially for out-of-school children, orphans, overstretched frontline workers and violence-affected schools in Tripoli. Hence, IAHV worked in public schools, private schools, unofficial Syrian schools, orphanages, juvenile centres, refugee camps, community centres for out of school children and local NGOs.

Some of the most vulnerable children we worked with, inside and outside schools, include:

- The most vulnerable children and youth from SOS Village Amman, which hosts Jordanian and Palestinian orphans and children whose families are unable to support/raise them. Many of these children suffered from a lack of hope in life, general distrust and indifference, and often expressed aggressive and uncooperative behaviour.
- Syrian children supported by Medical Relief in Jerash, Jordan, who escaped the war and were suffering from the toll it had taken on them and their families.
- Syrian girls supported by Child Care Jordan, most of whom did not attend school because their parents were afraid of the violence in schools towards Syrian children.
- Children from Beddawi – Wadi El Nahleh, who come from a Lebanese tribal community, affected by poverty, basic needs survival and conflicts. The area, which includes Lebanese, Syrian and Palestinian communities, was also known in Tripoli to be a breeding ground for recruitment into armed groups.

- Children from Ab Nadr Foundation in Deddeh, a juvenile centre hosting children with problematic or violent family backgrounds as well as orphans. Most of these children are extremely vulnerable, traumatized and at risk. They are generally coming from very poor backgrounds with big families (some have twelve brothers and sisters). Some children are totally abandoned by their families, and many of them have been physically abused by family members or exposed to other kinds of violence and abuse, including sexual. Before coming to the shelter, most of them dropped out of school and worked at a very early age. In general, the children lack trust and love, and have tendencies towards paranoia, thinking that everyone is conspiring against them to keep them away from their families. They display strong tendencies towards aggression and isolation.
- Children in Dar Zahra orphanage, Tripoli.
- Children from Barsa and Dahr El 3ein, who live in Syrian informal settlements and compounds. Common issues in the compounds are early marriage from the age of thirteen onwards, unsafe sexual intercourse and lack of sexual knowledge leading to pregnancies, school dropout, begging, undisclosed prostitution, lack of values, lack of hygiene, lack of well-informed understanding of their own religion and misunderstanding of religious rituals and symbols. Many social conflicts arise due to the intense proximity within the compound, including gossiping and hatred among families. Some of the children in the camps come from Bedouin families, who used to live in the rural areas of Syria.

Among the project participants was ten-year-old Kamal, who was shot during clashes in Tripoli and was suffering from anxiety and marginalization due to a bullet lodged next to his liver which cannot be removed without endangering his life. And there was Amjad, a refugee from Syria, who became the main provider for his family at the age of twelve, going to school in the morning and working at the barber's in the evening. And there was Nadia from Syria:

My name is Nadia. When I was a little girl I used to think that everything was possible. I had a very strong personality, no-one was able to say anything bad to me or scold me. So when I was in my country I used to dream big. However, when I came here [Lebanon] it all changed. If I need to go out anyone can affect me. I cannot do what I want anymore. I became so sensitive and depressed. I cannot tolerate this anymore. I'm so tired. There is nothing here . . . I have so many dreams but am unable to achieve them. I can't even have my most basic right to get the Brevet certificate here in Lebanon. And I can't go back to my country or travel abroad. We are suffering so much here. All I want is to have a future like all other children who dream.

Project results in numbers

Table 4.1 *IAHV Project Results in Numbers*

- **16,249 Syrian, Jordanian and Lebanese children** affected by trauma, conflict and violence received **basic training in stress-relief and resilience tools** (Stress-Relief and Resilience workshops – SRR)
- **636 children most at risk** of violent behaviour, self-harm, suicide, aggression or recruitment, received **deep trauma-relief, empowerment and human values training** (Trauma-Relief, Healing and Human Values training – THRH)
- **167** specially trained Youth Anti-Violence and Peace Ambassadors (YAVAP) got the confidence, well-being, skills and inspiration to prevent and reduce violence in their families, schools and communities
- **2,811 parents and caregivers** participated in Healing, Resilience and Empowerment Training to enable them to improve their quality of life and provide a supportive and violence-free environment for their children
- **477 Frontline Workers (teachers, social and youth workers)** participated in the Personal Resilience, Stress Management and Professional/Self-Care Training to prevent burnout and improve stress management, personal resilience, well-being and performance capacity
- **99 frontline workers graduated** from the Training of Trainers to keep multiplying stress-relief techniques in their schools and communities on a sustainable basis. New Syrian trainers provided Stress-Relief and Resilience workshops to 5,000+ refugees in Zaatari camp, Jordan.

- **Evaluative Statistics**
    - Hopelessness   − 44%
    - Sleeping problems   − 40%
    - PTS   − 37%
    - Sense of well-being + 49%
    - Care for others   + 34%

- Youth Peace Ambassadors designed and implemented **15 Peacebuilding Projects** to prevent and reduce violence in their families, schools and communities.
    - Topics they chose: domestic violence, early marriage, violence against women and children, violence from school dropout and drugs, bullying, cyber blackmail, conflict between Jordanian and Syrian youth, sexual harassment, violence from stress and negative coping strategies, peer conflicts.
    - Forms they chose: theatre plays, musical, flash mob, dance, songs, movies, football games, music classes, interactive discussions, silent tableaus, graffiti, social campaigns, workshops.

- Estimated **indirect outreach: 100,000+ people.**
    - Peace Ambassadors hosted **4 community celebrations with performances** to raise awareness and share the values of peace with wider communities.
    - **Media exposure** through 17 items, including 5 live TV coverages.
    - **2 Project Closure Ceremonies** attended by 1,500+ people.
    - **4** Multi-Stakeholder Meetings and dozens of individual Stakeholder Meetings.

The core principles of IAHV's conceptual framework and their concrete case study application

Below is a **more detailed overview** from theory (Chapter 3) to practice (Chapter 4), showing how the case study serves as an applied implementation of the conceptual framework presented in Chapter 3. I will provide deeper insights into how the core principles and theoretical models are operationalised and illustrate them with concrete examples and outcomes.

1. **The effectiveness of the evidence-based SKY breathing technique and related practices to reduce stress, trauma, depression and anxiety and strengthen overall well-being**

a. **Theory:**
- There are one hundred twenty scientific peer-reviewed articles on the physiological and psychological benefits of SKY, such as reducing depression, anxiety, PTSD, stress and burnout, and improving overall well-being, optimism, outlook on life, emotional regulation, cognitive clarity and aggression.
- Breathing practices can positively regulate the stress physiology and strengthen homeostasis in the autonomous nervous system.

b. **Practice**:
- Breathing exercises are at the core of all project activities described above, such as the Stress-Relief and Resilience (SRR), Trauma-Relief, Healing, and Human Values (THRH) training and the Professional Care Training (PC).
- Evaluative statistics of the THRH training showed a 44 per cent reduction in hopelessness, a 40 per cent improvement in sleep problems, a 37 per cent reduction in PTSD and a 49 per cent increase in overall well-being.
- Evaluative statistics of the PC training (self-assessment questionnaire) showed that 97 per cent of participants felt improvement in energy levels, 96 per cent in sleep, 94 per cent in stress management capacity, focus, mental clarity and communication, 87 per cent in anxiety, 86 per cent in anger and 85 per cent in depression.

'I used to always have nightmares about the bad things that happened to me in the past. I would re-live them in my dreams. Now I am not scared to sleep anymore. The breathing lets me sleep without nightmares and I wake up rested' (SRR Participant, Irbid, Jordan)

Since her husband disappeared during the war, a Syrian woman had been covering up her physical and emotional pain with jokes in order to look strong in front of her family. She was always suffering from many cramps in her body, which troubled her very much. During the HRE Programme, she felt her ailments relieved. *'Thanks for being able to remove some of the pain from our hearts'*

As told by Manal Karrara, IAHV trainer:

'A mother of a boy who died in battle was sitting on the side, not socializing much and interacting only with her daughter. Out of courtesy and with a feeling of obligation, she joined the group without speaking to anyone. At the end of the session she had a smile on her face. She hugged the trainer and shared that it was the first time since her son had died that she was smiling when thinking of him. Before, she always used to have tears when she closed her eyes and remembered him being dead. Her daughter was so grateful to see her mother smiling after a long time.'

Fatima is supporting her family and has always felt burdened with a lot of suppressed emotions. During the HRE Programme, she was able to eliminate these as she shared:

> 'The training was more than wonderful. It has changed my feelings and the extent of the inner sadness that I have put in myself. I have learned the correct way to breathe and to enjoy the daily exercises, which was the best I have experienced in my life. I got rid of the internal toxins and I came back to my house psychologically relaxed, calm and full of energy, the thing which I was looking for since a long time. I reached a deep peace of mind, which helped me to be content and endure all that is difficult in our daily lives.'

2. Profound and holistic intrapersonal transformation, including mindsets, attitudes, emotions, behaviours and outlook on life

a. Theory:

- Stress in body, mind or emotions negatively influences our perception, interpretation, decision-making and behaviour. When individuals are able to release stress and negative emotions, calm their worries and tensions in the mind, and are thus positively established in themselves, this reflects in their outlook, attitudes, interactions and behaviour. A positive psychosocial state is characterized by improved self-confidence, a broadened and shared self-identity, overcoming issues of trust, fear, suspicion and hatred, and an increased sense of connectedness.

- On a behavioural level, this can subsequently lead to a diminished need for negative coping strategies, improved communication and life skills to handle challenging situations, and increased inclination to take responsibility. It reduces inclination towards harmful behaviour towards oneself or others, such as reduced aggression. Similarly, individuals can feel more resilient against peer pressures, overwhelming emotions, discriminatory behaviours or intimidation.

- On the existential level, it can elicit and restore a sense of meaning in life, provide a way out of states of deep disappointment and despair, establish a reconnection within oneself and with existence, and restore fundamental trust. It can broaden one's outlook and perspective on life and life events and give a personal experience of being part of something larger.

b. Practice:

- In addition to advanced breathing techniques, physical exercises and relaxation, all project activities contain introspective tools, knowledge, processes and skills training, which foster the changes described above.

- The above effects were experienced by many of the project beneficiaries, as demonstrated by their testimonials and the observations of family members, teachers and the IAHV project team.

> 'I discovered that I am not that bad person I always thought I was. At last I felt it's possible for me to live my life, [I understand] why I am here, and why I shouldn't be sad. I used to find all the reasons to

> be sad, to be a miserable and depressed person; maybe I felt worthless; but now I know who I am. I have value; I don't need to remain sad. I need to stay happy.' (Hiba, YAVAP graduate, Sept 2018)
>
> An eight-year-old girl from Homs, Syria, living in Beddawi, Lebanon, was very shy, had low self-confidence and many suppressed emotions. She shared:
>
> 'I felt great rest and relaxation, as if I got rid of all the aches and anxieties that were inside me. When I opened my eyes, I felt reassured and safe as if I was reborn in a new world. I felt that the feelings which have been inhibiting my self-confidence and my courage have left my body... and when I got rid of them [negative feelings], I regained self-confidence and I felt the courage and determination filling my entire body.'
>
> 'Until now I lived because I was forced to live. But now I live because life is beautiful.' (THRH / YAVAP graduate)
>
> 'I used to be scared of everything. Through my fear, I would make others nervous and create tension around me. Now I am still a bit scared, but I don't make others nervous any longer and people stay peaceful around me.' (THRH / YAVAP graduate)
>
> 'Things used to bother me. Now I can control my anger better. I learned how to do it.'
>
> 'I cannot imagine my life anymore without it' (YAVAP graduate)
>
> 'We were able to be with ourselves and get to know who we are. I feel confidence and mental peace. I am a better listener now. I learnt that if I fail at something, I will continue until I succeed. Something has changed for the better.' (Nour, YAVAP graduate, Sept 2018)
>
> 'I was eager to keep coming to the follow-up sessions to be able to release what was inside me. I was able to relax. I now listen more to my family members. The activities made us less shy and increased our motivation. I learnt to keep working towards my goals however big or small. I feel so happy that I am sharing all of this with you all.' (Malak, YAVAP graduate, Sept 2018)

Participants often mentioned an increase in their **self-confidence**. They would no longer allow anyone to make fun of them or bully them. They felt they now had a practical toolkit of breathing exercises which they could use whenever they needed to feel better. Allowing participants to lead exercises and eventually their own community peace projects proved to be a successful method to ensure their confidence and their ability to take responsibility within their own schools, homes, and communities.

A twelve-year-old boy was very shy and introverted because he was bullied by his peers for his physical structure. He felt left out because other children were avoiding playing with him. He was suppressing much pain and sadness, but on the last day of the training, he was able to stand up for himself and politely stopped someone from mocking him. He also proved his importance in the team and showed those who were making fun of him how he could excel them in other areas and complement them instead of competing with them. He shared that he felt much stronger in his body and spirit, and that now he feels he can do anything.

Another twelve-year-old boy was strongly influenced by and following his friends' footsteps to the extent he was living in their shadows. He was suppressing lots of anger and frustration, which he succeeded in eliminating during the training. He was also able to experience great rest and calmness according to his sharing. On the last day of the training, he was very self-confident and excelled independently of his friends' influence, thus proving himself as a leader with his own personality.

> *'I used to be so insecure because of my glass eye. I couldn't even look people in the eye when they were talking to me. I always looked down. After working with IAHV, I'm no longer embarrassed of my eye. I'm proud of who I am. Not only am I proud, I appreciate everyone for their own stories and struggles rather than their looks and what they have.'* (YAVAP graduate, Zaatari Refugee Camp)
>
> *'A 14-year-old Syrian was crying on the first day of the training. Her parents, who are conservative, push her to be perfect, but she felt she cannot: "I cannot get 100 per cent on exams, only 98. If you ask me to dance, I won't, because I know I will fail. If you ask me to sing, I cannot, because I won't know word by word what the lyrics are." Afraid of failure, she refused to try while other girls were singing. When the last night of the training was nearing, she asked her parents if she could stay over for the night. After receiving permission, she packed her stuff and strutted happily to the training the next day. That night, after realizing that you need to live the moment as it comes, she got up to dance. First, she was scared, but when she saw the encouragement from everyone around her, the clapping and the smiles, she let loose. It was her first time dancing, ever. She didn't know what to do with her body, hips, hands and legs, but she didn't care. She just moved, laughed and shook with happiness, saying she finally felt free.'*
>
> *'This is the first time in my life that I have the willingness to really change.'* (YAVAP graduate, Boussayna)

3. Intrapersonal Transformation as the Basis for Interpersonal Peacebuilding

a. Theory:

- The Intrapersonal transformation described above, which is central to IAHV's conceptual framework, fosters inner peace, mindsets and emotions conducive to peacebuilding, resilience, and the cultivation of human values, which are essential for improving relationships and interpersonal peace.

b. Practice:

- Conflicts and fights between different groups of children transformed into increased understanding, acceptance and joint singing, dancing and celebration.
- Project participants shared that their relationships (between children and parents, children and teachers) within the families and the classrooms had improved.

> *'We used to hit each other. Now we talk to each other.'* (YAVAP graduate, Menshieh)
>
> *'When there would be problems at home or my parents would be fighting, I would be very affected, fall sick and go to hospital. Now I think positively. I don't fall sick anymore, but I see how to change the fights into something positive.'* (THRH / YAVAP graduate)
>
> *'I feel more sympathy and more empathy now for people. I feel more connected to others.'* (YAVAP graduate)
>
> *'I started to help others more, even with their personal problems. Am more outgoing to help now.'* (YAVAP graduate)
>
> *'This training taught us how to behave in society, stay away from violence, and learn how to solve problems differently.'* (Rayan, YAVAP graduate, Sept 2018)

When one day, one girl was bullying another girl in a sarcastic way, trying to provoke her, the other girl firmly and calmly asked her to stop it. The bullying girl became upset. Then the bullied girl told the bullying girl to calm down and do the straw breath technique.

'My students have become much better. They participate better and like the music lessons. They used to hit each other but that does not happen now anymore.' (teacher, Menshieh)

As told by Manal Karrara, IAHV trainer:

'A very athletic and energetic 16-year-old Jordanian orphan was constantly running around and very hyper. When you saw her, you saw pure confidence, but when you got closer, she pushed you aside. As the days went by, her tough act was dropped and her vulnerable side showed. After getting into a fight with one of the other girls, she stood for 10 minutes choking on her apology. Upon finally saying it, she collapsed, crying, repeating the words "I'm sorry". That same night, she interacted more with the girls. Before, the other girls would blast music and dance each night, but she would shrug and tell us it wasn't her thing. That night, however, she joined in, stood front line, and danced like she never did before.'

'A young teacher and mother totally veiled in Niqab was attending to her child during the first session. When I asked her to keep him with the nanny, she was at first annoyed and worried about him. When she then sent him with the nanny, she was shouting at the boy to stop crying. The following day, when passing the boy on to the nanny, she told him: "You see how we played and laughed better yesterday after mommy relaxed? Today we will do the same. Just go for a little time." The boy listened to her and left calmly. On the last day the mother was so grateful and shared that she feels more bonding with her children since she is able to feel relaxed and she can give them more now, with higher energy and enthusiasm.'

'I became more patient and more cooperative with colleagues. My relationships with family and friends have also improved.' (JRS refugee staff for house visits)

'When I am angry now, I stay relaxed and solve the problem instead of creating it.' (JRS refugee staff for house visits)

'These techniques help teachers to manage themselves and the (refugee) students better. We can react differently now on the way they behave.' (teacher with Jesuit Refugee Service)

'I am capable of handling more pressure . . . whether from the kids, or work, or at home, everywhere . . . we accept others' opinions more. I used to be so intolerant of people before. If there was a difficult situation, I didn't use to think, I just reacted straight away, and I would get angry. But I don't do this anymore. Now I understand events and situations better.' (TOT Graduate, ICCS)

4. Empowerment which creates leaders and agents of change

a. Theory:

- The IAHV framework supports individuals, through different stages of healing, resilience and empowerment, to become leaders in their communities and agents of change instead of being victims or staying at the receiving end of circumstances, conflicts and violence.

- Empowerment is framed not only as an individual process but also as a pathway to fostering collective action and social change.

b. Practice:

- The **Youth Anti-Violence and Peace Ambassador Programme (YAVAP)** empowered 167 youth as agents of change in their communities. The Programme is designed to build leadership and peacebuilding skills and foster a sense of agency. These youth transitioned from being beneficiaries to becoming leaders who spearheaded fifteen peace projects to address driving factors of violence in their communities, such as the anti-bullying campaign, the theatre for social change around early marriage and the friendly football competition to improve communal relationships, which sparked community dialogues, changed opinions, and garnered widespread media attention, thus influencing thousands.
- Through the Training of Trainers project, beneficiaries turned into empowered service providers after being supported and trained as facilitators of the workshops they had attended themselves, reaching hundreds and thousands of new beneficiaries.

'I always wondered why we are here on earth. Why Allah put us here. I always thought it's not just to eat and sleep. After doing these courses I got to know my mission was to make the world more beautiful. Also, I am going through a very difficult time in my life, but I was able to cope with it.' (Hiba, YAVAP)

'Before I was lost in life. IAHV is giving us a path to walk on.' (YAVAP graduate)

'Although in this course [advanced training which was a preparation for the Training of Trainers] I was keeping my eyes closed most of the time, I got a clearer vision for the whole world.' (Salim, YAVAP graduate)

'The programme taught us how to create goals and work towards them while giving our 100 per cent and how to achieve them. I used to dream a lot, but I never felt any of these dreams were possible. But now, after doing this programme, I feel that I can reach my dreams.' (Rayan, YAVAP graduate, Sept 2018)

'The peace that is inside of us, now we want to help others to find it, to find their inner peace and find more confidence and accept themselves. We do not know what the future holds, but we can work towards making it more beautiful and live and enjoy the moment. I now want to start improving myself, increase my self-confidence, and help people change the same way you helped us.' (Fadia, YAVAP graduate, Sept 2018)

'My name is Boussayna. I am sixteen years old. Honestly, I did not expect to reach this stage. I have been working on a play on early girls' marriage, and never in my life did I expect to do something like this. To stand on stage at this age and period in my life, it's something beautiful and it's so exciting. We evolved in many levels and fields during the training and the follow-up sessions. My personality is stronger. What was outside my circle of comfort has moved inside it. Is there anything more amazing than this? It is so wonderful, and I feel so proud of myself when I see how much I have evolved in such a short time. The training gives you back the basics that are supposed to be present in everyone. It awakened me to many things I was not aware of, be it on a social level or personal

> level. You start evolving, and the more you evolve, the better the society, and we can start changing people's mindsets. In the future I don't want to remain a student in peace building; I would also love to help in the same ways they helped me. I wish they keep spreading this message all over the world to the largest number of people. I will help develop such a society.' (YAVAP graduate, Boussayna)
>
> 'Since we took the title "Ambassadors of Peace", we feel that we carry a big responsibility.' Personally, I have changed a lot in terms of behaviour, like patience and calmness. I learned how to love everyone without thinking about their identity and background. I used to think about myself that I was a useless, obsessed, worthless and unlucky person. But now I am an ambassador of peace and I was very fortunate to have been a member of the family of love where I knew and understood why I was alive. I thank all those in charge of making these three years the most beautiful years of my life.' (Hiba Abboushi, YAVAP graduate, twenty-one years)
>
> 'I discovered my place in my community. I discovered my talent, which is teaching. I used to be bored, with nothing to do. Now I have something that wakes me up in the morning, something that makes me have fun, something I'm proud of, something that makes me special . . . I used to think about the past all the time and be sad about it, but now I think more about the future. I feel like I have a future in something, and it's called peace.' (Peace Ambassador, new IAHV trainer, Zaatari camp)

5. Addressing driving factors of conflict and violence and creating peace-enhancing systems

a. Theory:

- Sustainable peace requires addressing both direct, structural and cultural violence. IAHV focuses on transforming the psychosocial factors contributing to different kinds of violence and on strengthening psychosocial resources for peace, including for the development of peace-enhancing systems and structures in society. It creates a practice and culture of peace by transforming societal norms and promoting human values such as empathy, cooperation, and non-violence.

- The framework integrates personal transformation with community engagement to address the root causes of conflicts and violence. Individuals who are well established in themselves, healed and empowered, are more likely to bring a positive contribution to different aspects of society and to play a peace-enhancing role in developing peace-enhancing systems and structures.

b. Practice:

- Local NGOs and schools integrated IAHV's methods into their schedules and operations, thus improving the learning environment for children as well as their concentration and learning ability, and supporting the well-being of their staff.

- In the Youth Leadership Peacebuilding Training, the youth analysed the driving factors of conflict, violence and peace in their schools, homes, camps and communities, and designed specific interventions to address the root causes as well as the consequences.

- The peace projects addressed driving factors, attitudes, consequences, values and dynamics related to domestic violence, early marriage, violence against women and children, violence from school dropout and drugs, bullying, cyber blackmail, conflict between Jordanian and Syrian youth, sexual harassment, violence from stress and negative coping strategies, and peer conflicts. For example:
    - In Jordan's Menshieh community, Peace Ambassadors bridged existing conflicts and divides within the Jordanian and Syrian communities through friendly football matches while engaging parents and community leaders, reducing stereotypes, fostering cooperative attitudes, thus creating social cohesion instead of alienation, mistrust and division.
    - In Lebanon, youth participants highlighted the psychological and social harms of the traditional practice of early marriage, inspiring community-wide reflection and shifts in attitudes and opinions.
    - Anti-bullying campaigns raised awareness about the harmful effects of bullying in Lebanese society and helped participants identify and overcome the roots of bullying behaviours within themselves.

6. **Universally human approach and context-specific programming**

    a. **Theory**:
    - IAHV's holistic model, addressing physical, mental and emotional well-being, is applicable across cultures, nationalities, social backgrounds, age, gender, religion and other distinctions. At the same time, it adapts to local cultural and contextual needs, integrating universal principles of peacebuilding with culturally relevant knowledge, perspectives and practices.

    b. **Practice**:
    - Thanks to its universally human approach, IAHV was able to work with a wide spectrum of very varied communities and groups across the social mosaic of Tripoli, which few organizations have been able to reach simultaneously. Young people and adults from these diverse communities all recognized universal human values, became aware of their body, mind and emotions, recognized the impact of stress, and learned to use their breath to improve their well-being.
    - IAHV's and Art of Living breathing techniques, as practised around the world in 182 countries, have equally been practised by the variety of communities mentioned above with similar positive outcomes.
    - While universal, the knowledge and techniques of IAHV's programmes are introduced and presented in a context-specific way, for example with references to the importance of the breath in Islamic scriptures. The peace projects are created from the local context, examples and case studies in the project activities are

context-relevant, and the peace interventions and methods are embedded in the local culture. For example, the dabke flash mob and the traditional storytelling in the theatre peace projects resonated with the local communities in familiar, meaningful ways. The use of globally tested techniques like SKY breathing alongside culturally resonant tools and embedded in the unique cultural, political and social dynamics of Lebanon and Jordan ensured both measurable impact and local relevance.

7. **Wide range of Bio-Psycho-Social Factors addressed in the case study**

    With reference to the Overview of Bio-Psycho-Social Factors in Peacebuilding (Figure 2.1), the data and testimonials in the case study illustrate how most of the psychosocial peacebuilding factors in the model, across the bio-psychological, psychosocial, sociocultural and existential-spiritual dimensions, have been addressed in the case study. This illustrates that it is possible to lay a strong psychosocial foundation for peacebuilding through an integrated psychosocial peacebuilding approach.

8. **Theory of Change in action**

    a. **Theory**:
    - IAHV's Theory of Change posits that personal transformation at the individual level leads to improved interpersonal peace and broader peacebuilding impacts, addressing structural violence and promoting a culture of peace, ultimately laying the psychosocial foundation for sustainable peace.

    b. **Practice**: The cascading effects of individual transformation were evident in stories like those of the Peace Ambassadors who influenced peers, families, and communities. The theory of change was actualized through cascading impacts, for example, related to early marriage:

    - **Individual Impact**: Girls who had suffered from early marriage were trained and practised techniques to improve their overall well-being, reporting greater emotional resilience, reduced aggression and increased self-esteem. Having overcome negatively affecting experiences, they were empowered as agents of change to support people in similar circumstances.

    - **Community Ripple Effects**: The theatre play on early marriage shifted the views of community members and reached a large audience in the Middle East through live TV performances.

    - **Culture of Peace**: The project promoted the values of respect, freedom, care, responsibility, and nurturing a culture of peace.

    - **Institutional Integration**: Local NGOs adopted IAHV's methods, contributing to the sustainability of the interventions.

9. **The human being at the centre of peacebuilding and fostering human connection**
   a. **Theory**:
      - IAHV places the human being at the centre of peacebuilding and focuses on restoring a sense of connection with oneself, others, society and the planet.
   b. **Practice**:
      - The human being was the focal point of the interventions, whether children, youth, caregivers, teachers or community leaders.
      - Community ownership and multi-stakeholder involvement were essential aspects of the project in several ways: starting from stakeholder consultations, it involved not only children as the direct project beneficiaries, but also caregivers, parents, teachers, local authorities, service providers, national and international organizations. Stakeholders were involved in programme design and implementation. Nearly 3,000 caregivers participated in resilience-building programmes, enabling them to create nurturing environments for children. Teachers noted improvements in students' behaviour and relationships. Activities such as the art and music programmes engaged entire communities, creating long-term changes in social attitudes and reducing violence.

What worked well

The case study demonstrated multiple strengths in its design and implementation, both intended and indirect, contributing to its positive impact:

1. **One of the strongest positive side effects of this project was the widespread awareness it created at the community level about psychosocial support and peacebuilding. People got inspired by the simple but effective link between well-being, inner and outer peace**, and were eager to spread this further for the benefit of their families and communities.
2. **The effectiveness of the techniques in combination with the holistic approach** of the programmes created intrapersonal transformation as a foundation for interpersonal and social change.

    For almost all of the children, this was their first acquaintance with tools and techniques to relax, to become aware of their emotions and reactions and feel better in themselves. The simple but effective workshop of several hours spread over three days significantly improved their sense of well-being, emotional regulation, concentration, happiness and relations with peers and family.

    In the THRH programmes, IAHV's trainers witnessed how children who lacked self-esteem and isolated themselves opened up, those displaying aggressive behaviour experienced relief from long-term traumas, those suffering from anxiety, depression and PTSD became more positive and enthusiastic, and those who were shy transformed into effective leaders taking responsibility for peace projects.

3. Through **a comprehensive and multi-level approach,** the project addressed individual, community and cultural/structural issues simultaneously. By integrating stress-relief, trauma healing and community empowerment, it **exemplified a holistic psychosocial support model**. Tailored and synergetic interventions for specific age groups and contexts enhanced broad community participation and leverage of impact. The multiple (intra-)personal, interpersonal and social transformations described above converged and culminated in broad communal transformation during the closure activities of the project as well as beyond that.

4. Throughout the project implementation, the trainers and their team **'walked the talk'** in order to create a safe environment for the participants, to inspire as a role model, to teach by example, and to embody the human values of compassion, empathy, friendship, peace and responsibility.

Most participants felt that the IAHV training provided a **safe space**, one where participants were encouraged to express themselves without having to fear negative consequences, a space where they were comfortable.

'I feel like we entered a "room of Peace" when we entered the training. You release all the bad energy and return happy to your house when you finish the training'. (YAVAP graduate, Zarqa)

'IAHV gave us a safe environment where we can safely express and improve ourselves. I wish the whole world would be part of IAHV.' (Sarah, YAVAP graduate)

'The IAHV centre is a place where I can be my own personality. I can be me in this place. I finish all my things elsewhere so I can be here. Everything I can do is to be here with you. I want to come here until my last breath, in a space that I love that expresses me.' (Hiba, YAVAP graduate)

5. The **social bonding** was very supportive for the youth and adults participating in the project. Many of them were separated from their family members or had lost people close to them. It was also very meaningful for them to meet people from such different backgrounds with whom they would not have come into contact without the project.

Very early on in the trainings, a **sense of connectedness** was established among the youth from different regions, nationalities and backgrounds, as well as between the youth and their supervisors, trainers and communities, which lasted until well after the training. A positive environment where good communication, understanding and tolerance were practised supported the participants to bond with one another, the trainers and the broader community upon their return.

> 'When I'm in the classroom with the trainers, I feel like I belong to them, I'm not a student, they're not teachers, we all belong to each other ... When we first began the training, I felt like everyone just wanted to provoke each other. This person wants to fight with this person while this other person is making fun of anyone who participates. Everyone had an ego, but after the breathing and the games and the sleepovers, everyone was on the same level. Me and the rest of the kids started making friends, we started supporting each other and cheering for one another in the group activities and games. By the end, we were all one family. We all cared for one another, including the trainers. We didn't judge each other anymore.' (THRH Participant, Jarash)
>
> 'I have done many social things in my life, but this was the best experience I ever had. I feel closer to this group of strangers I was with here than to anyone I have met in my life. This project made us a family.' (THRH graduate)

6. **Training youth to act as peace ambassadors** not only facilitated personal transformation but also amplified the project's reach, as they implemented peacebuilding activities in their communities. These ambassadors became relatable role models, inspiring peers and younger participants. It also contributed to their overall development and life trajectory. Even though there was no longer-term impact evaluation, the project team regularly hears of their personal successes in the fields of study, competitions, awards, scholarships and positions. The project illustrated that peacebuilding with and for children and youth can be very effective both on a personal and social level.

7. The project became **strongly embedded in the local community** through active involvement of many stakeholders, the training of new local trainers, and the multiple community outreach and celebration events. Thousands of children, youth, parents, caregivers, teachers, partnering organizations and municipalities interacted and engaged with the project activities and with each other. Jordanian, Syrian and Lebanese parents, teachers and youth became themselves trainers of the trauma-relief workshops. Some of them trained in turn hundreds of children in their own schools and communities. Parents and caregivers gained tools to be able to better support their children and families, thus creating a ripple effect across families. Culturally resonant mediums like traditional dance, theatre performances, music, flash mobs and football tournaments, through which sensitive and important messages were shared, were relatable and accessible, leading to widespread community engagement. The level and spread of community involvement with the project and its objectives were very visible and culminated in the final project celebration in Tripoli:

The Final Closure Ceremony of the project took place in the midst of chaos and uncertainty in Lebanon, where widespread protests had started in October 2019. Roads and schools were mostly closed, many people chose to stay at home, waiting to see what was going to unfold, and most other organizations working on the ground had suspended their work. Apart from the protest movements, Tripoli was mostly empty and silent. There was a small, lively and enthusiastic group of youth though who were actively busy shaping their future into a positive and peaceful one. In the midst of heightened tensions, these inspired Youth Peace Ambassadors came to the IAHV office every day, many of them walking on foot from faraway parts of Tripoli, to prepare their own Final Closure Ceremony.

Some of them shared that if it were not for their increased understanding, more positive outlook on life, their team bonding and revival of peace values, they would probably either have stayed at home, watching television without getting involved, or they would have joined the aggressive and at times violent protesting groups. But instead, they had become non-violent agents of change!

The youth put together a very inspiring and touching programme for their Final Closure Ceremony

- to express their deep aspirations and hopes for peace,
- to share their experiences of empowerment and healing,
- to present their peacebuilding projects to create a more peaceful and violence-free Tripoli,
- to share with the audience stress management practices they had deeply benefited from,
- to inspire a broader community of non-violence and human values,
- to celebrate the positive changes they made inside and outside themselves.

The Closure Celebration took place at the Rachid Karami International Fair in Tripoli on 8 December 2019 in the presence of 800+ guests. It brought together a large community for peace in the midst of the turmoil of Lebanon's protests. Prejudices, conflicts and tension between different groups transformed into increased understanding, acceptance, joint celebration and cooperation.

> **The mayor of Tripoli, Riad Yamaq, who attended the Closure Ceremony, commended 'the group of Peace Ambassadors in Tripoli and their positive initiative to do these projects that will help the coming generations to overcome crises. Even if it was a difficult mission, to light a candle is much better than cursing darkness. In the name of the municipality of Tripoli and all its members, I would like to thank all who have been working on this project, which is positively influencing and contributing to the revival of the society and reducing the psychological pains of the coming generations to move forward from the current difficult period. We appreciate the support of the EU and the organizations who are running this project. We wish it would be a continuous programme for our children who are living these difficult situations.'**

Community awareness and engagement were evidenced by high numbers of participants and attendees in public campaigns and follow-up initiatives. This contributed to widespread awareness about the needs of children impacted by conflict and violence and generated discussions and solution brainstorming among stakeholders.

8. **The quantifiable impact** of this psychosocial project showed tangible improvements in participants' well-being (e.g. decreased PTSD and sleeping problems, increased sense of care for others). In addition, the project team and target groups indirectly reached an estimated 100,000+ people through several community celebrations in different locations and extensive media coverage, including several live TV interviews and performances.

9. **Building local capacity** by training teachers, caregivers and local stakeholders as trainers of the stress-relief workshops ensured that the knowledge and tools provided could outlive the formal project. It is **particularly effective to train youth and adults who were once beneficiaries to become new trainers**, since they have inside knowledge of the circumstances of workshop participants and have personally experienced the benefits of the workshops in these situations. They can therefore relate very well to workshop participants, connect to their experiences and support them in the best way possible.

10. **The agility and resilience of the project team** contributed to the success of the project. In a sociopolitical context where many NGOs halted their activities, the project team was able to continue. They also addressed daily challenges and came up with solutions in a context where opportunities arise last minute and plans are changed regularly. They ensured relevance and impact by flexibly tuning into the changing circumstances, such as facilitating the spread of the anti-bullying campaign during the protests. Their commitment to peace and human values and their resilience, supported by daily practice of the Art of Living techniques, allowed them to achieve a profound and large impact, and this with a relatively small budget.

11. **Upholding human values and integrity** in the operations creates long-term partnerships and trust. In a Lebanese context, where loyalty is often bought or linked to sectarianism, where project beneficiaries are awarded for their participation in order to meet donor targets, and where the reputation of the NGO sector is tarnished with hidden agendas and corrupted practices, IAHV stood out as 'an organization that is different'. Through consistently ethical behaviour, upholding human values in interactions and project implementation, the absence of hidden agendas, transparency and open communication, IAHV became known, trusted and respected as an organisation and a partner.

Qualitative understanding through stories, case studies and testimonials

Trauma-Relief, Healing, Resilience and Human Values Training (THRH)

The majority of the 636 THRH participants were Syrian refugee or Lebanese and Jordanian host community children residing in highly populated but marginalized areas. Many were negatively impacted by poor family conditions (parental divorce, loss of care), extreme poverty, school dropout, child labour, social violence, denial of basic rights or displacement due to Lebanese and Syrian wars, leading to mental disturbance and social disadvantage.

Based on IAHV trainers' testimonials:

> These trainings were both challenging and beautiful. Some of the boys were particularly aggressive towards one another and the trainers at the beginning of the training. Their hostile attitude towards life exposed insecurities and a lack of self-esteem, which could be traced back to different kinds of abuse they had experienced. Day by day, love and attention paired with the breathing techniques proved to be a remedy for the violence. The violent behaviour among the boys reduced dramatically by the end of the training; they were able to control their violent tendencies and eventually to control their reactions so they could avoid fights altogether. Also, certain girls under care were very rude in the beginning of the training towards girls from the other organizations. However, during the training, they actually made friends and at the end, they were sad to part ways. For example, one girl who was always trying to disrupt the class and distract her peers during the sessions experienced a clear change in attitude towards the end of the training. On the last day, she cried and asked to extend the training at least one more day because it became very important for her.
>
> Although initially reluctant to do the breathing techniques, most participants later looked forward to the rhythmic breathing portion of the training and became very keen on continuing the practice, since they saw it as the reason for their newly found relief. In the safe space of the training and through these rhythmic breathing techniques, the traumas these children had faced in their lives initially became more evident in the form of aggression, isolation and depression, but were then replaced with inner peace. Despite their burdensome past and traumas, the children developed deep connections with each other and their trainers.

The children and youth reported improvement in their sense of hopelessness (−44 per cent), sleeping problems (−40 per cent), PTS (−37 per cent) and sense of well-being (+49 per cent), as well as increased care for others (+34 per cent). Their testimonials also speak of the reduction in their stress levels, anxiety and tendencies towards violent behaviour, increased ability to control their reactions to fight with other participants and improved skills to express themselves. They also mentioned their deep relaxation, increased confidence, energy, positive outlook on life, and empowerment to shape their lives and live their dreams. Also, the parents, teachers and social workers observed the positive changes in the THRH participants, such as reduced aggression, more calmness, better focus and concentration, and improved well-being.

Following the THRH, the maturity of the participants made them stand out among their peers; they clearly became pioneers in their schools and communities and were eager to share what they learned with them. Teachers observed that, after participation in IAHV's programmes, the children showed more self-confidence, hope towards the future, reduced violence, more calmness, increased school participation, and a new sense of togetherness among Jordanian and Syrian children who used to separate themselves before. Most of the THRH participants attended follow-up sessions, during which the trainers could observe their continuous transformation. Coming from different schools and areas in Tripoli, they shared their stories during these sessions and became friends.

> 'Working with boys in the Lebanese high schools was very special at times. Sometimes the boys did not want to open their eyes, there was a deep sense of silence and depth. Some said they had never felt this peaceful before. There was a change in their eyes, the way they looked and how they looked at us. There was a deep sense of amazement and wonder after having experienced even simple breathing techniques.
>
> I am amazed every time our sessions turn 180 degrees from total chaos to deep peace and silence.
>
> Even in the more chaotic sessions, we always managed to have at least some of the participants experience a deep sense of relaxation and value the techniques. It is so beautiful when they open up, when they are able to value and experience deep rest from stress and trauma. When troubled youth who were behaving erratically and aggressively end up sshh-ing others because they want to enjoy that deeper rest. When they are not afraid to close their eyes, drop their hard shell and show their sensitive side. When girls tell each other enthusiastically at the end how they loved the session and how relaxed they felt.' (Christian Matta, IAHV Trainer)

Case study: Ab Nadr, juvenile institution, Deddeh

In 2017, IAHV implemented the first THRH training for children living in the Ab Nadr shelter in Deddeh, Lebanon. Following its success, the management requested THRH trainings for all the sixty-nine children living in the shelter, which were followed by several follow-up sessions.

> One of the IAHV trainers shares the transformation she observed in one of the boys:
>
> 'One boy of nine years old was avoiding any physical contact with anyone, whether from his caretakers, peers or trainers. He was not able to talk easily and not willing to make any eye contact with people. He was just throwing few words here and there, creating chaos among his peers, and then silently watching.
>
> At the end of the second day of the THRH training, he asked to talk to me privately. He told me that he misses his mother as he hasn't seen her for a whole year and said: "I love my family and miss them, even though they are hurting me!"
>
> This boy was repeatedly sexually assaulted by family members. When he tried to defend himself, he ran away and got arrested. The mother wasn't able to visit him, not only because she lives very far and is very poor, but also because she is trying to protect her family, including him, from her point of view, by asking him to change his testimony against those who abused him.
>
> During the training, we paid attention to enhance his confidence in himself and others. He was reluctant, though we saw a change in his body language. He was feeling a change inside himself, which he only expressed when I visited the institution a week after the training. To my amazement, he came running towards me and hugged me tight. With a sweet smile, he told me he was regularly doing the exercises we taught him. He looked so much accomplished after overcoming some of his

> inhibitions about physical contact with people, thanks to the transformational techniques he had been practising and the patience of our team to give him space to express himself.
>
> One year later I met him and saw him much more confident to talk and express himself. He was also able to see his mother without being influenced by any dictation regarding his testimony.'
> (Manal Karrara, IAHV trainer)

Case study: Dar Zahra orphanage, Tripoli

IAHV conducted SRR and THRH workshops for almost all the children in Dar Zahra orphanage, as well as one Professional Care Training for the staff.

> One of the IAHV trainers shared the experiences among the girls:
>
> 'The girls in the orphanage were full of suspicion and trying to push us to our limits by making fun and disrupting the session. While on the first day they were not able to trust and close their eyes at all, on the last day they were able to sit and rest for several minutes and then express in drawing what they felt. One girl had suicidal thoughts but was able towards the end of the workshop to transform her disaster into a strength. Another girl who was always bullying or being bullied and who had a sad expression on her face, started laughing out loud happily towards the end of the workshop. The other girls expressed their amazement since it was the first time they saw this girl so happy! One of the most disruptive girls in the workshop came back one week later to join the workshop for another group, because the exercises made her feel so happy and relaxed. Some of the older orphans eagerly started assisting and supporting our work with the younger ones when they heard we did not have assistants those days.'
> (Manal Karrara, IAHV trainer)

Case study: SOS children's village, Amman, Jordan

The SOS children used to live in isolation, not interacting much with society, distrusted and distrusting. In the SOS village in Amman, each house was more or less like a gang stronghold. Since they participated in IAHV programmes, there was a big positive change in the relationships within the village. After the Youth Leadership Training, the youth from different houses started meeting and studying together. Youth who were enemies before came together; there was more brotherhood and no more problems.

> 'When there is a problem among them, they are now less aggressive than before. There is a much more positive connection among them.' (SOS Manager)
>
> 'I used to be very stubborn, but now I am listening more and accepting others more. I hated socialising before, but now I have many friends. I never made so many friends in such a short time!'
> (YAVAP graduate, SOS)

One of the biggest successes of the project for the SOS organization was the positive change they observed in the personalities of the children. It was the first time that the SOS children started mixing and interacting with other youth outside the village. They lost their shyness and inhibitions, did not feel embarrassed and expressed their emotions freely. They became motivated from within. The management was (positively) shocked by the changes they observed.

When the SOS children started visiting cancer hospitals as part of their YAVAP project, all the boys decided to shave their heads as a sign of solidarity and empathy with the cancer patients. For these boys, for whom the haircut is a very important aspect of their outlook and personality, this was a very new and strong message of empathy with others, coming from their hearts.

> *'Normally our children think in the first place about themselves. Now, when they started thinking about their project, it was the first time they thought about others in the first place, such as the cancer patients.' (SOS manager)*

The Youth Coordinator from the SOS village informed us that the SOS children became more confident, calmer, and more hopeful towards their future. The supervisors of the youngest age group were very vocal about their appreciation for the positive energy boost that IAHV programmes instilled in their children. They also observed that earlier the children would separate themselves into groups according to nationality, with the Syrians on one side and the Jordanians on the other. Now they were all sitting together, sharing stories from their training, playing games and practising the techniques of the training together.

Empowering Youth Peace Ambassadors with confidence, skills and knowledge to build peace in their homes, schools and communities

> *'If there was a word stronger than "Thank you" I would say it. Discovering myself, the self that I love, that I have kept inside me for a long time, this is what I have achieved. We are born for a purpose. I know for sure that since the moment I was born I will do something good. The main purpose of course is peace building but first we need to start with ourselves to be able to make things better. IAHV is a road we can walk on, why go all over the place? I believe this was fate. As if there was a white door I have always been waiting for and now I have reached it.' (Hiba, YAVAP graduate)*

Shaped by their own specific experiences of violence, the youth overcame their personal traumas, obstacles and disappointments and gained healing, confidence, skills and inspiration to start making a positive impact on the people and environment around them. Passionate and trained to reduce stress and violence and bring peace in their schools and communities, the Youth Peace Ambassadors conceived and designed Peacebuilding Projects on topics which are part of their lives and close to their hearts.

> 'When people hear the word Tripoli or Lebanon, oh my God, they think, terrorism. I want them to have a positive idea about Tripoli. Tripoli is really not that ugly and that bad of a place as people think. There is goodness in people.' (Boussayna, YAVAP graduate)

As described earlier in this chapter, girls who had suffered the effects of early marriage healed their wounds, spoke out and changed the minds of their audience through their self-written theatre play performed on live TV. The anti-bullying flashmob campaign of the Youth Peace Ambassadors reached tens of thousands of people live and online. Syrian youth transformed a community through their friendly football matches, messages of shared human values, music and art classes, creating togetherness and peace instead of separation and conflict. Thousands of children and adults in Zaatari camp learned positive ways to deal with their stresses, taught by the locally trained youth themselves, following the production and screening of a powerful awareness-raising movie they produced themselves.

Several groups of youth also focused on the **violence** directly experienced **in their homes** and the violence they witnessed against women and children in their Lebanese and Syrian communities. They expressed their feelings in songs that were recorded and integrated into a musical they performed and in a series of very expressive silent tableaus depicting the oppression of women at home and in society. The songs and the plays inspired women to stand in their strength and encouraged them to take up their equal role alongside and together with men.

> 'I want to defend my right that you acknowledge me. I don't want to harm you, believe me. We complete each other. You are not supposed to control me until I am burnt out. I am not your slave. You are my partner in life.' (Lyrics from the song)

The youth participants from Beddawi, Tripoli, identified **sexual harassment** as one of the most disturbing forms of violence in their community. This made it unsafe for them and others to walk certain streets, and it had a strong psychological impact on its victims. Because of the sensitivity surrounding the topic, the Peace Ambassadors decided to make several graffiti murals highlighting various aspects of the issue, which were to be placed in the community and used in schools to start discussions on the topic.

In a SOS village for orphans in East Amman, the children felt that the angry and hostile environment among different children's groups prevented them from concentrating on their education and planning their future. A mixed group of boys and girls decided to create **a positive, conflict-free environment** in the village through a special Peace Day where they would run different stations to teach peacebuilding exercises and necessary life skills and values. Through the initiative, the disadvantaged orphans felt they could better focus on their future rather than worrying only about present threats to their happiness. Another group of SOS children created

social cohesion and integration between the SOS village and the wider society in East Amman through educational activities.

The youth had observed that violence in their communities also originated from children and youth who **dropped out of school and from the use of drugs**. In order to help prevent school dropout, violent tendencies and child labour, they wrote and performed two theatre plays. The first play was a silent play with strong impressive scenes showing a young boy being seduced by his peers to drop school, ending up wasting his life, until he accidentally comes across a school book, gets inspired, takes up his education again and gets reunited with his real, positive friends. The second play is a series of very vivid, real-life dialogues between different members of a family living in one house, showing how their behaviours make it impossible for the young boy to study or continue his education, which he desperately drops, until he reads a letter from his grandfather. . . . Both theatre plays, combining recognizable content, characters, issues and dialogues from real life, staged in a beautifully imaginative and artistic way, were an immense success with the audience.

In addition, this group of Peace Ambassadors went out to speak in person to children at risk of dropping out of school. They also brainstormed, acted and filmed a short clip 'Your reality is the dream of someone else' https://www.youtube.com/watch?v=2s2c_RXq69Q . In order to raise more awareness about the widespread problem of school dropout in Tripoli, they also launched a drawing and writing competition through which children could express their thoughts and feelings on the topic and find solutions. The winners of the competition were invited to and awarded at the Final Ceremony.

> 'I am very happy with the reactions of people on our competition. I started to talk with people and with the orphans; I played with them. I was really happy to be able to connect to people. Participants in the competition and the audience of our plays became much more aware about school dropout. They didn't know much about it. The orphans became more aware as well and said they were studying more now because they don't want to drop out of school.' (YAVAP Peace Ambassador)

The youth were equally worried about the use of drugs among their peers, which was making their communities unsafe, leading to crime and violence, and destroying the lives of their peers, sometimes up to suicide. They wrote a powerful song and play, expressing a message from their hearts: 'Don't try drugs because it will ruin your life.'

They also became aware of the disastrous effects of **cyber blackmail**, which usually shames and blames the victim while the blackmailer goes free. Touched by cases of injustice and suicide in their environment, the Peace Ambassadors wrote and filmed a powerful and creative awareness movie explaining cyber blackmail and encouraging the victims of blackmail to speak up in order not to stay a victim, to reclaim their dignity and support justice. 'Have the courage to speak out!'

Inspired by the positive effect of effective stress management on their own well-being, relationships and behaviour, the youth also recognized the need for **stress management in**

their communities in order to prevent and reduce violence. Therefore, the Peace Ambassadors put together an awareness campaign on the effects of stress and offered practical Stress-Relief and Resilience workshops in their communities.

> 'This organisation [IAHV] can remove many difficulties in a peaceful way. I was able to release a huge burden in a very comfortable way. The way we get rid of our burdens through the breathing, I wish other people can experience this, especially those who express themselves in a violent way.'
> (Rayan, YAVAP Peace Ambassador)

The Art Peace Performances in these projects were developed with the support of CrossArts, IAHV's local partner in Lebanon, which is specialized in empowering youth at risk and disadvantaged youth through different forms of art, giving them a voice of their own, skills to handle challenges, and a sense of meaning and empowerment. Facilitating positive identities and expressions among youth, CrossArts connects youth from different communities to share their messages against violence and extremism and in support of social peace. The youth participating in IAHV's project were excited to experiment and build skills in the different forms of art which they chose as their means of expression: theatre plays, musicals, flash mob, dance, songs, movies, music classes, interactive discussions, silent tableaus and graffiti.

While IAHV techniques restored the inner mental, emotional and physical well-being of children, Cross Arts supported the development of their own voice, ideas, talents and identity. This combined approach equipped the youth to create desired change within their communities.

> 'I am an eighteen-year-old girl. My identity is Syrian, Arab. The war in my country has forced me to live my life in exile since my childhood. Eight years of war, alienation, isolation, oppression, physical stress, fatigue from a harsh psycho-physical reality, pain, constant sadness, despair, frustration and loneliness. Despite all the assistance we have received, especially psychosocial support from some international organizations, it did not and will never be able to fix what I and many people, especially those of my generation, felt.
>
> When I participated in the programme "IAHV Peace Ambassadors", this was the best programme: effective and capable of making a change.
>
> We learned that to be a positive and effective human being in this society, which is full of corruption, violence and oppression, you need to change your life to be better, more beautiful and stable; you must be optimistic and love the small things of your day. You should not feel different from others, accept everyone without exception, have within you a radiant love, spontaneity, kindness and positive energy, and take responsibility because you are a human being. To be a member of the family of peace is to feel and be sensible to those around you, to be active, enthusiastic, understanding and humble. These are the simplest bases for peace, because peace carries many more of these deep meanings. The ambassadors of peace programme, with all its trainers, with their ideas,

> their love and trust in themselves and others, and their smooth handling, is enough to give this land a special name: to be the land of peace, safety, satisfaction, compassion and harmony, the land of humanity.
> So I would like to express my gratitude to everyone who contributed to the project. This land is in dire need of such projects.'
> (Bayan Alzhori, YAVAP graduate)

Creating a peaceful and supportive environment with parents and caregivers

Many times, the children shared how good they felt in the sessions and the training, but when they went home, they felt all stressed again. Therefore, IAHV also worked intensely with **parents, families and caregivers** to strengthen a more supportive environment for the children. The Healing, Resilience and Empowerment (HRE) trainings strengthened awareness, well-being and resilience to improve quality of life and the capacity to support their families.

> 'Especially for women it was really good. They had the chance to think about themselves for the very first time. They were able to improve relationships within their families.' (Representative partner organization Lebanon)

The majority of participants were women, many of whom were female householders, widows, bereaved mothers or single parents in the absence of their spouse.

> As told by Manal Karrara, IAHV trainer:
> 'An old lady was very serious the first session and sceptical about every exercise. She was giving sharp orders to people around her to maintain discipline in the session. During the session she started laughing, throwing away all imposed discipline. Afterwards she shared that for nineteen years she has never laughed from her heart as she did during the session. She used to smile politely to people, but she had never felt that genuine laughter and joy before.'

Occasionally the positive effect for the women was also transmitted to some male members of their communities who showed interest in participating in the programmes as well. Several dozen men, including in Zaatari camp, were able to benefit from the programmes and released the huge stress, burden and negative feelings they were carrying. The participation of men was rare, since their culture did not make it common for men to attend training of this nature, but it was equally important.

Case study: Unofficial Syrian schools, Tripoli

The unofficial Syrian schools were a network of schools in Tripoli and beyond which were run by Syrians for Syrian children. The fact they were not recognized by the Lebanese Ministry of Education caused a whole series of problems for both the staff and the children. In these schools, which were deprived of any regular support services, the impact of this project was especially strong. Not only thousands of children participated in SRR workshops but also hundreds of parents and teachers learned stress management techniques in the HRE and PC programmes in order to be able to support the children better.

> 'Many women called us to ask for more courses. They experienced physical, emotional and spiritual improvements. Same for the children and the youth. The children learned new techniques to break the cycle of bullying and being bullied. You offered children another way. The women practise the techniques you taught them at home and at work and they remember them when they are upset.' (Rita, director Syrian school)

Improving stress management, personal resilience and performance capacity for teachers and frontline workers

Four hundred seventy-seven staff of dozens of organizations, including **local, national and international NGOs, youth and refugee organizations, as well as teachers in official and unofficial schools**, benefited from IAHV's short and effective Professional Care (PC) training to prevent burnout and improve stress management, personal resilience, well-being and performance capacity.

According to post-training self-assessment questionnaires, **more than 94 per cent of participants experienced improvement in their sleep, energy levels, mental clarity and focus, ability to handle stress, communication and skills to deal with others, while 85–87 per cent experienced reduced depression, worry, anxiety, anger and loss of temper.** In addition, they reported increased levels of energy during the workday, which helped increase their productivity, tolerance and effectiveness at work.

> 'We are working in an environment that is in dire need of psychosocial activities. I have never seen such an effective stress-relief as in this workshop ... This will heavily reflect on the type of work that I do and will allow me to truly benefit the Syrian refugees that I work with.' (Social worker at Zaatari camp)
>
> 'We learned how to release stress and anger and control our emotions. In our job we go into much detail of each person's situation and make decisions that may change somebody's life. Sometimes we struggle with feelings of guilt when we refuse refugee status. This affects our emotions. In the Professional Care Training of IAHV, I experienced that there is hope in life. I don't need to go to the doctor. I can think better and come out of my negativity. I can release negativities and

> *can become a better human being. Twenty-five staff members did the programme and all agreed that they felt more improvement and awareness. This programme should be widespread, not just for refugees.'* (Director Refugee Center, Australian Embassy, Amman)
>
> *'It was the first time they thought about themselves as a person, about their own mind and emotions. For the first time their mind was able to stop. One staff member who was very depressed, started speaking and smiling again.'* (Manager, Handicap International, sharing about their staff who were working with war victims in Syria on a daily basis and who got very affected themselves)
>
> *'I always felt there was something missing in my personal and professional life. This gap has now been filled.'* (JRS refugee staff for house visits)

Training of trainers to facilitate Stress-Relief and Resilience workshops
Case study: Jesuit Refugee Service, Jordan

Jesuit Refugee Service (JRS) staff who completed the Training of Trainers integrated IAHV techniques in their classes for refugees. The refugee students were asking for it and it helped them to focus and study better. JRS staff became less affected by the stressful situations of the refugees and felt able to have a more positive impact on them. Also, their team relationships improved, as well as their family relationships, since they no longer took the stress home with them.

> *'I am teaching life skills to refugee children, but something was missing. IAHV's Stress-Relief and Resilience workshops give that. Children want more of it. I integrate it in my workshops now. Their energy levels used to drop but now stay high during my sessions.'* (teacher with Jesuit Refugee Service)

Lessons learned and challenges

While the project achieved significant success, several weaknesses and challenges were identified. Most importantly, the prolonged challenging implementation context of Lebanon combined with Covid restrictions and lack of human and financial resources unfortunately did not allow us to continue working on a sustained basis with the project participants in Lebanon and Jordan following project end.

1. **Contextual Challenges**:
   - Increasing and chronic political instability, economic hardships, and entrenched social issues in Lebanon created barriers to long-term engagement and follow-up. Project

beneficiaries became predominantly occupied with daily struggles and survival, preventing them from allocating time or space for anything else. In addition, the restrictions and challenges of the Covid pandemic interrupted the momentum of activities, interactions and bonding among children, youth and adults across Tripoli, which became especially strong following the Peace Celebration in Tripoli in December 2019.
- The ongoing exodus of families and youth from Lebanon and the mobility among the Syrian refugee population limited the possibilities for continuity.

2. **Sustainability and Resource Constraints**:
   - With a relatively small project team, it was challenging to adhere to the demanding and resource-intensive requirements of EU project management, administration and reporting. The task of ongoing project implementation, in a challenging context where every day is unpredictable and planning needs to be adapted continuously, in combination with intensive administration and reporting, fully absorbed the capacity of the team, and left little to no capacity for the equally demanding task of securing follow-up funding. Such funding was not available at the time inside Lebanon due to the economic and financial crisis and political decision-making, and would therefore have to be sought externally. Being a volunteer-based organization, the organizational development and resources of IAHV are disproportionately small compared to the extensive impact it creates on the ground. Unlike most other big NGOs, it does not rely on extensive headquarters run by huge overhead costs with special fundraising departments and professionals.
   - Even though the project aimed towards structural integration of IAHV's methods into sectors of society, such as frameworks for refugee response, education or staff well-being, this was poorly accomplished. While impactful on a personal and community level and even though its positive outcomes were shared with authorities and decision-makers, the socio-economic-political context and limited resources did not allow for long-term institutional integration. The crisis and emergency mode in which many international organizations were operating left little scope and attention to explore innovative approaches and scale up successful interventions or embed lessons into broader policies.
   - For the reasons mentioned above, it was challenging to follow up with the new trainees, support their engagement, or supervise where required. Many of them became preoccupied with survival and related challenges in daily life and could not continue engaging with the organization or implementation of stress-relief workshops.

3. **Local and cultural sensitivities**:
   - Issues such as early marriage, domestic violence, interreligious and intercommunal collaboration, recruitment into armed groups, support for refugees and needs of host populations, child abuse, physical punishment and harsh educational methods are very delicate issues and need to be handled with great sensitivity and skill. In some cases, the prevailing beliefs, stereotypes and customs were reflected in an attitude of resistance to the values and aims of the project.
   - Male participation was lower than female participation, reflecting cultural norms and economic and livelihood demands that were challenging to overcome.

4. **Possibility of Impact research study:**

During the project design, it was envisioned to include an impact research study. However, it was very challenging to find a researcher or team with the expertise of evaluating (1) intrapersonal transformation on physical, mental, emotional levels, (2) in children, (3) in a challenging context, (4) in Arabic and (5) the link between personal transformation and social peace impact. Especially the question of attribution to define the effectiveness of the intervention in reducing violence and creating a more peaceful society is complex. Given the challenges of such research study, it was not only difficult to find the right experts but also too costly to include in the limited budget. For the same reasons, it has not been possible to track the long-term outcomes of the project.

Conclusion: Psychosocial peacebuilding impact

This case study vividly demonstrates the practical application of IAHV's psychosocial peacebuilding model presented in Chapter 3. It shows how **the different components of the model, at different levels, come to life and deliver tangible results in line with the theory of change**. A comprehensive psychosocial peacebuilding approach, including personal transformation, community empowerment and structural change, can create sustainable impacts at both individual and societal levels. The case study shows the importance of evidence-based techniques which can provide healing, well-being and empowerment at the individual level, which are at the core of subsequent interpersonal and social change. It demonstrates the transformative power of inner peace in a community-based peacebuilding project. Intrapersonal transformation, creating ripple effects in families and communities, emerges as a catalyst for social peace and as a hallmark of a successful psychosocial peacebuilding approach. The case study also presents a compelling model for how **universally applicable evidence-based practices can be implemented through context-specific programming**.

One of the most unique, valuable and effective outcomes of this project was the widespread awareness about psychosocial support and peacebuilding that IAHV generated at the community level. People were inspired by the simple but effective link between well-being and inner and outer peace. Many testified that together with improved personal well-being, their relationships at home and with friends improved, mutual understanding improved, and they had fewer fights and conflicts or were able to solve them amicably. Seemingly small, individual stories of forgiveness were in fact life-transforming for the people involved.

> **Experience from a sixteen-year-old orphan living in the SOS village, as shared by IAHV trainer:**
> People around her claimed she was very violent and aggressive. Her supervisor stated that once she is triggered, she is like an 'untamed bull'. Six years ago, her father, not sober, beat her mother to death in front of her and turned himself in. Ever since then, any threatening situation triggers those memories, and then she attacks. A little comment from a friend at camp triggered her anger, and she lashed out and scratched her face. After sitting and talking, she remembered the techniques of the THRH training, calmed down and said: 'In these few days, I have learned to forgive my father and move on with my life. Life goes on, and if you don't move with it, your memories will suffocate you. I forgive him, I forgive my friend. Life is too short.'
>
> 'Everyone who participated in this project had some problem or the other, and you helped everyone to overcome these. Considering how many people have participated in this project, this is something really big, a real big positive change.' (YAVAP Peace Ambassador)

Rejuvenated individually, further empowered by skills training and supported by their teams, the youth also gained the strength and inspiration to contribute to society and actively work towards transforming factors of violence and building a foundation for peace. They experienced the transformative effects personally, could relate to it and were inspired to share and spread this further for the benefit of their families and communities.

> 'I felt so supported, empowered and grateful after the training. I wanted to share this feeling with everyone I know. I started to support my wife to pursue her dream and encouraged her to study and apply for a scholarship. She was awarded a scholarship for Japan to study a master's in women empowerment.' (TOT Graduate from Syria, Zaatari Refugee Camp)

The EU Ambassador to Lebanon, His Excellency Ralph Tarraf, received the Peace Ambassadors in Beirut on 13 December 2019. Their exchange was warm, honest and appreciative. The youth from Tripoli shared the big changes that happened in their lives, told personal stories of how their difficult family dynamics were positively impacted, and expressed their energy and vision to reduce embedded forms of violence in their society through the peacebuilding projects they had taken up. The energy and enthusiasm of everyone to continue on this mission were palpable in the room. 'You have changed our lives. We are so grateful. Now we will continue no matter what.'

Moving forward into the future, the Peace Ambassadors dreamt of

- Integrating Stress-Relief and Resilience workshops into the school curriculum all over Lebanon;
- Teach SRR, THRH and YAVAP to as many children as possible all over the Middle East;
- Becoming trainers themselves of all the programmes;
- Perform their Peace Art Performances all over Lebanon and the Middle East;
- Take up new causes for peace and develop new projects;
- Opening IAHV centres where people can come to release their stresses and bond with one another.

Often living with severe chronic stress and many of its psychosomatic symptoms, commonly just endured or managed through unhealthy coping mechanisms, broad sections of the target population came to know and experienced a different, healthy way to deal with the stresses of life. Life opened up from under a thick layer of stress dominating so many experiences. Attending to one's own stress levels came to be considered a practical, affordable and wise thing to do.

Children and adults who felt overcome by the events in their lives, powerless in the face of structural, cultural or direct violence, and subdued by a lack of self-worth, gained a new sense of self-importance. They realized that they matter as individuals and that it is important to take care of themselves, regardless of their circumstances and the viewpoints of others around them.

Functioning on the level of deeply shared humanity and designed as such, this project and its activities broke through barriers of generations, religions and social backgrounds, and increased social cohesion within and between different Jordanian, Lebanese and Syrian communities. For example, one local partner organization in Tripoli mentioned that *'Thanks to your trainers, who understood us, we were able to create trust with very conservative and cautious communities. Other projects come and go, but this is something that continues and we want to continue.'* In a gentle way, innovation was introduced into traditional cultures. Gender barriers and religious objections were softened. So it happened that several female participants spread such strong word of how good they felt after the HRE trainings, that the men in Zaatari Refugee Camp personally requested an HRE Training. Until then, specific cultural aspects and machismo attitudes made it almost impossible for most men to willingly attend a training of this nature. Also the Syrian parents in Menshieh, who did not trust to send their children anywhere, started trusting IAHV to let their children go to the programmes.

'The way they (IAHV) meet us is different from other organizations,' a staff member from a small local partner organization mentioned. Caring for the well-being of all individuals and communities, IAHV was seen as an organization that does not have a hidden agenda and that can be trusted. Through its way of working, IAHV restored some hope among people with regard to the NGO/humanitarian field, which had caused many disillusions in the past. One of our staff members in Jordan observed towards the end of the project: 'I worked with other organizations with bigger budgets and more staff, but we achieved less.'

This project worked with a wide scope of psychosocial factors among youth, parents, external staff and our own teams, laying a strong psychosocial foundation for sustainable peace, such as:

- The wholesome blossoming of children with fewer opportunities in life;
- Strengthening hope, energy, healing and confidence;
- Spreading human values, peace and a sense of belonging across boundaries;
- Bringing a sense of security and home to children in need;
- Creating a wave of peace in inner lives and outwards into society;
- And more.

> 'The youthful spirit that allows us to find ourselves was the best part of this project. Our inner world is like the ocean. We need fishermen like you to bring out the inner energy, light and strength. I found myself. The hope you give is the hope for the future.' (Suher, ToT graduate)

As a staff member of a partner organization in Lebanon observed: *'Most projects are just a sedative for problems. We need projects like this to work on the causes, eradicate the main problems and change society, not just giving a course'* (Representative partner organization Lebanon).

The impact evidence of this case study illustrates the necessity and possibility of integrating effective approaches to psychosocial peacebuilding into the core of local and international peacebuilding efforts in order to increase their impact and sustainability.

Videos
Available on YouTube IAHV Peacebuilding Channel

Project videos

Final Project Video: https://www.youtube.com/watch?v=7TPlTkPKHjg&t=605s

IAHV's Psychosocial Peacebuilding approach in Jordan and Lebanon: https://www.youtube.com/watch?v=0iprhqSSfUY&t=7s

Lebanon: Change in Tripoli: https://www.youtube.com/watch?v=yt7DDCiX0Ao

Lebanon: Final Closure Ceremony "Let's Breathe Peace": https://www.youtube.com/watch?v=5XJcki7Zbfo

Lebanon: YAVAP Training in Action: https://www.youtube.com/watch?v=9t8GCj_ncOM

Jordan: Professional Care Trainings: https://www.youtube.com/watch?v=x0k56g6gnts

Jordan: Stress Relief and Resilience Workshops: https://www.youtube.com/watch?v=LiA0eIl7y6c&t=4s

Jordan: Testimonials YAVAP participants: https://www.youtube.com/watch?v=SfZ_P-r-ISw&t=10s and https://www.youtube.com/watch?v=9pZe8ZsuqWw

Videos produced by the Youth Peace Ambassadors

Lebanon: Anti-bullying campaign 1 – Dabke Flashmobs in Tripoli: https://www.youtube.com/watch?v=z9lVLHO2pzg

Lebanon: Anti-bullying campaign 2: https://www.youtube.com/watch?v=ifxG8walmCc&t=3s

Lebanon: Awareness Campaign on School Drop-Out: https://www.youtube.com/watch?v=2s2c_RXq69Q

Video by filmmaker Tania Safi: https://www.youtube.com/watch?v=FgQS1pHEwrY&t=21s

---

Key points: Chapter 4

An IAHV project illustrates how the different components of IAHV's conceptual framework come to life in a real case scenario and how the conceptual model is operationalized on the ground.

The aim of the project was to facilitate the transformation of children and adults affected by violence, conflict, stress and trauma, into healed, resilient and empowered actors of change who have the well-being, confidence and skills to address the very driving factors of violence that caused them and others harm in the first place.

Applied implementation of the conceptual framework:

- The effectiveness of the evidence-based SKY breathing technique and related practices to reduce stress, trauma, depression and anxiety and strengthen overall well-being;
- Profound and holistic intrapersonal transformation, including mindsets, attitudes, emotions, behaviours and outlook on life;
- Intrapersonal transformation as the basis for interpersonal peacebuilding;
- Empowerment which creates leaders and agents of change;
- Addressing driving factors of conflict and violence and creating peace-enhancing systems;
- Universally human approach and context-specific programming;
- Wide range of Bio-Psycho-Social Factors addressed in the case study;
- Theory of Change in action;
- The human being at the centre of peacebuilding and fostering human connection.

What worked well

The case study demonstrated multiple strengths in its design and implementation, both intended and indirect, contributing to its positive impact:

1. The widespread awareness created at the community level about psychosocial support and peacebuilding. People got inspired by the simple but effective link between well-being, inner and outer peace, and were eager to spread this further for the benefit of their families and communities.
2. The effectiveness of the techniques in combination with the holistic approach of the programmes created intrapersonal transformation as a foundation for interpersonal and social change.
3. The comprehensive and multi-level approach that addressed individual, community and cultural/structural issues simultaneously and exemplified a holistic psychosocial support model.
4. The creation of safe spaces and 'Walking the talk' by the trainers, who inspired by example.
5. The social bonding that was integrated into the project and the resulting sense of connectedness across ages, nationalities and backgrounds, which was very supportive and enriching for the participants.
6. The training of Youth Peace Ambassadors, which facilitated personal transformation, contributed to their overall development and life trajectory, amplified the project's reach through peacebuilding activities in their communities, and inspired peers and younger participants. The project illustrated that peacebuilding with and for children and youth can be very effective both on a personal and social level. Youth Peace Ambassadors designed and implemented fifteen Peacebuilding Projects to prevent and reduce violence in their families, schools and communities. They had identified the following topics to work on, instead of being negatively affected by them: domestic violence, early marriage, violence against women and children, violence from school dropout and drugs, bullying, cyber blackmail, conflict between Jordanian and Syrian youth, sexual harassment, violence from stress and negative coping strategies, peer conflicts.
7. The embeddedness of the project in the local community through active involvement of many stakeholders, the training of new local trainers, and the multiple community outreach and celebration events.
8. The quantifiable impact which showed tangible improvements in participants' well-being and the indirect reach to 100,000+ people.
9. The development of local capacity for multiplication and sustainability, especially the effectiveness of training youth and adults who were first beneficiaries as new trainers.
10. The agility and resilience of the project team, which continued at times when many NGOs paused their operations, flexibly tuned into the changing circumstances and achieved a profound impact with a relatively small budget.

11. The upholding of human values and integrity in interactions and project implementation, consistently ethical behaviour, the absence of hidden agendas, transparency and open communication created long-term partnerships and trust.

Lessons learned and challenges

1. Contextual challenges of increasing and chronic political instability, economic hardships, entrenched social issues, Covid restrictions, and movement and exodus of Syrian refugees.
2. Limited human and financial resources for sustainability, lack of opportunities for institutional integration.
3. Local and cultural sensitivities around delicate issues needed to be handled with great sensitivity and skill.
4. Difficulty in finding experts and resources for a long-term impact research study.

Recommended reading: Chapter 4

International Association for Human Values (IAHV). 2020. 'Healing, nonviolent empowerment and preventing extremism. Final Project Report'. https://www.iahv-peace.org/jordan_lebanon/about-this-project/.

Note

1 This section is largely based on: IAHV. 2020. 'Healing, nonviolent empowerment and preventing extremism. Final project report'. https://www.iahv-peace.org/jordan_lebanon/about-this-project/.

5 Inner integration

A violence-free society,
disease-free body,
stress-free mind,
inhibition-free intellect,
trauma-free memory,
and a sorrow-free soul
are the birthright of every individual.
Unless every member of our global family is peaceful, our peace is incomplete.

—*Gurudev Sri Sri Ravi Shankar*

This chapter on the intrapersonal dimension of psychosocial peacebuilding starts with an opening reflection on the fundamental question as to who we aspire to be as peacebuilders and how we understand our role. The way we respond to these questions has a direct impact on how we understand and implement psychosocial peacebuilding. IAHV's Training on Psychosocial Wellbeing, Knowledge and Skills pays specific attention to the inner development of peacebuilders as an integral part of the peacebuilding processes and the environments in which they operate.

This chapter aims to develop our understanding of ourselves and the people we are working with, in line with IAHV's conceptual model of the seven different levels or layers of human existence: body, breath, mind, intellect, memory, ego and self.[1] We describe basic characteristics of these different layers in order to gain increased knowledge on how they function, both under excessive stress and in favourable conditions, along the scale between the restoration of well-being and optimal functioning. The importance of the role of the breath as a practical tool to manage stress, prevent burnout, release trauma, strengthen resilience and optimize overall well-being and potential is developed further. We explore in more detail the varied ways in which trauma affects the capacity for peace-oriented behaviours, both in theory and through an applied IAHV case study on trauma, adverse childhood experiences and criminality. Two case studies present firstly IAHV's effective approach to offender rehabilitation, as implemented with hard-core criminals in Denmark, followed by an examination of IAHV's trauma-relief work for war-affected communities and refugees around the world. We also explore the human potential for empowerment, inner peace and active non-violence. The chapter is supported by references to existing theories, evidence and insights from the fields of peace psychology, neuroscience, behavioural science and others.

Our role as peacebuilders

The second part of this book starts with an opening reflection on who we aspire to be as peacebuilders and how we understand our role. The way we implement psychosocial peacebuilding is related to our understanding of these questions. Are we inspired to bring important innovation into peacebuilding and open to dive deep into its core to generate increased and sustainable impact? Are we ready to look into ourselves while working with others, to take care of ourselves and to fine-tune our peacebuilding skills?

Sustainable integration of comprehensive psychosocial approaches into peacebuilding policy, practice and theory, and the resultant increased impact of peacebuilding work, will be embedded in and developed from the way we as peacebuilders connect and integrate within ourselves and our teams.

Until recently, attention upon the inner world of peacebuilders has largely been absent from mainstream peacebuilding, in the same way that the human being and psychosocial factors remained on the margins of peacebuilding theory and practice for a long time. This dimension has not been integrated conceptually into peacebuilding; neither has it been at the core of peacebuilding training and education, nor central to peacebuilding practice.

A few decades ago, peacebuilding was a rather unusual choice of study and an only vaguely understood occupation. Since then, it has rapidly expanded into a vast, professional field of its own, with the emergence of hundreds of universities and departments offering conflict and peace studies degrees, a wide range of new peacebuilding NGOs, dedicated think tanks, thousands of publications and policy papers, adapted systems and structures from local to national governments and international institutions, specialized training institutes and more.

While the expansive growth of the peacebuilding field has created vastly more opportunities, capacity, awareness, knowledge and skills in peacebuilding, it has also given rise to a form of industrialization of the field. While peacebuilding was certainly a mission for its pioneers, it has now also become a profession one can pursue like any other, with plenty of study and employment opportunities available. **The 'professionalization' of the field has come with increased technocracy, bureaucracy, specialized jargon and other forms of specialization that leads the field sometimes far away from the reality of people in conflict zones and from effective impact on the ground**. For example,

- Through collective learning processes, essential core elements of effective approaches to peacebuilding have been identified, such as 'do no harm', participatory approaches or gender-/trauma-/and conflict-sensitivity. However, through the formalization of the field, they have often become a tick-the-box practice rather than a conscious, lived and integrated approach.
- While supporting the measurement of impact, the focus on quantifiable indicators for peacebuilding often bypasses the real impact of peacebuilding initiatives, or the lack thereof. For example, reporting the number of peace agreements signed or workshops held does

not capture the nuanced and qualitative aspects of peace processes or the lived experiences and actual improvements in the lives of affected communities.

- The prescriptive, top-down approach rooted in the concepts and practices of outsiders does not always work for populations living in a particular conflict context. This is symptomatic of a lack of connectedness between peacebuilders and the people and their lived realities. The relevance and effectiveness of indigenous knowledge, practices and conflict resolution mechanisms have to be considered through joint, participatory ways of working.
- Time-bound peacebuilding projects organized within the parameters of donor requirements tend to focus on limited outcomes, while conflict and peace transformation is a longer-term commitment requiring transformation of deeper root causes and relationships.
- Peacebuilding interventions are at times defined more by the agendas and priorities of outsiders than by the needs and aspirations of people and populations themselves. There is often a disconnect between the priorities of local people and the peace they envision, and those of external and international actors and donors.

As such, the 'mainstream peacebuilding profession' moved away from human-centredness, even though many peacebuilders working actively on the ground remained human-centred.

Neta Crawford illustrates this challenge with the example of how external interveners deal, for example, with emotions of their target population. Pointing out the lack of 'expert' engagement with emotions, she stated that 'post-conflict peacebuilding efforts too frequently fail and wars re-erupt because peace settlements and peacebuilding policies play with emotional fire that practitioners scarcely understand but nevertheless seek to manipulate.'[2] An 'outward gaze' views emotions as exogenous to interveners and reinforces hierarchical relations between helpers and the recipients of help. The way peacebuilders include or exclude the power of emotions in their understanding and analysis of conflict has a direct impact on project design and the development of goals, strategies and activities. There is great potential in embracing the productive role of emotions and facilitating the 'social uptake' of certain emotions in the public sphere, for example in constructing and maintaining group identities and behavioural patterns conducive to peace.[3] A truly social and embedded view of emotions is a great asset to peacebuilding, but is not used when interveners stay in their isolated role as neutral external observers.

Working on conflict transformation, violence prevention and sustainable peacebuilding does not come down to only the administrative and logistical aspects of the peacebuilding activities and projects we implement. As the Swiss agency for Development and Cooperation pointed out: 'Successes and failures are also influenced by how we feel personally, how satisfied or dissatisfied, how stressed or relaxed we are, how well we manage to work in the team. We don't leave our personality at home when we arrive at work.'[4]

The quality and impact of our work is to a great extent defined by who we are as 'peacebuilders' and how we engage with communities and the people we work and

interact with on the ground. This idea has been beautifully formulated by peacebuilding expert Kai Brand-Jacobsen:

> *'Our words and how we behave as peace workers are the equivalent in our field to a surgeon's hand when doing surgery.*
> *Just as the slightest shake or mistake in surgery can cause harm,*
> *we also need to be intimately aware of how our words and behaviour are understood and perceived,*
> *and to ourselves model and manifest the values and practice we are promoting.'*
> *(Kai Brand-Jacobsen, peacebuilding expert and former Director of PATRIR (Peace Action, Training and Research Institute of Romania))*

After all, the core of peacebuilding touches upon deep human layers, upon pain, aspirations and values, and upon crucial and sensitive spheres of existence. Surgeons need to study more than ten years before they can operate on the tangible human body. Similarly, it is our responsibility as peacebuilders to prepare ourselves properly before 'operating' on more sensitive layers of human existence.

The **importance of the inner dimension of peacebuilders has surely been highlighted by individual peacebuilding practitioners and experts** who have developed various approaches, methodologies, workshops and training materials on this aspect. In particular, peacebuilders who have a personal practice of meditation, mindfulness, yoga, breathing or other self-awareness methods are very much aware of the positive impact of these techniques on both themselves and the people they are working with. Also in the training and development of peacebuilding leaders, facilitators or mediators, there is clear attention upon introspection, self-awareness, self-management and emotional regulation. Recently significantly more attention is paid within organizations to the well-being of humanitarians and peacebuilders and particularly to stress management, prevention of burnout, compassion fatigue and secondary trauma.[5]

In IAHV's approach the peacebuilder herself is central to the peacebuilding action: the qualities, skills, self-awareness and personality of the peacebuilder are not just a nice addendum, but core to the possible impact and effectiveness of peacebuilding initiatives. For example,

- Individuals with an inherent peacebuilding personality, such as a calming presence, emotional resilience, or a deep sense of empathy, can naturally inspire others to cultivate similar qualities.
- Self-awareness is essential for the accurate perception of people and situations around us, and self-management to skilfully respond.

- The extent to which we embrace and connect to painful or uncomfortable aspects within ourselves can increase the extent to which other people with similar experiences can relate to us.
- The understanding about ourselves and our identity can hinder or enhance our ability to connect to people on all sides of conflict.
- When we understand and acknowledge the power and dynamics of our own emotions, we will also acknowledge their role in other people's lives.
- Someone who is able to choose the right words at the right time can calm down tensions and allow solutions to emerge.
- Peacebuilders can inspire others through wisdom and their outlook on life.
- The love one has for people, and which finds expression in caring for their well-being, can be transformative in itself.

> 'Only one in whom human values have fully blossomed can be truly effective in promoting dialogue in areas of conflict around the world. The very presence of such an individual, considered by all to be a trusted friend, will soothe, calm and comfort. In creating arbitrators and negotiators to work in areas of conflict, primary consideration must be given to choosing individuals such as these, who exemplify the essence of what it means to be human.'[6]
> (Gurudev Sri Sri Ravi Shankar)

Exercise 1: Peacebuilding qualities

Think of one or more peacebuilders whom you really admire. What are the peacebuilding qualities you observe in them that make them so special, effective or admirable?

When Art of Living trainer Sanjay Kumar embarked on reaching out to the militants in Assam, he was worried that, as he did not speak a common language with them, gaps in communication could easily spark tension in the volatile and delicate situation he would find himself in.[7] He reflected:

'To my surprise, I soon discovered that language was not a barrier at all. There were powerful communication tools far beyond mere words: the greatest among them was commitment. When I arrived at the camp to meet the militant leaders, the locals were astonished to see me. In a place where people hesitated to step out after sunset, this unarmed boy had undertaken a three-day and night journey, braving dangers, to bring them the hope of peace. They recognized, respected and honoured my commitment. The fact that I belonged to an organization and had been sent by its leader became secondary to them. What mattered was the effort I had put in to cross treacherous

territories, risking my life for people I didn't know, and being a non-militant myself. My unwavering commitment towards a cause and my engagement spoke volumes, and their immediate trust in me and my intentions was a significant lesson I learned. This experience made me realize that commitment and personal engagement are the most potent tools for building trust. To gain trust, one must engage deeply, personally and demonstrate unwavering dedication to the cause. Words may falter, but genuine commitment can transcend all barriers and bridge gaps in understanding.'

IAHV's training for peacebuilders: Psychosocial well-being, knowledge and skills for increased peacebuilding impact

IAHV has developed a specialized training programme entitled 'Towards Integrated Peacebuilding: Psychosocial Well-being, Knowledge and Skills for Increased Peacebuilding Impact'[8] to address some of the important gaps in the way we have been practising peacebuilding, as mentioned above. This tailored programme is designed to equip professional peacebuilders and peacebuilding organizations with the well-being, knowledge and skills to incorporate psychosocial competencies and self-care into their work. The training consists of three major components:

1. **Resilience, Stress Management and Self-Care:** An experiential module with practical and evidence-based techniques to integrate psychosocial health and well-being, and personal resilience and stress management into effective peace work. It assists people working in difficult, challenging and often traumatic contexts to deal effectively with emotional and physical stresses. The module includes the SKY breathing technique, proven to improve health, immunity and sleep, and reduce anxiety, depression, PTSD and burnout. Participants learn a personal self-care package to strengthen well-being, stress management skills and mental and emotional resilience, which they can continue practising daily post-training.

'Now I work with myself in the same committed ways as I work with others.' (IAHV training participant)

'Peace building work can be so emotional and draining. With the SKY technique and the right skills, I am refreshed and good to go!' (IAHV training participant)

2. **Developing one's potential as a peacebuilder**: Inner resources and qualities for transformative and effective peacebuilding practice are nurtured, developed and finetuned through a combination of processes, knowledge, skills, reflections and insights, including active listening, compassion and empathy, holding multiple realities, patience and endurance, balancing simplicity and complexity, facilitation, tranquillity, discernment

and integrity. This module inspires peacebuilders to apply practical wisdom and skills to deal with challenging situations and people, and to improve personal and professional performance. It strengthens the experience of peace in the midst of conflict. The module also refines and strengthens self-knowledge, self-awareness and self-management.

> 'Life is utterly simple and yet most complex. You have to simultaneously attend to both facets. When life appears most complex, turn to simplicity. Simplicity brings peace. When you are peaceful, attend to the complexity; that will make you more skilful. If you are only with the simplicity, it makes you lazy and dull; growth is not there. Being only with the complexity makes you angry and frustrated; then there is no life at all. The intelligent ones skilfully balance these two and rejoice in both.' (Gurudev Sri Sri Ravi Shankar)
>
> 'When I am self-aware of my own biases, perceptions, thought processes and my whole being, then the real issues as presented by the parties are handled and peace follows.' (IAHV training participant)

3. **Skills Training in Psychosocial Peacebuilding Projects:** This model provides tools for the analysis, design and implementation of psychosocial interventions to increase sustainability and effectiveness of peacebuilding outcomes. Rooted in the personal experience provided in modules 1 and 2, this module offers participants insight and strengthens their confidence to work in an effective way with crucial psychosocial factors in order to make a meaningful impact on conflict and peace dynamics.

Through the above three modules, participants gain well-being, knowledge and skills for personal stress management, professional excellence and innovation in psychosocial peacebuilding. The training uniquely integrates personal experiential components with professional skills development to improve peacebuilding practice. Hence, it supports peacebuilding students and professionals to become more healthy, stress-resilient, smart, effective, creative, innovative, connecting, impactful, strategic and empathetic peacebuilders. In this way, IAHV's capacity building programme aims to provide current and future peacebuilders with the insight and practical tools needed to develop their full potential, both as individuals and as professionals in the field.

Stress, trauma and self-care
Stress

> 'The basis of terrorism and any conflict can be understood in this way: whatever may seem to be the cause, whatever excuses there are, these excuses arise on the surface of the human race only, but the underlying cause is a buildup of stress in the life of the people – stress in world

> *consciousness – and stress is not seen until it bursts out into violence and war. Only by relieving the individual and society of this buildup of stress can we ever hope to prevent war.'[9]*
> *(Maharishi Mahesh Yogi, Founder of Transcendental Meditation)*

The first important but still too often overlooked intrapersonal aspect of peacebuilding that should be addressed is stress, both among conflict-affected populations and peacebuilders.

The World Health Organization estimates that 20 per cent of conflict-affected people develop diagnosable long-term mental health disorders, in addition to non-clinical mental health issues experienced by the majority of conflict-affected people, such as shock, distress, disorientation, loss of self-confidence and identity, loss of sense of agency, insufficient coping mechanisms and lost hope.[10]

For peacebuilders, both work-related and personal stress are important to consider. Working on or in conflict poses great challenges for our inner selves and can be extremely demanding for our mental, emotional and physical well-being. Peacebuilding practitioners are often working under extremely challenging conditions, such as:

- Direct and indirect experiences of different forms of violence;
- Being confronted with the limitations of oneself or one's organization in supporting people, moral anguish about choices to be made, and insufficient training or resources;
- Exposure to horrific stories and despair of people, witnessing gruesome scenes, experiencing traumatic events;
- Harsh living conditions, movement restrictions, lack of personal space;
- Demanding work load without sufficient recuperation time, accumulated fatigue;
- Deterioration in contextual conflict dynamics and setbacks in peacebuilding processes;
- Difficulties in cultural adaptation;
- Chronic or episodic exposure to danger;
- Team conflicts, inadequate management;
- Isolation from support networks, separation from family;
- And many more.

While a healthy amount of stress can be beneficial for both personal and professional functioning, the adverse consequences of excessive stress include:

- burnout: It is estimated that around one third of humanitarian workers experience psychological distress or burnout,[11] which the World Health Organization defines as 'a syndrome based on chronic workplace stress that has not been successfully managed, with three dimensions:

1. feelings of energy depletion or exhaustion;
2. increased mental distance from one's job, or feelings of negativism or cynicism related to one's job;
3. reduced professional efficacy.'[12]

- depression and anxiety;
- psychosomatic complaints;
- over-involvement with beneficiaries;
- apathy, less commitment and higher rates of turnover, reduced efficiency;
- self-destructive behaviours such as drinking, substance abuse and dangerous driving;
- internal and interpersonal conflicts, scapegoating;
- higher accident rates, poor decision-making and risky behaviour;
- higher rates of illness and absenteeism.

The impact that stress has upon the quality of our work as peacebuilders is often underestimated. For example, when a highly stressful, traumatizing event is lodged unprocessed in our body-mind system, it affects our outlook, performance and interaction. The energy we use to contain and manage this affliction can wear us out or undermine our working capacity.

> **Exercise 2: Impact of stress**
>
> How does stress affect your personal life quality?
> How does stress affect your professional performance?
> How does stress affect your relationships / family / colleagues?
> What are your coping mechanisms?

Rarely have we been trained or educated in practical stress- and self-management tools to effectively handle this aspect of peacebuilding work. Stress management trainings are often theoretical or limited to cognitive approaches, which are often insufficient to effectively reduce stress levels and psychosomatic symptoms in one's daily personal and professional life.

When it comes to stress management, Gurudev Sri Sri Ravi Shankar emphasizes the importance and possibility of strengthening our own inner resources. If we understand stress as 'too much to do in too little time without enough energy' and we cannot increase the available time nor reduce one's tasks and responsibilities, the most feasible option to manage stress is to maintain or increase one's level of energy.

Below is a selection of testimonials from peacebuilding and humanitarian personnel in Lebanon and Jordan following participation in IAHV's Professional Care Training and practice of the SKY technique:

> 'I am under a lot of pressure. I need to find a suitable environment for the children and help them come out of the trauma of war and transform their situation and feelings into positive ones. I felt very relaxed after experiencing the breathing techniques. Day after day it turned out to be a positive experience and it helped me to come out of many difficult situations I am facing.' (Mustapha al Haj, Director, Toyour al Amal schools for Syrian refugees)
>
> 'These techniques are effortless and allow us not to let things pile up.' (JRS refugee staff for house visits)
>
> 'I work with war-affected children and get their stress as well. Now I feel more relaxed when I go home after work and I also changed my behaviour towards the children more positively.' (Teacher, Menshieh)
>
> 'Working with the refugees used to give a lot of stress and take a lot of energy. Their conditions, especially when they have disabilities, are so stressful. Before I didn't know how to deal with their anger when I was visiting them. Now that I have more energy [after the IAHV workshops], my perspective has changed. I can now give them hope and a positive outlook.' (JRS refugee staff for house visits)
>
> 'This project could take off a huge load from the refugee community.' (JRS refugee staff for house visits)
>
> 'I now keep a smile on my face when I teach my 300 refugee students.' (teacher with Jesuit Refugee Service)
>
> 'Now I am able to recover my energy during the week itself, so I don't have to catch up with sleep anymore during the weekend. I take more care of my health now.' (JRS refugee staff for house visits)

Raising energy levels

Life energy, well known in holistic medicine systems and yoga schools as prana or chi, is present in every atom of creation. We could say that it is the life energy that keeps life dynamic. It is present in our bodies and spreads through thousands of nadis or energy channels.

Practically speaking, we notice as human beings that at times our energy level is high or low. Our level of energy hugely defines our experience of life. When our energy level is low, we may feel negative, depressed, not wanting to do anything, irritable, lazy or complaining. When our energy level is high, we feel more motivated, inspired, positive, active, centred and resilient. Depending on our own level of energy, the way we perceive and experience the world, and also how we interact and respond to it differs significantly, even if the world as such remains the same. Therefore, it is important to take care of our energy levels and identify what gives us energy in life.

> **Exercise 3: Energy levels**
>
> Identify the sources of energy in your life: what gives you energy?
>
> Among the many sources of energy, the IAHV approach highlights four of the most important ones which we can manage ourselves:
>
> 1. Food: fresh food, not too little and not too much, and drinking enough water;
> 2. Sleep: not too little and not too much (average 6–8 hours for adults);
> 3. A calm and positive state of mind, such as when we do something we like or meditate;
> 4. Breath: we can imagine ourselves in an ocean of energy. With every inhalation, we gain energy, and proper breathing allows us to generate even more.
>
> Whenever we feel we become depressed or negative, we can check and manage our four main energy sources: Did we eat, and what? Did we sleep? What is going on in the mind? Did I do some breathing exercises?

Energy, as opposed to apathy, is necessary to create agency, ability and drive to achieve positive personal and social change. Drawing on the theory of emotional energy and positive emotions, the Berghof Foundation links different forms of interaction to specific emotional conditions and kinds of agency in conflict and conflict transformation:[13]

(1) cooperative interaction engenders positive emotional energy such as confidence and trust, promoting productive agency,

(2) dominating interaction energizes the dominant party and de-energizes the dominated ones, who descend into shame and hopelessness, fostering one-sided agency,

(3) conflictual interaction produces negative emotional energy such as anger and resentment, driving conflictual agency, and

(4) disengaged interaction leads to boredom, indifference and fatigue in all parties involved, diminishing agency.

It is therefore of crucial importance to learn skills and tools to raise individual and group energy levels regardless of the outer conflict dynamics and forms of interaction, in order to be less negatively affected and be able to exert a positive influence.

Trauma

An extreme form of stress is trauma. Trauma can be described as a **deep impact on our mind and body caused by an event that surpasses our normal coping capacity**. This can be an event that we were subjected to, but it can also be something that we have done ourselves, witnessed or learned about second-hand. Possibly traumatizing events include military combat, violent personal assault (sexual assault, physical attack, robbery, mugging), being forced to flee home and/or country, being kidnapped or taken hostage, terrorist attacks, satanic rituals, torture, incarceration as a prisoner of war or in a concentration camp, natural or man-made disasters, severe automobile accidents, being diagnosed with a life-threatening illness, adverse early-life experiences, emotional abuse or intergenerational trauma (e.g. Native Americans, genocide survivors, racism, colonialism). Trauma can affect large parts of the global population given the current prevalence of war and conflict, domestic and interpersonal conflicts, natural disasters and social, economic and environmental stressors.[14] The experience of several traumatizing events can create 'complex trauma'. Secondary or vicarious trauma refers to the process when we learn about a traumatizing event that happened to someone else, and our bodies and minds react as though the trauma is happening to us directly.

It is important to note that **it is the personal experience of an event or a situation which causes traumatization, not necessarily the actual event itself**. Two people can be in the same situation, but one of them may become traumatized while the other does not, or develops different trauma symptoms.

For example, two young men in a suburb outside Copenhagen started dealing drugs at the age of sixteen. The gang who controlled the drug trade in this area wanted to make it clear to them that this was a bad idea: They went to the apartment of the two young men and tortured both of them for several hours. IAHV trainer Jakob Lund noticed that afterwards, the reactions of the two young men to the same traumatic experience were very different: One started suffering from anxiety to such an extent that he could not even leave his apartment. The other became very aggressive and would not stand any kind of humiliation. After some time, the one suffering from anxiety went into treatment, and the other ended up in prison. While the one who went to prison had to answer for crimes he committed, he was actually as much in need of treatment as his companion.

Various factors, including the intensity and duration of the traumatizing experience, one's perception of the event, attribution of the cause, one's personality, the social support available and even genetic make-up, affect how an individual is affected by trauma.

Trauma is an all-encompassing experience: it causes adaptations in physiology and psychology, causing physical sensations, affecting the mind, emotions, nervous system, brain, endocrine system, the functioning of the organs and social interactions.[15]

Trauma has a direct effect on the **functioning of organs and systems in our body** through the vagus nerve, a central nerve with many branches throughout the body that connects body, heart and gut. Trauma can get lodged in the body in the form of sleeplessness, organ malfunctioning (including heart problems), digestion problems, irregular blood pressure, and can lead to fibromyalgia, chronic fatigue or other auto-immune diseases. These symptoms are often found to have no detectable physical cause. When we are under severe threat or attack, the vagus nerve can also turn off organs or slow heart rate and circulation in order to 'play dead' and deflect harm. The response of the vagus nerve and the nervous system to stress has been the main focus in the work of Dr Stephen Porges, professor of psychiatry at the University of North

Carolina.[16] Tests have revealed that people with impaired vagal activity have also been diagnosed with depression, panic disorders, Post-Traumatic Stress Disorder (PTSD), irritable bowel syndrome, anxiety, panic disorders, violent mood swings, early Alzheimer's and obesity.[17]

A traumatic reaction is a natural response to an overwhelming experience. This response is deeply rooted in our biological imperative for survival and embedded in our system which is prepared to **fight, flight or freeze** in case of danger. It is regulated by the autonomous nervous system and happens in milliseconds, bypassing the cognitive brain. The thalamus, amygdala and hippocampus in the emotional brain function automatically on the basis of the information they detect from the outside world in order to assess threat and danger, pleasure and pain, and to look out for one's welfare. In a situation of threat, they send signals which facilitate the release of stress hormones into the bloodstream and which create impulses into the nervous system to raise the blood pressure, heart rate and oxygen intake so that the body is ready for fight or flight. In normal circumstances, this **stress hormone system** returns to equilibrium after the stressful period is over. The body and brain quieten down, and the rational part of our brain processes the events so that we can move on with life.

However, when trauma is not healed, the **natural threat response system does not return to equilibrium** and becomes dysfunctional. It continues to send danger signals through the body and secrete stress hormones, long after the actual threat has disappeared, causing agitation, panic or collapse. A chronically activated threat response system, a hyperactivated (overly responsive) or hypoactivated state (underly responsive), can lead to complex physiological and psychological states and symptoms. Traumatized people can live in a state of constant arousal, having difficulty falling or staying asleep. They may be affected by protective or reactive states of rage and anger, have difficulty concentrating, be hypervigilant or anxious, or feel powerless. They may experience numbness, dissociation and disconnection, recurrent intrusive thoughts about the traumatizing event(s), visual or somatic flashbacks, negative thoughts about the self and the world, distrust in people and humanity, reckless or self-destructive behaviour, social withdrawal, and the avoidance of triggers that remind them of the traumatic event. Mildly stressful stimuli are sufficient to spike the stress hormones and symptoms quickly and disproportionately.

Lodged in the mind-body system, the trauma can easily be **reactivated by triggers**. People can re-experience the trauma as if it is happening again right now, with strong psychological distress and physiological reactivity. This re-experience can include a huge amount of stress hormones, unpleasant emotions, physical sensations and impulsive aggressive actions. People with retriggered trauma may experience recurrent and intrusive distressing recollections of the event, including images, thoughts and nightmares.

During a traumatic response, the emotional brain reacts faster and instinctively, while the rational, processing brain responds later or does not get involved at all. This explains why traumatized people sometimes have difficulty putting their experience into words or in a story, because the event itself passed through parts of the brain we are not aware of. Also, the memories of early childhood abuse are rarely found in explicit memory, where there are words to talk about them.

They are more often found in implicit memory, remembered by sensations and emotions of the body and the nervous system.

The function of the prefrontal cortex or rational part of the brain is to judge and interpret experiences, emotions and situations, give meaning and understanding to them, rationalize and then make informed decisions on that basis. In the absence of these processes, however, instinctive reactions and strong emotions take over and may whirl around uncontrolled.

The bypassing or dysfunction of the prefrontal cortex may also mean that the process of interpreting the information from the outside world can get distorted, so that **no meaningful, understandable 'story'** is formed but rather disconnected impressions such as smells, images and sounds which arouse strong emotional reactions. The filtering function of the emotional brain may also be affected, so that traumatized people may experience an overload of sensory information and be unable to shut down or calm down.

In order to avoid feeling these extreme sensations and emotions, another traumatic reaction can be the **avoidance of all associated thoughts, feelings and places or numbing** the whole system. Numbing can happen to such an extent that traumatized people do not feel anything anymore: no pain and no pleasure, no elevation or depression, no sensations and no feelings.

During a traumatic experience, the part of the brain that gives us a **sense of self** and orientation may also be affected. This can result in a reduced sense of oneself, of being someone, of feeling oneself, knowing oneself and one's needs, or even having the feeling of being alive. When we are unable to detect the signals that are coming from inside, or when we receive distorted, incomprehensible information, traumatized people may feel very uncomfortable with themselves. They may have a constant feeling of unease, gnawing discomfort, or even a chronic sense of being unsafe in their own bodies. Due to the lack of capacity to self-regulate, they may resort to ways of external regulation, such as medication, the use of substances, seeking constant external reassurances, extreme compliance or other forms of compulsive behaviour.

Survivors of trauma often use **enormous energy to suppress the inner chaos** and the re-emergence of unbearable physiological reactions in order to just stay alive or cope with life. Trauma can completely hijack people's lives. People living with trauma may have real difficulties living in the present. They are stuck in the past or their new experiences are contaminated by the past, so that the present eludes them.

After trauma the world is experienced through a different nervous system. Lodged in the body-mind system, trauma influences our **perception of the world as well as our interactions with it**. The emotional brain stores reactions and may therefore colour harmless events with past interpretations, triggering survival mechanisms and causing irrational and disproportionate reactions. A traumatized mind sees a threat in a stranger on the street, while a non-traumatized mind just sees a person there.

Looking into someone's eyes may evoke feelings of shame or survival reactions from the emotional brain, rather than a healthy processing of information, discernment and healthy social engagement from the prefrontal cortex. People who had **adverse childhood experiences** may not pick up others' emotions and actions accurately, since the process of mirroring can be distorted.

It is important to understand that the changes in brain, body, psychology and behaviour occur in order to keep individuals and communities safe in a situation of threat or danger. If they persist unaddressed, however, these adaptations can have longer-term negative effects on relationships, social interactions, work and performance.

At the **community level,** trauma leaves its imprint on cultures, narratives, norms, worldviews, families, histories, and even in the DNA of peoples. Collective trauma refers to the trauma of an entire group, community or society. The impact can move slowly through society at large and become embedded in a social ecosystem, changing its sense of identity, positive self-esteem, sense of strength, access to resources of resilience, rituals and communality. The whole of social life is impacted and previous social bonds are disrupted, especially in contexts where neighbours and friends become enemies. Collective trauma may be felt immediately but also be transmitted across generations over hundreds of years.

Overcoming trauma

Research and practice have shown that it is possible to come out of the trauma response and restore homeostasis. Even more, the experience of trauma can also lead to **post-traumatic growth**, when people successfully overcome the negative impact of it and actually gain increased strength and skills, purpose and meaning, improved functioning and social interaction.

Trauma can be overcome through one's own resources of resilience, one's social support network, different kinds of therapy (such as exposure therapy, cognitive behavioural therapy, psychotherapy, rapid eye movement EMDR), holistic body-mind interventions and other methods.

The **medical approach** involves taking psychotropic medicines to influence the hormones and change the brain's activity. However, this approach does not always work, may make people drug dependent and cause significant negative side effects. **Psychotherapy** involves talking about what happened in order to come to some sort of understanding of the experience and process it. However, talking about the experience can be difficult when it has bypassed the rational brain to begin with. As Van der Kolk wrote, 'the rational brain cannot talk the emotional brain out of its experience.'[18]

We can distinguish **two general approaches to trauma-relief: bottom-up, from the body towards the brain, and top-down, from the brain towards the body.**

The top-down approach strengthens the capacity of the rational brain to observe, discern, discriminate and manage the emotional experiences and the physical sensations in the body. It is about training the rational brain 'to become a competent driver of the unruly horse of the emotional brain'.[19] Thoughts about oneself, others and the world may have changed due to the impact of trauma. Since thoughts affect emotions and physical sensations, the top-down approach focuses on becoming more aware of the thoughts and starting to change them.

Bottom-up approaches start from the body. Recognizing that one's body is physiologically still responding as if the trauma is still happening, new body experiences are created which deeply contradict the known experiences of helplessness, rage or collapse. Movement, touch and breathing can all help to reregulate the autonomic nervous system. Here the survival response of the body is brought to a sense of completion so that a new input and memory based on safety, agency and success can be created.

Somatic experiencing, as elaborated by biophysicist and psychologist Peter Levine,[20] is especially important in cases of physiological numbing. Moving the body sends signals to the brain about the physical self, so that people can start feeling more and sensing themselves again in the present moment. It helps survivors to reconnect to their self and their resilience.

Interoception, or the capacity to perceive what goes on inside us, is crucial for recovery. Being able to feel and sense the feelings and sensations in one's own body is the first step to being able to start managing them and get a sense of agency back. The mind can be re-educated to feel physical sensations and the body can be re-educated to feel comfortable with them.[21] Getting back the sense of being in charge of oneself, including one's body and emotions, allows us to restore a 'friendly relationship' with our inner world and body. When we are more able to feel what is happening inside ourselves, we are more able to feel what is happening with others too, which can in turn greatly enhance relationships and communication.[22]

Important in the process of overcoming trauma is providing and **restoring a sense of safety**, so that the whole body-mind-nervous system can let go of the constant survival mechanism mode and start relaxing. The capacity to feel safe and to relax needs to be restored. This can happen from outside, for example through various forms of social support and existing resources and resiliencies within communities. In the case of collective trauma, drumming, dancing, singing, connecting to nature, prayers, chants and rituals all can increase a communal sense of safety and restoration. Reconnecting with such communal resources is vital in increasing resilience and rebuilding the community and social fabric.

The sense of safety can also be restored from inside. Stimulation of the vagus nerve through the activation of the parasympathetic system plays an important role in relaxing the body-mind-nervous system and balancing homeostasis. The proper functioning of the vagus nerve is said to promote the regulation of emotion, social competence, prosocial behaviour, and decrease aggression, hostility, depression and anxiety. Yoga, meditation, breathing, chanting, singing, laughter and electric impulses all stimulate the vagus nerve.[23] This not only helps us feel calmer, more resilient, and relaxed, but also fosters a sense of safety with others. It dissolves defensiveness and strengthens a more socially engaged state of mind characterized by trust and cooperation. A general 'neuroception of safety' can be restored when neural circuits indicate that situations or people are safe.

The breath is an important, practical and effective instrument to help overcome trauma. Cognitive approaches alone may not work because they may not address the deeper physiological impact.

As presented in Chapter 3, the breath is the only aspect of the autonomous nervous system which we can consciously use and adapt in order to reduce sympathetic drive and increase parasympathetic drive, restoring a more optimal balanced state of homeostasis.

Breathing techniques such as SKY help to restore a state of deep rest, which facilitates the healing of trauma that is lodged in our mind-body system. They also help to reduce trauma symptoms, such as heart palpitations, blood pressure, anxiety, emotional outbursts and hypervigilance. They improve overall physical and mental health and functioning, including sleeping problems, the sense of connectedness with one's body and oneself, a sense of empowerment, trust, a more balanced outlook on the world, and the ability to live in the present without the constant shadow of the past. The SKY technique may reduce and release deeply traumatic impressions lodged in the system, even without bringing them to the level of conscious awareness or clear, logical understanding.

Breathing techniques can also help to improve resilience to stress and the prevention of difficult episodes by widening the physiological window of tolerance.

Through physiological changes created through the breath, thought patterns are also more easily changed. The higher brain function stabilizes, allowing people to apply cognitive tools, emotion regulation and decision-making, even when under duress. Interoception in itself may be challenging without practical tools. Several studies have shown that mindful awareness alone is not enough and may even exacerbate traumatic symptoms when faced with internal states of distress without the tools to deal with that distress.[24] The breath helps with interoception, since it is a practical and easy tool for observing and bringing attention to the body, breath and present moment.

Testimonials from children, youth and adults affected by trauma after completing IAHV programmes:

> 'After IAHV's courses I feel our lives are safe now.' (YAVAP graduate from Syria)
>
> 'I saw my father die in Syria. But I couldn't accept it. I couldn't move on. I tricked myself into thinking he's still alive; I convinced myself he was just away and coming back. After the training, I acknowledged what happened to my father. I accepted his death and I was okay with it.' (THRH Participant, Jarash)
>
> 'As a KLA (Kosovo Liberation Army) soldier, I was wounded three times during the war. Since then, I feel a lot of pain and take painkillers almost every day. During my sleep, I hear my brother's voice who was killed in the Reqak massacre and voices of my friends who were killed in the war. I hear them calling me for help. I often jump from my bed searching for the gun and afterwards I cannot sleep. After taking the Art of Living Programme, I sleep much better and flashbacks and nightmares have reduced. Now I am using the AOL programme instead of painkillers. On the basis of my own experience, I find this programme so effective in giving relief to traumatized people and war victims.' (Afet Bilalli)[25]
>
> 'I am twenty-three years old and I come from Reqak where the massacre took place. Since the war and the massacre that happened in my birthplace, I have problems with sleep. I easily get tense, nervous or depressed. I was surprised when I experienced the power of breath and how easily

> the breath throws out negative, unwanted emotions. Each time I do Sudarshan Kriya, I feel reborn again. Free of painful memories and depression.' (Avdi Billali)

Application

All the above effects of trauma show how radically we can get disconnected from ourselves. This disconnect undermines our own quality of life and also affects the people around us. When we are disconnected from ourselves, we cannot fully or healthily connect to others either, and this undermines our social interactions. **'Psycho-biological traumatic re-enactment' stands in the way of peaceful relations with oneself and others.** When the world is seen through an over-active nervous system, the parts of the brain that are alert to danger, are constantly working, whereas the parts that are intended to be curious and open to new experiences and impressions are not stimulated. The sense of danger overshadows the capacity to see what is positive and interesting. **Faulty neuroception is one of the factors that perpetuates conflict. Therefore, regulation of the traumatic response system is crucial to restore the capacity for social engagement, communication and peaceful coexistence.**

This process is at work at both interpersonal and social levels. As long as the stressors and trauma are maintained in the individual, group or social system, conflict, tensions, misperceptions, traumatic reactions and social instability are easily perpetuated. In turn, these outer manifestations of conflict and rupture maintain the respective inner state of stress and trauma. This vicious cycle can continue until it is effectively interrupted or weakened.

Also for peacebuilders, it is important to take care of trauma processing, whether traumatizing events are experienced directly or vicariously, so that the trauma response is not interfering with the quality of their interactions with others and their work in society. Also, an activated trauma response among conflicted parties may negatively impact negotiation and mediation processes and outcomes. Therefore, Neuropeace states that 'peacebuilding efforts have the potential to have more effective outcomes if the neurophysiology of traumatic stress is addressed directly.'[26]

Indeed, the provision of tools to restore and strengthen homeostasis, to release stress and trauma from the body-mind complex, is a fundamental aspect of peacebuilding at the individual, interpersonal, intergroup and broader societal levels.

It is important to note that **trauma should not be generally assumed in contexts of conflict and peacebuilding.** Not all people experiencing traumatizing events develop trauma symptoms afterwards, and the majority of people may be able to cope within a relatively short period of time through their own resources. As we have seen, trauma can also lead to increased self-development and resilience in the form of post-traumatic growth.

Equally, trauma in conflict and peacebuilding contexts **should not be pathologized or decontextualized**. Standard Western-based MHPSS interventions often focus on improving mental health through counselling, medicines or other approaches which may not be appropriate, culturally adapted or may even do harm. Such narrow, medicalized approaches do not consider the broader context that causes or contributes to traumatic experiences, such as the impact of armed conflict, the legacy of historical injustices such as colonialism, racism, land dispossession, and wider social and political processes. They risk pathologizing individual and collective suffering in an ahistorical or decontextualized way. Peacebuilding does not just deal with trauma as an add-on health intervention, but is also about transforming the system that generates trauma, essentially looking into how psychosocial factors interact with different aspects in the broader conflict and peacebuilding context.

IAHV's personal transformation model: 7 levels of existence

The IAHV and Art of Living model of personal and social transformation is based on 7 intrapersonal levels of existence.[27] This specific paradigm is rooted in ancient spiritual and Vedic knowledge of human existence. When looking at these 7 levels, we notice that they function entirely differently when they are affected by stress or not (Table 5.1).

Body

Our body is the most tangible part of our existence. A healthy and energized body is generally supported by a healthy lifestyle, such as physical exercise, a nutritious and healthy diet, sufficient rest and a positive mindset. The increasingly popular practice of yoga also has significant physical benefits such as enhanced flexibility, muscle strength, circulation and cardiovascular health, and reduced blood pressure, cortisol and back pain.[28]

Vast resources of psychosomatic research and health science have shown that body and mind are closely linked.[29]

Table 5.1 *IAHV Model of 7 Levels of Existence*

Level of Existence	Stress-Free	Under Stress
Body	Relaxed, healthy, energized	Tired, deregulated, sick, tense, hurting
Breath	Smooth, deep, regular	Blocked, shallow, irregular
Mind	Clear, focused, positive	All over the place, occupied, restless, negative, worrying
Intellect	Sharp, positive, broad	Dull, negative, narrow
Memory	Functional, positive	Stuck, focused on the past, negative, dysfunctional
Ego	Connecting, helping, open, motivated	Aggressive, defensive, unhelpful, demotivated, superior or inferior
Self	Shines through and manifests itself	No access to or experience of this layer

First, a weak and sick body can negatively affect the mind while a healthy, rested and energized body can positively influence the mind. Research has shown that regular physical activity and exercise have positive effects on self-esteem and self-efficacy, mental health, improved cognitive function, enhanced mood, reduced fatigue, alleviating symptoms of depression and anxiety and altering the physiological response to stressors.[30] Studies have shown that people who exercise regularly and are physically fit have a bigger and more active hippocampus, which is associated with resilience to adversity.[31] Exercise also promotes the release of neurotransmitters such as serotonin and dopamine as well as endorphins, often referred to as 'feel-good' hormones, which can improve mood and alleviate stress.[32] Balance between physical activity and rest, with enough time to relax and rejuvenate, is important to stay resilient.

Also, a positive state of mind can support health and healing processes, while chronic stress and a negative mindset can negatively influence the well-being of the body.[33] The field of psychoneuroimmunology has shown that negative thoughts and stress can undermine every aspect of our health and well-being. The power of the mind for physical well-being has also been pointed out by Gurudev Sri Sri Ravi Shankar, who says: 'a strong body cannot carry a weak mind, but a strong mind can carry a weak body.'

Application:

IAHV programmes therefore include moderate to intense physical exercises, selected yoga postures as well as deep relaxation processes to support overall well-being.

Breath

The breath is the link between the tangible physical level of our existence and the more subtle, intangible layers of mind, intellect, memory, ego and self. The breath is both tangible in the sense that we can feel it and change it, but it is also intangible, a kind of mystery, and deeply linked to the core of our existence.

Our life started with breathing in, the first act of life, and will end with breathing out, the last act of life. In between this first inhalation and last exhalation our whole life passes, sustained by countless breaths keeping our body alive. However, most of the time we are not aware of our breath, unless we maybe run up the stairs, do some sport or face some breathing difficulty. And yet, the breath is a very precious but largely unexplored instrument that can greatly improve our sense of well-being, health and self-management.

The power of the breath has been understood and applied by ancient civilizations, such as the Vedic, Native American, Tibetan and Chinese wisdom traditions, as well as by many individuals, research institutes and experts around the world. The PubMed online database of articles from a wide range of medical, scientific and health-related journals, managed by the US National Library of Medicine, currently holds 12,000 studies on breathing exercises.[34]

In his book *Breath*, James Nestor gives an impressive overview of knowledge about the breath that has been accumulated throughout the ages and used for a wide spectrum of purposes.

Clearly, breath is not just an automatic function to be taken for granted, but the way we breathe directly and indirectly influences a wide range of indicators of our physical and mental well-being.

> *'Breathing, as it happens, is more than just a biochemical or physical act; it's more than just moving the diaphragm downward and sucking in air to feed hungry cells and remove wastes. The tens of billions of molecules we bring into our bodies with every breath also serve a subtler, but equally important role. They influence nearly every internal organ, telling them when to turn on and off. They affect heart rate, digestion, moods, attitudes. Breathing is a power switch to a vast network called the autonomic nervous system.'*[35]
> (James Nestor)

The breath is closely linked to the body, not only keeping the body alive but also enabling the **release of tension and stress from body and mind.**

The breath is also one of the major pathways for the release of impurities and waste products from our system. It does not just provide oxygen to all the cells, but also removes carbon dioxide and thousands of other waste products through the lungs.[36]

Through the breath, we can relax our whole system in the parasympathetic state by relaxing the vagus nerve. **By breathing slowly or fast, we can consciously access the autonomic nervous system and turn our system from stressed to relaxed or from relaxed to stressed at will**. In many cultures, there is an understanding that a deep breath in and out can bring release and relaxation. Scientifically, this is supported by the fact that many of the nerves connecting to the parasympathetic system are located in the lower lobes of the lungs, which are accessed and activated through deep breaths.[37] More at the top of the lungs is the network of nerves connecting to the sympathetic system, which can be activated through short, hasty breaths. The activated sympathetic system sends signals to the organs to slow down and to the brain and muscles to get into action, increasing heart rate, raising adrenaline and sharpening the mind. The sympathetic system is not meant to stay activated for a long time, but for short moments and only when required. Activating the sympathetic system takes less than a second, but bringing it back to a state of relaxation takes longer, a process in which the breath can play a major role.

Optimizing the breath can prevent chronic health problems and increase lifespan, while breathing badly can lead to a range of illnesses, such as deregulated blood pressure and heart rate variability. In his book, Nestor gives a wide range of examples of how **different ways of breathing affect physical well-being**. For example,

- Slow inhalation and exhalation balance oxygen and carbon dioxide levels in the body, which helps to maintain good health.
- Breathing through the nose heats, cleans, slows and pressurizes air so that the lungs can extract more oxygen with each breath. Breathing through the nose improves sleep, mental

clarity, circulation and oxygen delivery into the cells, and also boosts immune function, mood, and sexual health.

- The flow of the breath through the right and left nostrils controls body temperature, blood pressure and chemicals in the brain which alter our mood, emotions and sleep states.[38] Breathing through the right nostril activates the sympathetic nervous system, increasing circulation, body temperature, cortisol, blood pressure and heart rate. It gets the body into a more ready and alert state, including for fight or flight. Breathing through the left nostril, on the other hand, has the opposite effect: it activates the parasympathetic nervous system, decreasing blood pressure, body temperature and anxiety. It gets the body in a rest and relax state. Breathing through the right nostril also activates the opposite part of the prefrontal cortex associated with logical thinking, while breathing through the left nostril stimulates more abstract thinking and creativity.

- Through 'heavy breathing' people can learn how to control their heart rate, immune response and body temperature, for example enabling them to stay in ice water for almost two hours or living in the Himalayas without warm clothes or heating.[39]

- A range of other breathing techniques helped people to heal themselves from depression, diabetes and body pains. Nestor even gives examples of how certain ways of breathing have healed scoliosis.

The breath is also closely linked to our emotions. When we experience different emotions, our breathing pattern changes.[40] For example, we breathe faster when we are angry, lightly and easily when we are happy, heavily and long when we are depressed, or even stop when we experience a shock. Most of the time, this is a one-way process whereby our emotions change our breathing pattern. However, since breath and emotions are so closely linked, we can also make it a two-way process **and manage our emotions more easily by consciously using and changing our breath**.

Nestor cites examples of how different breathing techniques open up 'the brain's pharmacy, flooding the bloodstream with self-produced opioids, dopamine, and serotonin.'[41] Science may not yet fully understand why and how specific ways of breathing are so effective in curing ailments that could not be cured otherwise, but Nestor thinks it has much to do with raising the energy levels in the body/mind system through the breath.

Similarly, the breath is also linked to the mind and can be used to manage our mind more easily (see below), as well as the deeper layers of our existence.

Application

From the above and the research cited in Chapter 2, we have seen that **the breath is a practical tool to manage stress, prevent burnout, release trauma, strengthen resilience and optimize overall well-being and potential**. It is available to everyone, effective and cost-effective, stigma-free and without negative side effects.

The breath has a huge potential for generating improved well-being, but generally people do not have access to this because they use only a small part of their lung capacity. IAHV programmes include a variety of breathing techniques with different effects, one of which is to increase the lung capacity.

Mind

The state of our mind defines the quality of our life. When the mind is calm and positive, we can feel and function well even in the most stressful circumstances. However, when the mind is tense and negative, we feel bad and unable to function even in the best of circumstances. For example, we may work in uncomfortable, challenging emergency situations, but if our mind is calm and focused, we can maintain our state of well-being and performance. On the other hand, we may finally travel to a favourite holiday place with our family and loved ones after prolonged Covid restrictions, but if our mind is depressed, then we are not able even to enjoy such a perfect setting. This is how important the state of our mind is. Hence, it is essential to understand the mind and how to handle it.

Through the mind, three important functions occur: **perception, observation and expression**.

The mind has the capacity to perceive the world through the senses. For example, when someone is talking to you but you are thinking of something else, you do not actually hear what that person is saying. Even though the sounds are falling on your ears, the mind needs to be present in order to perceive. Deriving meaning from the impressions happens through the mind. We do not observe objective reality, but the mind interacts with the external world and interprets the impressions derived through the various senses, thus developing meaning from the perception.

Through the mind we also perceive our inner world and can observe our thoughts, emotions and inner state. Often we may feel that our lives are led by the state of our mind: whatever happens in our mind defines what we do and how we feel. However, we have an inbuilt capacity to actually observe what is happening in our mind and have the option to either hold on to or let go of certain thoughts and emotions. We can observe and select the thoughts and emotions that are beneficial, supportive or useful and let go of those which are harmful, detrimental or irrelevant.

The mind also functions as a vehicle for expressing our inner world outwardly through words and actions. There is a close link between one's inner state of mind and its external expression, which ultimately influences relationships and our impact on society. One who is unable to handle his/her own negative emotions and their expression can create misery for dozens, thousands and even millions of people.

The process of perception, observation and expression is very individual and influenced by a range of factors colouring this process, such as upbringing, education, life experiences, memories, expectations, culture, personal characteristics, motivation and context. That is why people living in the same situation or witnessing the same event usually do not perceive or experience it in the same way. This is illustrated with the famous image of six blind people describing an elephant based on their personal perspective and knowledge: the one holding the trunk may think it is like a vacuum cleaner, the ear is like a curtain, the flank is like a wall, the tail is like a broom, the leg is like a pillar and the tooth is like some ancient hand tool. Unaware of the full picture, they may each insist on their partial truth based on their personal perspective (Figure 5.1). A lack of openness or willingness to learn about other points of view and experiences may lead to fundamentalist positions. Realizing there are other options and consciously opening one's limited perspective to learn about them reduces the risk of fundamentalism and lays a foundation for enriched, mutual understanding. Recognizing and being able to hold multiple, diverse and often opposing views of reality is a precious skill for mediators.

When the mind is stressed, the ability to perceive the world around may be distorted or reduced. Perceiving in a selective manner, we may not perceive opportunities in the midst of crises, qualities of people beyond stereotypes, or situations as they are without our erroneous personal interpretation. Entangled in our own mind, we may not be able to accurately observe our inner world and our expression into the world may not be the most appropriate or skilful. The mind may get stuck in the past or the future, with certain events and people, unable to let go or to wind down. It may perceive the world more negatively than it is in reality.

When the mind is calm and clear, it is much more able to perceive the world around as it is, without biased interpretation and colouring. A clear observation of surrounding facts is a fertile basis for skillful interaction and appropriate responses to situations around us.

In addition, the mind leads a life of its own with all kinds of **thoughts** popping up and whirling around. **The mind has a tendency to go to the past and the future and accordingly brings a wide range of emotions with it.** For example, when the mind goes to the past it can bring emotions of regret, guilt, anger or sadness, or positive memories and feelings. When it swings to the future it can generate emotions of hope and expectation, but also worry and anxiety.

Figure 5.1 *Blind men describing an elephant (copyright: leremy/Adobe Stock).*

When our energy level is low, the mind clings more to negative thoughts and emotions. With the mind thus roaming around, a stream of related emotions continuously enters our life. These thoughts and emotions related to the past and future overwhelm the present moment in our lives, and may undermine our energy level, efficiency, focus, happiness and well-being. The present moment, however, is all we really have. The past is already over and the future is not there yet. Life happens in the present moment. Therefore, it is good to regularly bring the mind to the present moment. When the mind is in the present, we feel increased focus, productivity, efficiency, clarity, fulfilment and contentment.

A way to keep the mind in the present moment is to do everything 100 per cent. Often we are simultaneously involved in many things, reading while eating, calling while walking, checking messages while working, making plans while listening and so on. This habit may consume significant energy and contribute to an overall feeling of restlessness, dissatisfaction, non-accomplishment and distraction. When we do something 100 per cent, however, we feel clarity, focus, presence and lightness. This we can notice when we are engaged in something we like, for example, such as walking in nature, playing with children or animals, listening to favourite music, doing a job we love and so on.

The mind has a tendency to go outward into the world and engage with the world. It is a very subtle layer of our existence which is easily influenced, easily gets stuck and takes the form of what it is focused on, whether good or bad, interesting or irrelevant. The mind is often very busy, and it takes a conscious effort to disengage it from the outside world and redirect it inward, where it can relax and release impressions.

The nature of the mind is very sensitive and needs to be handled with skill. Whereas effort is required to keep the body in good shape, **effortlessness is key to the optimal functioning of the mind.** For example, the more pressure we exert on the mind to remember something, to forget something, or to fall asleep, the less it usually listens to us. 'What you resist, persists', a tenet of the IAHV programmes, describes a fundamental tendency of the mind. However, when we are able to relax the mind, then it functions optimally.

The breath is linked to the mind. Through the breath, we can handle the mind more easily. The mind is like a kite that is blown in all directions by the wind. Just as we have more influence over the kite through the thread, we have more influence over our mind through the breath. Every breath is always in the present moment. Through the breath we can bring our mind into the present moment, disentangle it from its occupations, raise its level of energy and positivity, and release unnecessary impressions. The breath has the innate ability to quieten the mind.

Therefore, practising certain breathing techniques makes it easier to meditate. Meditation is a state of relaxed awareness, or a state of profound rest with awareness, which provides deep rest for the mind, cleanses it from multiple impressions and brings it back to focus and clarity. Hundreds of studies have shown the benefits of meditation on mental, emotional and physical health: lowering blood pressure, improving immune function, reducing pain, enhancing sleep quality, reducing anxiety and depression, increasing energy and vitality, and improving cognitive function, emotional regulation and social interactions.[42] One of the effects of meditation is an increased ability for interoception, or the ability to be aware and feel what is happening inside oneself. Studies have shown that the right anterior insula in the brain responsible for delivering a sense of oneself becomes thicker in long-term meditators.[43] Interoceptive sensitivity is linked to increased sensitivity to feel the emotions of others, respond more sensitively to them, and improve relationships.[44] Meditation has also been shown to change the structure of critical areas of the brain, optimizing mental capacities, and increasing grey matter density in parts of the brain that are responsible for empathy and memory while decreasing those responsible for fear.[45] In addition, meditation practice can expand one's experience of life and provide a personal experience of something encompassing and transcendental.

Exercise 4: Mind

1. Sit with your eyes closed and observe the thoughts that pop up in the mind. When a thought pops up, give it a label (work, family, past, future, . . .) and drop it in an imaginary basket in front of you. Then wait for the next thought to come. Do this for 6–8 mins, observing every thought that comes into the mind, labelling it and dropping it. Open your eyes and reflect on what you observed during the exercise.
2. For one day, do everything you do 100 per cent and see if and how your productivity, focus and calmness during the day increase.

Application:

The mind functions optimally when it is relaxed, free of stress, and with its attention fully in the present moment. Breathing techniques and meditation are effective ways to bring the mind in the present moment, free it from its occupations and entanglements, raise its energy level to come out of negativity and worries, and remove unhelpful and unnecessary impressions.

The ability to observe and handle our mind has a direct impact on the **quality of our perception, observation and expression**, and therefore directly **influences our ability to interact skilfully and constructively to situations and people around us.**

Self-awareness and self-management are essential peacebuilding qualities. How aware are we of ourselves, the people we interact with and the environment? How finely do we perceive our own inner vulnerabilities, reactions and emotions? How much inner noise is filling our minds already when we interact with others? How open is our mind when we assess an environment? **Awareness and a stress-free state of mind are the foundation of most essential peacebuilding qualities.**

IAHV Programmes provide cognitive understanding about the functioning of the mind together with practical tools to manage the mind more easily.

Intellect

The intellect is the rational mental faculty that discriminates, judges, analyses and decides. It is the voice within us engaged in making sense of the experiences and impressions in the outer and inner worlds. It uses acquired understanding, logic and concepts to understand and respond to the experiences and inputs.

An intellect which is closed, therefore, does not really acquire new understanding or knowledge, since it hovers in existing understanding and judgements. When we carry certain judgements, concepts and prejudices in our mind, they will more often than not be reinforced by our experiences, since they form the perspective through which we perceive and engage with the world. The psychological notion of confirmation bias refers to our judgements being confirmed by our experiences and then becoming rooted even more strongly in our intellect.[46] Once we have labelled a person as intolerant or aggressive based on an encounter with them, it is likely that our next experiences with them will be coloured by similar feelings. Behavioural insights reveal, among other things, that people rely on a set of known mental shortcuts to make important decisions and are susceptible to systematic and predictable errors in judgement.[47]

Gurudev Sri Sri Ravi Shankar says that war is the '*worst act of reason*', or intellect: people may think they are doing what is right and find a justification for war, but in fact they are coming from a stressed state of mind and intellect.

> '*Every war has a reason and the reason justifies the war. But reason is limited, and as reasons change, justifications fall apart. All reasons for war appear to be justifiable only to some limited minds and for some limited time.*'
>
> '*No other species in this creation engages in war or mass destruction, because they have no reason to do so. Animals hunt and kill their prey to satiate their hunger. No animal kills to make a point. Man has to learn to transcend reason.*'
>
> '*A fight is rooted in righteousness and every side involved feels they are righteous. Your sense of righteousness depends on your perception and your perception can be erroneous. Only when people become sensible, rise above hatred and have heightened consciousness, can war be stopped.*'
>
> (Gurudev Sri Sri Ravi Shankar)[48]

Anecdote on the intellect

Mullah Nassrudin believed he was dead. His wife was very upset. She tried everything, but nothing worked. Then she went to a psychologist. He told her to ask Mullah to go for shopping. She asked him, but he would not go and said he was dead. Then the psychologist

> suggested asking him to take the kids from school, but again he said he was dead. Desperately, she went to another, very intelligent psychologist who came to see Mullah in person. He asked Mullah: 'Does a corpse have blood in it?' Mullah said: 'No, blood does not flow in a corpse.' So the psychologist smiled and pricked a pin in Mullah's finger. Blood came out. Mullah exclaimed: 'Oh, this changes everything!' The psychologist was very happy. But then Mullah said: 'Now I know that corpses also have blood!'

An open intellect, on the other hand, engages with interest and curiosity with the outer and inner worlds, wants to learn, questions, considers a range of possibilities and generates new insights and wisdom that are beneficial. It functions on the understanding that anyone and anything can change at any time.

Neuroplasticity, the ability of the brain and its neural networks to change and reshape themselves, shows that the brain and intellect can be rewired to function differently than before. In fact, the brain keeps changing according to what we repeatedly think, do or feel and can be seen as a muscle that can be trained accordingly. Through awareness, practice and discipline, we can change the way we perceive, feel and respond to the world by changing our very brain structure. For example, when individuals are aware of their own bias towards people or situations, they can start reducing its influence. Encountering and acknowledging positive examples that contradict negative stereotypes can also start weakening set beliefs.[49]

Therefore, the intellect, our judgements, understanding and knowledge are not carved in stone. They are flexible in nature and can be used in either a beneficial or harmful manner, to enrich and support our life and the lives of others, or to limit and undermine them.

Exercise 5: Intellect

During the day, observe any judgements, interpretations or concepts arising in your intellect, and consider whether they are helpful or not. If not, let them go.

The intellect can be nurtured by wisdom in order to discriminate, judge and respond beneficially to life's situations and direct one's life towards greater good for oneself and others (Table 5.2).

Exercise 6: Acceptance

Close your eyes. Think of someone whom you find very difficult to accept. Observe the feelings that arise in you when thinking about this person. Take a deep breath in and let go. Now think of someone you find very easy to accept. Again observe the feelings that arise in you when thinking about this person. Take a deep breath in and let go. You may open your eyes. Reflect on your respective inner state and which state you prefer to be in.

Table 5.2 *Wisdom Keys That Are Shared in IAHV's Programmes*

> **Wisdom keys that are shared in IAHV's programmes**:
> 1. Discriminate between what is temporary and what is permanent. Remember that many situations in life are of a changing nature.
> 2. Live in the present moment: The past is already gone and the future has not yet come. The present moment is all we have. It is where life is really happening.
> 3. The present moment is inevitable: However the present moment manifests, the situation is what it is. Noone has been able to change the present moment. Yet, we spend so much time and energy questioning it and wishing it to be different. We can only change the next moment, the future.
> 4. Accept people and situations as they are. When we are in a state of acceptance, there is calm and clarity in the mind, from which we can respond and take action. When we do not accept, we may feel frustrated, angry, hurt or agitated. Any reaction resulting from such a state of mind is less likely to be constructive, helpful or beneficial. Acceptance is not a passive state, but a settled state of mind from which we can better respond to situations.
> 5. Take responsibility for one's own actions and emotions. When we hold other people and situations responsible for how we feel and act, we give our power away. If, on the other hand, we take responsibility for how we feel and act, we retain our power and can grow through situations to become more free, self-aware and empowered.

Also at the societal level we can distinguish certain sets of beliefs, shared understanding and narratives, which guide people's behaviour, leaders' decisions and the functioning of society. Daniel Bar Tal calls this 'an ethos': a set of beliefs and understandings that is presented as a coherent body of knowledge that forms a comprehensive picture of the present situation, the past and the future aspirations, giving meaning and predictability. In a conflict ethos, certain beliefs are emphasized in particular, such as the justification of the goals and behaviour of one's own group, the delegitimization of the opponent and a sense of positive self-image and victimhood.

Application:

In order to resolve conflict, prevent violence and create peaceful relationships, it is crucial to work on the sets of beliefs, judgements, narratives, understandings and prejudices that are present in the intellect, both at the personal level and at the social level. Stress reduction tools such as breathing techniques relax and open up the intellect, while wisdom, knowledge and an education in human values nurture a stable, resourceful, open and peace-oriented intellect.

Memory

The memory is the layer of our existence where our past experiences are stored, together with the meaning or interpretation we have given them. The experiences of our daily life are stored in the conscious part of our memory, while the unconscious part stores deeper, older or vaguer impressions, emotions and patterns. The meaning or interpretation we give to impressions and memories is very personal, defined by genetic make-up, tendencies, socialization, culture and other factors, and can therefore be very different from the meaning and interpretation that other people carry for the same events or experiences.

When our energy level is low, the memory turns more negatively, focuses more on what does not work in life, and gets stuck in the past more easily. Challenges, problems and misery are magnified while the positive aspects of life are hardly acknowledged. Sometimes people are stuck in the past and live their present lives fully through the lens of the past. This is especially so in the case of trauma, which is lodged in the brain and the nervous system and influences how we perceive the present and act in it. According to psychological research, this negativity bias is an inherent characteristic of the so-called negative motivational system, the tendency for negative information or experiences to have a more significant impact on an individual's psychological state than positive ones.[50]

When our energy level is higher and we feel well, the memory records and revives experiences and memories more in accordance with what actually happened. It serves its main purpose better and remembers the things that are useful and important.

To some extent we can decide what we hold on to and what we let go of through conscious awareness: We can choose to let go of memories and impressions which are unhelpful and to hold on to those that are beneficial and life-supporting. This is true for the individual as well as the social level.

Societies too can make deliberate choices about their collective memories. The collective memory is usually not a factual representation of the past, especially in conflict contexts, but a specific representation in which certain facts are omitted, doubtful facts are added and interpretations are coloured or biased. For example, certain traumatic events can be selected to be remembered in order to keep the sense of victimization and injustice alive. The brutal acts committed by one's own group can be omitted to maintain a sense of one's own righteousness, while the brutal acts of the opponent can be emphasized in order to depict them as immoral enemies who can and should be harmed. Similarly, the collective memory can be shaped to present a less biased and more balanced account of the past which recognizes the beneficial and harmful acts on both sides.

Application
Individual and social memory can become an instigator of conflict, a major driving force for the perpetuation of conflict and an obstacle to its resolution. With higher energy and awareness, we can discern and select what we choose to hold on to and what to let go of on both the individual and social levels. That way, **the memory can function rather as a source of learning and wisdom, and an inspiration for progress and peace, instead of being an instigator of conflict and an obstacle to its resolution.**

Exercise 7: Memory

- Observe the memories that pop up in your mind. Which emotions arise with these memories?
- Which memories or events do you hold on to? (Do you hold on to the insults, blame, disappointments, conflicts? Or to the achievements, appreciation, heartwarming contacts?)
- Which memories or events do you let go of? Your aspirations, hopes and dreams? Or the disappointments and frustrations?

Ego

The ego is our sense of identity, of being a specific person who is different from any other person. We may associate with ourselves many identities, such as mother/father, sister/brother, son/daughter, male/female, of a certain age, geographic location, nationality, religion, social background, profession and so on. Thinking we are better than others is a manifestation of our sense of ego. Equally, thinking we are not good enough or unworthy is also our sense of ego playing out. When our ego is hardened, we feel a sense of separation between ourselves and the world around us, unconnected or ill at ease with certain people and situations. When the ego is softened, we feel comfortable, connected and at ease with everyone. In that state, we also have a sense of ourselves as being first and foremost human beings, this ranking ahead of other roles and identifications. The conversations we have about ourselves arise also from the ego.

Testimonials related to ego and identity from participants in IAHV's programmes

'The training helped me get out of the world that I was imprisoning myself in, out of the too serious character that I was stuck in because of my fear from people and society. After I came here and met very kind people and loving trainers, the fear got reduced and I knew that this character I was playing wasn't the real me. I finally know who I am and am able to be natural.' (Wassef, THRH / YAVAP)

'I used to be very shy. That is gone now. I was able to enter a new school and integrate quickly. I used to be very nervous and scared about this.' (THRH Participant, Jarash)

'I am usually introvert but now I start socializing every time I meet strangers in the office.' (THRH / YAVAP graduate)

'The training gave me so much serenity that I never experienced before in my life. I am usually an introvert person and don't mingle with people I don't know. I felt this was totally released out of me. I was able to mingle with others, talk to them, eat with them and joke with them very comfortably and naturally. Now I have more confidence in myself and I want to achieve more. Until I become myself the peace that will help others.' (Kheiro, YAVAP graduate)

> **Exercise 8: Connectedness**
>
> How connected do we feel with every human being, regardless of their background? Can you feel or imagine feeling connected to people from all races, social backgrounds, professions, ages, nationalities? When we work as a peacebuilder, can we connect to all people on all sides of conflict, including those engaged in violence, stuck in selfish desires, immersed in victimization or maintaining narrow ego positions?

Many people in the world identify themselves strongly with their religion, nationality, political views, race and sexual preferences. These strong identifications create in-groups and out-groups in society. When people perceive a threat or attack on that aspect of their identity, they may perceive it as an attack on their person or group. This happens when one's sense of self and self-interest are inextricably tied up to a group. Identity fusion with one's group predicts even willingness to fight and die for the group.[51] Similarly, the survival and welfare of the group can feel essential for the survival of the individual. The feeling of threat, attack or denial on these identities may trigger opposition, 'counterattacks', preventive attacks and defence mechanisms. Also, threats to other members of one's group may generate strong emotions and reactions among individuals who identify with the same group even when they are not directly involved in the events. One's own identity and in-group affiliations get reinforced while opponents are characterized negatively, derogated or even dehumanized. A new conflict-logic centred around identity may take over, aiming to protect one's sense of identity and related sense of survival. Individual and collective identity may become intrinsically tied up to the conflict and can easily start prevailing over original conflict issues. Moreover, conflict resolution initiatives which overlook or threaten these conflict-constructed identities may be opposed and obstructed.

Social identity is that 'part of an individual's self-concept which derives from her knowledge of her membership of a social group together with the value and emotional significance attached to that membership'.[52] Social identity can be strongly linked to territory, political-economic systems, culture, heritage, religion/beliefs, traditions, language or other factors. The extent to which individuals adhere to their social identities can differ, depending on their individual experience of feeling belonging to the given group, their willingness to belong, the importance ascribed to this belonging, the emotional attachment one feels towards the group, commitment to benefiting the group, or belief in the group's characteristics, norms and values.[53]

In conflict situations, these specific social identities are often stronger than the more universal identities of being part of the human race as a whole or being part of something bigger. It seems probable that if the prevailing sense of identity is reversed and people experience more of their interconnectedness and shared human nature, many conflicts in the world would not arise nor escalate into destructive violence. In this regard, Brewer has mentioned that the extent of in-group identification influences whether intergroup threats are perceived in the first place and then how likely individuals are to mobilize in defence of in-group interests.[54] People who strongly identify with the group 'hold more aggressive attitudes towards outgroup members, support more aggressive action, and express more willingness to participate in illegal and violent actions in order to protect their group'.[55] It seems important to give people an experience of multiple identities, to become grounded in the more universal identities of being part of something bigger and/or the human race as a starting point, and to strengthen the capacity to identify flexibly with, and engage, different identities if and where appropriate, especially in highly stressful, threatening or challenging situations. This more universal identification comes from the deeper level of the Self, which is experienced when the level of the ego is more expanded or relaxed. From this level, a sense of belonging to the broader human community is fostered together with the promotion of universal human values that transcend individual group affiliations.

Another challenging and frequently occurring dynamic at the level of the ego is the tendency to identify with the role of being either a **victim or perpetrator**. While these are understandable reactions to situations that we are subjected to or engaged in, at a deeper level they can cause and sustain conflicts as well as become a significant obstacle to their resolution and transformation.

When we identify with being the perpetrator, we may get stuck in a negative self-image and feelings of guilt without being able to move forward. When we identify with being a victim, we may limit our own sense of agency and power. We are likely to attribute the responsibility for the particular event or situation to the perpetrator, remaining stuck in our negative feelings of blame, revenge and resentment, sometimes also overlooking our own possible contribution to the situation. Thinking about the losses, deaths, harm, atrocities and violence committed by the opponent, and focusing on one's own gloomy fate or hopeless situation, easily puts one into depression or aggression. The sense of victimhood can become socially ingrained in a culture through narratives, commemoration of the dead, monuments and rituals, which all become part of social and individual identity. Victims often turn into perpetrators themselves in a vicious cycle of violence.

> *A mother of an ISIS fighter who died in Syria participated in an IAHV Healing, Resilience and Empowerment Programme in Belgium. She had been condemning herself for the fate of her son. She was also condemned by others for being a 'terrorist mother'. At the same time, however, she was also a mother who lost her child. Her life was stuck between sadness and despair, and guilt and condemnation, making it impossible for her to mourn. After realizing these feelings at the level of the ego and experiencing a deeper, freer sense of herself, she was finally able to let go of her self-condemnation, accept herself and her actions, mourn the loss of her son and move forward with her life.*

Application:

Unhelpful self-identifications can be limiting and create separation, aggression and tension, while a more expanded understanding of one's identity can lead to peaceful and meaningful interactions with the people and the world around us.

Identity is a psychosocial factor with a deep impact on conflict. In particular, group identities and specific conflict identities play a crucial role in the generation, escalation and resolution of interpersonal and intergroup conflicts and the creation of social cohesion. Remaining stuck in identification with being a victim or a perpetrator can have very unhelpful and even counterproductive, violence-escalating consequences. It is therefore important to engage profoundly with the identity factor in order to transform conflict dynamics.

An important way to engage positively with the identity factor for conflict resolution and peacebuilding is to cultivate the experience of having multiple identities, while developing a stable foundation with a broader, more universal identity, such as being part of something bigger and/or the human race. **The capacity to flexibly identify with and engage different identities as and where appropriate is an important skill for conflict prevention and source of resilience.**

Self

The Self is the deepest and most subtle layer of our existence. Since it is beyond the mind and the intellect, it is not so much something to understand as it is to experience. The following might give a clearer idea of the Self: You may remember moments when you are fully content and at peace, and experience a sense of expansion and lightness. This could be when you are very happy or in love, or in any situation when you are fully present in that moment and truly enjoying what you are doing. You may experience a subtle joyous level of yourself that suffuses life at that moment. This is the Self, which is the storehouse of love, peace, happiness and virtues. It is actually the core of our existence, which can be experienced when we are fully relaxed. As Gurudev Sri Sri Ravi Shankar says, the innate core of our being, the Self, is ultimately positive, while the so-called negative emotions lie out on the periphery of our existence. He compares us to the atom which is positive at the core and negative in the surroundings. When we are stressed in the other levels of our existence, we do not have much sense of our deeper essence, in the same way as we may not perceive the sun when it is covered by clouds. In young children who grow up healthily we can observe their revealed Self in their bubbling enthusiasm, liveliness, trust, and total presence in every moment. Through the journey of life most of us acquire stresses that block us from experiencing our deeper Self, but in fact it is always there with us, present but hidden. We never lose this essential core of our existence. The basis of the approach of Art of Living and IAHV is not to acquire anything new, but to reveal and access this innate Self through the removal of the stresses on all levels which obscure it. This is the deeper meaning of the SKY or Sudarshan Kriya technique: it is a purifying action that gives us a right vision of who we are, of our true Self. **The Self is where inner peace lies. And it is present in every human being.**

> *A twelve-year-old boy shared that during the relaxation after the practice of the breathing techniques he felt his heart was expanding and there was a strong energy flowing into his body, making him feel very strong and happy.*
>
> *A thirteen-year-old boy from Abou Samra suffered from breathing problems and a sleeping disorder. He was also very introverted and wasn't willing to take any initiative at the start of the programme. On the last day, he slept very deeply during the relaxation after the breathing exercises and shared that he had never felt that much rest.*
>
> *He shared:*
>
> *'I felt great rest. I felt the tiredness, dizziness and all the negativity being eliminated from my body.' He also showed great leadership skills and responsibility towards his team and was able to enhance his self-confidence.*
>
> *A twelve-year-old boy was feeling very angry and sometimes very aggressive with his peers. He said he was not able to relax. However, during the course, he was able to experience deep rest:*
>
> *'I was very relaxed when I was lying down. I am so rested and my happiness is indescribable.'*
>
> *'I cannot remember any happy moment in my life after the war, apart from this course. I really felt happiness coming from within me and I felt the happiness of my friends who were on the course.' (Bashkim, Kosovo Liberation Army soldier)*

This dimension of inner peace is essential for inclusive peacebuilding and global peace. 'Unless every member of our global family is peaceful, our peace is incomplete,' says Gurudev Sri Sri Ravi Shankar.[56] A human-centred approach to peacebuilding fully incorporates the intrapersonal dimension as an essential foundation for social peace.

As peacebuilders and mediators we can not only play an important role with our communication and mediation skills but also through our presence. The embracing, calm and connecting presence of a mediator can help people to open up to their deepest wounds, struggles, aspirations and hopes. Not addressing these psychosocial factors can obstruct the deep transformation of conflict, while conversely giving them space and integrating them can be the foundation for deep peacebuilding.

As human beings, we carry many emotional and mental impressions and experiences. When we push aside, ignore or run away from certain aspects of ourselves, these elements remain, reducing the 'space' that we have available inside ourselves that other people can connect with. What we have hidden within ourselves and what we prefer not to face, we may not perceive, ignore or mishandle when it is present in those we are aiming to work with and support. On the other hand, the more we can connect to the different aspects of ourselves, the more space and capacity there is for others to connect with us.

During the facilitation of a crucial breakthrough in the peace process with FARC leadership in Colombia, Gurudev Sri Sri Ravi Shankar was asked by a journalist what it was that he had said to change the mindsets and position of the FARC leadership, especially given the lack of success by previous negotiators and mediators. In response, he stated, 'It is not what I said, it is who I am.'

Ultimately, the Self can be compared to space. As a physical space, it is empty, but as an energetic field, it is full of vibrations. Like a mirror, it reflects the world around it, and through its energy field, it can positively transform other energies around.

> **Exercise 9: The Self**
>
> How connected do we feel with our Self? How relaxed can we be in our Self? Are there obstacles, stresses and blocks preventing us from really living and interacting from the level of our Self? There is a direct link between stress and the ability to connect. The extent to which we are connected to our Self also allows other people to relax and repose in our presence. How at ease can others be with us?
>
> A simple example: You are walking in a city in a stressed and hurried state. Most likely you are not very patient with others, perceptive of what is going on around you, or feeling much connectedness to your environment. However, when you are strolling very relaxed in the same city, you may feel very tolerant of whatever your fellow inhabitants are doing, finely perceive what is going on around you, and feel very connected to strangers and an environment you may have never seen before.

> **Exercise 10: Positive and negative qualities**
>
> Make a list of ten positive and ten negative qualities you have observed in yourself. Afterwards:
>
> - reflect how the negative qualities are not always present; they mostly come up when we are under stress. They do not really belong to your Self.
> - reflect on the positive qualities that have been given to us by nature; they are at the core of our existence and manifest when we are stress-free or able to handle our stress levels constructively.

On emotions

Emotions are linked to several levels of our existence: they are essentially connected to sensations in the body, often triggered by the mind, and exist closely linked to the ego or sense of 'I'. Different emotions cause specific sensations in our body in different places: anger we feel mostly in the head, sadness in the throat, love in the heart or jealousy in the stomach. Thoughts and emotions are often closely linked, with specific thoughts creating specific emotions, which in turn create related thoughts, interpretations, reflections and more emotions. These can go round and round in a vicious cycle. We tend to identify with our emotions: it is 'me' feeling this way or that way. When we experience emotions as 'ours', in the understanding 'I am sad' or 'I am happy', we easily become entangled in our inner field of emotions.

Some of the strongest emotions at play in conflicts are anger, fear, humiliation and hatred: Anger about the acts of the opponent. Fear about a real or perceived threat to one's interests, needs, beliefs, welfare, values or aspirations. Hatred over evil acts by an evil opponent that should be revenged. Humiliation as the experience of intentional demeaning treatment of individuals or a group.

According to insights from the field of psychology and neuroscience, human behaviour is more driven by emotions than by rational thought processes.[57] We are predominantly emotional beings, and behave rationally primarily when we feel secure and validated. So, for example, how we perceive an 'out' group different from our own is more influenced by affective (or emotional) processes than by cognitive processes.

Such **emotions, when acted out in destructive or aggressive ways, are a major contributor to ongoing cycles of conflict**: For example, groups who feel humiliated can rise up to put an end to that experience of humiliation, but this is often done with feelings of frustration, distress or even trauma, and they can end up committing the same acts of humiliation as their oppressors. In this way, humiliation as both antecedent and consequence can fuel conflicts for a long time.[58] Similarly, perceiving an external threat may lead individuals to attempt to regain control by adopting a simplistic worldview that categorizes people as either good or evil and by identifying exclusively with their own group. This, in turn, creates a heightened sense of threat towards those outside the group.

Therefore, it is important to be aware of one's emotions and to be able to manage them. **Emotional intelligence refers to the capacity to understand, regulate and manage one's own emotions while also understanding other people's emotions and needs and act in the most appropriate way according to the situation.** Generally, it helps to better understand the mechanism behind emotions when we see how they link up to mind, body and ego.

IAHV programmes focus on the capacity to observe the emotions without reacting to them or resisting them. As we have seen earlier, the breath is an important instrument to manage and transform emotions more easily, since the breathing patterns and emotions are closely interlinked.[59] Modifying one's breathing patterns can lead to changes in emotional states. In advanced IAHV programmes, participants are encouraged to focus on the bodily sensations associated with emotions, as well as on the more subtle experiences of energy. By cultivating gentle awareness of these sensations, individuals can gradually transform entrenched emotional patterns and maladaptive responses. This process creates a state in which the Self, characterized by an unchanging sense of peace, becomes more accessible. A stronger, more stable sense of the Self makes it easier to observe the changing emotional states without getting too absorbed in them negatively.

> A fourteen-year-old boy from Homs, Syria, now living in Beddawi, Lebanon, was at times reacting very aggressively and angrily towards his peers, and would then feel bad about it. During the SRR Programme, he felt he was able to release these suppressed emotions as he shared:
>
> 'There were all those emotions inside me: frustration, anger, hatred, pain. When I did this exercise, I felt that these feelings, which I have been using in my life, have all vanished. When I opened my eyes, I felt something went out of my body and I felt deeply rested, as if I became another person ... I felt calmness. Feelings of frustration, anger, hatred, sadness and pain have vanished from my body. Thank you very much for getting us out of this entanglement...'
>
> A Syrian mother in her early fifties who had lost both her sons in the war was very gloomy and crying most of the time. This bothered her husband and family and made her feel separated from them. She felt alone with her memories and felt that even if she were to smile, it would be a betrayal of the memory of her sons. However, during the HRE Programme, she was able to express all the suppressed feelings that she couldn't share with her near ones. She felt a deeper and more peaceful connection with them. She felt as if her heart had opened up to life again!

Restoring inner peace

The 7 levels of our existence can be compared to the strings of a guitar: When they are out of tune, they only produce sound. However, when they are tuned, they bring forth harmony. Similarly, when the levels of our existence are free of stress, our whole inner being is at peace and in harmony, and the layers function according to their original nature. With practice, such a state of inner calm can be maintained even in the midst of conflict, chaos and activity.

The levels of our existence can also be further developed and refined, not just to mitigate the negative effects of stress, but also to optimize the full spectrum of human potential. For example, the mind can be trained to become laser sharp and clear in its perception, to be centred on the Self rather than on the changing external events and experiences, thereby cultivating awareness and inner freedom over states of misery and constriction. Additionally, intuition, an innate capacity present in all individuals, can be cultivated through specific practice. Deep meditation can facilitate enhanced insights into past, present and future. Furthermore, through self-enquiry we can vastly expand our understanding of who we are as human beings, and through self-awareness and self-management practice we can master both intellectual processes and certain physiological functions. The exploration of the nature of the Self is boundless and can generate fundamental insights into existence and the link between the micro- and macro-cosmos. We can also attain a state of deep non-violence, not only in actions and in words, but also in thoughts and feelings.

Inner Empowerment through ownership and responsibility

The elements presented above, which are the foundation of IAHV's programmes, allow people to become aware and take charge of their own inner world. This is **the deepest level of empowerment: integrating the practice of mastering our own mind, emotions, impressions and reactions, and acting skilfully in the world.**

We can distinguish several aspects in this process: self-awareness, self-regulation, social awareness and self-management.

Self-awareness can be defined as the non-judgemental, conscious recognition of one's internal states, encompassing thoughts, emotions and bodily sensations. Key components of self-awareness include self-observation, introspection, the ability to reflect on one's own perceptions, and the recognition and acceptance of one's emotional experiences. This internal clarity serves as the foundation for self-regulation, as one can only manage what one is consciously aware of. Self-awareness plays a critical role in interrupting habitual behavioural patterns that are often driven by unconscious emotional reactions. It effectively creates a mental space, often described as a gap between stimulus and response, wherein lies the capacity to make conscious and deliberate choices. Self-regulation, then, refers to the capacity to monitor and modulate one's emotional and behavioural responses to internal and external stimuli. This includes managing reactions to intense emotions such as anger, frustration, or excitement, and restoring emotional equilibrium after distressing experiences.

This capacity becomes very clear and important, for example, in conflict situations and other interactions where our emotions, aspects of identity, needs and values are strongly triggered. Strong triggers can set of automatic thoughts and emotions which define our immediate reaction, like a bull reacting to a red flag. However, when we are able to pause and observe and master the processes of the inner world, we can choose a responsive action rather than reacting automatically as if pre-programmed.

Similarly, social awareness is the ability to observe and understand the moods of other people and groups, to empathize and to accurately realize what is really going on. Having social awareness allows you to choose your actions towards others based on the understanding and recognition of their feelings, needs and ways of thinking, and is the foundation for relationship management.

Self- and social awareness entail mental presence, a moment-to-moment awareness that facilitates an understanding of oneself, others and the broader context, thereby supporting the capacity to respond to situations appropriately and effectively.

Self-management builds on self-awareness, self-regulation and social awareness, and refers to the ability to consciously direct one's emotions, thoughts and behaviours towards desired outcomes. While self-awareness creates the mental capacity to choose one's actions, self-management entails purposeful behaviour, communication and decision-making. Transitioning from automatic, potentially maladaptive reactions to more proactive, constructive and creative responses fosters healthier interpersonal dynamics and enhances overall effectiveness. For example, a research study on 300 leaders showed that individuals who are more self-aware make better decisions and show better conflict management.[60]

Through these processes, we can decide the state of our inner world at any time, act instead of react in any situation, and define the quality of our interactions. 'Skill in action,' is how yoga is defined in the groundwork on Yoga by the ancient sage Patanjali.

In order to do this, we **need to take responsibility and ownership of our own thoughts, emotions and reactions**. As long as we keep holding other people responsible for how we feel and act, we are stuck in the same place: at the receiving end. This position often manifests in complaining, blaming and accusations towards people and situations, and also to the feeling of victimhood. We give more power away to the external factors. When we turn this around, however, and take responsibility for our inner reactions, then we hold the power with ourselves. With dedicated practice, we can cultivate the competencies of self-awareness and self-regulation, and move through the reactive patterns and grow out of them. This is the road to true inner freedom and to empowerment in the deepest sense.

> **Exercise 11: Responsibility and blame**
>
> Looking into your life, are there people and situations you are blaming for how you feel and react? What are the feelings and reactions that you observe inside yourself? How do you feel when you take responsibility for them?

Non-violence in feelings, thoughts, words and actions

The ideology and practice of active non-violence, aiming to achieve justice and peace through non-violent means, is an important strategy and core element of peacebuilding theory and practice. A distinction is made between the more pragmatic, technically oriented approaches to nonviolence and the more principled approach to non-violence, as propagated, among others, by Mahatma Gandhi, Lev Tolstoy and Martin Luther King.[61] **A deeper understanding and experience of non-violence includes non-violence not only in actions but also in words, thoughts and feelings**. In deep non-violence, not only anger and aggression dissolve but also subtle forms of violence, such as judgements, condemnations and irritation.

According to Gurudev Sri Sri Ravi Shankar, a non-violent act that is conducted with anger or frustration is not really non-violent, and a violent act that is conducted with inner peace and awareness is not really violent. He says that violence or non-violence are determined not by the act but by the attitude and intention behind it. A surgeon cuts open the belly of a patient in order to save him, while a criminal can cut the belly of a victim in order to kill. Violence springs forth from anger, lust, hatred, jealousy, greed, frustration or aggression. Non-violence springs forth from inner peace, centredness, awareness, compassion and connectedness. In that sense, even a war can be non-violent if it is devoid of anger, hatred, jealousy or greed and if it is the last resort to educate a group of people. Even charity can be an act of violence if it is conducted with disrespect, suppresses people and takes away self-esteem.

In order to cultivate deep inner non-violence, the inner tendency for conflict and the seed of negativity need to be removed. Conflict is part of the world, as Gurudev Sri Sri Ravi Shankar points out: the basic elements of creation are in conflict with each other, like water is in conflict with fire, and fire is in conflict with air. Since the mind is engaged with the world, conflict is part of the tendencies of the mind. As Gurudev Sri Sri Ravi Shankar explains, this inner tendency for conflict easily makes the mind pick up an excuse or reason for disharmony and conflict. This seed of negativity and conflict can be removed through spiritual practices, breathing exercises and meditation.

> *'Conflict is the nature of the world; comfort is the nature of the Self. Amidst conflict, find the comfort. When you are tired of conflicts and the games of the world, get into the comforts of the Self. When you are bored with comfort, get into the games of the world. If you are wise, you do both simultaneously.' (Gurudev Sri Sri Ravi Shankar)*
>
> *'People who love peace do not want to fight. And those who fight do not have peace. What is needed is to be peaceful within and then fight.' (Gurudev Sri Sri Ravi Shankar)*

Active non-violence is essentially an approach to conflict transformation which combines deep personal transformation with an authentic meeting with the other, and the transformation of society. Contrary to some popular perceptions, active non-violence is not an option for the weak, but requires significant inner strength and courage on a personal level. An active non-violent position is characterized by the absence of hatred or the desire for revenge and ideally comes forth from an inner space which is itself devoid of violence. To be able to break the cycle of hatred with positivity and empathy requires wisdom and moral courage. Such characteristics can be developed through self-reflection on one's own emotions, reactions and behaviour, and internal discipline. In addition, active non-violence implies a willingness to bear pain. By nurturing a sense of wholeness and inner integration in ourselves we can engage with more acceptance, empathy and skill with others. Essentially**, active non-violence is a path of deep personal transformation and self-realization, since the outer action of non-violence is inextricably linked to the inner workings of the heart, mind and spirit of the individual**.[62]

> *'I don't beat my friends or get angry at them anymore . . . Even whenever I get angry I now do the breathing. Then I make up with them and love them for the rest of my life.' (SRR participant, ten years, El Tal, Lebanon)*

Resilience

The widely used term of resilience refers to the ability of individuals and communities to cope, adapt and 'bounce back' from adverse events, and even to thrive despite adversity. We can distinguish individual, organizational and social resilience. Research into resilience has highlighted the importance of positivity, capacity for emotional regulation, coping skills, hope, sense of agency, meaning and purpose, as well as social support networks.[63]

The core of individual and collective resilience can be strengthened through awareness and practice, understanding the 7 levels of existence and managing them as proposed in IAHV's model of intrapersonal transformation.

> 'After I started working out according to the programme, significant changes happened to me. Now I mostly have a good mood; even if something happens, I quickly return to a state of balance. There was more resource inside, as if something had strengthened.' (participant from Ukraine after HRE trauma-relief workshop)

Case study: 'In every culprit there is a victim crying for help': Trauma, adverse childhood experiences and criminality – IAHV's approach to offender rehabilitation

The below case study is based on an article by Jakob Lund[64] as well as the experiences of myself and other IAHV Prison Programme trainers.

Jakob Lund is a senior Prison Programme trainer for IAHV, based in Denmark. He has pioneered IAHV's Prison Programme as it was developed by Gurudev Sri Sri Ravi Shankar in Europe, especially setting up a successful integrated prevention and rehabilitation initiative for offenders in and outside prisons in Denmark, including its gang-ridden capital Copenhagen. Specialized in the treatment of trauma in offenders, he also provides one-on-one rehabilitation training for hard-core criminals, violent extremists, terrorists and life convicts. The people described in the article are all hard-core criminals and gang members who have convictions for serious crimes, including one or more murders. The quotes used in this case study are from offenders Jakob has worked with over the years, unless stated otherwise, and are used here anonymously.

Gurudev Sri Sri Ravi Shankar says that **'in every culprit, there is a victim crying for help.'** Or, as Bessel Van der Kolk, Professor of Psychiatry and one of the world's leading trauma specialists, says: 'Re-enactment of victimization is a major cause of violence in society.'[65] Crime and violent behaviour indeed often stem from unprocessed painful experiences in the past, such as abuse, witnessing abuse, trauma, accidents and so on. Crime, violence and destructive lifestyles are often just symptoms or defence reactions provoked by underlying traumatic experiences. The psychological defence mechanisms that people develop when they are violated in their being, such as antisocial behaviour, lack of empathy, aggression or unfiltered expressions of emotion, are initially useful to survive and protect oneself against physical, emotional and mental destruction. Later, these same defence mechanisms can become a hindrance to living a fulfilling life. However, they are often an advantage in a criminal environment. Based on the experience of IAHV's Prison Programme trainers, it is possible to reduce crime and violent behaviour by healing the victim inside. As the trauma of the past gradually heals, also the perpetrator inside and her violent dysfunctional behaviours gradually disappear.

Adverse childhood experiences, trauma and criminality: Survival mechanisms that become life threatening

Traumatizing experiences, and especially those experienced in early childhood, can lead often to dysfunctional behaviour, violence and crime.[66] There are different ways in which early childhood trauma can create the seed for future delinquent behaviour.

Through a normal childhood, a child receives both mental and physical **nourishment from his/her surroundings** to grow and develop. When this environment is abusive or non-responsive, however, a child will instead have to protect oneself from these same surroundings, spending his/her energy on maintaining a **defensive strategy**, rather than developing the inner core and personality. Without a sense of safety, it is difficult for a child to be in contact with his/her core, feel his/her own emotions and simply be at peace within oneself. The experience of the lack of belonging, connectedness, loyalty and safety is often the root cause of attraction to gangs and similar groupings, which promise stable loyalty and brotherhood forever.

Early or chronic **exposure to or experience of violence and abuse** can programme the **nervous system** of a child in such a way that it is constantly on alert and ready to escape danger. For a child, the normal reactions of fight of flight in life-threatening or seriously destabilizing situations may not have been possible. Instead, the child is forced to experience an overwhelming threatening impact which it cannot really integrate physically or mentally. When the abuser is the person supposed to protect and take care of the child, there is no safe space for the nervous system and the body of the child to discharge, relax and recover. The energy, which at the time was mobilized for fighting or fleeing, is instead locked inside the body, together with a feeling of insecurity and uncertainty. With such a continuous feeling of insecurity within, the fight or flight mechanism remains activated in the body and nervous system, ready to be released at any moment against a possible threat. People in this condition usually keep scanning their environment to detect danger, or they are over-sensitive to criticism, which is perceived as a personal attack. When war veterans suffering from PTSD were asked in a study to look at pictures of faces with a neutral expression, they read the expression of these faces as being threatening because of their state of high alert and stress.[67] When the world is seen through an over-active nervous system, the parts of the brain that are alert to danger, are constantly working, whereas the parts that are intended to be curious and open to new experiences and impressions remain unstimulated. The sense of danger overshadows the capacity to see what is positive and interesting. Small offences or small amounts of stress are sufficient to think that there is a matter of life or death. Consciousness shifts from the cognitive part of the brain to the deeper and primitive survival mechanisms of the brain. This makes a person react automatically to a threat, overruling good sense and reason and often reacting disproportionately. In these cases, there is no capacity for self-regulation; the person does not consider and reflect on what is happening and does not consciously choose how to respond to the situation.

> *'I would always wear my bulletproof vest, even if I only visited my Mum. One could never know when it was time. All my sweatshirts and shirts are too big now because my clothes were bought to fit me when wearing my vest.'*
>
> *'I would constantly scan my surroundings. When I went out, I would look for whom I would maybe have to fight, possible exits, cameras or the police that might be following me. When I came into your room the first time, I looked around and saw that there was a bowl and a chair, that I could smash on your head. Not that I wanted to do you harm; that was how my brain was. I did not think that I was stressed out, but now I can see that I was.'*
>
> *'Only as I was washing the blood off my hands, I was able to actually remember what I had done.'*

In the criminal world, where there is real danger, this unfocused aggression and this inner fear of an undefined and unknown threat find a focus. **Instead of having to deal with what is going on inside, which is hard to tolerate, one can direct this energy towards an outer threat or enemy**. This gives a feeling of certainty, predictability and even safety. Some will even provoke a conflict or a fight just because it provides them with a sense of control. Jakob regularly heard from the people he worked with that they *'are always afraid, except when what they are afraid of, actually happens'*. Dealing with one's own conscious and unconscious anxiety is much more challenging than looking for danger in the outside world. One offender told Jakob that it was much harder for him to sit and talk about himself, which gives rise to much anxiety, than it would be if somebody had just been shot in the street outside.

> *'I have an old enemy, who used to give me trouble. Had this been before, I would just have wiped him out with a gun. This would have been easy for me to do. It is much harder for me not to do it, now that I have to handle all this pent up energy and uncertainty.'*

Inner pain can be externalized by being violent to another person. The suffering, which is so hard to bear, will no longer be carried by yourself, but by the person who is subjected to your aggressive behaviour. For some this feels like a relief, because the pain is over there, in another person, and not inside yourself. The feeling of power and invincibility relieves or erases anxiety and powerlessness for a moment. It makes the aggressor master of the pain that he alone cannot bear. Several people told Jakob that it is the hate and the thought of revenge which carried them through their time in prison as a kind of survival strategy.

The chemical substances that are secreted by the body during battle or when being victorious can be similar to the effect of drugs and can become addictive. Stress hormones, such as adrenaline, noradrenaline and cortisol, provide 100 per cent focus while in danger and make you almost insensitive to pain if you are beaten, shot or hurt in another way. The instinctive reactions during danger take blood away from the thinking part of the brain, the inner world and emotions, and towards the muscles. One becomes focused, with a strong feeling of being present in the now, and this is very alluring. Many people in the criminal world seek high intensity, action and potentially dangerous situations because they stimulate all the senses and are a way to feel really alive.

> 'Violence always gave me a kick. There is nothing better than a good fight. This is where I feel alive... where I get to that point.'

Inner aggression may build up over time and accumulate, to a point there may be an urge to let it out. Only after living out the aggression externally is it possible for some people to relax again, enjoy the release, and become more balanced.

> 'Some guy had fucked with me. I got the number of his ex-girlfriend and drove all the way to Jutland. I kicked in the door at the ex-girlfriend's and forced her to give me the number of the guy who had cheated me. I then forced my way into his house and smashed him up with the computer that he had used to cheat me. When I came home, I was still like on a high. I picked up my phone to see if someone else had fucked with me. I then went out and beat up two other guys. I felt totally relaxed for a week after this.'

When young children witness or experience violence or abuse, they may end up becoming a perpetrator themselves. Besides the mechanisms described above, this happens also because children **mirror**, imitate and copy the behaviour of their parents. At an early age, children do not have a sense of being different from their parents and learn through them how to handle and express emotion. If they see that emotions of anger, fear, loss or sorrow are expressed through aggression, it becomes quite natural for them to adopt that behaviour in their lives.[68]

Especially where children have witnessed or experienced violence without being able to intervene or defend themselves, they may carry with them feelings of **guilt, cowardice and helplessness**. One of the defence mechanisms to avoid feeling these unpleasant emotions is to prove the opposite by being overconfident, proud and shameless. Some people will pick up on or seek out any kind of challenge just to prove to themselves and the world that they are unafraid and not a coward. In order to avoid feeling like a victim of violence and abuse, which means being weak, powerless and not in control, they choose instead to become the abuser, with its associated feelings of being powerful, strong and in control.

Children tend to process early adverse experiences and feelings of unease by thinking there must be **something wrong with them**, rather than with the parents or caretakers. Instead of directing feelings of fear, anger or sadness towards the parents, they direct them against themselves. Later in life, these internalized feelings find expression in different ways, including through aggression, domination, rigidity or lack of empathy. The inner feeling of discomfort will be directed against other people through projection or externalization in the attempt to escape from oneself.

If parents are absent, not playing an active role in guiding the child, not responding to their feelings and actions, and not putting **boundaries** where needed, the child may grow up challenging her environment to see how far she can get. Children in these situations may have the feeling that the world owes them something, some response or reaction, and may challenge the world until they get this. Or they may grow up without a sense of boundaries, feeling that they can do whatever they like and that the world exists only for them. If something or somebody gets in their way, they may become aggressive or manipulative because they have never learned that boundaries and limits are a natural part of coexistence with other people. They may tend to seek the extreme in order to somehow, somewhere find a limit. They locate the boundaries which they are exploring or challenging outside themselves, rather than inside.

In the absence of a fatherly figure who embodies positive **masculinity**, boys may exhibit exaggerated masculinity in order to compensate for the lack they experienced in their life. Young men may also be at risk of being attracted to men who misuse their position as a male role model and leader.

When parents do not respond to the **emotional needs** of the child, the child may get lost, finding it difficult to get a sense of themselves and discern what they really need. When the deepest emotional needs have not been met in the early stages of life, it may become too painful for the child to identify these needs at all. A strong resistance develops to the pain of identifying the deepest needs, which experience has taught will never be got anyway. Rather than feeling the pain of what is missing, a defence mechanism develops which shuts down all emotion, including empathy for oneself and others.

The inner chaos of unpleasant and unprocessed feelings and experiences may be compensated for by extreme **rigidity** on the outside. Earlier in life, the experience of loss of control meant inner chaos. Rigidity is a way to distance oneself from this inner chaos and an attempt to re-establish a sense of safety that was lost long ago. One holds on firmly to notions of how things should be to avoid inner insecurity and uncertainty and to protect oneself against any sudden changes. To many criminals, uncertainty is the feeling they want to avoid the most, since it can evoke memories of past trauma, chaos and powerlessness. If anything deviates from their rigid will, they will use aggressive and violent behaviour to re-establish order and control. Thinking in black and white, dominance, a lack of empathy and fundamental mistrust of everyone and everything become part of a mental and physical defence. The defence constructed to prevent others from harming us also prevents them from coming close and connecting. Rigidity is meant to keep chaos at bay, but when unpleasant feelings are kept at a distance, positive feelings become distant too. Many participants have become so good at suppressing emotions that they do not notice when something feels uncomfortable or wrong and they do not feel negative sensations such as stress, anxiety or pain.

The rigidity is not only apparent in the way a person thinks, but also in the nervous system, which functions in an inflexible manner, and in the body, which is not able to relax and let go of tension.

As criminologist Larry Siegel explains: 'When we block our awareness of feelings, they continue to affect us anyway. Research has shown repeatedly that even without conscious awareness, neural input from the internal world of body and emotion influences our reasoning and decision-making. In other words, you can run but you cannot hide.'[69]

Feelings and bodily sensations may push from the inside to be expressed. Many offenders live in a state of constant restlessness, resembling ADHD, to unconsciously discharge this inner state of tension. Others act more like robots and it is difficult to detect any kind of emotion in them. They seem to have become prisoners even inside their own body. Yet others seem to be in a kind of dull emotional state, almost as if they were sedated, or as if something is dead inside them. When the lid is on for too long for any of them, it may lead to sudden explosions.

When children think there is something wrong with them when their parents are absent or not responding to their existence, they may find it **difficult to connect with themselves**. Children who grow up without a sense of who they are may only be able to have a feeling of who they are through the eyes of others and through their surroundings. They can only **see themselves from the outside**, without a sense of direct experience. Not their inner human qualities, but appearance, the things they do, big muscles, designer clothing, tattoos, and respect from others, become what they measure themselves by. When they grow up **without self-esteem**, they may strive as adults for status, respect, recognition, excitement or material status symbols to compensate the lack of inner self-esteem. In such cases, many criminals have developed a **grandiose self-image** which is very different from who they really are. The false self-image is freed from all needs and emotions that might indicate weakness, such as fear, sorrow, doubt, insecurity, longing or a need for help. Instead, the self-image is boosted with strength, courage, success, respect and will be shown as such to the surrounding world. However, inside an awareness remains, both consciously and unconsciously, about the falseness and fragility of this self-image, which may have taken years to build and could easily be torn to pieces in a few minutes. Therefore, many conflicts in criminal circles are as much about money as they are about one's name and reputation. The 'weak', underlying self-image is associated with shame and needs to be concealed at all costs. The smallest indicators of a possible revelation of this shameful identity are perceived as a threat against oneself. Some people are more willing to risk their lives to defend this false self-image than to feel the pain underneath.

> 'The violence begins little by little; when you become good at it, it becomes more and more until someday it is part of your everyday life. Later on, it provides you with enough money for you to live ... You feel that you are a success, just like a businessman. Everyone in the neighbourhood knew me. I felt like a rock star.'

All the above examples, mechanisms and patterns illustrate that it can be very unpleasant to be with oneself. When there are many disturbing and negative thoughts or painful and uncomfortable bodily sensations such as restlessness and stress, there is a tendency to want to escape from oneself and out of the body. One way out is through the use of drugs to change one's inner state. Hashish, which brings relaxation, and cocaine, which provides a kick, are part and parcel of the world of crime. In the absence of a capacity to self-regulate one's mental, emotional and physical state, **drugs are an attractive means of self-regulation**. However, the more drugs are used, the more the capacity for self-regulation is reduced, since the production of the naturally occurring substances that the body uses to regulate the emotional and physical state is repressed. People end up in a vicious circle, using increasingly more drugs to re-experience some degree of inner pleasantness.

Early trauma can both strengthen or weaken the resilience of a child. The defence mechanisms in the body and the nervous system which are described above initially serve to save and protect the child, but they can remain in the system and affect the child for the rest of her life. As life progresses these strategies and patterns limit the possibility of developing one's potential and living a life which is non-destructive for oneself and others. 'The child's interactions with his world are imprinted in his brain circuitry, which is reflected in his body. He is wired up and his body is shaped to suit his particular situation. This bodily held "memory" will profoundly affect later emotions, behavior patterns, beliefs and abilities to process information.'[70] These patterns are, therefore, difficult and painful to change, even if they only serve to maintain traumatization. Consequently, the way life is then lived only confirms and reinforces the experience that the world and other people are unsafe and potentially dangerous. Trauma is a force from the past, colouring the present reality with the old experience. When resilience is weak, further traumatization is more likely to happen later in life.

In addition, the mechanisms and skill sets developed during such an early life, for example the lack of empathy, accumulated aggression, the capacity to act in highly intensive and stressful situations, manipulation, the ability to detect the weaknesses of others and to shut out pain, can be very useful in the criminal environment.

These initial survival mechanisms, which can become life-threatening for oneself and others at a later stage, are deeply buried in the nervous system, brain and body, often in the non-verbal parts. Therefore**, deeply transformative and effective approaches are needed to transform the physiological, neurological and psychological circuits and patterns**. Below we will describe IAHV's approach to offender rehabilitation, which addresses this challenge.

Rehabilitation process through the IAHV/Art of Living Prison Program

Through IAHV's Prison programme, offenders experience profound transformation, including changes to the old and deep-rooted patterns and emotions described above.

As described in the Preface, the IAHV/Art of Living Prison Programme is a holistic stress management and rehabilitation programme providing in-depth inner transformation that consequently translates into improved relationships, outlook and engagement with society. The intense 12–20-hour programme contains intensive physical exercises and yoga followed by deep relaxation, advanced breathing techniques including the SKY technique, meditation, life skills, group discussions, self-reflection, cognitive input and wisdom. The effects on the Prison Programme participants described below relate to this whole, comprehensive Programme.

Reviving the capacity of the body to heal in deep rest

When we work with the breath, meditation and conscious body movement, in a bottom-up approach, we are able to access the vitality, resilience and adaptability of the body. Through the sets of profound stress release techniques offered in the IAHV Prison Programme, the body and nervous system become able to relax, permitting the release of accumulated and chronic tensions. As we have described in detail in Chapters 2 and 5, the breath is a central instrument in this process. Before participating in the Prison Program, many participants breathe superficially, don't take deep or full breaths in or out, and their breath has become stuck in a certain rhythm, ready for self-defence at any time. Releasing and changing the breath from this stuck pattern can bring up an initial feeling of defencelessness and lack of control. For some people, the process of letting go can be painful. They may shout, cry, tremble or have muscular spasms until they fully let go. The breathing techniques help to reduce and release emotions of guilt, shame, anxiety, helplessness and insecurity. The release of accumulated physical tensions and negative emotions is an enormous relief. Participants often experience a huge surge in energy, since the energy which used to be bound to the defence mechanisms is now freed up and can be used for positive actions. The nervous system becomes more flexible, homeostasis gets restored, the parasympathetic nervous system can do its work again, and the body and nervous system find their inherent capacity and intelligence to rebalance and heal themselves.

Relaxation of the body supports relaxation of the mind and release of emotions, and vice versa. In this state of deep relaxation, it is possible to leave behind rigidity, hypervigilance, numbness and aggression. In a state of inner calm and security, one finds freedom from the overthinking and overcontrolling brain and returns to the present moment. There is no need for defence mechanisms or aggression. On the contrary, body and mind now actually become able to process what they have experienced.

The experience and reinforcement of this calm inner state enables people to become aware of the deeper causes of patterns, emotions and behaviour within themselves, where previously these were invisible or too painful to face. It becomes possible to look within, and so to come face to face with unpleasant aspects and observe and experience the painful emotions without fully identifying with them and being overwhelmed. An experiential understanding dawns that there is a space that lies beyond all those negative feelings and experiences, a space inside them which is untouched by their false self-image, negative experiences and defence mechanisms. Even a glimpse of this experience helps many of them to believe that change is possible, and that it is attainable without the use of drugs. Many participants share that the effect of the SKY technique, the feeling of elevation, inner freedom, contentment, love, gratitude and deep rest that they experience, is actually better than any experiences they had with drugs.

> *One offender who used drugs to feel ok, came to realize during the programme how stressed he actually felt inside. As a child, at the age of one to six, his mother used to grab his hair and bang his head against the wall, and he had been continuously in a fight or flight mode since. The breathing techniques gave him a sense of joy and happiness without the use of drugs: 'The feeling was just like heroin. In the way that I would just feel present in the moment. I just wanted to lie down, and the only thing I felt was gratitude.'*
>
> *'I can't really begin to tell you the emotional and psychological feelings I'm having now after the course. The peace, serenity, and exhilaration I have got from doing the breathing techniques gave me more euphoria than any drug I've ever taken, and I know that if I continue this in my daily life I'll never use drugs again.' A.K., age twenty-four, Iraq.*

As discussed earlier, the breathing techniques positively affect the production of hormones and neurotransmitters that affect one's mood. This approach is therefore very helpful when one wants to quit drugs or come out of negativity or depression. It gives a feeling of great freedom when you can change how you feel by your own actions. IAHV teaches participants how to use the techniques to regulate their own nervous system, to reduce fear, to calm down or to raise their energy levels at will.

With continuous practice, participants progressively feel stronger and better mentally, emotionally and physically. The moments of peace last longer, until it becomes possible to affirm a positive experience of one's self and even to identify with one's core self. This provides a way to let go of the old self-image and old ways of being in the world. In their place, there develops a sense of a deeper inner self, the core of their being which they may not have felt earlier in life.

> *A very prominent criminal who felt himself to be a big failure and contemplated suicide after he had lost his money and status shared, after completing the Prison Programme: 'I feel that I exist, even though I have lost everything.'*

This process of transformation is not always easy. One participant shared that he had an ambivalent feeling stepping out of the world of crime because people were no longer chasing him or wanting to kill him. On one hand, it was a relief, but on the other hand, he had also lost his status.

One of the most important aspects of the IAHV Prison Programme is that it gives participants the sense that it is okay to be with themselves. They start accepting themselves more as they are, both the pleasant and unpleasant aspects, including those things they previously ran away from. Even more, they become interested and engaged in getting to know themselves better instead of running away from themselves.

They gradually become more aware of their inner 'climate' and build up a tolerance for what is happening inside them without automatically reacting to it. This is the first step for self-regulation.

These individuals develop a capacity to hold their attention in the present moment even when things become uncomfortable, rather than being swayed away into negativity by the effects of past trauma. There is suddenly a capacity to allow impulses, bodily sensations, and feelings to simply be there, without the need to react automatically. One of the most common experiences of participants is to notice that they now think before they act, whereas previously they would simply react mindlessly to situations, often in an aggressive or violent manner. Their rewired physiology allows them to be present and observant, while experiencing sensations that would normally prompt an inappropriate reaction. Many discover that they suddenly start to have a choice of how to respond. With this capacity, change becomes a possibility.

> 'Sometimes during meditation sessions, I suddenly feel angry. My body contracts, and I have a taste like shit in my mouth. Normally, if I feel like this, I find someone to beat up or I just get the hell out. But in here they taught me to sit still. I have now learned that when there is trouble in the prison ward, and I feel the stress, I can just go into my cell and meditate. After a little time, I end up being calm.'
>
> 'I backed out of a fight for the first time, and I just felt calm, sat down afterwards and had a cup of tea as if nothing had happened.'
>
> 'I always get so fuckin mad when doing that damn Sudarshan kriya, but actually it is because I feel so damn sad, and then it gets out. And I love it, because I feel so good afterwards.'

Emergence of empathy

When participants become more connected to themselves, they also start feeling more connected to others. For many participants, empathy emerges for the first time in their lives, or re-emerges after a long absence. Other people are seen again as human beings rather than simply as objects for one's actions. As a result, it becomes more difficult to hurt and harm others.

> 'I was sitting in my car, my heart pounding. I just felt like smashing the skull of that moron. For some reason, I began doing the breathing. Suddenly, my head went calm; it was wild. I would normally have to smoke two or three bongs to snap out of something like this.'

> 'It feels good to be out of this, not having to live up to anything. It was a lot of pressure. If somebody shows me the middle finger now, I no longer need to drag him out of his car and beat him up. And I do not need to look over my shoulder anymore. Empathy has become something valuable; it does something good to me when I feel it.'
>
> 'I am getting too nice, doing this yoga. I cannot maintain my [criminality] business.'

As we have seen earlier, through breathing and meditation it is possible to activate the prefrontal cortex, which strengthens the ability to connect with oneself, with one's own thoughts and feelings as well as with those of others. This makes it physiologically possible to stop and think before acting or reacting, and to feel empathy.

Turning aggression into a constructive force through vulnerability

A considerable part of IAHV's work with traumatized people consists of helping them to see the benefits in owning and containing the vulnerability, sensitivity and emotions they habitually push away. We have seen that aggression can become lodged in the system due to a past traumatic event. However, even when that event is over, people remain stuck with the resultant unhelpful and destructive patterns that remain active as a form of protection. Deep down, they are not only fighting against the actions of others and becoming provoked by what is going on around them. There is also an ongoing inner struggle against the way they perceive themselves, especially if they were to lose a fight, prestige or position.

> 'I wanted to be invincible; I did boxing, karate, and took anabolic steroids; nobody was to touch me. But today I have started being a bit jealous of "normal people", who are able to be close to one another. I would like to know how to do that.'

When past experiences of vulnerability are processed through the deep physiological relaxation experienced on the Prison Programme, the feelings of aggression diminish or can be better integrated as a constructive driving force, rather than destructive. Through experience and cognitive input participants realize that anger and aggression can 'burn' other people or themselves, but can also be used towards something constructive, just like steam.

Learning to choose not to behave aggressively can be a tough and difficult process if everything that has been achieved previously has been through aggressive behaviour. Those for whom this was previously the way to climb up the social ladder might feel this is the only means they know to progress and maintain status. However, where aggression and violence are used in this way, human qualities are also abandoned.

Being in contact with one's own vulnerability makes it possible to feel what you really want and what you really need. Knowing oneself increases the capacity to be able to steer the direction of one's own life, rather than being swayed away by destructive patterns and emotions.

Breaking the cycles of violence through a transformative human-oriented approach to rehabilitation

Traumatic experiences of early childhood are often the underlying cause of living a destructive lifestyle, which has serious consequences for the perpetrators themselves, for society, and for the victims of their violent behaviour. Through the profound bio-psycho-social approach of the IAHV and Art of Living Prison Programme, we have seen that these **deep-rooted patterns, traumas, defence mechanisms, self-identifications and other unhelpful patterns can be released or reduced. These profound transformations allow people to avoid instinctive harmful reactions and instead to respond differently physiologically, mentally and emotionally**. They become able to feel different, more positive emotions, to perceive others and the world around more accurately, and to have a say over their own decision-making process. They can discover and nurture a new sense of self, and envision a new life for themselves.

Offenders become more able and willing to strive for improvement and become more receptive to other forms of rehabilitation. They are empowered to better navigate life outside prison and are prepared with essential life skills to handle stressful situations, live up to their highest potential and contribute in a positive way to society. Over the years, the Prison Programme has given hundreds of thousands of offenders the practical techniques and knowledge to make changes in their lives. Among these are a great many hard-core criminals and those who have been given up on by all other authorities.

Effectively transforming the mindsets, attitudes and behaviour of offenders, the IAHV and Art of Living **Prison Programme provides a solid and effective foundation to break the cycles of violence in our societies at their root and reduce reoffending.**

Case study on the Healing, Resilience and Empowerment workshop: The trauma- and stress-relief intervention of IAHV and the Art of Living

The challenge

In any human crisis, the experience of loss, destruction, violence and trauma can have detrimental consequences for one's mental, emotional, physical and existential well-being. In the worst cases, this can lead to suicide, destructive behaviour, addictions, burnout, PTSD, depression or illness, while in less severe cases, individuals demonstrate the inability to function, decreased motivation and agency, and increased risk of somatic illness and substance abuse.

In these contexts, it is crucial to offer the best relief possible to address acute psychological and psychosomatic needs, and also to prevent and reduce long-term consequences.

While many people affected by trauma and crisis are able to overcome the resultant mental, emotional and physical impact through their own resources of resilience, others may need support to strengthen their coping mechanisms.

However, health care systems and mental health professionals in crises are often overburdened or dysfunctional. Standard psycho-pharmacological, psychotherapeutic and 1-on-1 interventions may be inefficient or ineffective in the face of large-scale disasters affecting millions of people. Also, socio-cultural, language and bureaucratic hurdles may prevent people from getting professional help.

The Healing, Resilience and Empowerment (HRE) workshop

The HRE workshop is a low-threshold workshop to address psychosocial consequences of conflict and violence. It aims to provide people with tools, knowledge and skills to maintain and strengthen their own well-being, releasing acute and basic stress and fears. It further aims to improve sleep, raise energy levels and calm the mind. The HRE workshop is a basic IAHV intervention programme that can reach a large number of individuals while still affecting strong personal benefits.

The HRE workshops are designed to be scalable in the context of large-scale disasters and are accessible and free from stigma for all individuals in need. They are grounded in evidence-based practices with demonstrated immediate impact and are cost-effective relative to pharmaceutical interventions or consultations with mental health professionals. The programme is applicable across diverse cultural settings and emphasizes self-empowerment, so that people do not become unduly dependent on external support. It empowers participants with techniques they can continue practising to independently maintain and improve their well-being without relying extensively on external support from scarce mental health resources.

Given the scale of natural and man-made disasters around the world and limited resources, the provision of self-empowering psychosocial support is crucial to prevent long-term negative consequences, break cycles of violence, and strengthen individual and communal resilience as well as social and economic empowerment.

HRE methodology

- Evidence-based and scientifically researched breathing and relaxation techniques to reduce distress and anxiety, improve sleep, and regain focus and clarity;
- Physical techniques to release tension and stress from the body;
- Knowledge and skills to raise energy levels and handle the mind;
- Interactive discussions and sharing;
- Games;
- The creation of a safe and connecting space.

Target groups

HRE is offered for those affected by violence, war, trauma and conflict. IAHV and the Art of Living Foundation have applied their global expertise in mental well-being, resilience and empowerment to provide support to hundreds of thousands of individuals facing acute crisis situations:

- Syrian refugees and vulnerable Lebanese communities,
- Ukrainians all over Europe and inside Ukraine,
- Afghans who fled the Taliban regime,
- Iranians and Belarusians living through political and social unrest,
- Survivors of domestic violence,
- Communities affected by school shootings in the United States,
- Families of political prisoners in Venezuela,
- People all over the world affected by earthquakes, floods and fires,
- Survivors of terrorist attacks (Manchester, Brussels, New York, . . .)
- Healthcare Workers in the Covid-19 pandemic,
- Families of hostages in Israel, and survivors of the war in Gaza.
- Vulnerable communities in South Africa,

and more.

The straightforward design and demonstrated efficacy of the HRE workshop have provided a lifeline for individuals during severe crises. In some cases, participants have maintained engagement with the workshops even under extreme conditions, such as during active sirens and urban bombings. When a bomb went off a few hundred metres from the course venue in Jaffna, Sri Lanka, the Art of Living teacher checked with the participants if they should postpone the programme. They replied: 'Sir, to these explosions we are all used . . . but the knowledge you are sharing is new and inspiring. So don't bother, let's continue.'[71] Similar situations happened in Kabul, Kiev and other places under bombardments, explosions and attack. It seems that in these intense situations, participants are even more strongly drawn to the life skills, stress management practices, wisdom and human connection provided through the Art of Living and IAHV workshops.

Hundreds of **Afghans** attended online and offline HRE workshops after the Taliban returned to power, which exacerbated the distress of decades of war and violence.

> 'For the last two weeks since being evacuated, every night I was having nightmares that some person was trying to kill me. After the first day of the workshop, that night I did not have any of those nightmares anymore.'

In September 2023, around one hundred thousand **Armenians** were forced to leave their homes in Artsakh/Nagorno Karabakh. In addition to being weak and malnourished after nine months of blockade, many were also caught in military attacks.

> 'I feel I have changed a lot during these days. My body has changed and opened up because of the exercises. I have positive feelings. I feel contentment and feel grateful.'
>   (Marietta, HRE workshop in Gyumri)

On 22 March 2016, **Brussels** experienced two terrorist attacks, during peak hours, at the airport and metro station close to the EU quarter, leaving thirty-two dead, hundreds injured and thousands traumatized.

> 'For two months I have been sleeping with a butcher's knife under my pillow, because I was engulfed by fear. And last night, I put the knife back in the kitchen where it belongs. I didn't sleep peacefully, but I know this is the way forward to break away from my pattern since the Brussels airport bombing.'
> (Survivor of Brussels airport attack, Participant IAHV workshop)

The attack by Hamas on **Israel** on 7 October 2023 and the subsequent war against **Gaza** left millions of people in shock, desperate, grief-stricken and afraid.

> 'I arrived to the HRE workshop exhausted, with a lot of pain, sadness and a sense of futility. Little by little, with each meeting, I felt relief. The day after each meeting, I woke up with more energy, more clarity and an understanding of what I should do in this situation. What's great about the workshop is that you don't have to think about how to feel. It happens spontaneously, like peeling onion skins ... emotions are released. Air enters and stays. Thank you.'
> (Galit Moor, Israel)
>
> 'This workshop should be called not the Art of Living but the Art of Surviving, as it has kept me afloat. This is my second war in two years as I escaped from the war in Ukraine and now I'm living in Israel. Your organization and the techniques which you teach us are probably the best thing which has happened to me during my whole life, but especially during the last twenty-two months ...
>
> I was not able to smile. I tried, but it was not possible for me. But today was different; I gained my smile back, and now I feel happy again, I can laugh again. Everyone should learn these techniques, from our children to the leaders of our countries. This way, we can have a war-free world.'
> (Irina (Ukraine / Israel))

Following the devastating explosion at **Beirut**'s port on 4 August 2020, numerous individuals suffered severe injuries, hundreds lost their lives and hundreds of thousands were forced to flee their homes.

> 'It was the most terrifying moment in my life. I started having daily nightmares, waking up terrified, my heart palpitating. I would imagine the same thing happening again. I had feelings of frustration and despair, and felt there was no solution. I didn't feel how much I benefited until two days

> *after the course. That annoying feeling in me which I didn't know how to kick out was released. I was back to who I was before.'*
> (Fatat Ayad, journalist, participant of HRE workshop in Beirut)

In **South Africa,** HRE workshops have been conducted over many years, in particular to support those badly affected during the Covid pandemic. They have also been run for communities in informal settlements who are struggling with the impact of violence, crime, drugs and poverty.

> *'Now my thoughts are wise.'*
> *'I feel cool within, peaceful, relieved and open-minded.'*
> *'I feel like a new human being.'*

On 6 February 2023, two earthquakes hit **Turkey** and neighbouring Syria, killing more than 65,000 people, levelling whole neighbourhoods and leaving over 3 million without housing.

> *'Before (meeting) you, following the death of my sibling, I did not want to go out at all – not even out of the tent. However, after completing the programme, I began holding myself together and felt much better. So glad that you exist and God bless you.'*
> (Feyza, elementary school teacher, Defne Region)

Ukraine

Living through an ongoing war since February 2022, the daily life of large parts of the population in Ukraine has been disrupted and detrimentally affected by personal losses, sirens, living in shelters, humanitarian crises and unemployment, water and electricity shortages, in addition to stress, anxiety and trauma. Also, those who left to go abroad often struggle with their memories and the trauma of war and their experiences while escaping. They also experience regrets for the life left behind, the loss of role and identity, family separation, adaptation stresses, financial stress, worries and guilt. The World Health Organization estimates that 15 million Ukrainians are in need of mental health and psychosocial support, but Ukrainians generally share that everyone needs support.

Since the war began in Ukraine in February 2022, more than 400 HRE workshops have been conducted for over 8,000 Ukrainians inside Ukraine, as well as for 8,000 Ukrainian refugees outside, including 2,000 children, in more than twenty different countries. The IAHV Ukraine team conducted workshops in frontline territories, de-occupied regions and across Ukraine for children, adults, soldiers, doctors and medical staff, teachers and social workers. They were given to those who escaped from the occupied city of Mariupol and to other displaced people across Ukraine. Workshops were given in shelters, under shelling and outdoors in the regions of Donetsk, Kharkiv, Dnipro, Uzhhorod, Cherkasy, Mykolaiv, Kherson, Odesa, Volyn, Kirovohrad, Kyiv and Zhytomyr.

'I was feeling that I was worth nothing; I was nothing. And now I came back to myself. I can feel myself again. I feel I am not alone'

'We had so much stress and anxiety, a lot to process. This workshop helped us to feel peace and serenity.'

'I now have a smile and I don't know why!'

'The knowledge we gained through the course changes our perspective on life and the way we live.'

'Here I rest, fill myself with energy and become cheerful and joyful. Full of energy I return to my children. I am very grateful for this opportunity to participate in this programme.'

'With the help of our trainers, I can now cope with stress. I have become more aware and centred. I did not feel the interconnection between my body and emotions before. This is a very very useful experience and a great help.'

'On the first day, there was a feeling of tension, fear and aggression among the participants from Ukraine. Within three days the energy and attitude had changed greatly and by Sunday many were able to relax and calm down.'

'The war completely unsettled me. There is a lot of pain inside that you don't know how to cope with and how to continue to live. During these three days, thanks to the techniques, I began to sleep, to worry less. I realized there is a long road ahead of you to work on yourself. Thank you for restoring faith in oneself and one's abilities. It's amazing!'

(Olga Kitchenko)

E. was a very successful fashion designer in Cherson. A strong lady who never cried, she ran a huge business and ran her family with authority. They lived under Russian occupation for eight months, witnessing how people were recruited to cooperate or otherwise locked up in cellars. They managed to be spared collaboration due to health and age. When their flat was destroyed and the art studio closed, they moved to their countryside house on the left bank of the Dnepr River. A few days later, this area became the frontline, and they found Russian soldiers inhabiting the neighbouring houses and entering their home with their weapons. One night under bombardment, they managed to escape through Russian-occupied territory, but while doing this, she fell and injured her arm. They stayed outdoors overnight and travelled for several days to reach Lithuania, where their daughter lives. However, the fireworks at New Year would send shocks through her system, and the image of people enjoying life would cause immense pain.

Following her arrival in Lithuania, E broke down. She could not stop crying, relived the whole awful experience of the war, of the people who died, the senseless destruction, and the looting of her beloved city. She felt pain for all the people who were left behind, moral disappointment in people she considered close, loss of purpose and meaning, lack of energy, loss of her identity and role, lack of any perspective and the feeling of being nobody in her family and in the world.

When she arrived at the HRE workshop, three months after their escape, E was still reliving this experience daily. In a state of shock, she talked continuously about all that had happened and how desperate she felt. Her body and nerves were visibly tense, and she would burst out in tears uncontrollably.

A few days into the workshop, she said she had stopped taking Valerian tranquillizers and she was now able to manage and sleep. Over the final days, she became very relaxed, her eyes started to shine, she started enjoying the blue sky with the white clouds, the company and the present moment. She said she felt grateful for life and for finding happiness again. Filled with gratitude, she has a vision to bring this knowledge and techniques to all the people in Cherson.

Key points: Chapter 5

Who are we as peacebuilders?

The quality and impact of our work is to a great extent defined by who we are as 'peacebuilders' and how we engage with communities and the people we work and interact with on the ground.

The 'professionalization' of the field has come with increased technocracy, bureaucracy, specialized jargon and other forms of specialization that leads the field sometimes far away from the reality of people in conflict zones and from effective impact on the ground.

Sustainable integration of comprehensive psychosocial approaches into peacebuilding policy, practice and theory, and the resultant increased impact of peacebuilding work, will be embedded in and developed from the way we as peacebuilders connect and integrate within ourselves and our teams.

In IAHV's approach the peacebuilder herself is central to the peacebuilding action: the qualities, skills, self-awareness and personality of the peacebuilder are not just a nice addendum, but core to the possible impact and effectiveness of peacebuilding initiatives.

IAHV has developed a specialized training programme entitled 'Towards Integrated Peacebuilding: Psychosocial Well-being, Knowledge and Skills for Increased Peacebuilding Impact' to equip professional peacebuilders and peacebuilding organizations with the well-being, knowledge and skills to incorporate psychosocial competencies and self-care into their work.

The role of Stress, Energy and Trauma

The impact that **stress** has upon the quality of our work as peacebuilders is often underestimated.

Energy, as opposed to apathy, is necessary to create agency, ability and drive to achieve positive personal and social change. It is therefore of crucial importance to learn skills and tools to raise individual and group **energy levels**.

The changes in brain, body, psychology, and behaviour due to **trauma** can have longer-term negative effects on relationships, social interactions, work and performance. 'Psycho-biological traumatic re-enactment' stands in the way of peaceful relations with oneself and others. Indeed, the provision of tools to restore and strengthen homeostasis, to release stress and trauma from the body-mind complex, is a fundamental aspect of peacebuilding at the individual, interpersonal, intergroup and broader societal level, and crucial to restore the capacity for social engagement, communication and peaceful coexistence.

IAHV's model of intrapersonal transformation: 7 levels of existence

The **breath** is a practical tool to manage stress, prevent burnout, release trauma, strengthen resilience and optimize overall well-being and potential.

The mind functions optimally when it is relaxed, free of stress, and with its attention fully in the present moment. Breathing techniques and meditation are effective ways to bring the mind in the present moment, free it from its occupations and entanglements, raise its energy level to come out of negativity and worries, and remove unhelpful and unnecessary impressions. The quality of our perception, observation and expression directly influences our ability to interact skilfully and constructively to situations and people around us. IAHV programmes provide cognitive understanding about the functioning of the mind together with practical tools to manage the mind more easily.

In order to resolve conflict, prevent violence and create peaceful relationships, it is crucial to work on the sets of beliefs, judgements, narratives, understandings and prejudices that are present in the **intellect**, both at the personal level and at the social level. They are flexible in nature and can be used in either a beneficial or harmful manner, to enrich and support our life and the lives of others, or to limit and undermine them.

Individual and social memory can function rather as a source of learning and wisdom, and an inspiration for progress and peace, instead of being an instigator of conflict and an obstacle to its resolution.

Unhelpful self-identification can be limiting and create separation, aggression and tension, while a more expanded understanding of one's **identity,** such as being part of the human race as a whole, can lead to peaceful and meaningful interactions with the people and the world around us. The capacity to flexibly identify with and engage different identities as and where appropriate is an important skill for conflict prevention and source of resilience.

The Self is where inner peace lies. And it is present in every human being.

Emotions, when acted out in destructive or aggressive ways, are a major contributor to ongoing cycles of conflict. Emotional intelligence refers to the capacity to understand, regulate and manage one's own emotions while also understanding other people's emotions and needs and act in the most appropriate way according to the situation.

The levels of our existence can be further developed and refined, not just to mitigate the negative effects of stress but also to **optimize the full spectrum of human potential**.

The **strongest empowerment** is the ability to master our own mind, emotions, impressions and reactions, and to act skilfully in the world.

Therefore, we need to take **responsibility and ownership** of our own thoughts, emotions and reactions, instead of blaming external factors.

Active non-violence is a path of deep personal transformation, since the outer action of non-violence is inextricably linked to the inner workings of the heart, mind, and spirit of the individual. A deeper understanding and experience of non-violence includes non-violence not only in actions, but also in words, thoughts and feelings.

Adverse Childhood Experiences and Criminality – IAHV's Approach to Offender Rehabilitation

Traumatizing experiences, and especially those experienced in early childhood, can lead often to dysfunctional behaviour, violence and crime. **IAHV's Prison Programme provides a solid and effective foundation to break the cycles of violence in our societies at their root and reduce reoffending.** Deeply transformative and effective approaches transform the physiological, neurological and psychological circuits and patterns. These profound transformations allow people to avoid instinctive harmful reactions and instead to respond differently physiologically, mentally and emotionally.

Natural and man-made disasters: The IAHV Healing, Resilience and Empowerment Workshop

The provision of self-empowering psychosocial support is crucial to prevent long-term negative consequences, break cycles of violence, and strengthen individual and communal resilience as well as social and economic empowerment.

Chapter 5 Recommended reading

Fitzduff, M. 2021. *Our Brains at War: The Neuroscience of Conflict and Peacebuilding*. OUP.

Hertog, K. 2019. 'Towards integrated peacebuilding: Comprehensively integrating psychosocial factors in peacebuilding trainings and programmes for increased impact'. *Journal of Peacebuilding & Development* 14:3, pp. 333–9. https://doi.org/10.1177/1542316619862766.

Levine, P. A., & Kline, M. 2006. *Trauma Through a Child's Eyes: Awakening the Ordinary Miracle of Healing*. North Atlantic Books.

Lund, J. 2017. 'Survival mechanisms that become life threatening'. In Hviid, S. (Ed.), *Traumebehandling og Resocialisering*. Turbine Akademisk.

Nestor, J. 2020. *Breath: The New Science of a Lost Art*. Riverhead Books.

Neuroscience and Peacebuilding Initiative. 2015. https://www.neuropeace.org/volumes.

Rausch, C. (Ed.). May 2021. *Neuroscience and Peacebuilding*. Neuropeace 3.

Van der Kolk, B. A. 2014. *The Body Keeps the Score: Brain, Mind, and Body in the Healing of Trauma*. Viking.

Notes

1 The model and layers presented here are more detailed than those described in Chapter Two, as they only pertain to the intrapersonal dimension.

2   Travouillon, K. 2021. 'Emotions and post-liberal peacebuilding'. In Jeong, H. W. (Ed.), *Transitions to Peace. Between Norms and Practice* (1 ed., Vol. 1, pp. 51–70). Rowman & Littlefield Publishers Inc., pp. 51–2.

3   Travouillon, K. 2021, pp. 62, 63, 65.

4   Swiss Agency for Development and Cooperation. S.a. 'Psychosocial conflict analysis'. Fastenopfer. p. 5. https://www.ziviler-friedensdienst.org/sites/default/files/media/file/2022/zfd-die-psychosoziale-konfliktanalyse-1958_184.pdf.

5   Antares Foundation. 2012. 'Managing stress in humanitarian workers: Guidelines for good practice'; Dunkley, F. 2018. *Psychosocial Support for Humanitarian Aid Workers: A Roadmap of Trauma and Critical Incident Care*. Routledge/Taylor & Francis Group. https://doi.org/10.4324/9781315201450.

6   www.iahv.org , https://uploads-ssl.webflow.com/60b0461ace7a9afaeb3f142f/60bb478d3288c5f9186cf225_Universal-Declaration-of-Human-Values.pdf

7   Kumar, S. 2023. *Militancy to Meditation*. Sri Sri Publications Trust, p. xxiv.

8   https://www.iahv-peace.org/services/professional-training-towards-integrated-peacebuilding-psychosocial-skills-and-professional-care-for-peacebuilders-in-the-field/.

9   Global Peace Initiative. 'Societal Stress'. https://globalpeaceproject.net/societal-stress/ (consulted 24 Sept 2024).

10 WHO. 'Mental health in emergencies'. 16 March 2022. https://www.who.int/news-room/fact-sheets/detail/mental-health-in-emergencies (consulted 24 Sept 2024).

11 Miolene, E. 'Burnout is hitting humanitarians — but not for the reasons you'd think'. Devex https://www.devex.com/news/burnout-is-hitting-humanitarians-but-not-for-the-reasons-you-d-think-108225 (consulted 7 Sept 2024); Lopes, C. B., et al. 2012. 'Psychological distress, depression, anxiety, and burnout among international humanitarian aid workers: A longitudinal study'. *PLoS One* 7:9, p. e44948. https://doi.org/10.1371/journal.pone.0044948. PMCID: PMC3440316.

12 World Health Organization. Kestel, D. 2019. 'Mental health in the workplace'. https://www.who.int/news-room/commentaries/detail/mental-health-in-the-workplace (consulted 24 Sept 2024).

13 Bramsen, I., & Poder, P. 2018. 'Emotional dynamics in conflict and conflict transformation'. Berghof Foundation, p. 2.

14 Rausch, C. (Ed.). May 2021. *Neuroscience and Peacebuilding*. Neuropeace 3, p. 25.

15 The below is largely based on van der Kolk, B. A. 2014. *The Body Keeps the Score: Brain, Mind, and Body in the Healing of Trauma*. Viking.

16 Porges, S. W. 2001. *The Polyvagal Theory: Neurophysiological Foundations of Emotions, Attachment, Communication, and Self-Regulation*. New York, NY: Norton.

17 Huguenard, F. 'The vagus nerve and the healing promise of The Sudarshan Kriya'. https://www.artofliving.org/us-en/the-vagus-nerve-and-the-healing-promise-of-Sudarshan-Kriya (consulted 26 Mar 2024).

18 Van der Kolk, B. A. 2015, p. 47.
19 Van der Kolk, B. A. 2015, p. 63.
20 Levine, P. A. 1997. *Waking the Tiger: Healing Trauma*. North Atlantic Books.
21 Rausch, C. (Ed.) May 2021, p. 32.
22 Ibidem.
23 Shah, S. '7 common ways of vagus nerve stimulation to nourish your body and mind'. https://www.artofliving.org/us-en/7-natural-ways-to-strengthen-and-stimulate-your-vagus-nerve-today (consulted 25 Mar 2024).
24 Rausch, C. (Ed.) May 2021, p. 46.
25 Art of Living. 2007. 'Rebuilding War Torn Kosovo: Art of Living Report', p. 24.
26 Rausch, C. (Ed.) May 2021, p. 31.
27 See Chapter 2.
28 Chu, P., Gotink, R. A., Yeh, G. Y., Goldie, S. J., & Hunink, M. G. 2016. 'The effectiveness of yoga in modifying risk factors for cardiovascular disease and metabolic syndrome: A systematic review and meta-analysis of randomized controlled trials'. *European Journal of Preventive Cardiology* Feb 23:3, pp. 291–307. https://doi.org/10.1177/2047487314562741. Epub 2014 Dec 15. PMID: 25510863.
29 From Engel, G. L. 1977. 'The need for a new medical model: A challenge for biomedicine'. *Science* 196:4286, pp. 129–36 to McEwen, B. S. 2007. 'Physiology and neurobiology of stress and adaptation: Central role of the brain'. *Physiological Reviews* 87:3, pp. 873–904 and more.
30 Biddle, S. J. H., Fox, K., & Boutcher, S. (Eds.). 2000. *Physical Activity and Psychological Well-Being*. Routledge. https://doi.org/10.4324/9780203468326; Penedo, F. J., & Dahn, J. R. 2005. 'Exercise and well-being: A review of mental and physical health benefits associated with physical activity'. *Current Opinion in Psychiatry* Mar 18:2, pp. 189–93. https://doi.org/10.1097/00001504-200503000-00013. PMID: 16639173; Dishman, R. K., et al. 2005. 'Self-management strategies mediate self-efficacy and physical activity'. *American Journal of Preventive Medicine* 29:1, pp. 10–18; Magnan, R. E., Kwan, B. M., & Bryan, A. D. 2013. 'Effects of current physical activity on affective response to exercise: Physical and social-cognitive mechanisms'. *Psychology & Health* 28:4, pp. 418–33; Taylor, C. B., Salli, J. F., & Needle, R. 1985. 'The relation of physical activity and exercise to mental health'. *Public Health Reports* 100:2, pp. 195–202.
31 Richter, A., Krämer, B., Diekhof, E. K., & Gruber, O. 2019. 'Resilience to adversity is associated with increased activity and connectivity in the VTA and hippocampus'. *NeuroImage: Clinical* 23, p. 101920; Killgore, W. D. S., Olson, E. A., & Weber, M. 2013. 'Physical exercise habits correlate with gray matter volume of the hippocampus in healthy adult humans'. *Scientific Reports* 3, p. 3457.
32 Basso, J. C., & Suzuki, W. A. 2017. 'The effects of acute exercise on mood, cognition, neurophysiology, and neurochemical pathways: A review'. *Brain Plast* 2:2, pp. 127–52. https://doi.org/10.3233/BPL-160040. PMCID: PMC5928534.
33 Segerstrom, S. C., & Miller, G. E. 2004. 'Psychological stress and the human immune system: A meta-analytic study of 30 years of inquiry'. *Psychological Bulletin* 130:4, pp. 601–30. https://doi

.org/10.1037/0033-2909.130.4.601. PMCID: PMC1361287; Fredrickson, B. L. 2001. 'The role of positive emotions in positive psychology: The broaden-and-build theory of positive emotions'. *American Psychologist* 56:3, pp. 218–26. https://doi.org/10.1037/0003-066X.56.3.218.

34 Website National Library of Medicine: https://www.ncbi.nlm.nih.gov/pmc/ (consulted Feb 2024).

35 Nestor, J., 2020. *Breath: The New Science of a Lost Art*. Riverhead Books, p. 143.

36 Popov, T. A. 2011. 'Human exhaled breath analysis'. *Annals of Allergy, Asthma & Immunology* 106:6, pp. 451–6. https://doi.org/10.1016/j.anai.2011.02.016. PMID: 21624743; Tien-Chueh Kuo, et al. 2020. 'Human breathomics database'. Volume 2020, baz139, https://doi.org/10.1093/database/baz139.

37 Nestor, J. 2020, p. 144.

38 See Nestor, J. 2020, pp. 41–2.

39 Nestor, J. 2020, p. 152.

40 Homma, I., & Masaoka, Y. 2008. 'Breathing rhythms and emotions'. *Experimental Physiology* 93:9, pp. 1011–21. https://doi.org/10.1113/expphysiol.2008.042424. Epub 2008 May 16. PMID: 18487316.

41 Nestor, J. 2020.

42 See dozens of meta-analyses in PubMed, USA National Library of Medicine (consulted February 2024): https://pubmed.ncbi.nlm.nih.gov/?term=meditation%5BMeSH+Terms%5D&filter=pubt.meta-analysis&filter=pubt.review&filter=pubt.systematicreview&filter=ds1.y_5&filter=species.humans&filter=language.english&sort=pubdate.

43 Rausch, C. (Ed.) May 2021, p. 32.

44 Ibidem.

45 Hölzel, B. K., et al. 2011. 'Mindfulness practice leads to increases in regional brain gray matter density'. *Psychiatry Research: Neuroimaging* 191:1, pp. 36–43. https://doi.org/10.1016/j.pscychresns.2010.08.006.

46 Nickerson, R. S. 1998. 'Confirmation bias: A ubiquitous phenomenon in many guises'. *Review of General Psychology* 2:2, pp. 175–220.

47 Tversky, A., & Kahneman, D. 1974. 'Judgment under uncertainty: Heuristics and biases'. *Science* 185:4157, pp. 1124–31.

48 Swami Virupaksha, 2022, p. 35, 46, 48.

49 El-Hibri Foundation. 2015. 'Neuroscience and peacebuilding: Reframing how we think about conflict and prejudice'. Jan 2015 Conference Proceedings, Washington DC.

50 Baumeister, R. F., Bratslavsky, E., Finkenauer, C., & Vohs, K. D. 2001. 'Bad is stronger than good'. *Review of General Psychology* 5:4, pp. 323–70. https://doi.org/10.1037/1089-2680.5.4.323.

51 Bar Tal, D. 2013, p. 81.

52 Tajfel cited in Bar Tal, D. 2013, p. 80.

53 Bar Tal, D. 2013, p. 80.

54 Bar Tal, D. 2013, p. 81.

55 Bar Tal, D. 2013, p. 82.

56 Sri Sri Ravi Shankar. "Unless Every Member of Our Global Family Is Peaceful, Our Peace Is Incomplete." Message on the occasion of the United Nations International Peace Day, September 21. The Art of Living Global. Accessed Nov 2, 2025. https://www.artofliving.org/'unless-every-member-our-global-family-peaceful-our-peace-incomplete'

57 Damasio, A. R. 1994. *Descartes' Error: Emotion, Reason, and the Human Brain*. New York, NY: Putnam; Loewenstein, G., & Lerner, J. S. (2003). 'The role of affect in decision making'. In *Handbook of Affective Science* (pp. 619–42). Oxford University Press; Lerner, J. S., Li, Y., Valdesolo, P., & Kassam, K. S. 2015. 'Emotion and decision making'. *Annual Review of Psychology* 66, pp. 799–823. https://doi.org/10.1146/annurev-psych-010213-115043. Epub 2014 Sep 22. PMID: 25251484.

58 Lindner, E. 2006. *Making Enemies: Humiliation and International Conflict*. https://doi.org/10.5040/9798400681479.

59 Homma, I., & Masaoka, Y. 2008.

60 Dierdorff, E., & Rubin, R. 2015. 'Research: We're not very self-aware, especially at work'. Harvard Business Review, March issue.

61 Kool, V. K., & Agrawal, R. 2020. 'The psychology of nonviolence: Models and their validation'. In *Gandhi and the Psychology of Nonviolence*, Volume 1. Cham: Palgrave Macmillan. https://doi.org/10.1007/978-3-030-56865-8_7; Chenoweth, E., & Stephan, M. J. 2011. *Why Civil Resistance Works: The Strategic Logic of Nonviolent Conflict*. Columbia University Press; Sharp, G. 1973. *The Politics of Nonviolent Action*. Porter Sargent Publishers.

62 Hertog, K. 2010. *The Complex Reality of Religious Peacebuilding: Conceptual Contributions and Critical Analysis*. Rowman & Littlefield, pp. 53–4.

63 Graber, R., Pichon, F., & Carabine, E. 2015. 'Psychological resilience: State of knowledge and future research agendas'. Working paper, Overseas Development Institute. https://www.odi.org/sites/odi.org.uk/files/odi-assets/publications-opinion-files/9872.pdf (retrieved on 19 Dec 2020).

64 Lund, J. 2017. 'Survival mechanisms that become life threatening'. In Hviid, S. (Ed.), *Traumebehandling og Resocialisering*. Turbine Akademisk.

65 Van der Kolk, B. A. 1989. 'The compulsion to repeat the trauma: Re-enactment, revictimization, and masochism'. *Psychiatric Clinics of North America* 12:2, pp. 389–411.

66 Ardino, V. 2012. 'Offending behaviour: The role of trauma and PTSD'. *European Journal of Psychotraumatology* 3, Article 18968. https://doi.org/10.3402/ejpt.v3i0.18968; Greenwald, R. (Ed.). 2002. *Trauma and Juvenile Delinquency: Theory, Research, and Interventions*. NY: Haworth Press; Neller, D. J., Denney, R. L., Pietz, C. A., & Thomlinson, R. P. 2006. 'The relationship between trauma and violence in a jail inmate sample'. *Journal of Interpersonal Violence* 21:9, pp. 1234–41. https://doi.org/10.1177/0886260506290663. PMID: 16893968.

67 Morey, R. A., et al. 2015. 'Fear learning circuitry is biased toward generalization of fear associations in posttraumatic stress disorder'. *Translational Psychiatry* Dec 15; 5:12, p. e700. https://doi.org/10.1038/tp.2015.196. PMCID: PMC5068591.

68 Levine, P. A., & Kline, M. 2006. *Trauma Through a Child's Eyes: Awakening the Ordinary Miracle of Healing*. North Atlantic Books.

69 Siegel, L. J. 2011. *Criminology*. Wadsworth Publishing. ISBN 10: 0495912468, p. 125.

70 Chefetz, R., Solomon, M., & Siegel, D. J. (Eds.). 2003. 'Healing trauma: Attachment, mind, body and brain'. New York: W. W. Norton. *American Journal of Clinical Hypnosis* 47:4, pp. 265–7. https://doi.org/10.1080/00029157.2005.10403641.

71 Swami Virupaksha, 2022.

6 Weaving a peaceful social fabric – Interpersonal and intergroup peacebuilding

The socio-psychological repertoire, infrastructure and culture of conflict and peace – generation, escalation and resolution of interpersonal and intergroup conflicts

Conflict, violence and war are most often characterized by dysfunctional or broken connections and relationships between individuals, groups and societies. **The restoration of social connections at different levels, the reweaving of the overall social fabric, and conscious transformation of conflictual relationships into peaceful ones, are a critical foundation for sustainable peace.** Strong social cohesion can in itself serve as a prevention for social ruptures.

In this chapter, we will unpack some of the psychosocial dynamics of interpersonal and social conflict with reference to existing theories, evidence and insights on social identity and psychodynamics. With reference to Bar-Tal's framework, we will describe the different stages of the development of a socio-psychological repertoire, infrastructure and culture of conflict and peace. **Psychosocial factors are crucial in the generation, escalation and resolution of interpersonal and intergroup conflicts and can be addressed and transformed at the roots at each of these stages.** The in-depth insights of Bar-Tal, together with IAHV's philosophy and methodology, form the basis of the analysis in this chapter and of the practical model suggested to help in the understanding and handling of the 'psyche' of individuals and collectives involved in conflict and peacebuilding. Bar-Tal has studied centuries of intergroup and intractable. Conflicts around the world, with a special focus on the transgenerational conflict in Israel-Palestine. IAHV's model of intrapersonal transformation presented in the previous chapter is elaborated upon as the foundation for interpersonal peacebuilding and the creation of cultures of peace. We will propose how the transformation of psychosocial factors can prevent violence, break the cycles of conflict, create cultures of peace and lay the foundation for sustainable peace. Through the practice of Psychosocial Peacebuilding it is possible to transform the values, emotions, beliefs, attitudes and behaviour of groups in conflict, and so to transform cultures of conflict and war into cultures of peace. This will be illustrated with a practical case study on reconciliation between warring tribes in Ivory Coast. **Through the transformation of**

psychosocial factors at the interpersonal and intergroup levels, we lay a foundation for peaceful coexistence, social cohesion and eventually sustainable peace.

The challenge of conflict

Conflict is a natural phenomenon and part of life among people who differ in multiple ways, such as in their interests, beliefs, values, socialization, cultures, worldviews and so on. Interpersonal conflict emerges when two or more parties perceive an incompatibility in their goals or interests and express this or act on that.

Conflict and its management can be positive when it generates dynamism, progress, evolution and necessary change. This can be the case, for example, when innovative policies are developed, immoral practices opposed or cultural and structural violence transformed.

The challenge that peacebuilders seek to address is the negative, harmful or violent expression and management of conflict, as well as the transformation of the root causes of conflict. Conflict resolution can be understood in a limited way as the finding of solutions for conflict issues that will satisfy the parties involved. In this book, however, **we focus on an approach to conflict transformation and peacebuilding that entails a deeper transformation of attitudes, emotions, mindsets, relationships, behaviour, communication and social systems.**

How do we respond to conflict? Interpersonal conflict and conflict styles

When interpersonal or intergroup conflicts arise, people and groups have different ways of responding. **At the initial stage of conflict generation, the way we respond to the challenge of conflict can greatly influence the process and the outcome of these conflicts.**

How we respond to the challenge of an arising conflict depends on many factors, such as upbringing, context, culture and experience. Bar Tal speaks of **inner constructs or schemas, which define how we perceive a certain situation, whether we identify that situation as a conflict, and how we respond to it**. For example, people who find it difficult to deal with ambiguous situations tend to view ambivalent situations more often as conflicts.[1] Our conflict schema can be either non-hostile or hostile. Hostile conflict schemas cause a sharper detection of conflict and are characterized by a preference for the application of harsher measures to address the situations perceived, while non-hostile conflict schemas may not even perceive conflict in the first place. Our inner schemas and patterns generate different emotions when faced with conflict, ranging from anger, hatred and frustration to challenge and excitement. Inner schemas also define **preferences to avoid conflicts, to settle them constructively or to engage with them in a firm or forceful manner**. This corresponds with different behavioural responses, such as flight, appeasement, ignoring, compromise or fight. These schemas can change through life and are also flexible according to the spheres of life (e.g. at work or at home).[2] Just as these schemas and patterns are different for different individuals, different cultures will also identify and respond differently to conflicts.

In conflict resolution theory, generally **five different conflict styles** are distinguished (Figure 6.1).

Animal	Conflict Style	Behaviour	Benefits	Limitations
TURTLE 	**AVOIDING** • Denying a problem • Pretending not to notice	• Leaving a situation • Holding back feelings and opinions	• When confronting seems dangerous • When you need more time to prepare	• The problem may never be resolved • Emotions may explode later
SHARK 	**CONFRONTING** • Getting what you want no matter what • Some people win, some lose	• Interruption / taking over • Ignoring other's feelings and ideas • Loud tone of voice • Sometimes use physical violence	• When immediate action is needed • When you believe in the absolute rightness of your action and don't see any other choice	• This style can make people defensive and can make a conflict worse • This style can make it hard for others to express how they feel
CAMELION 	**ACCOMODATING** • Giving in to other person's point of view • Paying attention to other's concerns and not your own	• Apologising / saying yes to end the conflict • Letting others interrupt or ignore your feelings, ideas	• When you think you've made a mistake or that you don't really understand the situation • When smoothing over is important for keeping a relationship	• You may work hard to please others but never be happy yourself • Being nice doesn't always solve the problem
ZEBRA 	**COMPROMISING** • Each person wins some and loses some	• Interested in finding a solution • Show desire to talk about the problem	• When you need a fast decision on a small issue • When nothing else works	• You may fix the immediate conflict but not the bigger problem • Each person may not end up happy
OWL 	**PROBLEM SOLVING** • Finding a solution that makes everyone happy • Looking closely at the sources of the conflict	• Addressing your feelings, needs, and wants • Listening to others	• Can make someone who is stubborn move towards resolving a problem	• This requires Time and good communication skills

Figure 6.1 *Conflict styles.*

When we are negatively affected by stress or pressure, such as strong negative emotions or an acutely activated stress response system, our conflict style may become more destructive and unhelpful. It is understood that different conflict styles may be useful in different situations. For example, it may be better to avoid engagement in a conflict in times of heated and dangerous escalation, while it may be necessary to actively confront a conflict to save people's lives in a critical situation.

As individuals, we may all have one or more personal conflict styles that feel most natural to us. In some situations, however, it will be more appropriate, safe or constructive to adopt a conflict style that is different from our usual default pattern.

Application

In order to be able to **apply the most appropriate conflict style in any situation, clear perception, self-awareness, self-management and skilful expression are crucial.** This requires an inner state and sensitivity to be able to perceive, feel and connect to one's own needs, feelings and values. The interoception and self-awareness to sense and distinguish one's feelings and needs include acknowledging and coming face to face with deeply hidden, unpleasant and potentially traumatic experiences and emotions. This process requires courage and sincerity. At the same time, skilful conflict management and resolution also require the inner state, sensitivity and empathy to be able to connect with the needs, feelings, values and interests of others. **When one is centred and connected, it becomes easier to simultaneously consider one's own needs and those of others without violating any of them.**

In order to keep the mind clear, manage strong emotions and stay centred in stressful situations and conflict, it is important to have practical and effective tools for stress-relief and stress management. Breathing and meditation practices can significantly calm down the stress response system and reduce and remove feelings of negativity and hostility, the inclination to conflict and confrontation, and the seeds of anger and discontent. At the same time, these practices nurture feelings of contentment and compassion and foster tendencies to bring peace and harmony. Awareness and an understanding of human behaviour, a broader perspective on life and applied wisdom can strengthen emotional, mental and physical stability during conflict and chaos. When we are centred, we can **perceive, observe and express ourselves in the most appropriate way according to the situation**. This greatly influences how we perceive and respond to conflict.

In order to handle conflicts with more empathy, effectiveness and balance, individuals with a passive turtle and chameleon-like conflict style may need to strengthen their connection with themselves, increase inner strength and self-confidence. Conversely, individuals with a more aggressive shark-like conflict style may need to strengthen anger management, patience and sensitivity.

In all conflict situations, communication is key.

> 'Effective communication is necessary. Wars begin when communication breaks down. When words do not work, then we try to do it with weapons, and when weapons don't work, we try to come back to words.'
> (Gurudev Sri Sri Ravi Shankar)

The **practice of non-violent communication (NVC) encompasses the strengths of the different conflict styles** and aligns with the balance between one's own interests and those of others (Table 6.1).

Table 6.1 *The 4 Main Steps in Non-violent communication*

The 4 main steps in non-violent communication
1. Observation: Clearly and objectively describe what you are observing in a situation without projections, interpretations, judgements or blame. In order to observe facts and behaviour as they are, it is important to keep a clear mind, be aware and have an open intellect.
2. Feelings: Express your feelings related to the observation. Identify, articulate and connect to your emotions, without assigning blame.
3. Needs: Communicate the underlying needs or values that are causing your feelings. This step helps to connect your emotions to your deeper needs.
4. Requests: Make a specific, actionable request that could help meet your needs. Ensure the request is clear and doable, and is framed as a positive action.

Stress management, self-awareness and self-management are necessary for skilful perception, observation and expression in conflict situations. These elements form the foundation for achieving the most constructive and appropriate outcomes in any conflict situation. Based on the words of Patanjali, the propounder of yoga, we could say that 'Yoga is skill in action, including in conflict.'

Intergroup conflict

In addition to the dynamics of interpersonal conflict, intergroup conflict brings with it specific psychosocial challenges as well as opportunities.

The origin of intergroup conflict: Perception of threat, real or imagined, and lack of trust

Intergroup conflict often arises from a perceived threat, real or imagined, towards one's security, prosperity, identity, worldview and other interests and values. Researchers have found that the human mind is more responsive to indications of threat and risk than to indications of peace, safety and coexistence.[3] Therefore, both real or perceived threats can easily instigate and escalate conflict. **Perception of threat increases stress levels, and increased stress levels cause groups to become more vulnerable and sensitive to threats.** This in turn easily leads to a breakdown of effective communication and an inability to perceive or listen to the other's point of view, which is essential for the management of conflicts.

Application

It is therefore important for leaders in society to analyse a situation as it actually is, rather than as it is imagined or projected to be. It is essential **to manage effectively the community's stress response to the perceived threat**. To do this, it is necessary to maintain open communication with the other party so as to address the issues, while also communicating the best possible course of action to one's own group and avoiding unnecessary stress and harm. This requires clear perception, wise and correct interpretation as well as clear and appropriate communication.

The emergence of intergroup conflict

When intergroup conflict breaks out, Bar Tal distinguishes three important psychological challenges:

(1) The psychological need for safety and for having a say over one's destiny

(2) The need to learn to cope with stress, fears and other negative psychological phenomena

(3) The need to develop psychological resources to win over the rivalry

According to Bar Tal, the study of intractable conflicts shows that it is much easier to mobilize people on a path to violent conflict than on a path of peace making. He sees a variety of combined reasons for this:[4]

- Firstly, human beings are more perceptive of threats and risks than they are of peaceful indicators. This is a built-in mechanism to ensure survival and the preservation of life and security. Threats and risks are perceived to require immediate action and response.
- Fear is activated without effort and cognitive control, while hope, which is essential for societal peacemaking, requires some cognitive processing. People may be programmed with specific responses to fear from past experience, such as defence or aggression, while hope requires the conceiving of new behaviours towards a new desired goal.
- People are more perceptive to negative information about potential harm than to positive information about peace opportunities.
- The psychology of terror management has shown that the threat of death can create constant terror and the belief in the need to defend oneself against it.

Application

Even at this initial stage of emerging group conflict, the resourceful application of psychosocial resources can influence the experience and the course of the conflict.

Individuals who are resilient and have a larger 'window of tolerance' to stress, whose nervous system is stable and not prone to traumatic reactions, and who can remain centred in the face of challenge with a clear and focused mind, will be able to respond to the conflict in the best possible way. Fears, stress and anxiety can be significantly reduced through effective breathing techniques. Raising the energy levels of individuals can help reduce the negativity bias. The individual ego and collective willpower can be engaged positively for rising to the challenge. Regardless of the outcome, there will be a sense of empowerment in the directing of one's destiny rather than of being helpless and at the receiving end. Leaders and groups comprised of such individuals are more likely to discern the best course of action and possess the resources to successfully implement it. Leaders and groups with unprocessed trauma and its associated symptoms and reactions, who are governed by existential fear, driven by a sense of victimhood from the past, who are more affected by events and less able to self-master, and who react to situations rather than respond to them, will more likely be caught up in the escalating dynamics of conflict and violence, without having much sense of a say in their own destiny.

The polarization of intergroup conflict and the development of a socio-psychological repertoire

In order to meet the challenges of intergroup conflict, societies develop a socio-psychological repertoire that includes shared beliefs, attitudes, motivations and emotions. The function of such a repertoire is **to enable sense to be made of the situation, to provide a meaningful and coherent narrative, to construct a strong identity which is distinct from and superior to the opponent, to motivate the population to mobilize for action and withstand losses and difficult life conditions. It also justifies any violent actions of the group against the opponent.** Such a socio-psychological repertoire on the ethos of the conflict has different elements:

- *Conflict narrative and justification*: a coherent narrative about the conflict is constructed, which includes related collective memories from the past, an agreed history of the conflict, societal beliefs concerning it, the risks and threats involved, as well as the conflict justifications and goals. Engagement in the conflict is justified, because its goals are presented as being just and of great and sometimes even existential importance. Hence, the human sacrifices made in pursuit of these goals and the violence committed against the opponent also become justified.

- *A positive collective self-image*: As part of the conflict dynamic, the binding and integrating elements of the group identity – such as a shared past, destiny, culture, beliefs and sense of belonging – are strengthened, while differences with other groups are emphasized. A positive, glorifying image of one's own group is reinforced and propagated, providing a sense of security and boosting motivation. Group members become emotionally involved or participate directly in conflicts as part of their collective, driven by shared goals and interests. The own group is ascribed a range of positive characteristics and is humane and moral, in contrast to the evil nature of the opposing group. Bravery and heroism in withstanding the enemy are emphasized. Elements of social identity that are not helpful – such as atrocities committed by one's own group – are denied and censored, or they are minimalized, rationalized and justified as exceptional and due to circumstances.

- *Delegitimization of the opponent*: Delegitimization denies the humanity of the opponent and justifies harming them. The opponent is considered responsible for the outbreak of the conflict and its continuation. They are viewed as lacking peaceful or positive intentions and are seen instead as intending to cause harm or even to pose an existential threat to one's own group. The goals of the opponent are negated, presented as unfair, unjustifiable and unreasonable. Their violent acts and immoral behaviour – such as violence, atrocities, cruelty and the lack of concern for human life – are emphasized, and sometimes even linked to the genetic make-up and disposition of the group. Various negative characteristics are attributed to the opponent and strong negative emotions, such as animosity, mistrust and hatred, are directed towards them. Differences are experienced as a threat to one's own reality, leading to denigration of the other as a defensive response. Delegitimization impedes the capacity for empathy with the opponent's needs and suffering. The opponent is often depicted as a homogenous evil entity, without individualization or nuance.

- *Self-collective perception as the victim*: Often one's own group is presented as the victim of the conflict and the opponent's aggression. A sense of victimhood is easily developed and maintained when one's own group is presented as justified and at the receiving end of the opponent, who is associated with evil, harm, injustice, atrocities and blame for the harm experienced. This sense of victimhood denies one's own role and responsibility for the conflict dynamics. Victimhood can be objectively real, but when it becomes embedded in the social psyche and culture, it can become a paralysing force undermining peace-oriented attitudes.

- *Collective emotional orientation*: The dominating emotions in a conflict ethos are fear, anger, hatred, revenge and humiliation. Sentiments of empathy and compassion are often muted.

These beliefs and mechanisms serve to strengthen in-group cohesion and wage psychological warfare against the opponent. Such conflict ethos promotes 'othering', drives radicalization and furthers social fragmentation in societies at conflict. All this further undermines the trust, which is essential for readiness to engage in steps towards conflict resolution or a peace process.

Application

As Bar-Tal confirms, conflicts cannot be resolved without addressing this socio-psychological conflict repertoire which feeds, maintains and escalates the conflict.

In times of conflict, society members are often discouraged from questioning the set of beliefs that have been formed to interpret and perpetuate the conflict, in the interests of their own group. The more strongly society members adhere to the ethos of conflict, the less likely they are to support steps towards conflict resolution.[5] Those who disagree with the goals of the conflict and its management, who question, criticize or put forward a differing ethos, or who do not ascribe to the binding group identity, are likely to be censored or considered non-patriots or traitors.

In order to break the escalating cycle of conflict and move towards de-escalation and conflict resolution, **engaging the following psychosocial factors would be of importance**:

- At the level of the **mind**, to maintain and nurture a clear perception of the conflict, the opponent, one's own group and the dynamics, and to distinguish people from their behaviour.

- At the level of **the intellect**, not to be closed to new information and possibilities.

- At the level of **memory**, to keep in mind a representative record of wrongdoings on both sides in the past and the present.

- To take **responsibility** for the behaviour of one's own group and not justify its violent reactions through comparison to the activities of the opponent. To have a clear perception of the connection between harm caused and harm received.

- Not to simply **blame** the other group, thus giving away one's sense of power and weakening one's own capacity to respond and to act instead of reacting.

- To manage strong **negative emotions** and strengthen resilience and centredness in order to take the right action with the right intention. Acting with hatred, revenge and humiliation sustains the cycle of violence and does not lead to constructive outcomes.

- To uphold **moral values, human rights and dignity**. Delegitimizing the opponent and justifying harm to them amount to oppression and aggression.

- To abandon the **sense of victimhood**, which leads to the vicious cycle whereby victims turn into perpetrators and vice versa. Instead, to nurture and strengthen self-esteem and confidence independent of the attitude of others. Rather than remaining on the receiving end of events as a victim, to take responsibility and agency and become agents of change.

- To avoid being stuck in **limited self-identifications** from which unhelpful reactions spring forth, and to instead acknowledge multiple self-identifications. To remain aware that all people, first and foremost, share a common identity as human beings.

Active non-violence

The suggestions above on **how psychosocial factors can be engaged with to interrupt the escalation and polarization of conflict and violence bear many similarities to the methods of active non-violence**. Active non-violence implies a specific kind of interpersonal relationship.[6] A basic tenet of active non-violence is to fight wrongful behaviours instead of people, to focus on the conflict issue instead of on the person and to see the other party not as an enemy but as a partner in the struggle to satisfy the needs of all. Research has shown that better outcomes are achieved when negative emotions are targeted at behaviours rather than at people, and when specific conflict issues are addressed without attacking the people involved as such.[7] Non-violence is based on a positive view of human nature and sees the potential for good in every living person. This attitude allows one to consistently affirm the human dignity of the other and to offer to both oppressed and oppressors the possibility of safeguarding their honour. The relation towards the other is based on empathy, the will to place oneself in their world and to arrive at an understanding. Active non-violence aims to open up the mind of the adversary, touch his conscience, and change his attitudes, convictions, will and behaviour. The goal of the personal and interpersonal dynamics of active non-violence is to bring about deeper unity and cooperation between groups and to create a harmonious society.

The practice of principled active non-violence stems from a strong intrapersonal foundation of self-awareness and self-management. When individuals feel connected within themselves, they are more likely to develop interpersonally and within communities, creating inclusive relationships and greater community resilience to conflict, and contributing to the preservation and restoration of the social fabric after conflict.

In addition to the intrapersonal and interpersonal dimensions of active non-violence, several other core elements are emphasized in prominent models of non-violent action. These include strategic planning, the distinct nature of transformative power that operates without coercion, the practical methods and techniques employed to facilitate change, and the influence of the specific political, social and cultural context in which non-violence is enacted.

A solidified socio-psychological infrastructure and a culture of conflict

When not interrupted, the socio-psychological conflict repertoire described above turns into a *socio-psychological infrastructure* and begins to penetrate institutions and communication channels. It can evolve into a *culture of conflict* when the psychosocial infrastructure is integrated into the political, social and educational context as a dominant repertoire. This new culture of conflict provides meaning to the experience of prolonged conflict, **encompassing collective life**. It is present in public discourse, mass communication, cultural products and educational materials. The conflict becomes central to the lives of individuals and society, where they are emotionally and cognitively preoccupied by it, consciously as well as unconsciously. There is a sense of **normalization** around it, often without realizing the strong impact this has on individual and collective life or the possibility of living in a different way. The new generation that grows up in such a culture of conflict does not know anything else and easily absorbs and adopts it.

The psychological infrastructure of prolonged conflict has various embedded elements

The **use of violence** often changes the experience of the conflict, impacts the perception of reality and leaves a strong imprint on individual and collective memories. The dynamic escalates and the conflict becomes more entrenched once human lives are lost, soldiers as well as civilians are killed, women and children suffer and die, violence and atrocities are committed, and lives are destroyed. Escalation is especially severe when mass killings, ethnic cleansing or genocide are committed. The conflict develops the **characteristic of totality**: one's own values, interests and goals become existential, indispensable and non-negotiable for the group's existence. They are challenged by the opponent, who is increasingly seen as inhuman and evil. As a result, one's own violence becomes more and more justified and essential. Increasingly, there may develop a strong desire to inflict maximum harm on the opponent. In a rigid zero-sum logic, others' losses are perceived as one's own gains, and others' gains are seen as one's own losses.

Collective memory is shaped and reshaped in accordance with changing conditions, providing an interpretation of the past, serving the goals and needs of the present, and providing an orientation towards the future. The collective memory is not necessarily a shared memory of a fixed history or a factual representation of the past. In order to serve specific societal goals, certain facts can be omitted, doubtful facts can be added, interpretations can be coloured or biased. As a result, groups in conflict often have contradictory and selective historical collective memories of the same events. In intergroup conflict, collective memory has social, cultural and political functions, serving their own group, delegitimizing the opponent, imbibing a sense of collective victimization or superiority, justifying their actions against the opponent, and describing a biased history of the conflict. Such memory is often clad in black and white, offering a simplified understanding of complex history. Dysfunctional aspects that no longer serve a purpose are omitted or modified, for example where atrocities committed by one's own group are denied or minimalized. Useful aspects are included and emphasized, such as particular 'selected traumas and selected glories'. Events of glory are chosen to be remembered and nurtured in identity and culture, since they raise a sense of success and triumph, and inspire the group to believe that the challenges can be overcome and the conflict can be won.

'Selected traumas' are events of extensive suffering, defeat or loss, arousing feelings of anger, grief, frustration and the desire for revenge among the community. The remembrance of these events through narrative, culture, commemorations, monuments, cemeteries and rituals maintains a sense of injury, irreversible loss and injustice. The cost of the conflict as well as the guilt and malevolence of the opponent are constantly remembered and reinforced, justifying the investment in the continuation of the conflict. When they are not healed or allowed to heal, these traumas continue to affect whole societies, leaving an imprint on the psyche of the group, constituting a defining element of identity and culture, influencing the norms and worldview, and being transmitted from generation to generation.

According to researchers and the insights of psychology, negative events are more held on to and ingrained in the collective memory than positive ones.[8] Therefore, members of society tend to be more affected by negative events and selected traumas than by the selected glories.

What is held in the memory has a direct influence on **emotional responses**. As at the individual level, the collective memory also evokes specific emotions corresponding to the held memories. These could be fear and distrust based on past traumatic events, anger and hatred based on unjust acts of the opponent, or pride in past victories or in heroic acts. These dominant emotions of hostility, radicalization, fear and anger influence social behaviour and how people relate to each other.[9]

As a foundational aspect of a culture of conflict, these conflict-related emotions are integrated into the public discourse, social norms and institutions, and are mobilized for political ends.

A culture of conflict can also lead to the formation or strengthening of new conflict-related social **identities**. The primary identification of oneself and one's own group with their actual or perceived role in the conflict, including the suffering and injustice experienced, influences and narrows the scope of possibilities to think and engage from different and broader perspectives. Increasingly, opposing groups 'close themselves in an ethnocentric closet, focused on own needs and goals, building a psychological fence that prevents them from seeing the rival as fellow human beings with their own needs and goals.'[10] The focus on differences perpetuates mistrust and suspicion, and the out-group is further demonized through 'negative narratives'. In-group cohesion becomes very strong and at the same time the boundaries of exclusion are clearly marked, entrenching social division and fragmentation. In his elaborate works on social psychology, Volkan shared his insight that the central psychological factor in starting and keeping alive large-group conflicts is the protection and maintenance of large-group identity.[11]

The identity groups thus formed can significantly alter the behaviour of individuals in ways they would not adopt when alone. The group dynamics related to social identity, including peer pressure, groupthink and mob mentality, can influence behaviour in both prosocial and antisocial activities. In situations of heightened tension, individuals may act in ways they would not normally consider, when they are driven by the collective emotions and actions of the group.

Often the **values** in intractable conflict are considered sacred and non-negotiable when they are considered as fundamental to the identity, worldview or ideology of the group, such as those related to territory, justice, independence, holy sites and so on. The culture of conflict is usually more centred on norms and values that perpetuate the conflict, justify violence, normalize intolerance and aggression, and glorify martyrs and heroes, in preference to consideration of peace-promoting values and norms of non-violent conflict resolution, peacebuilding, wisdom, inclusion, reconciliation or justice for all.

In an established socio-psychological infrastructure and culture of conflict, various groups have **vested interests** in perpetuating hostilities because they derive power, profit, or a sense of identity and meaning from the ongoing discord. Consequently, even the most advanced conflict resolution strategies may prove ineffective if they do not adequately address the underlying incentives driven by greed and self-serving interests.

Through this solidified socio-psychological infrastructure and culture of conflict, **beliefs become rigid** and new information is perceived in selective, biased and distorted ways. The differing frames through which each party sees and understands the conflict contribute to intractability over time. Frames are the coherent cognitive constructs people use to make sense of complex information or situations.[12] They usually simplify complex realities, abandon nuances for clarity, reject contradictory information and disregard seemingly irrelevant aspects of observation. Reality is interpreted in ways internally consistent with one's worldview and thus one's vision is narrowed. This restricted prism defines perception, interpretation and action, and becomes in itself an obstacle to peaceful resolution. Communication becomes more difficult and parties polarize and radicalize further. Such frames become self-reinforcing because they filter information, colour interpretation, and thus strengthen the parties in their respective positions and sense of righteousness. Such frames are usually quite stable, even when some people or groups leave, as they are easily passed on through discourse, culture and systems.[13]

The belief that the conflict can ever be resolved evaporates and disappears. Accordingly, there is **no trust** or cooperation in attempts to solve it, and behaviour remains informed by the logic of the conflict.

Changing cultures of conflict is challenging, particularly since they are reinforced by supportive ideological beliefs and alternative ideas are suppressed.

At this stage, it is not the disagreements over the goals that are crucial to the conflict analysis, but the social-psychological repertoire that includes hostility, hatred, fear, resentment, anger, delegitimization and mistrust. Whereas this repertoire initially fulfilled important functions to cope with and respond to the conflict, with time the repertoire itself becomes the main motivation and justifying factor. **It serves as a major factor in the continuation of the conflict and as a major barrier to its resolution.** It excludes empathy, denies responsibility for one's own actions, justifies harming the opponent and prevents minds from seeing alternatives. The negative actions taken by each side confirm the negative psychosocial infrastructure in a vicious cycle. The culture of conflict can thus last for decades and centuries, continuing as a **self-fulfilling prophecy**.

Application

In order to move towards peace, a new repertoire needs to be formed and disseminated in society, including the need to resolve the conflict peacefully and to humanize the opponent. In addition to the factors mentioned in the previous section, we can present additional points for attention at the stage where conflict infrastructures are solidified and cultures of conflict have become entrenched.

To counter the culture of conflict and violence, it is important to **nourish a culture and practice of peace, including peace-oriented values** and strategies. In IAHV's view, an ethos and culture of peacebuilding is based on universal human values that support life for all, such as non-violence, respect for life, service and responsibility, peace, compassion, friendliness and cooperation, generosity, belonging and integrity. Values that foster divisiveness, hatred, discrimination and conflict would be challenged by values of inclusion, harmony, unity and collective solidarity. Norms and values that associate heroism and courage with violence and selfishness are realigned to non-violent conflict resolution, service to society and wisdom. For example, Gurudev Sri Sri Ravi Shankar often calls upon the youth to re-instil a sense of pride in being non-violent, compassionate, helpful and friendly, instead of being aggressive and violent. Also, Coleman identified these as core psychosocial components of sustainable peace: active recognition of basic human values and rights that are shared among all human beings and a shared social agreement that violence is not a way to solve conflicts.[14] New role models who exemplify these qualities need to be promoted in public life. Earlier in this book we have seen that the practical nourishment and manifestation of universal human values in individuals and communities are enhanced by stress reduction and the raising of awareness. The nourishment and promotion of human values in individuals and communities as well as in social, cultural and political life would then reflect in the attitudes, mindsets and behaviours of individuals and communities. It would positively impact the way individuals and communities think and interact at every level of society and inspire them to contribute to a more peaceful and prosperous world. It would be the foundation to address conflict issues without violence or unnecessary harm. Conflict would not compromise the value of life. By promoting, nourishing and instilling life-supporting human values we lay a psychosocial foundation for a culture and practice of peace.

Both leaders and members of society are developing and adhering to a socio-psychological repertoire and culture of conflict, and so both must change in order to de-escalate and terminate conflict and pursue a peacebuilding process.[15] While leaders can steer the direction and make decisions, members of society also need to be engaged in the transformation of the socio-psychological framework and peaceful settlement of the conflict.

While the dominating culture of the conflict is known, solidified, unambiguous and predictable, the culture of peace is unknown, uncertain, ambiguous and unpredictable. Exploring opportunities for peace in the midst of a culture of conflict therefore requires **strong inner resilience**, as well as vision, courage, inner strength, skills, intuition, empathy and many other qualities which can be nurtured in individuals and society. In his well-known book 'The Moral Imagination: The Art and Soul of Building Peace', peacebuilding scholar and practitioner John Paul Lederach emphasized the call for peacebuilders to step into the unknown, take risks and challenge existing power dynamics, norms and narratives to create new possibilities for dialogue and coexistence and to break cycles of violence.[16] This requires upholding a **hopeful vision** despite the challenges and obstacles, the skill of creativity, the ability to hold together conflicting truths, and the capacity for moral imagination, envisioning and creating an alternative future in the midst of existing conflict and violence.

Case study: 'How a Few Women Stopped a War.'

(from Lederach, John Paul. The Moral Imagination: The Art and Soul of Building Peace.)[25]

The women of Wajir did not set out to stop a war. They just wanted to make sure they could get food for their families. The initial idea was simple enough: make sure the market is safe for anyone to buy and sell.

Located in Northeast Kenya, Wajir District is made up mostly of Somali clans. With the collapse of the Somali government in 1989, Wajir soon found itself caught up in interclan fighting with a flow of weapons and refugees that made life increasingly difficult. Our colleague Dekha Ibrahim recalls one night in mid-1993 that shooting erupted outside her home. She ran for her firstborn child and hid under the bed while bullets crisscrossed her room. While under that bed, she had a distinct memory of her mother holding her, huddled, under the same conditions when she was a child. By morning, she had decided this had to stop. Other women shared similar stories.

So they gathered. Less than a dozen of them at first. 'We just wanted to put our heads together,' they said, 'to see what we know and to see what we can do. We decided the place to start was the market.' They agreed on a basic idea. The market should be safe for any woman of any clan, any background, to come, to sell and to buy. Women were looking out for their children. Access and safety to the market were what they needed. They spread the word. They established monitors who would watch every day what was happening at the market. They would report incidents and infractions. Whatever issues emerged, a small committee of women would move quickly to resolve them. Their initiative resulted in the creation of the Wajir Women's Association for Peace.

They soon discovered that broader fighting still affected their lives. Sitting again, they decided to pursue direct conversations with the elders of all the clans. Getting the men on board was not an easy thing to do in this highly patriarchal society. 'Who are women to advise and push us?' was the response they feared they might get. So they sat and thought through their understanding of the elder system, the actual key elders, the make-up of the Somali clans in Wajir. Using personal connections, they worked with concerned men and succeeded in bringing together a meeting of the elders. They aligned themselves carefully not to push or take over the meetings. Instead, they found one of the elderly men, quite respected, who came from the smallest and therefore the least threatening of the local clans. And in the meeting, he became their spokesperson, talking directly to his fellow elders, appealing to their responsibility. 'Why, really,' he asked, 'are we fighting? Who benefits from this? Our families are being destroyed.' His words provoked discussions. The elders, even some of those who had been promoting revenge killings, agreed to face the issues and stop the fighting. They formed the Council of Elders for Peace.

Engaging fighters in the bush took them to the youth, where they formed Youth for Peace. Youth need a job, so they formed Businessmen for Peace. Soon the question

> became, how do you bring this all together? It finally happened in the formation of the Wajir Peace and Development Committee.
>
> Ceasefires came into place. Local commissions were created to verify and help the process of disarming the clan-based factions in conjunction with the local authorities in the Kenyan district police. Ten years later, Wajir District still faces serious problems though the Wajir Peace and Development Committee actively works and has continued to expand. Fighting has not stopped in Somalia and still spills into Wajir. The elders meet on a regular basis. There is now much greater cooperation between the local villages, clans and the district officials. And the women who stopped the war still monitor a much safer market.
>
> When I recently spoke with Dekha, she said that since 11 September 2001, there has been an increased presence of US personnel based in Wajir focused on antiterrorism in Somalia. 'Our challenge now,' she said, 'is to engage the US government and convince them of better ways to approach this. Inshallah, we shall be successful.'

In order to counteract the negative impact of limited and narrow conflict-related identities, it is important to raise awareness of the **multiple identities** we all have, and above all of our mutually **shared identities**, such as our primary identity as human beings. Many authors agree that the only way to make long-term, intractable conflict more tractable is to address the underlying identity issues so that the parties come to see themselves and one another differently.[17] Among the psychosocial components of sustainable peace, Coleman also identified a strong sense of global as well as local loyalty and patriotism, the ability to have dual and multiple identities, and a strong sense of positive interdependence among the units making up a society.[18]

Gurudev Sri Sri Ravi Shankar consistently promotes the bigger vision of a one world family and emphasizes that we are all interconnected with each other and with the planet we all live on.

Even though this vision may seem far-fetched in view of all the human conflicts happening in the world today, it is still possible to seek to identify commonalities and connections. People can re-identify 'identity' connections that link them across conflict divides, such as being a woman, journalist or religious person. This, thus, reduces 'othering', hostile beliefs and intergroup tension.

The well-known example of the Parents Circle in Israel-Palestine unites Israelis and Palestinians across the divide of the entrenched conflict in their shared identities as parents and family members who have lost a loved one in the conflict and who want to work together to prevent further violence in the future and to build a more peaceful society.[19]

Well-established methods for the resolution of conflicts and the **improvement of intergroup relations are problem-solving workshops, sustained dialogue, negotiation and mediation**. For these peacebuilding processes to be effective, transformative and sustainable, and not just superficial quick fixes, they need to address deeper underlying issues as well as shifts in thinking, feeling and relating to each other. For example, the 'Improbable Dialogues' initiative in Colombia developed a methodology to initiate and support dialogue processes between unlikely dialoguers with antagonistic views and positions, through the application of alternative conversation frames, the transformation of biases and the re-humanization of the other.[20]

Scholars and practitioners from the fields of conflict resolution and psychology have developed various positively framed models focusing on successful cooperation, positive interdependence, constructive conflict resolution, sustained dialogue and creative problem solving.[21] They have defined psychological characteristics and requirements that lie at the basis of these models, such as empathy, trust, cognitive flexibility, emotional regulation and a willingness to collaborate towards a solution. In the midst of intractable conflict, these can be quite challenging. Therefore, the practices described earlier in this book, including the Sudarshan Kriya technique, are well-positioned to support a strong psychosocial foundation for such peacebuilding processes, including strengthening trauma-relief, stress reduction, self-awareness, emotion regulation, empathy, connection, communication and other skills.

In order to rebuild social cohesion, it is important to reduce negative perceptions and beliefs about the 'other' and restore a sense of trust and connection. In this regard, the importance of having different, **positive experiences of intergroup encounters** has been emphasized and practised. Exposing people to counter-intuitive exemplars from the dehumanized group which contradict the common stereotypes about them is a specific, recognized method to reduce prejudice and create openness to interaction.[22] 'Contact theory' posits that under certain conditions, direct contact between members of different groups can reduce prejudice and promote humanization, empathy and compromise. Through humanization of the other and the reduction of fears, anger, resentments and one's own sense of victimization, openings for forgiveness may emerge as well as the will and capacity to live or work towards a better future together. Storytelling among opposing groups, when well organized and properly embedded, is a specific method that can change the perception of 'the other'. It individualizes members of the opposing group, weakens tendencies to dehumanize and strengthens empathy.

Intergroup contacts between crisis-affected people have been organized by thousands of peacebuilders with differing results. While a 'meta-review' of 515 studies undertaken between the 1940s and 2000 concluded that there is a positive relationship between higher contact and lower prejudice, the author Tropp highlights that the type of contact matters. Neuroscience gives us a new perspective on the effectiveness of such initiatives: 'Many practitioners assume that contact + knowledge leads to reduced prejudice. In reality, lower anxiety and a reduced sense of threat produce less prejudice, as does increased empathy. This is because prejudice is based more on emotional processes than on rational thought.'[23] To reduce conflict between groups, therefore, reducing stress and anxiety and encouraging perspective sharing are fundamental elements.

Another example of an intervention that challenges prejudices and stereotypes occurs when former adversaries collaboratively propose initiatives or undertake concrete steps towards peacebuilding. Such efforts disrupt instinctive reactions and encourage others to re-examine and potentially reconsider their established assumptions.

Many peacebuilders and psychologists have emphasized that the **irrational aspects of conflict** are more important to be addressed than the rational ones. As Volkan said, 'If the irrational aspects are not first addressed then the substantive issues cannot effectively get solved because rituals, symbols, traumas, and the like will make any substantive suggestions psychologically unacceptable.'[24] Therefore, trauma, emotions and identity aspects must be addressed.

The threat coming from the opponent needs to be assessed as accurately as possible and responded to adequately, rather than exaggerating or exploiting it. Enabling peace-oriented strategies and choices requires trauma-relief and the cessation of the activation of the old stress/threat-response mechanism, and its replacement with a new system.

Educational systems and school books, culture, media and politics, can **reshape the collective memory** into a less biased and more balanced account of the past. Just as individuals can choose what memories to hold onto and which to let go of, societies too can make deliberate choices about their collective memories. That way, the memory can function as a source of learning and wisdom, and an inspiration for progress and peace, rather than as an instigator of conflict and an obstacle to its resolution.

We have also observed that when people have higher energy levels, their memories are less likely to be fixated on the past and tend to be more positively oriented. Therefore, raising the general energy levels among the population could play a crucial role in helping individuals to let go of the past, balance positive and negative events, and move forward towards the future.

The process of transforming the socio-psychological infrastructure of conflict can also be supported by adequate institutional and structural reforms, which will be discussed in the next chapter.

Understanding the psychosocial processes related to intergroup conflicts can inform many strategies to help reduce, reframe or transform those conflicts. The socio-psychological roots of prolonged conflict are not easily eliminated, but the psychosocial infrastructure is not carved in stone. It can evolve over time, alternative cultures and narratives may emerge, it can be actively influenced, and its grip on the population can change. The road may seem hard, long and difficult when the conflict permeates the minds, emotions, attitudes and behaviour of people, and when the repertoire has become so entrenched that it has become an institution and a culture, that it perpetuates itself in a vicious cycle. As a last resort, Gurudev Sri Sri Ravi Shankar also calls at times upon people in entrenched conflicts 'to snap out of it', to take the decision to let go of the past, take a fresh look at the current situation and reorient themselves towards a brighter future.

Reconciliation as a psychosocial process[26]

Reconciliation is an exemplary psychosocial process, revolving around deep inner and interpersonal factors and dynamics. Lederach speaks about reconciliation as 'the social space where truth, justice, mercy and peace come together.'[27] Similarly, Louis Kriesberg explains how truth (revelation, transparency, acknowledgement), justice (restitution) and mercy (acceptance, forgiveness, compassion, healing) lead to peace (security, respect, harmony, well-being). Reconciliation is a multidimensional process with seemingly opposing components. It deals with the past while looking for a shared future. It openly addresses wrongs while repairing relationships. It aims for truth about what happened while opening up for mercy and renewed relationship.

In order to heal a fractured society, it is necessary to confront the past in an appropriate way. Past injustices and wrongs need to be acknowledged. This can be done by creating a safe space in which the various truths from the different sides can be told and listened to (narrative truth) or through a process of public truth-telling. It is possible that this space will contain varying, sometimes contradictory, perspectives on the truth. **Truth** is a precondition for the social acknowledgement of the significance of the suffering on all sides and can help to restore self-esteem and confidence of the survivors (restorative truth). Truth is commonly understood as a necessary but not sufficient condition for forgiveness. Perpetrators are called to recognize their mistakes and accept responsibility for the physical and psychological injuries they have caused. If truth and accountability for past acts are not established, it is difficult to envision an inclusive future. Without the truth about injustices ever being spoken out or acknowledged in some way, injustice and conflict are likely to be repeated over and over again.

At a deeper level, truth is not limited to the recognition of facts and behaviours, but truthfulness is a way of living and relating authentically to oneself, others and the whole of existence. It means embodying truth in one's thoughts, actions and way of being. Truthfulness is mentioned as one of the basic qualities a yogi must practise, according to Patanjali, the propounder of yoga, and was clearly exemplified by Mahatma Gandhi and his Satyagraha (Power of Truth) movement for social justice. Truthfulness includes speaking truthfully, avoiding lies and manipulations, using clear language, and considering the impact of our words on others. Acting truthfully implies consistently behaving in harmony with one's inner truth, values and integrity, without being hypocritical or pretending to be someone we are not, and courageously facing the facts of life. Truthfulness also implies self-reflection, being honest with oneself, acknowledging life as it is without trying to conceal difficult aspects, and recognizing biases, patterns, fears and uncomfortable truths about oneself. It also means respecting others' perspectives and truths, recognizing that everyone's experiences and truths might differ from our own. In alignment with the truth of respect for life, truthfulness goes hand in hand with compassion and non-violence, the aim of not doing harm to others or oneself. Truthfulness implies living a life of integrity, honesty, inner strength and steadfastness, while fostering authentic connections with others and the world.

When truth has been spoken and acknowledged, some form of **justice** has to be done. The actual need for justice can be interpreted and translated in many different ways. Retributive justice focuses on revenge and the punishment of the offender. Restorative justice focuses on the restoration of social order, the rebuilding of social relationships, and the personal transformation and social reintegration of both survivors and offenders. The concept and practice of restorative justice restore the humanity of both the survivor and the offender. If carried out in a genuine way, such a process can be an opportunity for the offender to give expression to his remorse and to overcome feelings of guilt.

A process of true reconciliation not only entails initiatives to reveal truth and restore justice, but also ultimately aims to restore or build relationships across divisions. A first step perceived as a necessary condition for many survivors to be able to consider a renewed relationship and to forgive is a form of apology or expression of repentance by the offenders. The process of **apology and forgiveness** becomes possible as all sides get to a space where they are better able to humanize and empathize with each other. This process is often facilitated through **storytelling**, listening, sharing experiences, dialogue and meaningful encounters, which generate empathy towards the storytellers, deepened understanding of each other's lives, a safe space for all sides to express loss and grief, and increased trust among individuals and groups. As acts of compassion, forgiveness processes can greatly contribute to creating a peaceful society. The dynamic of forgiveness following apology can bring real liberation for both survivors and offenders and can be experienced as a form of healing.

For the **offenders** themselves, they can recover their humanity by acknowledging and repenting their wrong deeds. Gurudev Sri Sri Ravi Shankar emphasizes the importance of taking full responsibility for one's actions, emotions and responses, but not to linger in guilt. He suggests that guilt can be a learning tool if it leads to self-awareness and growth, but it should not be a lingering weight that hampers progress. He promotes self-forgiveness and asking for forgiveness, and emphasizes the importance of moving forward with a clear conscience. By accepting one's imperfections and learning from the past, one can cultivate a more positive and constructive mindset. Overcoming guilt involves accepting oneself, learning from mistakes, empowering oneself in a positive way and not allowing the past to dictate the future.

Survivors are encouraged to be compassionate, accept apologies, find mercy in their hearts, let go of the past, be strong to embrace the reality, and move on. Forgiveness not only forms the basis of a renewed relationship but, importantly, also frees the survivor from a vicious cycle of anger, revenge, reproach, self-pity and pain: 'Forgiveness entails a shift in understanding of the other party, the development of a sense of compassion towards the other and a personal release of anger, pain and suffering which leads to inner peace.'[28] According to Gurudev Sri Sri Ravi Shankar, the highest form of forgiveness is to realize that the other committed a mistake out of ignorance and to have a sense of compassion for them. He emphasizes that holding onto grudges and resentment only harms the person who harbours this. By forgiving others, we release ourselves from the burden of negative emotions. He often says that forgiveness is not about condoning the wrong actions of others but about freeing oneself from the cycle of anger and hurt, releasing the grip of past hurts and re-embracing the present moment with an open heart.

The subjective experience of peace is an important aspect of a reconciliation process. Developing **inner calm and tranquillity** and a sense of harmony and well-being can greatly contribute to sustaining a reconciliation process and enhancing the experience of security. **Fear** is one of the most important factors which has to be overcome in order for a community to be rebuilt. It is equally important to enliven or sustain **hope** in order to nourish a process of reconciliation. At a deeper level, a process of reconciliation can entail the development of **new self-images and the redefinition of one's relation to others and to the world,** from narrowly defined images towards a more inclusive, holistic understanding. Both perpetrators and survivors of violent conflict can be encouraged to develop multiple identities as well as a shared identity with humanity. To begin with, reconciliation requires humanization and legitimization of the opponent, but it can become very strong and sustainable when conflicting groups become aware of their fundamental interdependence, of their ultimate belonging to one another, and come to an **understanding of unity and inclusiveness**. An inclusive vision, together with the affirmation of the life of every human being, can lead to a rediscovery of the **humanity** of the other, to mutual acceptance and respect, and to the ability and creativity to live with diversity without fear. In turn, the sense of interdependence, belonging and inclusiveness will foster a **sense of responsibility** for oneself, the other, the immediate environment and the whole of creation. A process of reconciliation is only sustainable if it is built on trust that the injustices and wrongs committed previously will not be repeated again. It is very important to restore a sense of **social morality** after a period of violence in which all norms and rules have been broken. This trust can be created through **meaningful actions** that restore relationships and express a serious commitment to a new future. For example, publicly affirming the human dignity of survivors and empowering them can be one way to prevent further victimization and dehumanization. Through the reduction of both real and perceived threats, collective trust can (re)emerge. Still, apart from guarantees in the form of personal commitments, promises and institutional reforms, embarking on a renewed relationship with former adversaries entails a great risk. It always requires **courage** to risk peace and to trust the path of reconciliation. Reconciliation requires the transformation of relationships as well as restoration of a sense of community and purpose to society at large. True reconciliation entails overcoming estrangement in favour of **cooperation and harmony**. As people feel empowered and start changing their attitudes towards each other, openness towards joint activities may arise. Meaningful collective engagement can strengthen the social fabric after war. **Relationship building** on a daily level can be supported through concrete initiatives that aim to foster cross-community cooperation, break down stereotypes, support (re)integration, enhance respect, honour, foster mutual understanding and humanization, and reduce levels of hate and suspicion between people. Reconstructed relationships constitute the necessary thread to reweave the social fabric of a community and to reconstruct the physical infrastructure after conflict.

Reconciliation as a process happens **across the personal, interpersonal, communal, intercommunal, national and international levels**. Since antagonistic relationships are driven by subjective factors, it is important to overcome at a personal level, grief, loss, fear, misperceptions and mistrust. As Rasmussen points out: 'For any transformation to occur, a change of awareness, attitude and conduct must begin on an individual basis and eventually spread to the collective.' Personal psychological recovery and changes of attitudes and perceptions are the basis of renewing interpersonal relationships. The accumulated hurt and hatred suffered by the hundreds of thousands of war victims have to be addressed as one of the major obstacles to social and psychological healing. These personal and interpersonal transformations lead in turn to the healing of a society that has become dysfunctional by the ravages of war.

A process of reconciliation is not a strictly psychological phenomenon; there are also **social and structural dimensions** to it. For example, institutional frameworks, such as truth commissions, can be created to foster national reconciliation. If provided with a broad mandate, truth commissions can play an important role in writing an official history of past wrongs, cutting through myths and false pictures of the past, allocating moral blame, promoting psychological healing (survivors are listened to, acknowledged, and can express themselves), and uncovering broad patterns of past abuses and root causes. Reconciliation processes are also underpinned by structural reforms relating to, for example, economic justice or social and political power-sharing.

Art of Living, IAHV and Gurudev Sri Sri Ravi Shankar have facilitated reconciliation initiatives around the world, such as:

- In Kashmir, between family members of soldiers of the Indian Army and family members of militants killed by the Indian Army, in 2017–18.
- Between Israelis and Palestinians during a special training programme in Germany, 2012.
- In Colombia, between family members of parliamentarians who were killed by the FARC and the FARC rebels and leaders.

Case study: Reconciliation between Dioula and Guéré tribes in Ivory Coast

The civil war in Ivory Coast, which began in 2002 following a prolonged political crisis, saw the division of the country into a rebel-led north and government-controlled south. Long-standing political and economic divisions and inequalities among the country's diverse ethnic groups were exacerbated and exploited for political goals. Through a nationalistic and xenophobic discourse, immigrants and certain groups of Ivorian citizens were marginalized and excluded. Ethnic violence, targeted attacks and widespread human rights abuses against perceived political or ethnic adversaries were rampant. In the absence of a strong government and with multiple militias roaming widely, the tribe served for many as their central reference point. Origin and religious affiliation became prime markers of identity in Ivory Coast and an attack on a member of one's tribe was an immediate trigger for tribal warfare. The civil war saw neighbours turning against each other, communities divided along ethnic lines and long-standing grievances boiling over into violent confrontations, ultimately destabilizing the nation and leaving deep scars on its social fabric.

In the West of the country, the Dioula and Guere tribes had been living peacefully next to each other for generations, but triggered by escalated land conflicts, their members started attacking and killing each other. Members from the other tribe were chased out of mixed neighbourhoods, resulting in Guere staying in predominantly Guere neighbourhoods and Dioula in Dioula neighbourhoods.

Between 2005 and 2007, Art of Living conducted several programmes to support people to cope with the trauma of the civil war, to improve the quality of life through developmental initiatives and to promote harmonious coexistence of different factions.

As a pilot project to reduce conflict and build a sense of trust, the Art of Living invited and selected fifteen youth from the Dioula and Guere tribes for an 8-day Youth Leadership Training Programme (YLTP).[29]

YLTP empowers youth with well-being, confidence, values, skills and tools to become effective agents of change in their communities. It provides seven days of hard and soft skills development, focusing on personal development, leadership training and locally owned development strategies. The intense empowerment programme trains participants in deep trauma-relief and stress management techniques, project development, communication skills, leadership qualities, teamwork, decision-making, dynamism and entrepreneurship, interpersonal skills, creativity and innovation, and promotes a volunteering spirit. Its unique strength lies in the powerful combination of physical, emotional, mental and social empowerment so that the youth can become effective, inspired and skilled agents of change who take responsibility for the upliftment of their communities.

To start with, the effective breathing techniques, physical exercises and relaxation gradually reduced the accumulated stress and trauma among the participating youth. Whereas many of the youth were used to taking alcohol to shut out the horrific memories of the civil war, they were now able to sleep peacefully without the aid of any substance. They found inner peace again and could reconnect with themselves.

> *'I was the most traumatized from the war. The traumas that I saw, I cannot explain. But now I am totally free from stress and trauma.' (Benjamin Yene)*
>
> *'I am free once again. My heart is full of joy.' (Bonaventure Kuassi)*

At the start of the programme, there was enmity, distrust and division. When groups were formed the Dioula would be on one side and the Gueres on the other. Through the joint activities and exercises, the youth started warming up to each other. Instead of strife and division, they started appreciating the values of togetherness, solidarity, cooperation and peace. Attitudes of mistrust gave way to renewed trust. Interaction and encounter changed the beliefs about each other as well as about the conflict. They realized that their identity of being brothers and sisters is stronger than their tribal identity. Slowly their attitudes became warm and friendly. At the end of the programme, they admitted that they had never thought that they could live in such harmony with the opposite tribe.

> *'We lived together and discovered our ways are so similar. There is no fear. We are brothers.' ~ (Adama Bamba)*
>
> *'After the training we saw that it was useless, one tribe here and the other there. It was futile. We saw that we were all brothers and sisters. We had spent our time fighting uselessly, for nothing.' (YLTP participant)*

> 'With the Art of Living course we started forgiving each other.' (Jean Claude Kouassi)
>
> 'Since the training I can control myself. I can talk calmly to anyone without any problem.' (YLTP participant)

Having restored their well-being, inner peace and interpersonal connections, the youth were inspired to take up projects to spread peace and uplift their communities. The Dioula youth decided to rebuild the abandoned houses of the Gueres that they had destroyed during the conflict and invite them back to their repaired houses.

> 'What made us reconstruct the houses of the Gueres was that feeling of solidarity, of union. We felt a little obliged to do it because after all they are our brothers and each one of us is indispensable. Also, it was a signal to the other community that we have nothing in our hearts; we are ready for reconciliation.' (Adama Bamba)
>
> 'When we constructed the houses of the Gueres, they said that we had reconstructed their houses so that they would live in them and we could attack them again. We said, no, after Art of Living we can no longer do that. To have peace we need to live in peace. If we reconstructed these houses for you it is because we wish you well.' (Alexis Yoboue)
>
> 'We are together now. We work together. So thank you for this course! It allowed us to work towards peace.' (Adama Bamba)

The YLTP participants together with local organizations and community members continued renovating and cleaning hospitals and orphanages, repairing roads, cleaning public places and engaging in other service projects for the community.

> 'When we started cleaning the marketplace, hundreds of other youths joined us!' (Bangaly Soumahoro)
>
> 'After seeing the good work that we did, they decided to help us. That is why today they constructed a school, so that our children can go to school at last.' (Maikoue Kone)

Inspired by the first group, the YLTP programme was conducted for close to 100 youths from opposing ethnic groups, including in Bouaké, which was known as the headquarters of the rebels. After the programme, the participants admitted that they found peace and were committed to building a harmonious community. Impressed and touched by the impact of the programme on personal and social peace, they were inspired and motivated to see such programmes implemented across Ivory Coast to lay the foundation for peace.

> 'Sri Sri's initiatives consider human beings in their entirety, and heal the body, mind and spirit. The Art of Living is one of the rare NGOs which works at the grassroots level, close to the population and goes to the core of the problem.' ~ (Djedje Dano Sebastien, Minister of National Reconciliation, Ivory Coast at a Peace Conference in Duékoué)
>
> 'My wish is that all cities in Ivory Coast would do this course. Then the war would be over in two days.' (Bangaly Soumahoro)
>
> 'This course can bring about peace very fast. Instead of giving millions to someone who organizes only endless meetings, the money should be given to you to have such courses.' (Moussa Diomande)
>
> 'Who am I to keep ill feelings to anyone? I am ready to go anywhere. Even the thugs that steal from my house, I pray to God that I might meet them so I can train them. That they do this course, then there will be peace in Ivory Coast.' (Benjamin Yene)

Today, harmonious coexistence has helped the areas to prosper in many ways. People have dropped their prejudices and are willing to come together to work for their community.

> 'Kokoman is the biggest locality in Duekoue. I assure you that within one year of this course, you could not find one youth fighting on the streets.' (Mr Amara, Head of Dozo)

Art of Living shifted the paradigm of violence and retribution into one of forgiveness and cooperation. Inner peace led to interpersonal and social peace. The local culture of violence was transformed into a culture of peace.

From inner peace to social peace: Culture of conflict and culture of peace

Based on the above analysis, I want to present an overview of crucial psychosocial dimensions and dynamics which are present in a culture of war and conflict and which need to be turned around in order to create cultures of peace (Table 6.2).

Table 6.2 *Characteristics of Cultures of War and Cultures of Peace*

Culture of War	Culture of Peace
Centred on **norms and values that perpetuate the conflict**, justify violence, normalize division, intolerance and aggressiveness, glorify martyrs and heroes who engage in violence or die in battle Non-negotiable values Use of violence justified and glorified	**Peace-promoting values and norms** of non-violent conflict resolution, peacebuilding, wisdom, inclusiveness, reconciliation, solidarity, cooperation, respect for life, dignity
Attitudes of mistrust, humiliation and enmity Focus on Win – Lose outcomes	**Attitudes** of cooperation, respect and empathy Focus on Win-Win outcomes, sustainable conflict resolution
Reactivity, impulsivity	Inner calm, centredness, resilience
Rigid **beliefs** New information is perceived in selective, biased and distorted ways Ideological beliefs that support the conflict Suppression of alternative ideas Belief that the conflict cannot be resolved	Clear perception Open and sharp intellect Ability to hold multiple realities Innovation, hope and creativity
Black and White thinking Opponent is wrong, own group is right Opponent is homogenous group without differentiation Own group is intolerant of diverging opinions Conflict is between the good and the bad parties Focus on contradiction between good and evil, right and wrong	Awareness of grey areas, complexity, multifaceted reality, range of opinions and perspectives Maintain clear perception of the conflict, the opponent, the own group and the dynamics Conflict involves multiple and varied parties and stakeholders Remain open to new information and possibilities Focus on the issue and needs to be addressed, not on the person; acknowledgement that there may be some wrong and right on all sides; search for common ground and solutions
Dominating **emotions** of hatred, anger, revenge, humiliation Conflict-related emotions in the public discourse, social norms and institutions, and mobilized for political ends	Peace-oriented emotions of love, compassion, connection Emotional intelligence and resilience
Identity of superiority, positive self-image Identity of victimhood Primary identification with role in the conflict, including the suffering and injustice experienced Focus on differences Strong in-group cohesion Social division and fragmentation Outlook of Us versus Them Emphasis on in-/out-group divisions	Nurture and strengthen self-esteem and -confidence that are independent from the attitude of others Take responsibility and agency Foster multiple identities and a universally shared identity as human beings Connection and shared relationship, shared humanity

Table 6.2 *Continued*

Culture of War	Culture of Peace
Opponent is negatively portrayed, delegitimized, dehumanized, ascribed negative characteristics, even demonized Goals of the opponent are negated, presented as unfair, unjustifiable and unreasonable	Uphold moral values, human rights and dignity Distinguishing people from their behaviour Humanization of everyone Overcoming stereotypes Recognition of positive role everyone can play towards resolving conflict Promoting understanding See opponent not as an enemy, but as a partner in the struggle to satisfy the needs of all
Memory Serving the own group Biased and simplified history of the conflict Negativity bias 'Chosen traumas and chosen glories' to perpetuate the culture of conflict and related suffering, anger, grief, revenge, woundedness, sense of injustice	Representative record of wrongdoings on both sides in the past and the present Memory serves as source of learning and wisdom Cultivating a collective memory including peace and justice components
Behaviour Forceful means, reduced freedom and choice	Dialogue, freedom of choice, inspiration,
Responsibility for conflict and violence put on opponent Responsibility for own atrocities denied or minimized	Take responsibility for the behaviour of the own group and not justify the violent reactions of the own group by those of the opponent

Through the practice of Psychosocial Peacebuilding it is possible to transform the values, emotions, beliefs, attitudes and behaviour of conflicting groups, and to lay the foundation for sustainable peace. 'This struggle, which is conducted within the psychological domain, is as intensive as some of the violent confrontations,' Bar-Tal states in conclusion.[30]

> **Key points: Chapter 6**
>
> The restoration of social connections at different levels, the reweaving of the overall social fabric, and conscious transformation of conflictual relationships into peaceful ones, are a critical foundation for sustainable peace.
>
> Psychosocial factors are crucial in the generation, escalation and resolution of interpersonal and intergroup conflicts and can be addressed and transformed at the roots at each of these stages, thus laying a foundation for peaceful coexistence, social cohesion and eventually sustainable peace.

Conflicts and how we respond

At the initial stage of conflict generation, the way we respond to the challenge of conflict can greatly influence the process and the outcome of these conflicts. Our inner constructs or schemas define how we perceive a certain situation and how we respond to it.

In order to keep the mind clear, manage strong emotions and stay centred in stressful situations and conflict, it is important to have practical and effective tools for stress-relief and stress management.

Stress management, self-awareness and self-management are necessary for skilful perception, observation and expression in conflict situations and to apply the most appropriate conflict style in any situation.

The practice of non-violent communication encompasses the strengths of the different conflict styles and aligns with the balance between one's own interests and those of others.

The origin of intergroup conflict

Since the perception of threat, real or imagined, and lack of trust lie at the origin of intergroup conflict, it is important to manage effectively the community's stress response to the perceived threat.

The emergence of intergroup conflict

During the emergence of intergroup conflicts, escalating dynamics can be reversed when individuals are resilient and have a larger 'window of tolerance' to stress, when their nervous system is stable and not prone to traumatic reactions, and when they can remain centred in the face of challenge with a clear and focused mind.

The polarization of intergroup conflict and the development of a socio-psychological repertoire

In order to meet the challenges of intergroup conflict, societies develop a socio-psychological repertoire that includes shared beliefs, attitudes, motivations and emotions. Such repertoire consists of a meaningful and coherent conflict narrative and justification, a positive collective self-image which is superior to the opponent, delegitimization of the opponent, self-collective perception as the victim and a collective emotional orientation. It promotes 'othering', drives radicalization and furthers social fragmentation in societies at conflict.

At this stage, it is important to engage with psychosocial factors such as the mind, intellect, memory, responsibility, blame, moral values, dignity, sense of victimhood, emotions and self-identifications.

How psychosocial factors can be engaged with to interrupt the escalation and polarization of conflict and violence bear many similarities to the methods of active non-violence.

A solidified socio-psychological infrastructure and a culture of conflict

A solidified socio-psychological infrastructure and a culture of conflict start permeating the political, social and educational context as a dominant repertoire, encompassing collective life and creating a sense of normalization around it. It contains elements such as escalatory use of violence, the conflict's characteristic of totality, conflict-related identities, values, collective memory, emotions, vested interests, rigid beliefs and lack of trust. Such culture of conflict serves as a major factor in the continuation of the conflict and as a major barrier to its resolution.

To counter the culture of conflict and violence, it is important to nourish a culture and practice of peace, including peace-oriented values, strong inner resilience, a hopeful vision, multiple and shared identities, positive experiences of intergroup encounters, and reshaping the collective memory.

Reconciliation

Reconciliation is an exemplary psychosocial process, revolving around deep inner and interpersonal factors and dynamics, including truth, justice, apology and forgiveness, storytelling and connection, inner peace, emotions of fear and hope, new self-images and attitudes towards the world, humanity of the other, inclusive vision, sense of responsibility, cooperation and harmony, meaningful restorative actions, courage and relationship building.

Cultures of war and peace

Crucial psychosocial dimensions and dynamics which are present in a culture of war and conflict and which need to be turned around in order to create cultures of peace include norms and values, attitudes, beliefs, black-and-white thinking, identities, view of the opponent, behaviours, memory and responsibility.

Chapter 6 recommended reading

Bar Tal, D. 2011. *Intergroup Conflicts and Their Resolution: A Social Psychological Perspective*. New York: Psychology Press.

Bar Tal, D. 2013. *Intractable Conflicts: Socio-Psychological Foundations and Dynamics*. Cambridge University Press.

Deutsch, M. 2012. *The psychological components of sustainable peace*. New York London: Springer.

Kelman, H. C. 1997. 'Social-Psychological Dimensions of International Conflict'. In Zartman, W., Rasmussen, J.L. (eds.) *Peacemaking in International Conflict: Methods and Techniques*. Washington: USIP Press.

Kelman, H.C. 2008. 'A social-psychological approach to conflict analysis and resolution'. In Sandole, D., Byrne, S., Sandole-Staroste, I. & Senehi, J. (Eds.) *Handbook of conflict analysis and resolution*. London and New York: Routledge [Taylor & Francis]. Pp. 170–183.

Lederach, J.P. 1997. *Building Peace: Sustainable Reconciliation in Divided Societies*. Washington: USIP Press.

Lederach, J. P. 2005. *The Moral Imagination: The Art and Soul of Building Peace*. Oxford University Press.

Volkan, V. D. 1988. *The Need to Have Enemies and Allies: From Clinical Practice to International Relationships*. Northvale, NJ: Jason Aronson.

Volkan, V. D. 2020. *Large-Group psychology: Racism, Societal Divisions, Narcissistic Leaders and Who We Are Now*. UK: Phoenix.

Notes

1. Bar Tal, 2013, p. 9.
2. Ibidem.
3. Baumeister, Roy F., et al. 2001. 'Bad is stronger than good'. *Review of General Psychology* 5:4, pp. 323–70. https://doi.org/10.1037/1089-2680.5.4.323.
4. Bar-Tal, D. 2013.
5. Bar Tal, D. 2011.
6. Hertog, K. 2010. *The Complex Reality of Religious Peacebuilding: Conceptual Contributions and Critical Analysis*. Rowman & Littlefield, pp. 53–4.
7. Jameson, Jessica Katz, et al. 2009. 'Exploring the role of emotion in conflict transformation'. *Conflict Resolution Quarterly* 27:2, pp. 167–92. https://doi.org/10.1002/CRQ.254.
8. Baumeister, Roy F., et al. 2001.
9. Crawford cited in Travouillon, K. 2021, p. 64.
10. Bar Tal, D. 2013, p. 44.
11. Volkan, V. D. 2020. *Large-Group Psychology: Racism, Societal Divisions, Narcissistic Leaders and Who We Are Now*. UK: Phoenix.
12. See, for example, Grey, B. 1997. 'Framing and reframing of intractable environmental disputes'. In Lewicki, L. R., Gray, B., & Elliott, M. (Eds.), *Making Sense of Intractable Environmental Conflicts: Concepts and Cases*. Washington, DC: Island Press, pp. 5–31; Neale, M. A., & Bazerman, M. H. 1985. 'The effects of framing and negotiator overconfidence on bargaining behaviors and outcomes'. *Academy of Management Journal* 28:1, pp. 34–49.
13. Shmueli, D., Elliott, M., & Kaufman, S. 2006. 'Frame changes and the management of intractable conflicts'. *Conflict Resolution Quarterly* 24:2, pp. 207–18. https://doi.org/10.1002/crq.169.
14. Coleman, P. T., & Deutsch, M. 2012. *The Psychological Components of Sustainable Peace*. New York London: Springer.
15. Bar Tal, 2013, p. 2.
16. Lederach, J. P. 2005. *The Moral Imagination: The Art and Soul of Building Peace*. Oxford University Press.
17. Galtung, 1996; Northrup, 1989; Rothman, 1997.
18. Coleman, P. T., Deutsch, M. 2012.
19. https://www.theparentscircle.org/en/homepage-en/.
20. https://dialogoimprobable.org/ (consulted 15 Sept 2024).
21. Johnson, D. W., & Johnson, R. T. 2005. 'New developments in social interdependence theory'. *Genetic, Social, and General Psychology Monographs* 131:4, pp. 285–358. https://doi.org/10.3200/MONO.131.4.285-358; Bercovitch, J., Kremenyuk, V., & Zartman, I. W. 2009. *The SAGE Handbook of Conflict Resolution*. SAGE Publications Ltd. https://doi.org/10.4135/9780857024701; Deutsch, M., Coleman, P. T., & Marcus, E. C. (Eds.). 2006. *The Handbook of Conflict Resolution: Theory and Practice (2nd ed.)*. Wiley Publishing.

22 Neuroscience and Peacebuilding, p. 17.
23 Neuroscience and peacebuilding, p. 15.
24 Volkan, V. D. 2004.
25 Oxford University Press, 2005, https://www.johnpaullederach.com/2023/03/the-moral-imagination-the-art-and-soul-of-building-peace-2/)
26 Based on Hertog, K. 2010, pp. 50–3.
27 Lederach, J. P. 1997, p. 31.
28 Citation from Abu-Nimer, M. 2001, p. 41.
29 Citations in this section are from the documentary clip Ivory Coast, A United Africa, https://www.youtube.com/watch?v=yNjuJelF59g, consulted on 18 July 2024.
30 Bar Tal, D. 2013, p. 168.

7 Creating peace-supporting systems and structures and addressing global challenges

The political, economic, legal, educational, health and security structures and systems in our societies can either promote or undermine peace.
With reference to the definition of peace presented in the introductory chapter, we postulate that the systems which are more likely to be peace-promoting are those that provide, for example, basic needs and well-being for as many people as possible without discrimination, functional channels to effectively address grievances and conflict, and human value-based education.

Systems and structures are made up of people. They are not just nouns, but verbs as well, constituted by the actions of their personnel and their 'users'.[1] Social constructionism, networking theory, and system theories all offer insights on how social systems are created, maintained and transformed through human action and interaction. Some theories emphasize the role of culture and societal norms in shaping particular social systems. Others emphasize the role of relationships, perceptions, interactions, language and communication in creating the social sphere and systems. Others again focus on economic resources and power relations. Across the various theories, it is clear that **human agency creates social reality. The well-being, mindsets, values, beliefs, attitudes, emotions, memories, social and economic conditions, relationships and other factors all influence how people shape and interact with social systems. Therefore, the psychosocial dimension within all the systems and structures that make our social environment is crucial and cannot be overestimated**.[2]

Systems and structures can change in response to internal and external factors, such as innovations, institutional reforms, social movements, crises (such as environmental disasters and war) and cross-cultural influences. It is possible to consciously transform peace-inhibiting systems and structures and to envision and install peace-enhancing structures, systems and institutions. Throughout history, there have been many examples of movements, innovations and initiatives that have fundamentally changed old systems and structures which gave rise to discrimination, injustice, poverty and violence. The movements for civil rights, women's vote and LGBTQ+ rights have all challenged systemic inequalities and advocated for social justice. More recently, the environmental justice movement is addressing the systems aggravating environmental degradation, social inequality, power and exploitation, while advocating instead for sustainable and equitable solutions.

As human beings, we have the possibility to choose and create a more positive future for society and ourselves, rather than passively just allowing events to unfold. We don't have to simply remain at the receiving end of all that happens, with its potential negative effects. **Social transformation requires awareness, social empowerment, vision, imagination, resources and collective action, among other things.** These psychosocial factors and dynamics at the intrapersonal and interpersonal levels have been described in detail in Chapters 3, 5 and 6. Nurturing and strengthening these psychosocial factors lays a strong psychosocial foundation for social change and sustainable peace. For example, when people are too traumatized or stressed, they often lack the sense of belonging or the inner resources to contribute positively to society. Stress management and the enhancement of the overall well-being of individuals are crucial to empower citizens who feel connected and are positively engaged to make a difference in the world. We saw the crucial importance of enhanced emotional and self-management skills, because people and movements for social change that act and react with hatred or anger often perpetuate vicious cycles of action and reaction, in which victims become perpetrators and vice versa. We also saw that through the development of our human potential, we can become very skilful, creative, courageous and intuitive agents for change.

While we have previously described how the psychosocial foundation is the cornerstone for peace-enhancing personal, interpersonal and social change, in this chapter we will look into some of the psychosocial factors at play in different peacebuilding sectors, such as security, governance, economy, development, justice, education, health and others. A detailed and comprehensive analysis of the operation of psychosocial factors in the different peacebuilding sectors is outside the scope of this work, however, since it would require an extensive cross-disciplinary study. Therefore, we will focus on highlighting in this chapter some of the **crucial psychosocial factors to be taken into account in the envisioning, creation and operation of peace-enhancing systems and structures in society**. Practical examples of effective transformation of some psychosocial dimensions in different peacebuilding sectors will be drawn from the work of Art of Living and IAHV. It is also beyond the scope of this work to identify, select and include a representative overview of examples here, given the countless, worldwide, positive practices that exist.

Psychosocial dimensions in the security sector

The security sector, usually considered to be very technical, also responds to, interacts with and functions through some very important psychosocial factors.

- Firstly, there are the **subjective and objective experiences of threat, danger, fear, anxiety, safety and security**. Psychosocial factors and dynamics relating to how individuals and communities perceive, respond to and manage security threats play a significant role in shaping security strategies and outcomes. Leaders, media and public discourses can ignite a climate of fear, threat and danger, which can then generate support and lead to decision-making for more military spending, surveillance, repression and stricter laws. On the other hand, they can also help create a climate of trust and assurance, allowing for the reduction of military spending and increased investment in development and other initiatives for the prevention of violence, crime and war. At the local level, citizen and community initiatives can improve the sense of security and prevent violence by fostering dialogue, cooperation, social cohesion and mutual support within their communities. On the other hand, they can also ignite tensions, distrust, polarization and radicalization, resulting in overt violence, hate crimes and clashes.

- **Individual and community resilience** plays an important role in the response to security threats and incidents and in recovery from them. As we have discussed earlier, overcoming trauma and stress resulting from violence, crime or war is essential to mitigate their long-term psychological impact, prevent cycles of violence and rebuild society.
- Security policies aimed at providing **security for all segments of society without discrimination** prevent the sense of heightened insecurity among certain, often minority groups of the population.
- **Psychosocial peacebuilding and the transformation of the causes of conflict** can lead to a secure foundation for long term safety and security.
- The **state of mind and stress levels of security personnel** can increase insecurity when they are too stressed to manage themselves or take the appropriate action according to the situation, or they can lead to positive outcomes and increased security when they are centred, focused and able to self-regulate.

Radicalization and violent extremism

Radicalization and violent extremism are a specific security challenge to peacebuilding and manifest in many forms and at different levels. Non-state armed groups worldwide use violent means to address real and perceived injustices and grievances and to achieve their goals of creating political and social change, bringing about a new religious or ideological order, gaining legitimacy, controlling territory and resources or acting in self-defence. Youth and other individuals from varied social backgrounds and with varied ideological, religious and political beliefs radicalize in thoughts and behaviour, go on to join gangs or extremist movements, or act as 'lone wolves' in shooting, sabotage or suicide attacks. Individuals who have been engaged in armed conflict and war, whether as fighters, rebels or soldiers, experience difficulties reintegrating peacefully in society upon their return. Communities and societies hosting small or large numbers of refugees and groups of 'others', radicalize from a perceived or instigated sense of threat to their own identity, security or prosperity. Governments and security forces undertake extreme anti-terrorist operations, often violating human rights and thus generating further radicalization. Radicalization and violent extremism can undermine social cohesion, hinder economic development, increase levels of militarization and generate widespread instability.

International institutions, national governments, think tanks and civil society organisations have been developing responses to the challenge of radicalization and violent extremism. There is now increasing evidence and acknowledgement, including from within security circles, that military and harsh punitive responses are insufficient at best, and counterproductive at worst, let alone contribute to prevention and transformation. While governments and intergovernmental institutions have developed a wide variety of strategies to tackle the root causes of extremism and terrorism within a more comprehensive approach that includes the reduction of poverty, the improvement of the socio-economic situation and the provision of education, these efforts do not always reach into the deeper aspects of the inner personal lives and mindsets of those targeted and so often lead to limited positive outcomes. Meanwhile, effective practitioners on the ground often struggle to bring their transformative responses and good practices to scale.

IAHV approach and methodology in the Prevention and Countering of Violent Extremism (PCVE)

IAHV has been advocating as well as actioning an innovative paradigm for the understanding and countering of violent extremism. Its approach broadens the efforts for prevention, intervention and rehabilitation through the effective transformation of individuals and groups involved in or affected by radicalization, as well as the transformation of wider conflict dynamics. **The approach is fundamentally human, situated in a broader peacebuilding framework, and tackles the psychosocial roots of the challenge.** IAHV Peacebuilding programmes bring about a profound transformation in attitudes, mindsets, well-being and behaviour of individuals and communities involved or affected by violence and extremism. They inspire and train participants to **use non-violent means** to achieve legitimate needs and mobilize them to become **agents of positive change** within their own communities.

It is commonly understood that both external environmental and internal psychological factors are crucial in the prevention and transformation of violence and extremism and that violent radicalization happens at the intersection of an enabling environment and a personal trajectory. IAHV programmes focus explicitly on the personal and relational aspects involved, and to a lesser extent on social, political or geopolitical aspects. Among the **psychosocial drivers of violent extremism**, as identified through research into best practices, IAHV addresses in particular those presented in Table 7.1.

Given these psychosocial drivers of extremism, the strength of IAHV's programmes lies in the **integrative approach towards empowerment**, addressing different individual and relational aspects such as presented in Table 7.2.

Exclusive ideologies and universal human values

Ideologies play an important role in mobilizing individuals and groups towards peace- as well as violence-enabling action. Specifically, those ideologies that justify and exacerbate extremism, conflict and war have a tendency to be expressed in black and white terms, deny the responsibility of their own group and blame others for the suffering inflicted. This transference of responsibility to others goes hand in hand with processes of dehumanization, moral disengagement and

Table 7.1 *Psychosocial Drivers of Violent Extremism Addressed in IAHV's PCVE Approach*

Personal, such as:
- Sense of rejection, exclusion, isolation, humiliation
- Negative feelings (hatred, frustration, desire to provoke, despair, fear, hopelessness)
- Idealism and a strong sense of justice
- Fascination for violence and fights
- Disbelief in non-extreme alternatives
- Identity questions or problems
- Lack of a meaningful purpose in life
- Tendency to search for simple ways to understand a complex world

Relational, such as:
- Negative or lack of positive personal experiences with certain groups of people.
- Desire to belong to a group.
- Interest in alcohol, drugs, or other group-binding factors.
- Peer pressure.
- Negative home/family experiences.
- Connection with a charismatic leader

Societal/Political, such as:
- Fear of / strong dislike for multiculturalism or certain groups of people.
- Divisive us-them paradigms.
- Lack of brotherhood, sisterhood or belonging to a community.
- Lack of trust in others / society.
- Real and perceived injustice, persecution, discrimination, oppression, marginalization

Global/Geopolitical, such as:
- Rapid changes within society.
- Resentment of Western supremacy
- Feelings of inequity and injustice on a global level, and a sense of humiliation
- Encroachment of modernity on 'traditional' values
- Highly symbolic conflicts on the global scene with broad repercussions

collective identity building based on us-them paradigms. Narrow ideologies promote cognitive shifts that erode moral inhibitions, so that immoral behaviour is considered dignified and necessary.

On the other hand, **broader ideologies based on shared humanity and interconnectedness can play an important role in redefining moral and ethical boundaries, creating psychological reluctance and barriers towards dehumanization, while providing a more inclusive and non-violent lens** through which identity and relationships are approached. IAHV's approach engages with and transforms psychosocial factors that support destructive ideologies and fosters a strong, experiential foundation of universal human values to support more positive worldviews, discernment and decision-making.

Working inclusively across affected populations

IAHV's programmes to prevent and transform violent extremism and radicalization are applicable widely across diverse personality types, ideologies and contexts. Individuals involved may come from very different social backgrounds, undergo different processes of radicalization and be

Table 7.2 *Intrapersonal and Interpersonal Factors Addressed in IAHV's PCVE Approach*

Identity:
- Broadening of identity and a diversified understanding of oneself.
- Fostering of self-esteem.
- Fostering of a sense of belonging, counter social isolation.
- Fostering of positive intergroup contact through meetings and meaningful acts towards 'the other group'.
- Prevention and reduction of fear and dislike of multiculturalism.
- Prevention of labelling and stigmatization, fostering of empathy and compassion.
- Reduction of perception of discrimination and a sense of victimhood

Empowerment and responsibility.
- Addressing of injustice and empowerment for positive action.
- Fostering self-confidence.
- Stimulation of the acquaintance with positive role models.
- Moving from blame to taking responsibility.
- Strengthening action instead of reaction

Healing and emotional well-being
- Releasing negative emotions (anger, revenge, hatred, frustration, loss, depression, etc.).
- Strengthening emotional resilience and coping capacity.
- Healing and release of trauma.
- Strengthening positive emotions.
- Increasing a sense of security, social trust.
- Reflection on the meaning of life

Mental training
- Breaking of destructive cognitive patterns, countering dichotomizing, black and white thinking.
- Fostering broadened perceptions and open mindset.
- Contributing to critical thinking capacity and questioning, openly discussing violence-promoting beliefs.
- Decreasing worry and tension, and increasing inner peace and contentment

Physical Health and Stress Resilience
- The release of deep stress and the strengthening of resilience to stress.
- Restoring a well-functioning neurobiological stress response system.
- Increasing the sense of well-being

Providing an Alternative
- Awareness raising and skills training for alternative strategies and the power and effectiveness of non-violence.
- Developing an alternative community supporting positive choices

---

influenced by various combinations of motivations. Based on universal human values, and practical, non-religious techniques and processes, IAHV and the Art of Living provide flexible programming for all individuals and communities directly or indirectly affected by violence and extremism, including former extremists, ex-combatants, militants, prisoners and offenders, gang members, convicted terrorists, radicalized youth, affected communities and relatives, social/youth/prevention workers, survivors of violence/terrorist attacks and more.

Radicalized and extremist individuals and groups, if not engaged, can undermine the prospects of sustainable peace for entire societies. Political labelling and condemnation often preclude the possibility of strategic engagement with them. Excluding them from peace processes, denying their claims and violating their human rights have proven to be counterproductive, as evidenced by the widespread radicalization occurring in prisons or triggered by harsh treatment from security forces. Reducing complex phenomena to simple punitive responses does not resolve conflict in the longer term. IAHV approaches radicalized and extremist individuals first and foremost as human beings, proactively reaching out to them and supporting them to achieve their objectives nonviolently and create alternative communities in which they feel included.

Constructive

IAHV's constructive approach builds on the positive potential in every human being and applies an evidence-based methodology to transform the individual's inner environment, releasing negative tendencies in thought and behaviour and strengthening positive ones. Focusing on the core dignity and universal values shared by all people, IAHV trainers have witnessed even the most hard-lined extremists renounce violence and transform into agents of peace.

Working across all stages of radicalization

IAHV programmes are able to address the full spectrum of radicalization, from recruitment to demobilization, including prevention, intervention, rehabilitation and reintegration.

Empowering non-violent mobilization

Recognizing that many grievances, such as injustice, violation of human rights, exploitation, discrimination and unequal opportunities, are justified, IAHV programmes empower stakeholders to address conflict constructively and to bring about desired change through non-violent means. They channel the inherent drive of youth, empowering them with confidence and techniques to become self-reliant agents of non-violent, strategic peacebuilding. As such, the programmes aim to provide an attractive, alternative non-violent paradigm of discourse, strategy and community to replace extremist ideologies, violent engagement and mobilization.

Engaging formers, survivors and other positive role models

IAHV engages and integrates former militants and extremists into their programmes as trusted insiders to support participants of similar backgrounds. Having left the path of crime and violence to become trainers and peace workers, they function as inspiring, positive role models with a wealth of experience to share.

Addressing individuals and their environment

IAHV programmes strengthen the impact of their initiatives for prevention and resilience by also reaching out beyond individual combatants and survivors to work with and support their relatives, peers and communities. In addition, IAHV also assists staff and professionals working on radicalization and violent extremism to integrate effective techniques for stress management, personal resilience and well-being into their work.

Systemic approach in collaboration with ongoing initiatives

IAHV's expertise, combined with identified best practices from the field in an inclusive, integrative approach, can lay a strong psychosocial foundation that complements and strengthens ongoing initiatives.

The psychosocial dimensions of the reintegration of ex-combatants

The rehabilitation and reintegration of ex-combatants entail diverse challenges for ex-combatants themselves, communities of return and other actors involved. Disarmament, Demobilization and Reintegration (DDR), the mainstream approach in peacebuilding and post-conflict settings to transition combatants back into civilian life, is not merely a technical process with distinct components to be completed according to certain guidelines. It has profound psychosocial dimensions at both the individual and community levels. From the perspective of ex-combatants, important psychosocial factors for reintegration include (Table 7.3):

Table 7.3 *Important Psychosocial Factors for the Reintegration of Ex-combatants*

- Post-traumatic stress
- Addiction issues
- Mistrust and alienation experienced
- Depression, apathy and the perception of being disempowered
- Victimization and an inability to take responsibility for past acts or current behaviour
- Negative emotions such as anger, blame and a desire for revenge
- Cognitive reliance on violence to achieve power or fulfil feelings of masculinity
- Other identity challenges related to re-entry.

Families of combatants and surrounding communities are indirectly involved in or affected by violence and other extremist activities, and are also often deeply impacted. Through the actions of relatively small groups, large parts of affected communities live in fear and suffer from post-traumatic stress.

Even where security, military, judicial, economic and social measures of a standard DDR process are implemented, effective rehabilitation and reintegration may remain shallow if no attention is paid to more integrative, psychosocial issues. Given the varied and long-standing impact of armed violence, comprehensive DDR processes are necessary to help divided communities and returning combatants break cycles of mistrust and violence and ensure a sustainable peacebuilding process.

IAHV programmes and training to prevent and counter violent extremism and break cycles of violence

While the methodology of IAHV has been described in detail earlier in this book, its application for the prevention and countering of radicalization and violent extremism is carried out through various different programmes, such as:

1. *Preventing and Countering Violent Extremism for young people at risk, in the earlier stages, or seeking re-entry from periods of radicalization*:

   - Transforming the attitudes and behaviours of youths and young adults from being at risk to become high-performing, responsible, confident and empowered populations;
   - Providing alternatives to radicalized narratives and destructive behaviour towards themselves and others;
   - The provision of practical tools and life skills to relieve stress, master emotions, withstand radicalization and peer pressures, and resolve conflicts using non-violent action.

   > *'I thought I would go to Heaven by killing. Now I know that Heaven is right here on Earth by loving.'*
   > (Former Al Qaeda member imprisoned in India)[3]

2. *Youth Leadership Peacebuilding Training (YLPT). This* empowers youth to become dynamic leaders and role models who are the driving force behind the prevention and transformation of radicalization and violence and the development of a process of deep peacebuilding.

   YLPT facilitates the physical, emotional, mental, social and spiritual empowerment of youth, along with training in peacebuilding skills. This enables them to take responsibility for transforming their communities into more peaceful societies and to become effective and skilled peacebuilders within their own communities. YLPT provides hard and soft skills development, focusing on individual empowerment and locally informed and owned peacebuilding strategies.

   - Its comprehensive set of tools and techniques builds and enhances: stress management, trauma-relief and healing, resilience, self-knowledge and self-management, creativity and innovation, communication skills, value-based leadership, teamwork, decision-making, dynamism and entrepreneurship, interpersonal skills and a volunteering spirit.
   - In addition, YLPT includes training in peacebuilding skills such as effective communication and conflict resolution techniques.
   - Participants are supported to design peacebuilding projects that are context-relevant, effective, feasible and scalable through applied conflict and peace analysis, focusing on

the factors, actors and dynamics most relevant to the local context. They subsequently implement this project as part of their training.

- In addition, they are trained to facilitate low-threshold and accessible workshops on resilience and stress-relief, thus multiplying the benefits of the workshops in their communities.

> **As related by IAHV trainers in Iraq.**
> *Farhaan was supposed to have joined three of his friends that morning. They had driven to the front to join a militia to fight against the Islamic State (IS). Filled with fury and hatred for the brutalities IS had inflicted on his family and others, including the kidnapping and rape of his own sister, he had been pushed over the edge and was ready to take revenge. As a young man in his early twenties, he had volunteered to document the crimes against humanity committed against his own Yazidi people, taking pictures of corpse after corpse, often of people he knew. However, one of his friends spoke to him that morning and managed to persuade him to come to a peacebuilding workshop and later to an IAHV Youth Leadership Peacebuilding Training. As a result of that, Farhaan instead started giving Stress Release and Resilience Workshops for displaced people, from his base in an internal displacement camp in Dohuk.[4]*

In order to make a significant impact in conflict dynamics and make peacebuilding effective and sustainable, IAHV's programmes are guided by 'inside out' strategies, developed and driven from the inspiration, ideas and commitment of empowered, local people themselves. The Youth Leadership Peacebuilding Training strengthens the non-violent empowerment of youth who may otherwise follow a path of radicalization, aggression or violence. It also aims to create Ambassadors of Peace in societies afflicted by conflict, violence, gangs and extremism. These agents of change can counter the culture of despondency, helplessness, resignation, demoralization, grief and anxiety that may prevail in societies dominated by violence. Instead, they can help to restore self-esteem and confidence to change society for the better. As Gurudev Sri Sri Ravi Shankar says, the people who use violence are very active and loud, while the people who are peaceful are passive and quiet, so 'it is time for the voice of peace to be heard loud and clear'.[5]

3. *Rehabilitation & Reintegration of Ex-Combatants into society, including current and former extremists as well as war veterans.*

IAHV's programming specifically focuses on the psychosocial factors which are often missing in mainstream reintegration and DDR planning, helping them to re-enter society as contributing and peaceful members (see Table 7.3).

> 'I was a district commander of a military outfit. I used to carry a gun with me all the time. Sleep would come hard, so engulfed was I with worries and guilt that I had to resort to taking sleeping pills. After I underwent The Art of Living programme, I realized the futility of what I was doing and gave up the path of violence. My life has changed.' (Mansoor Ahmed, former militant from Kashmir)[6]

4. *The IAHV/Art of Living Prison Programme*

   The Prison Programme aims to break the cycles of violence, reduce recidivism and create a humane, rehabilitative prison climate by effectively transforming psychosocial factors of crime, aggression and radicalization. (See Chapter 5)

5. *Healing, Resilience and Empowerment (HRE) training for survivors, relatives and affected communities.*

   In a comprehensive, community approach, IAHV also supports survivors and communities affected by violent extremism as well as relatives of extremist offenders to cope with their situations, manage strong emotions such as fear and anger, and strengthen their own well-being and resilience. The HRE workshop is a low-threshold workshop to address psychosocial consequences of conflict and violence, releasing acute and basic stress and fears, improving sleep and providing relief.

> 'I felt so calm and good that when I talked to my son who is still in jail, he told me that he would love to learn the breathing techniques ... This workshop gives me the strength to keep being there for him ... ' (Mother of current prisoner in Venezuela)

6. *SKY Resilience and Professional Excellence training for PCVE, security and law enforcement personnel.*

   In addition to the Self-Care Programme described in Chapter 5, this training also includes:

   - Introduction to IAHV's approach, methodology and case studies on PCVE and offender rehabilitation;
   - Analysis of the psychosocial factors at the core of rehabilitation, reintegration and transformation of radicalization, violent extremism and offending;

   Ideally, each training programme mentioned above is supported by a tailored 3 to twelve-month follow-up period, in which participants engage in ongoing learning and advanced training programmes or implement local violence prevention initiatives.

Examples of IAHV and Art of Living Implementation in the security sector and in 20+ conflict- and war zones

- *7,400+ fighters renounced violence* (Kashmiri militants, Naxalite terrorists, FARC rebels, Kosovo Liberation Army veterans, the LTTE in Sri Lanka, militants in Assam, Maoists in Nepal) – see case studies below

Case study: Tamil Tigers, Sri Lanka

The conclusion of the war in Sri Lanka in May 2009 saw the displacement of over 275,000 people. Some of those who were serving in the erstwhile Liberation Tigers of Tamil Eelam (LTTE) were placed in the custody and care of government rehabilitation centres. IAHV and Art of Living Sri Lanka delivered their rehabilitation programmes to ex-LTTE combatants placed at the Boosa Prison and the rehabilitation centres in Omanthai and Maradamadu. The programmes helped more than 1,800 ex-LTTE combatants to meaningfully reintegrate within mainstream society.

- *Rehabilitation and reintegration of 5,000 criminals, gang members and ex-prisoners in Copenhagen.* In Denmark, former gang members, criminals, drug addicts and prisoners are training and supporting thousands of others both inside and outside of prison, following their own rehabilitation journey via IAHV's and Art of Living's Breathe/Prison programmes. Grateful for their 'new lives', they are committed to preventing others from going down a similar destructive path and providing support to them as they turn their backs on a life of crime, violence, stress and disillusion.

- *Iraq Trauma-Relief and Women and Youth Empowerment*
  Since 2003, IAHV and the Art of Living have been working actively and continuously in Iraq, promoting the message of non-violence and providing trauma-relief. They organize empowerment and leadership training for youth and women, support women to be financially independent through vocational training, and organize initiatives and collaborations to protect women and advance their leadership roles in Iraq. In addition, they also facilitate improved interreligious and interdenominational understanding and cooperation. Hundreds of youth have graduated from the Youth Leadership Training Programme and thousands of people from all denominations have received trauma-relief. *'Until now we have only known the art of dying,'* one Red Crescent official said, as he praised Sri Sri for bringing the *'art of living'* to the victims suffering from the long-drawn-out war.

  Former prime minister of Iraq, Nouri Al-Maliki, expressed his appreciation for Gurudev Sri Sri Ravi Shankar's support for the Iraqi people, stating: *'There are big powers who have big might, but they are not able to unite the hearts and minds of people. This work can be done only by a spiritual leader.'*

> 'I did the life skill course and it helped me recover fast and to have hope again for my life and my future.' Ibtisam suffered from a stroke after her husband was killed by terrorists.
>
> 'It feels like breathing out all the stress of war and breathing in a new life.' (Ahmed Hinoon)
>
> 'We knew only death and despair. Now we can smile. This is the greatest gift that the Art of Living has given us.' (Shafiqur Rehman)
>
> 'I feel like I went through a mental shower. Before, I was very angry and very sad about everything in the past. Now I'm just filled with joy and gratitude.' (Course participant)
>
> 'Before this experience, I was sad, depressed and starting to lose hope because of the situation here in Iraq. Now, after only four days, I feel confident about myself, happier, I have hopes and dreams again and I feel that life is so beautiful. I have started to love everyone and physically I have much more energy. I want to thank you very much for helping all of us feel better.' (M. Ali Bankat)
>
> 'We had no hope and we could only pray for some power to come and take us out of the situation. We think the Art of Living is that power.' (Ramia Sagban from Baghdad)[7]

- *In Ukraine*: The IAHV Ukraine team has been providing rehabilitation and reintegration of war veterans and of civilians released from captivity (including hostages) to improve their mental health and alleviate symptoms of trauma. They are also working with the populations of frontline and de-occupied territories and the families of the deceased and captured, to alleviate trauma, develop resilience and empowerment.

> 'I believe that the methodology and scientifically proven methods of IAHV Ukraine should become part of the training for new recruits, as well as to improve the leadership qualities and self-regulation skills of command staff, and be a part of the recovery of soldiers after service.' (Major V. Z. Derevyan'ko, Deputy Commander of the 1st Separate Assault Battalion named Dmytro Kotsiubailo)

- *Colombia*
  Since the crucial mediation role Gurudev Sri Sri Ravi Shankar played at a very critical stage in the peace negotiation process in 2015 (see Chapter 2), Art of Living has continued its special involvement with the peacebuilding process in Colombia. More than 20,000 people from vulnerable communities (victims, demobilized, interns, displaced, among others) in different areas of the country have benefited through humanitarian and peacebuilding work. Some of the initiatives include:
  - Empowering 800 women and community leaders as agents for peace (Department of Cundinamarca in the framework of the programmes of Reconciliation Colombia and Publications Semana 'Women Leaders Build Peace' and 'social leadership in times of reconciliation').

- Training youth in areas of risk in leadership skills and in implementing healing, resilience and empowerment workshops for the broader population (Department of Chocó, in alliance with Shakira's Foundation, and with financial support from USAID).
- Accompanying and providing psychosocial support to the families of the Valle del Cauca deputies (in 2016, with support of UNDP and the international community).
- Facilitating and mediating among the family victims and the FARC for the realization of the early act of recognition of collective responsibility in Cali.
- Accompanying and supporting the indigenous Awa community in the process with the FARC aimed at the performance of early acts of recognition of collective responsibility, including forgiveness and reconciliation, 2017.
- Trauma-relief support programme for FARC members in the process of receiving prosthesis, 2017.
- Trauma-relief and reconciliation event with thirty-two ex-combatants from the FARC, the AUC (paramilitary group Autodefensas Unidas de Colombia), the Colombian army and 160 victims, 2018, Remedios Antioquia.
- Trauma-relief and stress management programmes for vulnerable children, healthcare workers during the pandemic, prisoners, women affected by gender-based violence and defenders of human rights in Cuba (Civil Right Defenders).

  The work was conducted in partnership with different organizations such as: the Agency for Reintegration and Normalization (ACR), Victims Unit, High Counselling for the Victims of the Mayor of Bogotá, Reconciliation Colombia and others.
- *Belgium: Healing, Resilience and Empowerment Training for mothers in Belgium whose children left as foreign fighters.*

> 'I learned to accept the situation, to live with it. I am able to forgive myself and to forgive my son now.' (Mother of a foreign fighter, Antwerp, Belgium)
>
> 'I learned to be more in the present moment. I learned that instead of being stuck in the past, it is best to go through the pain and suffering in order to transform it into something better. It's a real-life training this programme. It should be accessible to all communities.'
>   (Mother of two sons gone to Syria, Molenbeek, Belgium)

Belgium: Training in Professional Excellence at the Court of Antwerp for Youth Lawyers interested in exploring alternative options to prison sentences for young returnees from Syria.

> 'This was very enriching, hopeful and encouraging – according to me an enormous potential for our society! This seems very applicable for many youth and children, not just radicalized but also

> victims of child prostitution, youth who are lost and estranged from themselves, as well as for youth workers to increase their capacity to deal with stressful situations.'
> (Youth Lawyer in Antwerp)

- *SKY Resilience Training for police officers, peacekeeping personnel and law enforcement officers, from Brazil to Kosovo,* aimed to reduce stress and trauma, increase resilience and focus, thus strengthening well-being, improving job performance and reducing risks of escalation and violence in critical situations.

Commanders and hundreds of members of the Special Police Units from different countries, that were part of the United Nations Mission in Kosovo (UNMIK), participated in the Art of Living's Stress Management Training at a critical time in their deployment, allowing them to release stress, sleep better, release worries and anxiety, have more energy and focus, and feel stable and calm in tense situations during their peacekeeping mission.[8]

> 'Almost one hundred police officers have taken the training and they reported release of negative emotions, increased energy and vitality. The Art of Living Programme has the potential to keep police officers free from internal stress and help them to remain stress free in critical situations.'
> (Rahahleh Mazen, Commander Special Police Unit Jordan, UN Mission in Kosovo)

The SKY Resilience Programme with over 3,000 officers from the Bahia Military Police in Brazil resulted in a 60 per cent reduction in the use of force and a 70 per cent reduction in community complaints.[9]

> 'I did the Programme and it helped me a lot to be more calm. In my work, as in life, we suffer from several kinds of tension. This helped me to control them. I feel much better; it helped me a lot to recover, to be more calm and to think positive. It changes your life.' (Matías Ferrito Mordillo, Police Officer, Buenos Aires)

- *Rehabilitation and reintegration of youth gangs in Panama and Mexico* – see case study below;
- *Healing, Resilience and Prevention of Extremism for 18,000 war-affected children in Lebanon and Jordan* – see Chapter 4;
- *Prisons worldwide*: rehabilitation programmes for 800,000 prisoners and staff – see Chapter 5.

> As one prisoner in the UK remarked, 'I spent my whole life trying to destroy society. After doing the Art of Living Prison Programme, I now want to spend the rest of my life contributing to society.'

Case study: Reintegrating gang members in the ghettos of Curundu, Panama City (2008)

The IAHV and Art of Living group were approached with the request to conduct a twenty-month rehabilitation and empowerment programme for eleven members of the gang of Los Cicarios in the ghettos of Panama City.

Gang members in the slums grew up in very poor living conditions, with families struggling to put food on the table and a prevalent lack of parental care and affection. It became natural for members to bond with each other and form a gang to help provide income for their families and to secure protection from rival gangs. Young members were often forced into criminal activities against their will and got caught up in a vicious cycle of violence and crime as a way of life. Without proper education or parental support, their options were limited, and many felt they had no choice but to go along with it. Violence, vandalism and robbery became the most straightforward strategies to get what they needed and stay alive. However, walking freely in the streets became impossible because of the threat from other gangs, and 'doing time' in prison became a pattern as a result of their illegal activities.

These gang members underwent a profound transformation during the Youth Leadership Training Programme. It gave them the discipline to develop healthier habits and provided them with practical life skills and techniques, which reinforced self-esteem, opened their minds to new possibilities, and empowered them with a new sense of purpose in life. This was then directed into the initiation of service-oriented activities. In partnership with local organizations, the Art of Living participated in mediation between rival gangs, which generated more peace in the area. There were weekly meetings in which the former gang members discussed and exchanged ideas and possible solutions for the difficult situations they found themselves in. They also participated in the Art of Living follow-up sessions to release freshly accumulated tensions as they arose and to reconnect with their own personal inner space of tranquillity and peace. Before too long, the former gang members began carrying out service activities in orphanages and gave mentorship to younger children, becoming known as the 'Youth for Change'.

> *One ex-gang member sincerely shared: 'We used to behave even worse than them. Now we've changed, and we come to teach them that there can be a change. All of them deserve a chance, just as we had too. One of us could have died with all these problems; we could have gone to jail. I don't know, but if we can change and take advantage of that, I think everybody can do the same. We have to stretch out our hand to help other people who also deserve a chance. We can teach them to change as a person and to shift their mind, to become a good person and not to fix things only with bullets, but to see there are different ways.'*

Through this comprehensive approach, Art of Living was able to provide a transformative solution to cyclical violence and crime.

Here are some testimonials from the former gang members of Los Cicarios:

> 'I have found the same belongingness of a group here, but it's not for vandalism; it's a group to help others who need it and were in the same situation as we were before.'
>
> 'I want to move forward, I want to know more, and to learn more things that I don't know. That's what I want for my future, to have a good family, to be able to help my mom and my grandma because they deserve it. I am sure I'll be able to get out of the ghetto and many more of us are going to get out.'

Case study: Reduced PTSD symptoms in US war veterans

Military life brings with it extreme stress due to multiple deployments, dangerous missions, traumatizing events and the subsequent challenges with reintegration back home into family and community. The US National Institute of Health estimated that, of the approximately 2 million veterans returning from Iraq and Afghanistan, up to 20 per cent suffered from post-traumatic stress (PTS). Veterans of previous wars also continued to experience symptoms of PTS. In addition to standard PTS symptoms, the signature wound among war veterans from Iraq and Afghanistan was moral injury, which is the psychological injury of having done, experienced or witnessed something against one's moral code. Symptoms of moral injury include feelings of guilt or shame, worthlessness, despair, and remorse, loss of meaning and interest in life, feelings like 'I've lost a part of myself' and/or 'I do not know who I am anymore', intense distrust and depression.

Traditional treatments for veterans with PTS do not always work for them, because recounting traumatic events in traditional therapeutic regimes can be too intensely emotional, while drug treatment has negative side effects. Despite advances in traditional therapy and drug-based treatments, there is a critical need for complementary approaches to alleviate the anxiety, trauma, anger, sleeplessness and other side effects of military service.

The SKY Resilience Training of IAHV's Project Welcome Home Troops restores well-being, mental focus and a renewed sense of connection and purpose. Veterans from Iraq and Afghanistan experienced significant reductions in PTSD in just one week, with sustained benefits after one year. The integrated body-mind programmes have multiple benefits. They are effective, evidence-based, have no known negative side effects, do not require participants to revisit and talk through traumatic events, and are self-empowering. This fits well for veterans, who are generally courageous, self-reliant people, who do not easily embrace the label of 'victim, or person with a diagnosis'.

> 'A few weeks ago shooting, cars exploding, screaming, death, . . . That was your world. Now back home, no one knows what it is like over there, so no one knows how to help you get back your normalcy. They label you as a victim of the war. I am not a victim! But how do I get back my normalcy?' (Nathan Hruska, US Marine Corps, Operation Enduring Freedom)

In preference to drug dependence or therapy, they value educational self-help tools which they can use to manage themselves. The Power Breath Meditation Workshop allows veterans to regain a sense of self-mastery and control because they can self-administer the techniques.

IAHV provides its training through military institutions, Veterans Affairs Hospitals, Veteran Centres and communities around the United States.

> 'I have done my best to battle my demons through physical activity and counselling; however, nothing has come close to the healing that occurred during the SKY Breathing Workshop. I honestly feel like I have been given a second chance at life.' (Travis H., USMC Veteran)
>
> 'This workshop has done more than I ever could have imagined. Not knowing there were any underlying issues made it hard to even acknowledge or accept them. After doing the workshop and continuing my home practice, I have opened the door to my emotions. I am happy to say that I can feel happiness as well as sadness, and both are great. Just being able to feel has been an amazing experience for me, and has made me become connected with friends and family. I have been given a new life, and I feel empowered to share my new self with everyone. It has been a very interesting journey for me, coming from a cold person who judged and criticized everyone to an open and loving person who is dedicated to serving my community and helping others make the same transition that I went through. Thank you for giving me a life worth living.' (Travis Leanna, US Marine Corps, Operation Iraqi Freedom)
>
> 'The course was very beneficial for me, uncovering things about myself that I never realized had been bothering me. It helped me be at peace with myself from issues, feelings and the things that I participated in at war ... Through that I have been able to come to peace with some of the things that I did and the way I felt about them. I wish I could have learned this breathing forty years ago.' (Noel, Vietnam Combat Veteran)
>
> 'After getting out of the Army I did not adjust well to civilian life. I was short-tempered towards everyone. After learning the breathing techniques most of my anger dropped away. Now I approach life with a calmness I never had before. On the rare occasions when I do get angry, I have easy-to-use techniques to relax and get rid of the stress. I have a newfound confidence to meet any challenge that arises.' (Ron Bayes, US Army, Desert Storm, Gulf war)

Rehabilitation programmes were also conducted for veterans of the wars in Vietnam, Kosovo and Ukraine.

> 'I have survived the Reqak massacre and I will never be able to forget it. I myself was beaten and my kidneys were severely damaged due to being beaten. My family members were killed in the massacre and since then I have suffered from depression and take medications (mostly tranquillizers). Disabled KLA (Kosovo Liberation Army) veterans do not get proper health protection and institutions seem to have forgotten us. All this adds to our depression and feeling of loneliness. Art of Living (AoL) gave me a feeling that somebody sincerely cares for us. The AoL course has helped me to see my future in a new, brighter perspective. After the breathing exercises I feel lighter and

> happier. From my own experience, I can tell that the AoL programme can bring relief to all those who went through the traumas of war.' (Ram Shabani)
>
> 'I was seriously wounded while I served as a KLA soldier during the war. My leg was amputated and I was left with many psychological problems like insomnia, flashbacks, irritability, anger and depression. Since the Art of Living programme, I feel more centred, peaceful and more satisfied. I have experienced that I am not just this body, but something much more.' (Enver Krasniqi)
>
> 'As a KLA soldier, I was wounded three times during the war. Since then, I feel a lot of pain and take painkillers almost every day. During my sleep, I hear my brother's voice, who was killed in the Reqak massacre, and voices of my friends who were killed in the war. I hear them calling me for help. I often jump from my bed searching for the gun, and afterwards I cannot sleep. After taking the AoL Programme, I sleep much better and flashbacks and nightmares have reduced. Now I am using the AoL programme instead of painkillers. On the basis of my own experience, I find this programme so effective in giving relief to traumatized people and war victims.' (Afet Bilalli)

Case study: Militant groups (ULFA and UPLA) in Assam, India

For many years, Assam had been a hotbed of militancy of various kinds related to tensions between the Indian government, indigenous people and immigrants, and among the many different tribal groups. The Northeast regions of India felt neglected by the central Indian government. Economic and infrastructure development had stagnated, and there was little communication or mutual understanding. As a result, there was a sense of alienation, isolation and emotional disconnect from the rest of India. Negative judgements and prejudices from the rest of India towards people from the Northeast aggravated these sensitivities. The huge influx of immigrants challenged the social fabric, communal harmony and rights of the indigenous people. The tribes wanted to defend and preserve their specific identity, cultures and traditions against the immigrants from neighbouring countries and against other tribes and groups. Autonomy and independence were seen as solutions to overcome these challenges. There was a general lack of trust among the different groups and actors, aggravated by a lack of effective communication and understanding. The situation required that the psychosocial driving factors of the conflicts should be addressed through a deeper process of conflict transformation rather than through simple discussions or superficial solutions.

The United Liberation Front of Assam (ULFA) was one of the strongest militant groups in the area, reportedly comprising more than 20,000 armed militants at its peak. ULFA had been fighting for the independence of Assam since 1979 in response to the neglect and exploitation of the Indian state and to address social and cultural grievances. Thousands of youth had joined what was initially a non-violent struggle, but which later turned into an armed insurgency, using extortion, kidnapping and killing as part of their methodology. Some died and some became disillusioned. While the original rebellion received significant social community support to defend the common cause, this changed over time as the general population suffered from the armed conflict and the actions of the ULFA. After extended struggles without concrete positive outcomes, many militants surrendered to the army, ended up in jail or in isolation in their villages. They had often invested many precious years of their lives in a cause which had hardly progressed. Whereas they had previously been respected and supported as freedom fighters, they were now rejected as militants. They also had difficulty integrating into community life after years of hiding in the jungle and were prevented from getting jobs or earning a living through other means. Reportedly, for many of them, it had been a long time since they had felt really happy. Without proper rehabilitation or reasonable prospects for leading a successful civilian life, they could easily return to the path of violence. In 2012, the Art of Living, in cooperation with the state of Assam and the Indian government, became engaged to rehabilitate hundreds of former militants who had surrendered and to support their peaceful return to society.

The Art of Living provided a one-month training, at its Bangalore ashram, for the rehabilitation and reintegration of 350 militants, many of whom belonged to different extremist groups from an early age. For most of them it was the first time in twelve years that they had been acknowledged by the government, so they did not ask further questions and simply undertook the travel and attended the training. The training included the standard programme curriculum of the Art of Living and IAHV, as well as the Youth Leadership Training Programme along with a special advanced meditation programme. They were able to release memories and traumas related to the violent acts they had faced and committed. As part of the reintegration programme, they also learned vocational training and training in organic farming to enable them to earn their living in a non-violent way.

Gurudev Sri Sri Ravi Shankar related to them on a very personal level, as he relates to everyone, regardless of where they are from. He commended their commitment, discipline, and dedication to a higher purpose, and he actively listened to their concerns. He also expressed concern about the use of violence and the resultant harm it inflicted on both themselves and others.

During the training, deadly riots broke out in Assam between indigenous Assamese people and Muslim inhabitants. Houses were burnt, families were killed, and half the population of a district had to flee and move into army camps for their safety. Being a mixed group of indigenous Assamese, tribal and Muslim people, tensions arose within the participant group. Many of them wanted to leave the training to check on their families. However, after discussion and practice, tensions calmed and the participants decided to continue with the training. The path towards rehabilitation for these former militants, and with it the choice for peace in Assam, could move forward. At the end, they were deeply touched by the hospitality, love and support they had received during their entire stay in the Art of Living ashram.

One hundred per cent of the participants felt their lives had changed for the better. Many renounced violence, took up agriculture, started small businesses and became willing to contribute to the sustainable and peaceful development of their communities. Many shared they took up volunteer roles to improve the lives of their communities, helped to set up schools for children, were able to provide for themselves and their families and became successful in farming. They also inspired and trained others, and persuaded other militants to leave the path of militancy and join the programmes. Others stayed back in Bangalore and became teachers of the Art of Living.

Here are some of their comments after the programme (where needed, names have been excluded for security reasons):

> 'My fight was for the people. So maybe I have no regrets. But I realized that violence is not the path. I am now determined to build a strong harmonious community. I want to go back and resolve conflicts in my region, now that I am at peace with myself.'
>
> 'I was merely eighteen when I joined the ULFA. From my early childhood, I had the zeal to serve my country and to do it proud. Like most of the lower middle-class households in Assam, the condition of my family was also very pathetic. There was just enough to fill our bellies and, at times, not even that. Whenever I saw people indulge in corrupt acts, hatred welled up within and I wanted to drive my village people on the right path and do something greater for society. When I joined the organization, the objective of the organization was perfect. The course of action was non-violent and the local Assamese people connected with our ideals and wholeheartedly stood by us. They would host us and keep us safe. Groups who joined later damaged the reputation of the organization. I surrendered in 1999. We were told that if we surrendered, we would be given many opportunities and rehabilitated. But nothing of that sort happened and I became depressed. I could not find social acceptance, nor wanted to return to the path I had abandoned. Many who had surrendered had inflicted atrocities and had mercilessly gunned down unarmed and harmless civilians. It disgusted the local population, and society not only feared but also disliked us, even after we had surrendered. I took to alcohol. I helped found the Ex-ULFA Coordination Committee to demand the rights promised to us by the government. For more than a decade, nothing happened. I continued drinking because I didn't know what to do or where to go. I felt as if my existence was of no use. It wouldn't make a difference to anyone if I died that very day. I didn't know who to look to for help. In 2012, I was part of the 300 Ex-ULFA members team that arrived at the Art of Living ashram for a month-long vocational and leadership training. Initially, I thought the government had promised rehabilitation but they had shirked their responsibility again and put us in this ashram. We used to get up early, exercise and meditate. I could not fathom how yoga and meditation would be helpful to us but decided to give the training a fair chance. Unknowingly, some transformation was already taking place by some grace which was beyond my minimal understanding. By the end of the training, I sobbed and wept my heart out. I was freed of the burden of all that I had done and not done. It dawned on me, during and after the training, what life was really meant to be. This training should have come much earlier in our lives. I told the Assam government I didn't need any rehabilitation. I was taken apart and put together in the most beautiful way possible and I was an island of bliss within. I had found the strength to live on my terms and could stand alone, tall and proud as the real Ramen Deka. I returned to Assam and conducted the first Art of Living workshop in my village, as I was taught during the training. People were so happy. They had never experienced anything like that before. But more than that, they were surprised by the transformation they witnessed in me. They said: "Is this the same Ramen that left then and has returned now?" I volunteered for three years and organized various Art of Living trainings in Assam for local and village youth. When I was in ULFA, people showed me respect out of fear, but now they respect me out of love. In 2016, I, a

trained ex-ULFA militant, completed my Teacher Training Programme with the Art of Living. My sole purpose is to inspire and empower people and spread happiness, peace and harmony in people's lives. I have Gurudev to thank for my new life.' (Ramen Deka, Ramjhuri village, Darrang district)[10]

'Coming here, I feel a lot of belongingness and respect for others. It is because I was given the same respect and I was welcomed with belongingness. I now recognize the struggle I was going through mentally. It seems I have found a tool to solve my problems. I can now see a way ahead. I have some land back home. I would like to take up organic farming.'

'The experience of the Sudarshan Kriya was unique. All the scars, physical, mental and emotional, that I had been carrying since my days in the organization, slowly faded and finally disappeared, leaving me light and calm. Alongside was the feeling of immense inner strength.' (Uday Brahma, Kosubil Village, Panbari, Chiran)[11]

'I have turned over a new leaf, fresh, green and tender. I don't know where the anger, guilt and darkness have disappeared.' (Tapan Kumar Sharma, Taragaon village, Darrang, Assam)[12]

'It's a new life for me. I find a lot of enthusiasm and determination to lead a new life. I had a lot of physical and mental strain, but just after two days of doing the Sudarshan Kriya and other practices, I can sit on the ground and sleep soundly at night. I have a new zest to live life.'

'It has changed the equation I had with the village people. Their aloofness had melted and they became very positively inclined towards me. They accepted me with open arms. My changed attitude and pleasant behaviour surprised the village people. I also felt a sense of fulfilment and happiness.' (Sidananda Deka, Doha village, Chamunpara, Darrang, Assam)

'When I became a teacher with the Art of Living and reached out to many people like me and saw them transform, I felt that I was still working for a better Assam but the method had changed. Was this the bigger purpose? Indeed, it was. I was putting my best foot forward, minus the stress and the fear.... There was a time when I was moving from village to village to take up arms to redress their grievances. Today, I am moving from village to village imparting spiritual knowledge to them. I experience the grace of Gurudev Sri Sri Ravi Shankar every moment of my life."[13] (Maneka Dihingiya, Nou-Hati, Dimow, Sibsagar)

When the general secretary of the ULFA was released from prison after eighteen years, he already knew about the support that the Art of Living had been providing to help his militiamen reintegrate into society. Having seen the ineffectiveness of armed struggle to achieve their objectives, he became a strong advocate for peaceful development and reaching objectives through non-violent means. He continued partnering with the Art of Living to bring other armed groups into the mainstream in Assam.

For eight years, the United People's Liberation Army (UPLA) fought an armed struggle for autonomy in the Karbi Anglong district in the Indian state of Assam. Gurudev Sri Sri Ravi Shankar and his team had been in intense discussions with members of the group for eighteen months. After thirty-five high-ranked members of the armed group, including its chairman and general secretary, attended an Art of Living programme in Bangalore, the leadership pledged to 'suspend armed struggle, declare a ceasefire with the State and Central Government of India and explore the possibilities of pursuing our demands through dialogue'.[14] Songsarpo Tungjang, UPLA joint secretary in charge, explained: 'Gurudev Sri Sri Ravi Shankar's vision has inspired us to look for democratic ways of fulfilling the aspirations of Karbi Anglong people. They have guided us to come to the mainstream and inspired us to see our demands with a bigger and long-term vision. We have learnt that we need to adopt peaceful, non-violent and loving ways to fulfill our aspirations and resolve our issues with the Government.'[15] The unilateral ceasefire by the UPLA in October 2018 was followed by peace negotiations resulting in the signing of a Peace Agreement in September 2021, the subsequent disbandment of the armed group and integration of some of its members in the Karbi Anglong Autonomous Council.[16] The Government and Art of Living continued to support the reintegration of former militants in mainstream society.

Case study: Naxalites, India (2002–Present): From bullets to ballots

The Naxalites are a group of left-wing communist militants in India, supportive of Maoist political ideologies and armed violence. What began as a revolutionary peasant movement in Naxalbari, West Bengal, in 1967, evolved into an ongoing armed uprising of mostly tribal inhabitants. Militant activity became concentrated along state borders in an area known as the 'Red Corridor', which runs through West Bengal, Jharkhand, Odisha, Andhra Pradesh and Chhattisgarh. Districts within this region are among the poorest in the country and have large indigenous tribal populations.

This conflict between Naxalite insurgents and the Government of India (GOI) posed a grave threat to India's peace and security. By 1980, the communist factions comprised of thirty different militant groups with more than 30,000 official members. In 2007, it was estimated that Naxalites were active across 40 per cent of India's geographical area. India's Ministry of Home Affairs asserts that more than 6,000 civilians died in the crossfire during more than twenty years of violent conflict. Since 2002, the Art of Living has been actively involved in providing trauma-relief, healing and reconciliation programmes as well as conflict resolution skills training throughout Naxal-affected areas of India.

From 2002 to 2010, more than 500,000 people benefited from Art of Living's trauma-relief techniques. This contributed to increased peace and security in more than 1,000 villages in Naxal-affected areas throughout nine states. In addition, the teams provided programmes for all actors engaged in Naxal-related violent conflict, including Naxal militia cadre, members of the Central Reserve Police Force, tribal villagers caught in the crossfire of conflict, as well as tribal villagers living in Government Relief Camps who were forced to migrate as a result of the violent conflict.

Art of Living trainers facilitated the reintegration of former Naxalite militants into society, encouraging them towards political participation and positive contributions to society. The programmes aimed to demilitarize mindsets, break down negative thought patterns and reconcile adversarial relationships, thereby strengthening social cohesion and conflict resilience. Deeply embedded attitudes of hatred and fear among many of them dissipated and transformed into non-violent behaviour.

> 'We were indoctrinated with words of confrontation and hatred. Now, Sri Sri has filled our lives with love and we want to spread love, not hatred.' (Shiv Prasad, former Naxalite, Bihar)[17]

This foundation for peace was strengthened by human values-based peace education that provided practical skills in conflict resolution and encouraged harmony in diversity. In addition, Art of Living trainers mediated between the Government of India and former militants and facilitated high-level policy and peace agreement negotiations to seek a resolution to the conflicts.

Case study: The upper-caste Ranvir Sena – Left-wing Maoist conflict in Bihar, India

Since the 1980s, left-wing militants, including Naxalites and Maoists, waged a war against Bhumihars in the poverty-stricken state of Bihar in India. They aimed to defend the rights of the lower-caste and landless peasants against the Bhumihars, who were an upper caste in the classical Hindu social hierarchy system, comprising mostly landowners. Caste violence in Bihar was widespread and caused serious social challenges. The Bhumihars established their own militant faction, Ranvir Sena to fight the left-wing militants. The massacres and killings between both factions claimed thousands of lives over the years.

In the year 2000, with ongoing fatalities, Gurudev Sri Sri Ravi Shankar asked Art of Living trainer Sanjay Kumar to bring the Ranvir Sena and the Maoist militants (Communist Party of India – Marxist-Leninist CPI-ML group) together in Rishikesh to meet with him. Sanjay got to work and found a contact with the Maoists through one of his acquaintances. He travelled deep into the forests of Bhojpur district in Bihar to meet with their leaders. Similarly, he reached out to Ranvir Sena and met with their leaders as well. The conversations with both groups were challenging, both justifying the violence because of the actions of the other group and the injustice they had experienced. Through sincere persuasion, Sanjay managed to bring both groups to Rishikesh, where they first participated in the Art of Living courses.

> One of the Maoist commanders shared his experience: 'I had all this rage inside me a day back. I could do anything for my brothers, harm anyone, kill... I suddenly find that all those emotions... have subdued suddenly. They are being replaced with something else. Something that makes me feel light... here. (pointing towards his chest) My brain is not able to understand. How is this possible?'[18]

After the courses, they met together with Gurudev Sri Sri Ravi Shankar as well as with each other. The Maoist chief said that it was the first time in decades that both groups were in the presence of each other without feeling the need for any violence. He then shared the intention of wanting to bring their families and friends along as well. In his words, he had forgotten what relaxation and freedom felt like: 'I had to question myself: is this how peace feels like?'[19] In the next months close to a thousand people from both groups travelled to Rishikesh to participate in the Art of Living courses. Reportedly, those who attended the courses did not feel like fighting any longer and did not engage in violence after their visit to Rishikesh.

In parallel, Art of Living also worked at the grassroots level in Bihar, restoring education for children and building additional schools, spreading the message of human values and social harmony, addressing the widespread problem of alcoholism, building and rebuilding homes and creating gatherings that bring communities in conflict together.

Case study in the Philippines: Addressing the psychosocial gaps in government-led interventions to prevent and counter violent extremism in Mindanao

IAHV Philippines has provided healing to impacted communities in ISIS-affected areas, as well as Youth Leadership Peacebuilding Training for Muslim youth leaders, while also supporting the military and police with stress management training.

The Philippines has a long history of violence and armed conflict in the southern region of Mindanao among insurgents, clan militias and criminal groups. More recently, there has also been a growth of violent extremist groups pledging allegiance to the Islamic State (IS). In May 2017, such groups besieged Marawi City in an attempt to establish an IS caliphate, displacing over 350,000 people. Since 2014, these IS-linked groups have increased their recruitment activities among youth who are out of school and among students in high schools, universities and madrassas (Islamic schools).

IAHV Philippines launched the programme 'Strengthening the Psychosocial Foundation of Vulnerable Populations: A New Paradigm for Preventing and Countering Violent Extremism'. This aimed to address the psychosocial gaps in the ongoing PCVE work in Mindanao, 2019–22.

It was implemented in partnership with:

- The United Nations Development Programme (UNDP Philippines), which provided financial support to launch IAHV's SKY Campus Programme for youth vulnerable to violent extremism;
- The Government's Department of Interior and Local Government, which is in charge of the national programme for preventing and countering violent extremism;
- The Armed Forces of the Philippines to integrate MHPSS into the main curriculum of the Philippine Military Academy.

Peacebuilding Activities delivered:

- Joint introductory peacebuilding workshops in three ISIS-affected areas in Lanao del Sur brought together the Armed Forces of the Philippines, 160 members of the insurgency group the Moro Islamic Liberation Front (MILF), thirty-six Maute-ISIS returnees and local government representatives. This was the first time these groups had been brought together in the same room, according to the Armed Forces of the Philippines. (June 2019)
- The SKY Campus Programme at Xavier University – Ateneo de Cagayan taught university students in conflict-affected areas to (1) release stress, master emotions, withstand radicalization and peer pressure, and solve conflicts using non-violent action; and (2) use emotional intelligence, social connection, service and leadership for personal well-being, social change and peacebuilding. (December 2019)
- Youth Leadership Peacebuilding Training (YPLT) for eighteen Muslim youth leaders who were directly affected by the 2017 Marawi Siege and members of the Thuma Ko Kapagingud Service, a youth-led civil society organization targeting out-of-school and excluded youth in conflict areas. (December 2019)

Political systems and good governance

Political systems and governance are permeated by a wide range of psychosocial factors and dynamics.

- **Values, interests and ideologies of different groups** in society differ and conflict with each other. They are responded to or manipulated by political leaders in beneficial or harmful ways.
- People with similar values, interests or ideologies group together, often strengthening a strong in-**group identity**. Prioritization of their own group can then lead to **intolerance and discrimination against other groups**, as well as to social polarization, enmity and conflict. Divided societies where governance structures, institutions and processes favour certain groups and exclude or discriminate against others, installing political, social and economic **inequalities**, are more prone to violent conflict.[20]
- Conflicts can escalate into violence, and the willingness for dialogue and compromise can be stifled. On the other hand, a **culture and practice of dialogue, negotiation and conflict transformation** can be upheld and implemented as part of political processes. Mechanisms and processes such as coalition-building, negotiation and consensus-seeking are essential for effective governance and rely on attitudes and skills such as empathy, communication and trust-building. In a worsening political climate, the public debate and political discourse no longer address the important issues to be resolved but are dominated

by personal attacks, misinformation and the depiction of one's opponents in negative personal characteristics.

- **Values of progress, peace and prosperity aimed for all people**, regardless of their differences, can lead to positive political outcomes, broad-based support, stability and progress.

- The responsiveness of political leaders to citizens' needs is an important source of legitimacy for political systems, and this in turn tends to increase their stability and effectiveness. Governance institutions that are unable or unwilling to respond to citizens' needs have been associated with increased instability, unrest and violence in a variety of conflict settings. While responding to citizens' needs, it is not only important to deliver services but also to respond to grievances and to involve citizens in decision-making through participatory processes. An attitude of being of **service to the people** as much as possible, and the translation of that into concrete action, can create positive political dynamics for the betterment of the general population, influence the perception of citizens and increase trust in and legitimacy of the government.

- **Greed, hunger for power and unprocessed experiences** of past injustice are, on the contrary, strong driving factors for political strife and mobilization, leading to deprivation, marginalization and injustice for large segments of the population.

- **Fears and anxieties** in the public can be ignited and used to justify protective policies or to start wars against opposing groups. Such political discourses and programmes refer to, exploit and manipulate emotions, collective memory and the manner of presentation of specific topics and situations.

- **Public opinion and sentiment** are sometimes measured through polls, which political leaders can use for public benefit, to design political campaigns and programmes. Sometimes leaders refrain from opposing dominant public trends, out of fear of losing popularity, power and position, even if that leads to long-term problems. Tendencies for order, stability and conformity among segments of the population can lead to support for authoritarian measures and leadership and the harsh treatment of dissent.

Good governance is an important contributing factor to peace, potentially enabling the prevention of violent conflict, but such governance **cannot be created without strong positive psychosocial dynamics**.[21]

A challenging issue in the field of conflict transformation and peacebuilding is the issue of **power** and, in particular, how the public should respond in the context of overwhelming coercive power, repressive authoritarianism or mass atrocities. Schools of active non-violence have identified various forms of power and developed distinct strategies tailored to different stages of power imbalance. For example, the Quakers have developed different intervention strategies depending on the situation: When unequal parties in a conflict are not aware of the situation, it is appropriate to start with awareness raising. When a conflict takes place between unequal parties who are aware of their situation, one must empower the less dominant party and work for change in a non-violent way. When a conflict takes place between equals who are aware of the situation, communication needs to be established along with engagement in conflict resolution. Scholars and practitioners have distinguished different kinds of power which work in different ways.[22] While coercive power typically rests with a single source and aims to dominate and enforce, pluralistic power refers to power that is not concentrated upon a single source but is shared among people. Integrative power stems from love, connection and inspiration, and it bonds, uplifts and transforms. 'Power over' refers to dominance, 'power with' to joint forces when people come together, and 'power within' to resilience. Deutsch also emphasized that power is not merely a resource for coercion, but can support equitable collaboration and influence change.[23] Effective conflict resolution requires a fair redistribution of power that empowers all parties and allows them to participate equally in the process, through strategies that reduce imbalances and promote shared decision-making. It also addresses the structural power dynamics underlying persistent conflict.

Case study on village councils in India

Between 2018 and 2020, Art of Living implemented village development programmes for 13,600 village representatives, volunteers and members of the councils of local self-governance in India. The Art of Living trainings had a huge impact on the participants themselves but also on the way they administered their locality and their political decision-making. According to Bholanath Jena, the Art of Living trainer in Odisha: 'Village council leaders are usually driven by the political agenda of their parties. In one village, a well had to be built and each member was fighting to build the well in his section. After they finished the [Art of Living] programme, they sat together and did what was best for the entire village. This is just one of many outcomes. Entire communities transformed after their leaders attended our Good Governance workshops.' The programmes were implemented in partnership with the state governments of Odisha, Maharashtra and Jharkhand with the aim of raising administrative capabilities and building good governance among the village councils, which are key stakeholders in integrated development. The combination of the rigorous curricula required by the governments with the holistic approach of the Art of Living led to very tangible changes in outlook, behaviour, decision-making and cooperation.[24] Village council members renewed their vision and felt greater resilience and enthusiasm, which resulted in increased community engagement and collective action at the local level. It also improved dialogue and harmony within the villages. These programmes for governance and development were eventually attended by local leaders from 50,000 villages in India and have had a strong positive impact on good governance and development.

Case study on the Kurdistan Parliament in Iraq

In 2014, amidst the deep crisis in Iraq marked by political instability, sectarian violence and the rise of the Islamic State of Iraq and Syria (ISIS), thirty-five Members of Parliament in Kurdistan participated in an Art of Living programme in Erbil focused on stress management and leadership.[25] Heightened tension, anger, hatred and confusion were palpable among the participants. Coming together from different political parties, they experienced big changes in personal well-being, which reflected in improved interpersonal relationships, trust, a shared vision and collective action. These changes are reflected in some of their testimonials:

> 'We are here from four different political parties in Kurdistan, but if we can talk and work together the way we are doing in this workshop, then we can solve all our problems.'
>
> 'If everybody in Iraq could do this, we would live in peace!'
> 'This course made us have a good relationship with each other.'
> 'Before we did not know each other, did not want to know each other personally. Now we trust each other!'
>
> 'Before this course we had not a good idea about the members of the different political parties. Now we all know that we have a goal we want to work for; we have a joint vision. And our whole goal is to serve our people.'

A strategy that Gurudev Sri Sri Ravi Shankar employs to promote peace is to create **platforms that bring people with opposing views and varied political, ethnic, religious and social backgrounds together in the midst of conflict**, often for the very first time. Examples of this are the conferences: 'Protecting Women and Bringing Stability and Peace', a Conference in Erbil, Kurdistan, in November 2014; the 'Back to Paradise' Conference in Kashmir, in November 2016; the 'Strength in Diversity' Conference in Assam, India, in September 2017. These conferences serve as platforms where different groups can express their grievances and views, listen and learn from each other, and together develop joint action plans for peace and prosperity. They transcend victim-perpetrator dynamics, blame and the sense of victimhood, by acknowledging that everyone involved in or affected by violence is, in a sense, a victim. This paves the way for joint sharing and collaboration towards agreed solutions which are implemented through non-violent and democratic means. This collaborative approach creates ownership and a sense of responsibility. Participation and effectiveness are supported by the joint practice of breathing and meditation, which help to clear the mind, foster equanimity and inner peace, and allow people to listen and engage in dialogue with a clearer perception and a more empathetic attitude. All these are essential for such collective transformative processes. Gurudev Sri Sri Ravi Shankar recounted that during his speech declaring the first International Yoga Day in 2015, former UN Secretary-General Ban Ki-moon remarked, 'We need this (meditation) before every negotiation. If we had this before every negotiation, we would be more successful.' Throughout his conflict transformation work, Gurudev Sri Sri Ravi Shankar consistently emphasizes the promotion of human values such as diversity, non-violence, respect and cooperation.

Economy and sustainable development

A peace-enhancing economic structure supports sustainable development, guarantees the satisfaction of basic needs, reduces inequalities and improves the overall quality of life for individuals and communities. Psychosocial factors at the basis of such peace-enhancing economic and development systems include:

- Values of trust and cooperation;
- Positive organizational cultures, inclusive policies, mutual support and positive relationships among colleagues, well-functioning and participatory organizational and management practices;
- Care for the planet and environment, commitment not to do harm and sense of social responsibility;
- Psychological well-being and energy among individuals, and resilience to manage adverse economic times;
- The creativity and capacity to innovate, interest in obtaining skills and knowledge, motivation and sense of empowerment, entrepreneurial mindsets and bravery, adaptability and strength when faced with loss or adversity, and a sense of purposeful engagement;
- Strong social networks for exchange of resources and information, the creation of joint initiatives and opportunities, and resilience in times of crisis;
- Economic activity, when balanced with well-being and positive values, can be a source of contentment, fulfilment, social connections, life opportunities and more.

The challenge of mental health in the workplace is in itself a hugely defining factor of the economy. According to the International Labour Organization (ILO), an estimated 12 billion working days are lost every year to depression and anxiety at a cost of US$1 trillion per year in lost productivity.[26] The World Health Organization's 2019 report 'Mental Health in the Workplace' also highlights the significant economic costs associated with mental health issues globally, mentioning figures that reflect 4 per cent to 6 per cent of GDP in terms of economic loss due to reduced productivity and increased healthcare costs.[27] In addition, employees who are not fully engaged or actively disengaged at work, estimated at 77 per cent of employees globally, may cost the economy $8.9 trillion per year, or 9 per cent of global GDP, according to Gallup.[28] The accelerated pace of today's working environment in an increasingly demanding, digitalized and complex world opens up new opportunities, but also leads to higher performance demands and a growing workload. It takes its toll on employee engagement, productivity, creativity and well-being.[29] Rather than being ambitious to earn more, seek promotion or follow preordained career paths, the younger generation seems to seek meaningful activity and careers that fulfil a sense of purpose, are in line with their values, and contribute positively to the world. People who 'live their purpose' at work are much more likely to sustain or improve their levels of effectiveness in work, with four times higher engagement and five times higher well-being, compared to those who do not.[30]

Case study: Women empowerment in Iraq[31]

IAHV has been working in Iraq continuously since 2003 with a strong focus on women empowerment. Women in Iraq, and especially those widowed in the wars, have been affected by discrimination, marginalization, domestic violence, poverty, stigma and lack of opportunities. The accumulation of stresses takes a huge toll on their mental, emotional, physical and social well-being. Major stress factors include insecurity, the fear of attack, the loss of family members and friends, as well as the responsibilities of being a family's sole breadwinner and caregiver.

To address these needs within a comprehensive approach, IAHV Iraq offers women stress management, healing and resilience workshops to reduce trauma and stress and strengthen their overall wellbeing. Having graduated through these, participants are ready and able to engage with other training programmes for well-being, to make life changes, to achieve economic and financial stability for themselves and to care for their families. They become able to engage fully with training content, absorb new knowledge and find inspiration and the confidence to implement their newly learned skills. Vocational training was given in computer skills and tailoring, with support in finding work placements. Survivors of rape, domestic and other forms of violence received free education in legal rights and professional support to pursue their cases. Feeling supported and empowered through peer support and collaborations, some women speak out for women in similar situations, thus enhancing their role and standing in society. At community and national level, task forces, expert groups and stakeholder meetings were organized to further protect and empower Iraqi women for the advancement of their leadership in society, and to eliminate gender-based violence. Community and national leaders from different sectors, such as business, law, politics and civil society, were mobilized and supported through Leadership Training Programmes to launch initiatives in support of Iraqi women, including the shifting of public attitudes.

> 'We knew only death and despair. Now we can smile, and that is the greatest gift that Sri Sri has given us.' (Shafiqur Rehman, trauma-relief participant)

Suad is a 35-year-old widow with five children. Because she is an immigrant without identification papers, it was very difficult for her to find a job. After taking the IAHV tailoring and trauma-relief courses, she had the vocational skills and self-assurance to start working and earning a living as a tailor in her neighbourhood. Now she is one of the most active tailors in her community and can confidently support her family.

Case study: Healing the farmer[32]

Hundreds of thousands of farmers in India have committed suicide over the last decades due to the interrelated challenges of debts, low crop production, chemical farming methods, personal and family problems, droughts and floods.[33] The Art of Living responded to this challenge by implementing a specially designed integrated programme, which includes stress and trauma-relief workshops with training in organic farming and associated subjects.

Firstly, the farmers learned techniques to combat depression, fear and stress. With their well-being restored, they gained the energy, motivation and inspiration to learn new knowledge and skills to transform the root causes of their problems. They were trained in methods and techniques for organic farming, water conservation and zero-budget farming. As a result, their crops increased, their income grew and they could start repaying their debts. This programme enabled the farmers to live their lives with confidence and self-esteem. At the communal level, the sense of community and resilience grew, along with economic prosperity and strengthened resilience of the local ecosystems.

One of the trainers was Sharad, who as a youth had fallen into bad company and become addicted to alcohol and tobacco. His life had become worthless and aimless, and his relatives lost hope of his recovery and rehabilitation. His sister insisted, and he participated in the Art of Living Youth Leadership Training Programme. As a result of this, he felt a significant personal shift and began a new chapter in his life. He became involved in service activities and gave up his addictions following the realization that he was capable of uplifting others and making a difference. He taught more than 300 village programmes in Vidarbha, an agricultural belt in Maharashtra, where farmer suicides were particularly high, and trained many more youth to become involved in the programmes.[34]

> 'Before undergoing the Art of Living programme, I was in a state of depression and worried about my debts. Now, I feel confident that with the breathing techniques and zero-budget farming methods, I will be able to improve my outcomes and repay my debts. I am grateful for this new hope in life.' (Devendra Borde, farmer)
>
> 'The Art of Living has given a new lease of life and stopped the suicides. This is what Sri Sri has been able to do, for which the Government is very happy. I am happy that the organization has given the farmers the strength to live.' (Vilasrao Deshmukh, Former Chief Minister, Maharashtra)

Across India, youth, women and farmers are trained in vocational, entrepreneurial, organic farming and natural resource management skills while being supported personally with techniques to manage their stress and maintain their own well-being. Special attention is paid to at-risk and disadvantaged groups, such as those in prison or with addiction issues. They are supported with self-development programmes, which enhance behavioural and attitudinal changes, as well as with vocational training in the skill centres that are set up within the prisons, to help bring them out of unemployment and poverty.

Case study: TLEX[35]

IAHV and Art of Living have a designated programme 'Transformational Leadership in Excellence (TLEX®)' to support employers and employees in the corporate sector to thrive and excel. Today's workplaces are increasingly characterized by unpredictability, an ongoing flood of information, complex and unforeseen challenges, fast technological developments and changes. Focusing solely on strategies and processes is insufficient to sustain good company performance. Teams and leaders need mental clarity, adaptive thinking, emotional resilience, inspiration and social connection for enhanced engagement and teamwork.

Starting with the individual, TLEX® offers participants a range of tools for greater personal calm and clarity. From a relaxed, calm and clear state of mind, imagination, intuition and creativity arise more readily, and opportunities and risks are perceived more clearly. Employees and leaders feel more connected to their teams and the organization, resulting in intrinsic motivation, creativity and enthusiasm at work. Empowered employees and leaders can maintain strong work performance with greater collaboration and innovation, despite high complexity and demand, even during challenging times.

An internal evaluation of TLEX®[36] showed that

- 90 per cent of participants felt enabled to adapt, initiate change and envisage better.
- 90 per cent of participants agreed that TLEX® techniques increase their ability to stay calm in difficult situations.
- 87 per cent of participants agreed that after TLEX® they feel enhanced social connectedness with other participants.
- 93 per cent of participants agreed that TLEX® techniques will have a positive impact on their working day.
- 85 per cent of participants agreed that TLEX® techniques increase ability to listen to and accept multiple perspectives.
- 96 per cent of participants had a better understanding of what blocks innovation.

TLEX® has facilitated training and talks to nearly 500,000 employees of over 500 client organizations across the globe.

Justice

Psychosocial dimensions permeate the legal justice system in its functioning and effectiveness and are very present among all those interacting and involved with it, including law enforcement officers, judges, lawyers, defendants, victims/survivors, and the broader community.

- Firstly, **psychological, social and cultural factors underlie and influence the norms, values and expectations concerning the justice system and the nature of the justice delivered**. The legal system can be designed and run to strengthen social cohesion, fairness, peace and reconciliation within society, or to increase fear, repression, division and revenge.
    - **Retributive justice** aims primarily to punish the perpetrators for the harm inflicted. This form of justice can restore a sense of moral order, give a sense of justice to the victims and serve as a deterrent to crime and violence. However, it can also overlook the human factor, the possibilities for rehabilitation and perpetuate cycles of violence.
    - **Restorative justice** aims to restore relationships and repair the harm done to the victims and communities. It is a form of justice that is people-centred and naturally integrates the psychosocial dimension: victims/survivors can express themselves, and this can lead to healing and empowerment; perpetrators are made aware of the impact of their behaviour and can take responsibility for it, and they can also be supported in rehabilitation and reintegration into society; the community involved can become more aware of their shared responsibility and stronger and more resilient against crime and violence going forward.
    - **Transitional justice** refers to the process of achieving justice and reconciliation in societies in the aftermath of war, large-scale violence, genocide or war crimes. The process entails both technical and psychosocial dimensions, such as war tribunals, truth commissions, prosecution, official apologies, reparation, reconciliation, community involvement, institutional reforms and initiatives around collective memory and prevention.
- Whether the handling and delivery of justice are **perceived as fair or unfair, discriminatory or preferential** during both processes and outcomes, is an important factor in the creation of a solid foundation for peace.
- **The perception, interpretation, values and cognitive frameworks of judicial decision makers** play a crucial role in the delivery of justice, directly impacting the lives of individuals and communities. Often very different and complex values, ethics and viewpoints need to be considered and balanced when reaching a judgement. The decisions made can have a huge impact on the direct lives of people and communities, creating either trust, restoration and relief, or resentment, anger and conflict.

- The quality of **interpersonal conduct and interaction during legal processes**, and the extent to which this includes respect, dignity and clarity of communication, can either improve or undermine mutual understanding and good relations.

- The evidential content of **legal cases can be distressing, shocking and even traumatizing**. Also, **the legal processes** themselves, with the time they take, obstacles, setbacks and outcomes, can be **highly stressful and draining**. All this can lead to high levels of stress, anxiety, depression, suicidal tendencies and PTSD among the survivors, defendants, jury and legal personnel. The harm, injustice, violence, crime and human rights violations do not only impact the survivors and perpetrators, but also their broader social environment, those involved in the cases, the wider population as well as other spheres of society.

- The **network of social relationships, whether supportive or aggravating**, plays a crucial role as a resource of support and resilience or as an aggravating factor. 'Victim groups', which aim to provide a safe space for sharing experiences and mutual support, are a positive example in this regard. **Victim-centred justice approaches** can help victims/survivors to have a sense of empowerment, regain a sense of control and agency, feel surrounded and supported. They in turn can then support acceptance and reintegration in society where needed, help with healing and preserve or recover self-esteem and dignity.

- By bringing legal issues and cases into the public domain, the media reinforces or corrects **perceptions, judgements and stereotypes among the general population** with regard to individuals or groups involved. They can instigate more hatred, intolerance and resentment or instead foster more mutual understanding, acceptance and compassion.

Therefore, the way justice is designed and implemented has a major influence on conflict and peace dynamics, and the effective integration and transformation of psychosocial factors play a crucial role in this.

Education

Many reports highlight the important role that education plays and the wide range of benefits it brings in reducing the likelihood of war, increasing social cohesion, promoting understanding and respect among diverse groups, reducing poverty, increasing economic development, improving health and promoting gender equality.[37] The extent of schooling within the population, the absence of discrimination in education, the objective teaching of history, and the integration of peace education are all factors contributing to a sustainable peace.

Strengthening peace-enhancing psychosocial dimensions in the education system is an important foundation for the educational sector to contribute to peace generally. 'Schools and classrooms are sites of intense psycho-social activity because it is there that young people learn to express their thoughts and emotions via interactions with teachers and other students. The importance of these individual and collective psycho-social experiences cannot be understated.'[38] **An integrated, holistic educational experience supports not only academic achievement but also personal development and social good.** Below we present some of the important psychosocial dimensions of education in this regard:

- The **overall well-being of children and youth**, including physical, mental, emotional and social aspects, is a crucial factor for their development and academic performance. Issues like anxiety, depression and stress can affect concentration, memory and overall learning capacity. Well-being, inspiration and intrinsic motivation can positively impact students' interest, persistence and enjoyment in learning.[39]

- **Effective stress management and coping strategies** can help students to deal with the pressures of academic performance and the challenges in their lives. Resilience and agility help students to overcome failures, disappointments and setbacks and enable them to persist in their educational journey.

- The overall educational experience of students plays a role in shaping their sense of **identity and self-worth.**

- At the social level, **negative peer pressure, bullying and exclusion** can negatively affect students' well-being, behaviour, motivation and academic performance, as well as lead to dropout from school. **Cooperation, teamwork and conflict resolution skills** can positively enhance the students' experience and social skills to navigate the challenges and conflicts in life. **Peace education** is a specific curriculum for school students in which they learn practices of peace and how to manage and resolve conflicts through non-violent means. It includes various communication and conflict resolution skills, the fostering of peace-enhancing attitudes, the strengthening of values of empathy, respect, non-violence and compassion, as well as the development of emotional intelligence, critical thinking and awareness of human rights, injustice and global issues.

- The school can be a learning environment for students to become aware of local and global challenges, to start taking responsibility through the setting up of initiatives and campaigns, to express their views and take part in decision-making within the school, and to become **active and aware citizens**.

- **The well-being, inspiration and commitment of the teaching personnel** can positively or negatively impact the education experience.

- Positive **relationships with teachers** can enhance students' self-esteem, motivation and academic success, while negative relationships may lead to demotivation and school dropout.[40] The teachers' sensitivity, their **responsiveness to and awareness** of the students' emotional and academic needs, can positively impact their learning experience and the sense of support throughout. Educators can be **inspiring role models** of respect, care, cooperation and skillfulness through their behaviour in and outside the classroom.

- Creating a **safe and supportive environment** in the classroom and the school is conducive to the students' well-being, their sense of emotional safety, and their readiness and capacity to learn.[41]
- The school environment can contribute to **community building and social cohesion** among the families and neighbourhoods through the values and practices it promotes and implements.

Today's world is full of challenges, complexity and uncertainty, brought about by globalization, climate change, war, technological developments, health crises and information overload. Traditional educational approaches, however, have been dominated by a culture of clarity and certainty, transmitting 'exact information in classrooms by very convinced teachers and measured with very accurate means of measurement, which will later provide the young people a very clear place in society.'[42] Educational systems have often been informed by neo-liberal values which focus on social and economic success but do not always include a broader understanding of life and who we are as individuals.

In order to prepare young people to navigate the uncertain, complex and changing world, more recent theories on integral, holistic and future education emphasize the importance of providing education in a more holistic way.[43] A more updated understanding of the meaning and purpose of education would include providing young people with self-awareness, self-knowledge and the skills to remain centred and confident: 'The only place that is not affected by duality and uncertainty, from which they can receive guidance, which can be the compass to navigate through life: their heart and soul.'[44] Through a multidimensional view of our human nature that honours body, heart, mind, and spirit, and through multiple ways of knowing that facilitate non-linear, in-depth and complex modes of perception, understanding, thinking and action, students may be able to live a fulfilled life for themselves and others.[45]

> 'Unless and until we develop an integrated personality in human beings and teach them that they can do anything as long as it is with care and concern, with a vision and with a goal in life, we will not be able to solve the larger issues.'
> (Gurudev Sri Sri Ravi Shankar)

The education initiatives of the Art of Living and IAHV are focused on the holistic development of children and young people. Students receive the modern standard education curricula but are also provided with programmes to develop their personality and to strengthen their physical and mental well-being. They also engage in a host of extra-curricular activities which encourage a greater contribution to society. The learning environment itself is made relaxed and enjoyable. This educational approach aims to create educated, skilled, healthy and connected individuals and communities.

Case study: SKY Schools

SKY Schools is a programme that has been developed to find sustainable solutions for school communities to deal with challenges such as school dropout, low academic results, bullying and violence, teachers' burnout, mental health challenges and the erosion of human values, while also increasing optimal well-being and performance for all. SKY Schools engages with the entire school environment, including administrators, teachers, parents and students.

It aims to transform

- The lives of youth and adults, to gain improved mental and emotional well-being, increased energy and focus, clearer awareness of their aspirations, and a deepened connection to oneself and others.
- Classrooms, to become spaces of respect, enthusiasm and creativity;
- Schools, to promote and implement attitudes of service, leadership skills, sense of belonging and responsibility.

A 2023 study on SKY Schools in the United States reported alarming baseline data on the well-being of adolescents in the United States, with approximately 40 per cent of high school students engaging in health risks and problem behaviours, including substance use (e.g. nicotine, alcohol and opioids), risky sexual behaviour and violence:

> More than 1 out of every 7 high school students reported using illicit or injection drugs (e.g. cocaine, heroin, and ecstasy) or misusing prescription opioids within the past 30 days, 1 in 7 report using e-cigarettes, and 1 in 5 reported consuming alcohol. Approximately 1 out of every 5 students dropped out of school or failed to graduate on time. Even adolescents who are free from apparent problem behaviours do not appear to be thriving. Statistics document alarmingly low rates of adolescent well-being. 42% of high school students have experienced periods of persistent feelings of sadness or hopelessness that interfered with daily activities, and 1 in 5 12–17-year-olds, across all genders and ethnicities, reported a major depressive episode within the past 12 months. In addition, approximately 22% of high school students seriously considered attempting suicide in the past year and suicide is currently the second leading cause of death for adolescents. Suicide rates for adolescents in the middle school age group (10–14 years) tripled from 2007 to 2017. Girls fared significantly worse than boys across nearly all measures including sadness, suicide risk (one in three seriously considered suicide), and violence. The new report also confirms extreme distress among teens who identify as LGBTQ+, with over half having recently experienced poor mental health, and 1 in 5 attempting suicide in the past year.[46]

SKY Schools is a holistic bio-psycho-social programme designed to reduce risk and problem behaviours in youth as well as to strengthen core aspects of psychological thriving. It is an empirically validated and evidence-based social emotional learning (SEL) programme that integrates risk reduction and personal development with a biological component, namely IAHV's and Art of Living's transformative physiological restorative practices. These include the

SKY breathing technique, which relieves stress, reduces emotional arousal, improves focus and concentration, and creates psycho-physiological calm and well-being (see Chapter 3). These different components are integrated into a powerful, experiential and fun social-emotional-physiological learning curriculum. It thus creates a highly effective strategy and environment for empowering youth, supporting overall student health and success, reducing conflict and apathy, and nurturing a positive, supportive, happier school climate and culture. The curriculum includes core evidence-based practices that have been shown to lead to student well-being, emotional intelligence and social intelligence, including:

- Evidence-based breathwork and neural restorative practices (including yoga and meditation);
- Emotional intelligence training;
- Leadership training;
- The learning of the principles of service;
- Social connection and belonging;
- Self-management tools;
- Positive psychology;
- Conflict management.

> *'To have a violence-free world, it is important to foster the spirit of friendliness right from childhood. In a classroom of fifty children, if you ask any child how many friends he has, he will count on his fingers – three, four, five. If a child cannot be friendly with the fifty children in his classroom, how is he going to live with 7 billion other people in the world? Technology has made our world into a global village. Right education can make this village a close-knit family.'*
> (Gurudev Sri Sri Ravi Shankar)

Youth, educators and communities learn practical tools and life skills to increase self-awareness, build resilience, manage stress and emotions and make responsible life choices. As students learn to reduce stress and manage emotions, they gain the ability to focus and perform well academically at school. They also develop the ability to build more positive relationships with their peers, parents and teachers. School management and teachers are supported by the SKY Schools programme to alleviate their stress, boost team morale and promote a general positive attitude to support a healthy learning environment. Regular practice of the SKY breathing technique and related practices engages all members of the school community in daily resilience building and strengthening of positive relationships.

The effectiveness of the SKY Schools programme is supported by three types of data, in addition to the research on SKY already presented in Chapter 3:

(1) Neurophysiological assessments of the physiological impact: Biometric measures have shown that SKY breathing improves the overall rate of emotion regulation, the capacity of prefrontal control for emotion regulation and the success of youth in utilizing cognitive strategies for the regulation of emotion. By reducing stress and calming the sympathetic nervous system, SKY also stimulates the higher brain centres responsible for both the suppression of inappropriate, destructive and impulsive responses, and for the enhancement of learning and recalling of adaptive skills.[47] SKY practices also increase the capacity of students to absorb the social emotional learning tools they are given and to recall and practise them during times of challenge when they are most needed. It equips student populations physiologically with the assets needed for effective and lasting change.

The limited available data suggest that combining social emotional learning curricula with biologically impactful tools in a bio-psycho-social approach can produce more robust outcomes than either a purely biologically impactful or social emotional learning approach alone and suggests that further examination of this approach is warranted.[48]

(2) Social Emotional Learning and Mental Health assessments:[49] SKY Schools programming shows significant increases in self-awareness, self-management, relationship skills and responsible decision-making. This includes specific improvements in emotion regulation, identity formation, planning and concentration, empathy, executive function, anger management, self-esteem and self-efficacy, as well as a reduction in aggression, impulsivity, distractibility, fear, anxiety and susceptibility to and exposure to substance use and antisocial behaviour.

Students report:[50]

- 70 per cent reduction in perceived stress;
- 70 per cent increase in emotion regulation;
- 77 per cent increase in resilience;
- 56 per cent increase in growth mindset;
- 58 per cent increase in caring and cooperative behaviour.

(3) School-based data that demonstrate the impact on behaviour and social determinants of health:[51] Implementation of the SKY programme in various educational settings led to substantial improvements within school communities, including increased academic performance, reduced bullying and acting out, reduced disciplinary actions and referrals, decreased substance use and violence, improved emotional regulation and well-being, significant reductions in anxiety and high-risk behaviours among students and increased class participation and social connectedness in SKY students.

Schools report:[52]

- 64 per cent sustained reduction in disciplinary infractions;

- 90 per cent reduction in violent infractions;
- 80 per cent decrease in suspensions;
- 45 per cent decrease in drug and alcohol use;
- 350 per cent increase in students making adequate yearly performance;
- 700 per cent increase in students on the honour roll;
- Statistically significant increase in average grades among participating students.

> 'The SKY Schools programme provided our students with a comprehensive toolbox to manage their emotions and stress as well as dynamically navigate through adolescence. After only a few days of taking part in the programme, faculty members could see a measurable growth in class cooperation and confidence.' (Dr Santos, Principal, East Side High, Newark NJ)
>
> 'I have never had a programme that was so universally embraced by students and teachers. Disney School has a student population where 80 per cent belong to minority groups and 70 per cent come from low-income backgrounds. Despite these challenging circumstances, our students' achievement rates have significantly improved, increasing from 52 per cent meeting or exceeding standards to 87 per cent over the past seven years.' (Kathy Hagstrom, Principal, Walt Disney Magnet School)
>
> 'In the last two weeks, we have had more problems with violent episodes and drug use than during the rest of the year combined, probably due to the pressure of the state exams. However, not one of the SKY participants has gotten involved with this, although there were a lot of problem students in the SKY programme. That says a lot! My observation is that students (who took SKY) handle anger and other issues differently. SKY gives them a concrete tool to calm their mind and find alternative solutions in times of stress and conflict, that they may not have been aware of before.' (Melissa Wolin, Principal, Palm Springs Middle School, Hialeah FL)

Over the past twenty years, the SKY Schools programme has been run in 243 schools across twenty-nine states, mainly in the metropolitan areas of New York, Washington, DC, Chicago, Milwaukee, San Francisco, Los Angeles and Pomona, benefiting more than 135,000 students. In addition, more than 3,000 educators have received the SKY Educators Programme in North America. More than 15,000 students have SKY Schools' restorative practices as part of their daily school schedule. The SKY Schools programme has also been taught to students across five continents.

Case study: Tribal and slum schools

The Art of Living and IAHV have established 1,200 schools in India since the 1980s, where more than 100,000 students have graduated. Tribal schools were opened in rural as well as violence-affected areas, for children who were often the first generation of learners in areas where no schools existed before. Slum schools were opened in some of the biggest slums in urban areas, such as Mumbai, where children were often entangled in a web of crime and violence.

The schools are set up as a community initiative, with the involvement and support of parents and caregivers. The teachers are trained and empowered to be agents of change for both the children and the parents in the community. Special attention is paid to the enrolment of girls in education in areas where they are traditionally discouraged or prevented from attending school. Their safety and comfort in the school and on the way to school are specifically taken care of. These schools are instrumental in transforming the lives of communities through the focus on human values and social harmony, social gatherings with families and specific school-driven projects for the neighbourhood and community.

Case study: SKY Campus Happiness

At the higher education level, IAHV and the Art of Living implement the **SKY Campus Happiness Programme:** creating happy and mindful campus communities to support students, faculty and staff to achieve their fullest potential, thrive in life, lead with clarity of mind, resilience, purpose and belonging. The SKY Campus Happiness Programme has similar, comparable components as the SKY Schools programme described above, but adapted to the age and context of higher education. The Programme has reached 550,000 students across 147 campuses in the United States.

- The comparative research study at Yale University which evaluated the impact of three well-being interventions in university students showed that the SKY programme was most effective, not only in improving mental health, stress reduction and the relief of depression but also in enhancing mindfulness, positive emotions and social connectedness.[53]
- A randomized controlled study run by Harvard University scientists showed that SKY demonstrated greater improvements than the cognitive behaviour intervention in perceived stress, sleep, social connectedness, distress, anxiety, depression, conscientiousness, self-esteem and life satisfaction.[54] Results were observed immediately after and three months after the workshop.

Health sector

Holistic approaches to health comprise 'physical, mental, and social well-being', as it was put forward by WHO. **The multidimensional concept of health encompasses psychological, emotional, and social well-being, including resilience, emotional stability, positive relations with others, social acceptance, contribution, support, sense of connection with a larger community and a commitment to a greater social cause.**

- Holistic health interventions, taking into account not only the **physical dimension but also mental, emotional and other psychosocial aspects**, can help to address the fundamental roots of health problems. They can provide more effective treatments, contribute to the prevention of illnesses and to the overall well-being of individuals.[55] This serves as a strong foundation for healthy and energized citizens, who are more likely to bring an active, positive contribution to society than individuals with negative mindsets, low energy or chronic health problems.

- Addressing the **stress factor**, a major contributing factor to most illnesses, is crucial for prevention and recovery, as are lifestyle, diet, physical exercise and mental fitness. A holistic view of health considers people healthy when they are not only physically fit, but also mentally calm and emotionally steady. Psychoneuroimmunology, which studies the interaction between psychological processes, the nervous system and the immune system, has shown that the strengthening of both mental and physical resilience has a positive effect on immunity, reducing the likelihood of falling ill.[56]

- Effective approaches to holistic health for both intervention and prevention can significantly reduce the burden on the healthcare system and related financial costs. An effective and sufficiently resourced healthcare system could **take care of the health needs of all**, without discrimination, and this would also contribute to **social cohesion and stability**. In public health campaigns, these values of solidarity, mutual support and shared humanity can be promoted to contribute to a peace-enhancing climate. The promotion of health as a human right around the world can help reduce discrimination and marginalization and strengthen health efforts where needed. Health policies can be designed in such a way that they explicitly involve and include marginalized and vulnerable populations, thus reducing social divisions.

- In times of conflict, the provision of **non-discriminatory, humanitarian health assistance to all in need**, on all sides, can act as a reminder of **shared humanity** and as an avenue to build connections and trust.

- Also community health initiatives, whereby communities come together to respond to certain health challenges, can foster collaboration among different groups, reduce social fragmentation and build **social cohesion**. Health is a universal good and challenge and can unite people and communities in a shared goal.

- Health policies can also contribute to peace at the local level by addressing the issues of poor mental health, substance abuse and domestic violence. Through a comprehensive care system and referrals, the health sector can play a critical role in identifying, intervening and supporting people affected by substance abuse, mental health challenges or domestic violence. By addressing both the immediate health needs and the broader social determinants of health in these cases, and adopting a comprehensive approach, the healthcare system can contribute significantly to the **prevention and mitigation of violence and crime at the community level**.

- Making **mental health a priority at the national level** would contribute to creating healthier, safer, happier and more productive nations. The WHO Mental Health Action Plan 2013–2030 encourages countries to develop national strategies for mental health, integrate mental health into primary care, and reduce the stigma associated with mental disorders. WHO's most recent Mental Health Atlas showed that in 2020, governments worldwide spent on average just over 2 per cent of their health budgets on mental health and many low-income countries reported having fewer than 1 mental health worker per 100,000 people.[57] In 2023, the European Union developed a new comprehensive strategy for mental health, recognizing that 84 million people in Europe were struggling with mental health issues and estimating the cost of non-action at 600 billion euro per year.[58] Closely linking mental health with physical health, the new strategy addresses mental health across all sectors of society, from prevention through to treatment and rehabilitation. Making mental health a visible priority in society reduces stigma, promotes equal access to underserved sectors of the population, helps in the prevention of mental health issues and can provide practical solutions and effective treatments to those in need. On a broader scale, improved mental health across society can foster increased societal well-being and happiness, innovation and creative contributions to the community, strengthened cohesion, and community resilience to large-scale stressors such as natural and man-made disasters.

- The effectiveness and sustainability of the healthcare system also depends on the **mental fitness, resilience and well-being of its personnel**. Burnout among healthcare personnel is widespread and undermines the provision of basic care to people in need, thus prejudicing stability and support systems in society.[59] Even more in times of crisis, the resilience of healthcare professionals can be a strong source of support and stability for people.

The Art of Living and IAHV provide knowledge, awareness and techniques to maintain and strengthen physical and mental health. The comprehensive set of physical exercises, breathing and relaxation techniques taught in their programmes has significant positive outcomes on physical and mental health indicators, as described in Chapter 3. Holistic health systems, such as Ayurveda and Naturopathy, are promoted to help in the prevention of illness and to strengthen overall health. In addition, specific Stress Management and Resilience programmes for health professionals ensure their well-being, resilience and capacity to perform.

Case study: Holistic support throughout the Covid-19 pandemic[60]

The global Covid pandemic which started at the end of 2019 was a multifaceted crisis. In addition to physical health issues, people had to cope with mental health issues such as depression and anxiety, and a sense of isolation and loneliness. In addition, their lives were disrupted by unemployment, financial stress and increased poverty, domestic tensions and violence, the premature, isolated deaths of family members, discrimination and insufficient public services. The health professionals experienced heightened stress and burnout due to constant exposure and risk of infection, the death of colleagues, work overload, excessive overtime shifts, the shortage of personal protective equipment and patient care supplies, staff shortages and challenging working circumstances.[61] The high stress and strain experienced by the healthcare professionals regularly led to illness, absenteeism, lack of motivation, low morale, and affected their families, the quality of care for the patients, and the overall good functioning of the health care system.

In November 2021, the World Health Organization (WHO) reported that the Covid-19 pandemic has had a severe impact on the mental health and well-being of people around the world, including a 27.6 per cent increase in cases of major depressive disorder and a 25.6 per cent increase in cases of anxiety disorders, worldwide.[62]

In this time of uncertainty, anxiety and multifaceted challenges, volunteers from IAHV and the Art of Living, sustained by their personal resilience practices, started helping out all over the world. They provided meals to hundreds of thousands of daily wage earners, particularly in India, who were left without the means to make a living. They raised funds to buy masks and other essential equipment and distributed them to health care facilities in need. In addition, they also supported tens of thousands of stressed and overworked health professionals with much-needed stress management and resilience training online.

In 2021–2, the Art of Living and IAHV conducted a randomized clinical trial to assess the potential efficacy of SKY compared with a stress management education training for physicians from Turkey, Germany and Dubai. Compared with the control group, participants in the SKY group had significantly decreased stress, depression, anxiety and insomnia post-training and post-intervention. The SKY group also showed significantly increased professional fulfilment as well as significant decreases in work exhaustion, interpersonal disengagement and burnout. This data suggested that SKY may be an effective, practical and safe strategy to increase wellness and mitigate burnout in physicians.[63]

During the Covid-19 pandemic, Gurudev Sri Sri Ravi Shankar personally guided two online meditation sessions per day for a global audience. These sessions aimed to help participants manage fear, anxiety, lockdown-related stress, grief over separation, family losses and uncertainty regarding employment and the future. Over several months, millions of individuals attended these regular meditation sessions. In addition, he engaged with various segments of society by offering practical advice for navigating lockdown measures, maintaining health and immunity, and guidance on leadership, remote work, the strengthening of relationships, and the care of children and adolescents.[64]

The global challenge of climate change

Psychosocial factors influence how individuals and communities perceive, respond to, and are affected by climate change, and in shaping policies and decision-making related to climate change mitigation and adaptation.

- The way the climate crisis is **perceived and understood** varies significantly among individuals and communities, depending on mindsets, attitudes, personal experiences, culture, public discourses and other factors. Processing information related to the climate crisis is affected by biases, misinformation, information overload and crisis fatigue. Large groups of people exhibit denial, avoidance and psychological defences that prevent them from acknowledging the significance of the climate crisis.
- For others, the climate crisis instigates feelings of fear and worry, which have been termed as **climate anxiety** in recent years.
- **Eco-grief** is another recent term, referring to sadness and mourning about the loss of species, natural environments and ecological balance.
- The lack of effective policies and implementation to tackle the challenges of climate change gives rise to widespread **anger, frustration** and disappointment.
- In view of the massive challenge humanity is facing, some people feel a sense of **helplessness.** Important supportive factors to enable **positive action for climate change** mitigation and adaptation can be listed as: personal energy levels and well-being, a sense of connectedness with the planet, resilience and agility, and an outlook on life which transcends the strictly personal. Ancient wisdom, systemic worldviews and indigenous cultures most often include **intrinsic respect, care and gratitude for nature and the planet**.
- **Resilient and empowered individuals and communities can protect, restore and promote sustainable use of ecosystems and natural resources**, which in turn strengthen community resilience.

IAHV and Art of Living's initiatives for protection of the environment and for adaptation to climate change and its mitigation stem from awareness raising and empowerment at the individual and collective levels. Through the reduction of stress and pressure in daily life, individuals and communities can develop the capacity to care for nature and the environment and feel able and empowered to start implementing more sustainable practices. This in turn positively affects well-being and resilience on environmental, community and individual levels.

For example, to improve the well-being and prosperity of farmers and the health and productivity of their land, farmers are provided with stress management techniques along with extra skills training. This integrated approach facilitates a sustainable shift from chemical farming using genetically modified crops and seeds, to natural, chemical-free farming with high-nutrition crops. As a result, there is less pollution through the abandonment of chemicals and huge water savings which can be used for other purposes. Food security is also improved due to climate-resilient farming techniques. All of this is achieved along with an increase in the farmers' income, an improvement in their quality of life, and the enhancement of the nutritional value of their crops, benefiting also the health of their consumers.

Awareness raising, empowerment training and skills development are also provided to guide communities and villages away from the use of fossil fuels to renewable and green sources of energy, and to the adoption of a wide range of improved practices including more sustainable methods of consumption, improved waste management and recycling, the reclamation of wasteland, the implementation of large-scale tree planting campaigns, improved management of groundwater, the rejuvenation of rivers and the cultivation of highly nutritious indigenous seeds resilient to climate change. In addition, there is encouragement and training to halt and reverse land degradation and biodiversity loss. In this process, local people are trained as entrepreneurs to make a living from renewable and sustainable goods and services.

This integrated approach aims to improve the well-being of people, their livelihood, overall economic development, healthy lifestyles, the empowerment of communities and marginalized groups, the protection of the environment and sustainability of the planet.

The River Rejuvenation Project is an inspiring example of a highly impactful integrated project. It was launched by IAHV and the Art of Living in 2013 to address the rising water crisis in India.[65]

India is a vastly agrarian economy, with an estimated 65–70 per cent of the population depending on farmland for sustenance either as a landowner or farm worker. Inefficient and unsustainable agricultural practices, deforestation and poor groundwater management played a big role in the loss of access to water for agricultural and household use in rural India. The tragic culmination of these factors led to the migration of hundreds of thousands of families and an epidemic level of farmer suicides, with 100,474 farmers committing suicide in the period between 2014 and 2022.[66]

Through comprehensive, scientific and eco-friendly planning and implementation, forty-seven rivers spread across the states of Karnataka, Maharashtra, Tamil Nadu and Kerala have been rejuvenated, including the planting of 600,000+ trees. This has resulted in an estimated 2,500 trillion litres of increased water storage capacity, generating employment for 10,000+ people, and benefiting 6,186 villages and several million people altogether.

The projects are informed by the latest scientific insights and technology and guided by environmentalists and river experts. They involve groundwater management, biodiversity regeneration, tree planting and chemical-free agriculture combined in a coordinated, integrated effort.

The river rejuvenation teams are committed not only to reviving rivers but also to rebuilding lives by empowering individuals and renewing hope for the preservation of their communal way of life.

The consistency in water supply has augmented farmers' incomes through improved agricultural yields and increased the number of crops per year, directly reducing farmer suicides.

'(In the) last 8 years there was no water. Farming was dependent only on rains, hence we managed only one crop a year. Now water is available throughout the year and I grow three crops a year. My annual income has also grown 10 times to 300,000 rupees now from 30,000 earlier,' says Dayanand, a small farmer in Kalaspur village in Maharashtra.[67]

Farmers who had left to find work in the cities returned back to their lands to take up farming once again, thus reversing the migration trend from the rural to urban areas.

In addition, the river restoration projects generate direct rural employment for thousands of people.

Volunteers are trained through capacity building workshops to take up leadership roles in the villages and to inspire and strengthen community involvement. This approach to community engagement facilitated women's empowerment and social equity, since a large number (sometimes 90 per cent) of the ongoing project workers are women. Groups and committees are set up for the sustainable local management of natural resources and the ecosystem.

The success of the projects undertaken in partnership with local governments has resulted in major changes to water policy.

The sustainability of the approach not only resolves the immediate requirement for safe water for populations but also creates systems that ensure reliable supplies in the future.

Peacebuilding leadership

Peacebuilding leadership is an important factor to de-escalate conflict and prevent violence, and to inspire and lead societies towards more sustainable peace. Leaders play a critical role in shaping public perceptions of security and coexistence and can prevent the escalation of fear and violence. Peacebuilding leaders can emerge from every sphere of society and at every level of society, as school directors, scout leaders, political leaders, business leaders, artists, influencers or others.

Peacebuilding leaders are described as courageous men or women, well acquainted with non-violent methods, having a high level of integrity and adaptive and flexible ways of behaviour. Building sustainable peace also requires long-term commitment, endurance, belief, self-sacrifice, physical courage and serious engagement on the emotional, mental and even spiritual level. The many challenges and setbacks with which long-term peacebuilders are confronted can be significantly addressed by commitment, passion and emotional energy. These can be generated by a deeply rooted motivation, inspiration, or even calling for peacebuilding, and sustained with the support of personal practices and community resources.

In addition to the self-awareness, self-management, qualities and skills described earlier as optimal functioning of the human potential, psychosocial dimensions of peacebuilding leadership include the ability

- To envision a shared, clear, and mutually attractive peaceful future and to inspire and motivate others towards such a vision;
- To identify and grasp the full complexity of the challenges with which they are confronted;
- To develop collaborations among different groups, and to create social networks and alliances to enhance resources and capacity for peacebuilding initiatives;

- To be a positive role model for values and personal behaviour that inspires and supports others, including emotional management, staying calm in times of crisis, 'living peace', listening and being available for others
- To positively influence public perception, opinion and behaviours through charismatic peacebuilding leadership;
- To engage with conflict in a way that includes critical self-reflection, awareness and checking of assumptions and biases; to use techniques such as active listening, empathy and mindfulness to help conflict parties recognize and address the underlying emotional and psychological factors driving the conflict; to create safe spaces.

Mediators are no longer seen as neutral, objective, external third parties without feelings, interests or needs of their own, as was a common understanding in the earlier days of conflict resolution. Mediation is now increasingly entrusted to people whose moral character and wisdom are respected and who are appreciated for their personal qualities such as integrity, political insight, commitment to non-violent management of differences, humility, the ability to postpone judgement, psychological strength, dedication, the sacrifice of ego, spiritual discipline of discernment, empathy to suffering on all sides and the ability to relate. Gopin also characterizes a peacemaking personality as having an understanding of silence, welcoming open discussion, not seeing every conversation as a win-lose phenomenon, strong personal discipline, a very long view of time and outcomes, a strong degree of personal inner peace, deeply felt patience, a basic trust of humanity and the world, and a love of imperfect human beings as such.[68] Mennonites too have paid much attention to the key moral characteristics of the mediator, since for them 'the biggest obstacle to peacebuilding efforts is for peacemakers to live by the values they teach.'[69] The personality and moral character of the peacemaker are an important factor, because the more upright or honourable a third party is in her own right, the more powerful her example will be for change in the parties.

Peacebuilding leaders such as Mahatma Gandhi, Martin Luther King, Desmond Tutu and Ghosananda are not only revered for their moral courage but also for their ability to inspire change through personal example. Personal transformation is the foundation for dynamic and effective leadership in the pursuit of social justice and reconciliation. For example, Gandhi's philosophy of non-violent resistance, or Satyagraha, was rooted in the belief that true power comes from inner strength and moral conviction. His commitment to personal discipline and spiritual practice allowed him to challenge oppressive systems and mobilize millions in the struggle for independence. Similarly, Martin Luther King drew heavily on his deep religious faith and moral vision to lead the civil rights movement in the United States. These leaders possessed not only a strong moral character and well-developed personal qualities, but also insight into the challenging situation, a vision for the future, and the necessary skills to take concrete steps forward. They naturally addressed not only the external manifestations of injustice but also the internal conditions, such as fear, prejudice and anger, that sustained them. The lives and work of such transformative leaders exemplify how personal transformation and a steadfast commitment to inner peace can translate into profound social and political change. Their legacy serves as a powerful reminder that the journey towards a more peaceful world begins with the inner work of transforming oneself.

Challenges and conclusion

This chapter demonstrates how psychosocial factors permeate and intersect the different peacebuilding sectors, such as security, governance, development, justice, education and health, and illustrates how these factors can be leveraged to create and reinforce peace-enhancing systems and structures within society. Such peace-enhancing systems, in turn, exert a positive influence on individual and community well-being as well as on intrapersonal and interpersonal psychosocial dynamics.

The examples provided above indicate possibilities and modest successes. However, a significant challenge remains in scaling individual transformation to achieve broader social impact, such as addressing structural inequalities, entrenched political divisions, mass atrocities, economic disparities and climate change on a global scale. The systemic and structural impact of IAHV and the Art of Living remains relatively limited compared to the pronounced impact at the intrapersonal and interpersonal levels. While the volunteer-driven nature and organic development of both organizations is a strength in terms of fostering self-motivation, rapid response and local contextual relevance, these characteristics may also constrain their systemic and structural impact. The decentralized organizational structure, the absence of a robust and sustainable fundraising strategy and the lack of a centralized support system, providing expertise in financial, administrative, communication, security and human resource management, appear to limit their capacity to achieve broader global systematic impact. Although thousands of local initiatives have been initiated, these efforts have not yet been scaled to effect structural changes in national or global economic, social or governance models. This may be just a matter of time, however, given the strong intrapersonal and interpersonal psychosocial foundations laid in so many parts of the world.

Another challenge relates to the effectiveness of psychosocial peacebuilding when a conflict has already escalated to the stage of overwhelming coercive power, repressive authoritarianism or mass atrocities.

The psychosocial peacebuilding approach lays the groundwork for the development and support of peace-enhancing systems through fostering a healthy psychosocial foundation within individuals and communities. However, achieving large-scale system transformation through this method is inherently a long-term process. In the shorter term, the examples discussed demonstrate that the psychosocial approach can enhance well-being, productivity, social cohesion, a positive value base and other beneficial outcomes within existing societal systems. This development is increasingly and exponentially occurring worldwide across the various sectors mentioned.

Psychosocial factors at the intrapersonal, interpersonal and group levels are central to system transformations. Consequently, integrated psychosocial approaches across the various peacebuilding sectors are well-positioned to eliminate structural violence and to respond to current global challenges by working on various dimensions such as intrapersonal transformation, group dynamics, value systems, social stress levels, overall well-being, resilience, empowerment, individual and collective identities, public sentiment and social cohesion.

Key points: Chapter 7

The political, economic, legal, educational, health and security structures and systems in our societies can either promote or undermine peace.

Psychosocial factors permeate and intersect the different peacebuilding sectors, such as security, governance, development, justice, education and health. These factors can be leveraged to create and reinforce peace-enhancing systems and structures within society.

Systems and structures are made up of people. Human agency creates social reality. The well-being, mindsets, values, beliefs, attitudes, emotions, memories, social and economic conditions, relationships and other factors all influence how people interact with social systems.

Social transformation requires awareness, social empowerment, vision, imagination, resources and collective action, among other things.

Peace-enhancing systems, in turn, exert a positive influence on individual and community well-being as well as on intrapersonal and interpersonal psychosocial dynamics.

Crucial psychosocial factors to be taken into account in the envisioning, creation and operation of peace-enhancing systems and structures in society:

Security

- Subjective and objective experiences of threat, danger, fear, anxiety, safety and security; individual and community resilience; the provision of security for all segments of society without discrimination; psychosocial peacebuilding and the transformation of the causes of conflict as a secure foundation for long term safety and security; the state of mind and stress levels of security personnel.

IAHV's approach to Preventing and Countering Violent Extremism is fundamentally human, situated in a broader peacebuilding framework, and tackles the psychosocial roots of the challenge. It aims to empower former extremists as non-violent agents of positive change, many of whom become positive role models in turn.

Intrapersonal and interpersonal factors addressed in IAHV's PCVE approach include mental training, stress resilience, identity aspects, healing and emotional well-being, sense of empowerment and responsibility, and the provision of an alternative community and non-violent strategy.

Throughout the stages of radicalization, IAHV offers a systemic, inclusive, constructive approach to PCVE rooted in human values.

Political systems and good governance

- Values, interests and ideologies of different groups in society; in-group identity and out-group intolerance and discrimination; a culture and practice of dialogue, negotiation and conflict transformation; values of progress, peace and prosperity aimed for all people; an attitude of being of service to the people; greed, hunger for power and unprocessed experiences of past injustices; fears and anxieties; public opinion and sentiment.

Economy and sustainable development

- Values of trust and cooperation; positive organizational cultures, well-functioning and participatory organizational and management practices; care for the planet and environment, and sense of social responsibility; psychological well-being and energy of individuals, resilience in adverse economic times; the creativity and capacity to innovate, entrepreneurial mindsets and bravery, adaptability and strength when faced with loss or adversity, sense of purposeful engagement; strong social networks for exchange of resources and information, the creation of joint initiatives and opportunities.

A peace-enhancing economic structure supports sustainable development, guarantees the satisfaction of basic needs, reduces inequalities and improves the overall quality of life for individuals and communities.

Justice

- Perception of justice as fair or unfair, as discriminating or privileging; the interpretation, values and cognitive frameworks among justice decision-makers; the quality of interpersonal treatment during legal processes; the content of legal cases can be very traumatizing, emotional and shocking, the legal processes can be highly stressful and draining; the network of social relationships, whether supportive or aggravating; perceptions, judgements and stereotypes among the general population.

Education

- The overall well-being of children and youth; effective stress management and coping strategies; identity and self-worth; negative peer pressures, bullying and exclusion; cooperation, teamwork and conflict resolution skills; peace education; the well-being, inspiration and commitment of the teaching personnel; relationships with teachers; a safe and supportive environment; community building and social cohesion in the broader school environment.

Health sector

- Mental, emotional and other psychosocial aspects of health; the stress factor, a major underlying cause of most illnesses; taking care of the health needs of all; health strategies that support social cohesion and stability; the importance of mental health; the mental fitness, resilience and well-being of its personnel.

Climate change

- Perception and understanding of the climate crisis; climate anxiety; eco-grief, anger, frustration and disappointment; sense of helplessness and positive action for climate change; intrinsic respect, care and gratitude for nature and the planet; resilient and empowered individuals and communities.

Peacebuilding leadership

- To shape public perceptions of security and coexistence; to prevent the escalation of fear and violence; to envision a shared, clear and mutually attractive peaceful future; to inspire and motivate people; to create social networks and collaborations; to be a role model; self-reflection and self-management; active listening and empathy; well acquainted with non-violent methods; high level of integrity; long-term commitment, endurance, belief, self-sacrifice, physical courage; motivation and inspiration.

Notes

1. Forst, R. 2017. *Normativity and Power: Analyzing Social Orders of Justification*. Oxford University Press; Archer, M. S. 2012. *The Reflexive Imperative in Late Modernity*. Cambridge University Press; Giddens, A. 1984. *The Constitution of Society: Outline of the Theory of Structuration*. University of California Press.
2. See also Bar Tal, D. 2013, p. 17.
3. IAHV. 'Beyond Violent Extremism'.
4. As related by IAHV trainers in Iraq.
5. https://wisdom.srisriravishankar.org/time-has-come-for-the-voice-of-non-violence-to-be-heard-loud-and-clear/ (consulted 16 Aug 2024).
6. Art of Living Impact Report, p. 96.
7. https://www.srisriravishankar.org/work/peace-initiatives/peace-initiatives/ *(consulted 24 Sept 2024)*.
8. Art of Living. 2007. 'Rebuilding war Torn Kosovo: Art of living report', pp. 30–44.
9. https://skyresilience.org/research/ (consulted 24 Sept 2024).

10. Kumar, S. 2023, pp. 30–34.
11. Kumar, S. 2023, p. 39.
12. Kumar, S. 2023, p. 44.
13. Kumar, S. 2023, p. 66.
14. 'Encouraged by sustained interventions UPLA pledges for peace on Gandhi Jayanti'. https://www.srisriravishankar.org/work/peace-initiatives/encouraged-by-sustained-interventions-upla-pledges-for-peace-on-gandhi-jayanti/. 3 Oct 2018.
15. 'Inspired by Gurudev, UPLA declares unilateral ceasefire'. 2018. https://www.youtube.com/watch?v=AIY6ktCC5o0.
16. The Sentinel. 4 Sept 2021. 'United Peoples' Liberation Army disbands organisation across Karbi Anglong district'. https://www.sentinelassam.com/north-east-india-news/assam-news/united-peoples-liberation-army-disbands-organisation-across-karbi-anglong-district-554565.
17. Art of Living. 2008. 'Voice of Nonviolence'. p. 26.
18. Duseja. 2022. *The man who froze fire*. Garuda. p. 58.
19. Duseja. 2022, p. 63.
20. Sipri. 2019. 'Governance as a root cause of protracted conflict and sustainable peace: Moving from rhetoric to a new way of working'. https://www.sipri.org/commentary/blog/2019/governance-root-cause-protracted-conflict-and-sustainable-peace-moving-rhetoric-new-way-working (consulted at 24 Sep 2024).
21. The close link between good governance, stability and sustained peace is also reflected in the UN Sustainable Development Goal 16, the Building Stability Framework of the United Kingdom's Department for International Development (DFID) and the States of Fragility Framework of the Organisation for Economic Co-operation and Development (OECD). (Sipri, 2019)
22. Sharp, G. 1973. *The Politics of Nonviolent Action*. Boston: Porter Sargent; Boulding, K. E. 1990. *Three Faces of Power*. Thousand Oaks, CA: Sage Publications; Starhawk. 1987. *Truth or Dare: Encounters with Power, Authority, and Mystery*. San Francisco: Harper & Row.
23. Deutsch, M., Coleman, P. T., & Marcus, E. C. (Eds.). 2006. *The Handbook of Conflict Resolution: Theory and Practice*. Jossey-Bass.
24. Art of Living. 2022. 'Impact Report 2018–2020'. p. 51.
25. https://www.srisriravishankar.org/work/peace-initiatives/art-of-living-conducts-programs-for-kurdish-parliament/ (consulted 24 Sept 2024).
26. https://www.ilo.org/resource/news/who-and-ilo-call-new-measures-tackle-mental-health-issues-work-0 (consulted 18 Dec 2024).
27. https://www.who.int/news-room/commentaries/detail/mental-health-in-the-workplace (consulted 18 Dec 2024).
28. https://www.gallup.com/workplace/349484/state-of-the-global-workplace.aspx (consulted 18 Dec 2024).

29 TLEX. 'Resilience training: Materials', p. 4.

30 McKinsey & Company: https://www.mckinsey.com/business-functions/organization/our-insights/covid-19-and-theemployee-experience-how-leaders-can-seize-the-moment (retrieved on 12 Aug 2024).

31 Based on The Art of Living. 2013. *The Voice of Non-Violence*. Volume Two, pp. 1–8.

32 Based on The Art of Living. 2008, pp. 29–32.

33 https://en.wikipedia.org/wiki/Farmers%27_suicides_in_India (consulted 18 Dec 2024).

34 https://www.artofliving.org/us-en/reformed-alcoholic-maharashtra (consulted at 24 Sep 2024).

35 https://tlexinstitute.com/.

36 1,258 participants from seventy programmes were chosen as respondents. Companies included: AL Rajhi Capital, American Express, Abbott, Accenture, AIESEC, BCG, Beiersdorf, BSL, Canada, Coca Cola, Deloitte, Educomp, Frontier, GE, Healthcare, Harvard Business School, Microsoft, Ministerie, MIT Sloan, Plinovodi, Samba, Shell, Star Division LTD, Supercell, Technip, Swiss Tennis, TLS, Università Commerciale Luigi Bocconi, Verivox, The World Bank, World Vision, Yale University, Beach, Capital One, Wharton, World Health Organization.

37 A 2005 World Bank report stated that 'If the enrollment rate for secondary schooling is 10 percentage points higher than the average, the risk of war is reduced by about 3 percentage points.' https://www.globalcitizen.org/en/content/the-value-of-education/ (consulted at 21 July 2024); https://www.worldbank.org/en/topic/education/publication/.

38 Berger, N., & Archer, J. 2020. 'Understanding the psycho-social dimensions of schools and classrooms'. *Oxford Bibliographies in Education*. Oxford University Press. https://www.oxfordbibliographies.com/display/document/obo-9780199756810/obo-9780199756810-0266.xml.

39 Ekornes, S. 2021. 'The impact of perceived psychosocial environment and academic emotions on higher education students' intentions to drop out'. *Higher Education Research & Development* 41:4, pp. 1044–59. https://doi.org/10.1080/07294360.2021.1882404; Grøtan, K., Sund, E. R., & Bjerkeset, O. 2019. 'Mental health, academic self-efficacy and study progress among college students – the SHoT study, Norway'. *Frontiers in Psychology* 10:45. https://doi.org/https://doi.org/10.3389/fpsyg.2019.00045; Lipson, S. K., & Eisenberg, D. 2018. 'Mental health and academic attitudes and expectations in university populations: Results from the healthy minds study'. *Journal of Mental Health* 27:3, pp. 205–13. https://doi.org/https://doi.org/10.1080/09638237.2017.1417567

40 Hamre, B. K., & Pianta, R. C. 2005. 'Can instructional and emotional support in the first-grade classroom make a difference for children at risk of school failure?' *Child Development* 76:5, pp. 949–67. https://doi.org/https://doi.org/10.1111/j.1467-8624.2005.00889.x; Montalvo, G. P., Mansfield, E. A., & Miller, R. B. 2007. 'Liking or disliking the teacher: Student motivation, engagement and achievement'. *Evaluation & Research in Education* 20:3, pp. 144–58. https://doi.org/https://doi.org/10.2167/eri406.0; Quin, D. 2017. 'Longitudinal and contextual associations between teacher–student relationships and student engagement: A systematic review'. *Review of Educational Research* 87:2, pp. 345–87. https://doi.org/https://doi.org/10.3102/0034654316669434.

41   Hovdhaugen, E. 2019. 'Causes of dropout in higher education: A research summary of studies based on Norwegian data'. NIFU Labour Note 2019:3. http://hdl.handle.net/11250/2593810.

42   Neagoe, L. 2023. 'Psycho-sociological aspects of education in the 21st century'. In Soare, E., & Langa, C. (Eds.), 2022. *Education Facing Contemporary World Issues – EDU WORLD 2022, Vol 5. European Proceedings of Educational Sciences,* pp. 387–97. European Publisher. https://doi.org/10.15405/epes.23045.40.

43   Ibidem.

44   Ibidem.

45   Ibidem.

46   Newman, R. I., Yim, O., & Stewart, M. C. 2024. 'Breathing life into social emotional learning programs: A Bio-Psycho-Social approach to risk reduction and positive youth development'. *Journal of Adolescence* 96, pp. 1065–77. https://doi.org/10.1002/jad.12317.

47   See also Arnsten, A. F. T. 2009. 'Stress signalling pathways that impair prefrontal cortex structure and function'. *Nature Reviews Neuroscience* 10:6, pp. 410–22. https://doi.org/10.1038/nrn2648.

48   Akinsola, E. F., & Nwajei, A. D. 2013. 'Test anxiety, depression and academic performance: Assessment and management using relaxation and cognitive restructuring techniques'. *Psychology* 4:6, pp. 18–24. https://doi.org/10.4236/psych.2013.46A1003; Seppälä, E. M., Bradley, C., Moeller, J., Harouni, L., Nandamudi, D., & Brackett, M. A. 2020. 'Promoting mental health and psychological thriving in university students: A randomized controlled trial of three well-being interventions'. *Front Psychiatry* 11, p. 590. https://doi.org/10.3389/fpsyt.2020.00590.

49   Newman, R. I., Yim, O., & Stewart, M. C. 2024; Newman, R. I., Yim, O., & Shaenfield, D. E. 2020. 'Gender and ethnicity: Are they associated with differential outcomes of a biopsychosocial social-emotional learning program?' *International Journal of Yoga* 13, pp. 18–24. https://doi.org/10.4103/ijoy.IJOY_64_19; Ghahremani, D. G., Oh, E. Y., Rana, S., Agarwal, P., & Dean, A. C. (N.D). 'Effects of a social-emotional life-skills workshop that includes controlled breathing on emotional empathy in adolescents', unpublished; Ghahremani, D. G., et al. 2013. 'Effects of the youth empowerment seminar on impulsive behavior in adolescents'. *Journal of Adolescent Health* 53:1, pp. 139–41; Toumbourou, J. W. 2015. 'Social and emotional skill questionnaire'. Centre for Social and Early Emotional Development and School of Psychology, Deakin University, Australia; Seppälä, E. M., Bradley, C., Moeller, J., Harouni, L., Nandamudi, D., & Brackett, M. A. 2020; Goldstein, M. R., Lewin, R. K., & Allen, J. J. B. 2020. 'Improvements in well-being and cardiac metrics of stress following a yogic breathing workshop: Randomized controlled trial with active comparison'. *Journal of American College Health* 70:3, pp. 918–28. https://doi.org/10.1080/07448481.2020.1781867.

50   See studies mentioned above.

51   Newman, R. I., Yim, O., & Shaenfield, D. E. 2020; Ballard, D. J. (N.D.) 'The transformation of a middle school through the implementation of a social and emotional development and learning program: A case study'. St. John's University, PhD Dissertation.

52   See studies mentioned above.

53   Seppälä, E. M., et al. 2020.

54 Goldstein, M. R., et al. 2020.

55 Bolton, D. 2023. 'A revitalized biopsychosocial model: core theory, research paradigms, and clinical implications'. *Psychological Medicine* 53:16, pp. 7504–11. https://doi.org/10.1017/S0033291723002660; Wade, D. T., & Halligan, P. W. 2017. 'The biopsychosocial model of illness: A model whose time has come'. *Clinical Rehabilitation* 31:8, pp. 995–1004. https://doi.org/10.1177/0269215517709890; Roz, S., Bennett, S. D., & McKenzie Smith, M. 2017. 'Interventions to support integrated psychological care and holistic health outcomes in paediatrics'. *Healthcare* 5:3, p. 44. https://doi.org/10.3390/healthcare5030044.

56 Segerstrom, S. C., & Miller, G. E. 2004. 'Psychological stress and the human immune system: A meta-analytic study of 30 years of inquiry'. *Psychological Bulletin* 130:4, pp. 601–30. https://doi.org/10.1037/0033-2909.130.4.601; Janice, K., Kiecolt-Glaser, McGuire, L., Robles, T. F., & Glaser, R. 'Emotions, morbidity, and mortality: New perspectives from psychoneuroimmunology'. *Annual Review of Psychology* 53, pp. 83–107. https://doi.org/10.1146/annurev.psych.53.100901.135217.

57 WHO. 'COVID-19 pandemic triggers 25% increase in prevalence of anxiety and depression worldwide'. 2 March 2022. https://www.who.int/news/item/02-03-2022-covid-19-pandemic-triggers-25-increase-in-prevalence-of-anxiety-and-depression-worldwide (consulted 18 Dec 2024).

58 European Union. 2023. 'A comprehensive approach to mental health'. https://health.ec.europa.eu/publications/comprehensive-approach-mental-health_en (consulted 18 Dec 2024).

59 West, C. P., Dyrbye, L. N., & Shanafelt, T. D. 2018. 'Physician burnout: Contributors, consequences, and solutions'. *Journal of Internal Medicine* 283:6, pp. 516–29. https://doi.org/10.1111/joim.12752; The 2019 'National Physician Burnout, Depression & Suicide Report' by Medscape highlighted a burnout rate of 44 per cent among US physicians. https://www.medscape.com/slideshow/2019-lifestyle-burnout-depression-6011056 (consulted 18 Dec 2024).

60 The Art of Living and IAHV's response to the global Coronavirus pandemic, https://gurudev.artofliving.org/wp-content/uploads/IAHV-corona-intl.pdf (consulted at 24 Sep 2024).

61 Jalili, M., Niroomand, M., Hadavand, F., et al. 2021. 'Burnout among healthcare professionals during COVID-19 pandemic: A cross-sectional study'. *International Archives of Occupational and Environmental Health* 94, pp. 1345–52. https://doi.org/10.1007/s00420-021-01695-x; Ros, L., & Bruisic, J. 2024. 'The impact of stress and burnout on the quality of life of healthcare workers during the COVID-19 pandemic'. *International Journal of Critical Care* 18:1, pp. 5–17. https://doi.org/10.29173/ijcc88; Çelmeçe, N., & Menekay, M. 2020. 'The effect of stress, anxiety and burnout levels of healthcare professionals caring for COVID-19 patients on their quality of life'. *Frontiers in Psychology* 11, p. 597624. https://doi.org/10.3389/fpsyg.2020.597624; Matsuo, T., et al. 2020. 'Prevalence of health care worker burnout during the coronavirus disease 2019 (COVID-19) pandemic in Japan'. *JAMA Netw Open* 3:8, p. e2017271. https://doi.org/10.1001/jamanetworkopen.2020.17271.

62 WHO. March 2022. 'Mental health and Covid-19: Early evidence of the pandemic's impact'. Scientific Brief.

63. Korkmaz, A., et al. 2024. 'Sudarshan Kriya yoga breathing and a meditation program for burnout among physicians: A randomized clinical trial'. *JAMA Netw Open* 7:1, p. e2353978. https://doi.org/10.1001/jamanetworkopen.2023.53978.

64. https://gurudev.artofliving.org/wp-content/uploads/IAHV-corona-intl.pdf (consulted 18 Dec 2024).

65. Art of Living. 2022. Impact report. pp. 100–11.

66. 'One farmer/farm labourer dies by suicide every hour in India: NCRB data'. https://web.archive.org/web/20240408180626/https://www.downtoearth.org.in/news/agriculture/one-farmer-farm-labourer-dies-by-suicide-every-hour-in-india-ncrb-data-93184 (consulted at 24 Sep 2024).

67. https://www.iahv.org/in-en/rejuvenating-rivers-reviving-life/ 300,000 rupees is approximately 3,200 euros in September 2024.

68. Gopin, M. 2002. 'Religion as an aid and hindrance to post-conflict coexistence work'. www.gmu.edu/departments/crdc/docs/relasaidandhindrance.html.

69. Lederach and Sampson. 2000, p. 44.

8 The psychosocial peacebuilding project cycle

How can individuals and organizations implement integrated psychosocial peacebuilding projects in practice? We propose that the methods and approaches already typically used in humanitarian, development and peacebuilding projects can also serve as a foundation for psychosocial peacebuilding projects, provided they are complemented with a specific psychosocial lens and perspective. In practice, this means that psychosocial factors are integrated at all stages of the project cycle, from conflict analysis and needs assessment, formulation of goals and objectives, strategy design, activities development, monitoring and evaluation, to capacity building among staff and in organizations. Theories of change and assumptions about the effectiveness of peacebuilding need to be reviewed from the additional perspective of psychosocial factors. Throughout, the aim is to identify peace-contributing and -inhibiting psychosocial factors in programming contexts and to design and implement effective psychosocial peacebuilding interventions accordingly.

The short practical overview in this chapter aims to increase the confidence and skills of practitioners to implement psychosocial peacebuilding in practice. We will conclude with reflections and suggestions on how to build psychosocial peacebuilding capacity within organizations.

Psychosocial factors throughout the project cycle

Here, we revisit the overview of the (bio-)psychosocial factors introduced in Chapter 2 (Figure 8.1), which can serve as a foundation and guidance throughout all phases of a psychosocial peacebuilding project cycle (Figure 8.2).

Analysis and assessment

Project design starts with an assessment or analysis of the current situation, the challenges, problems, needs and conflict factors, but also the resources, opportunities and positive dynamics. There exists a wide variety of templates and methodologies for conflict analysis,

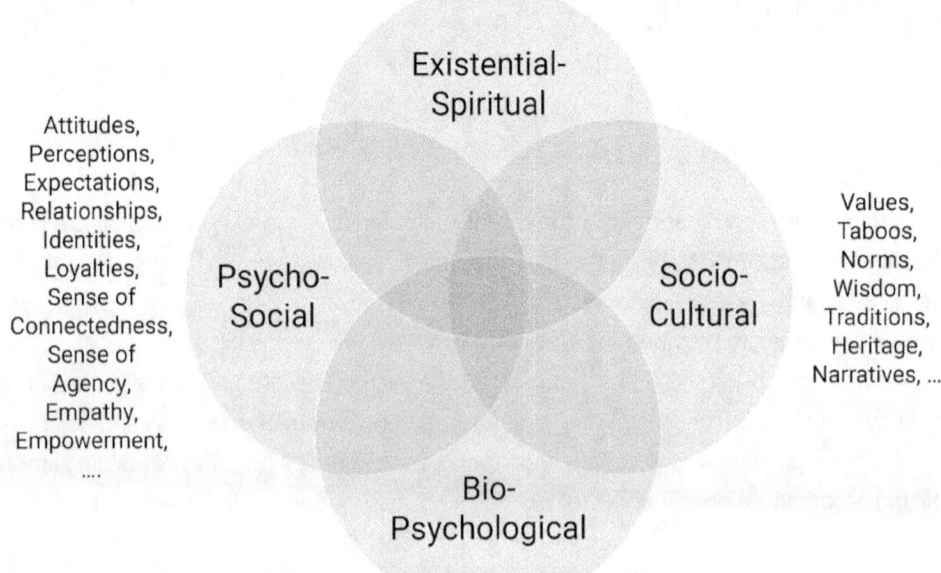

Figure 8.1 *Overview of bio-psycho-social factors in peacebuilding (Katrien Hertog).*

needs assessment, context analysis and baseline assessment, including more specialized tools for the assessment of risks, the need to do no harm, gender, environment, human rights, conflict sensitivity, security and others.

Psychosocial Peacebuilding analysis and assessment include identifying peace-contributing and -inhibiting psychosocial factors in the context of the specific conflict. This can be done with reference to the overview of psychosocial factors presented in Chapter 2. In order to illustrate how the psychosocial lens can be added in conflict and peace analysis, we will present two analysis tools which are widely used by peacebuilding practitioners: the stakeholder analysis or actor mapping and the conflict (and peace) tree (Figure 8.3 and Figure 8.4).

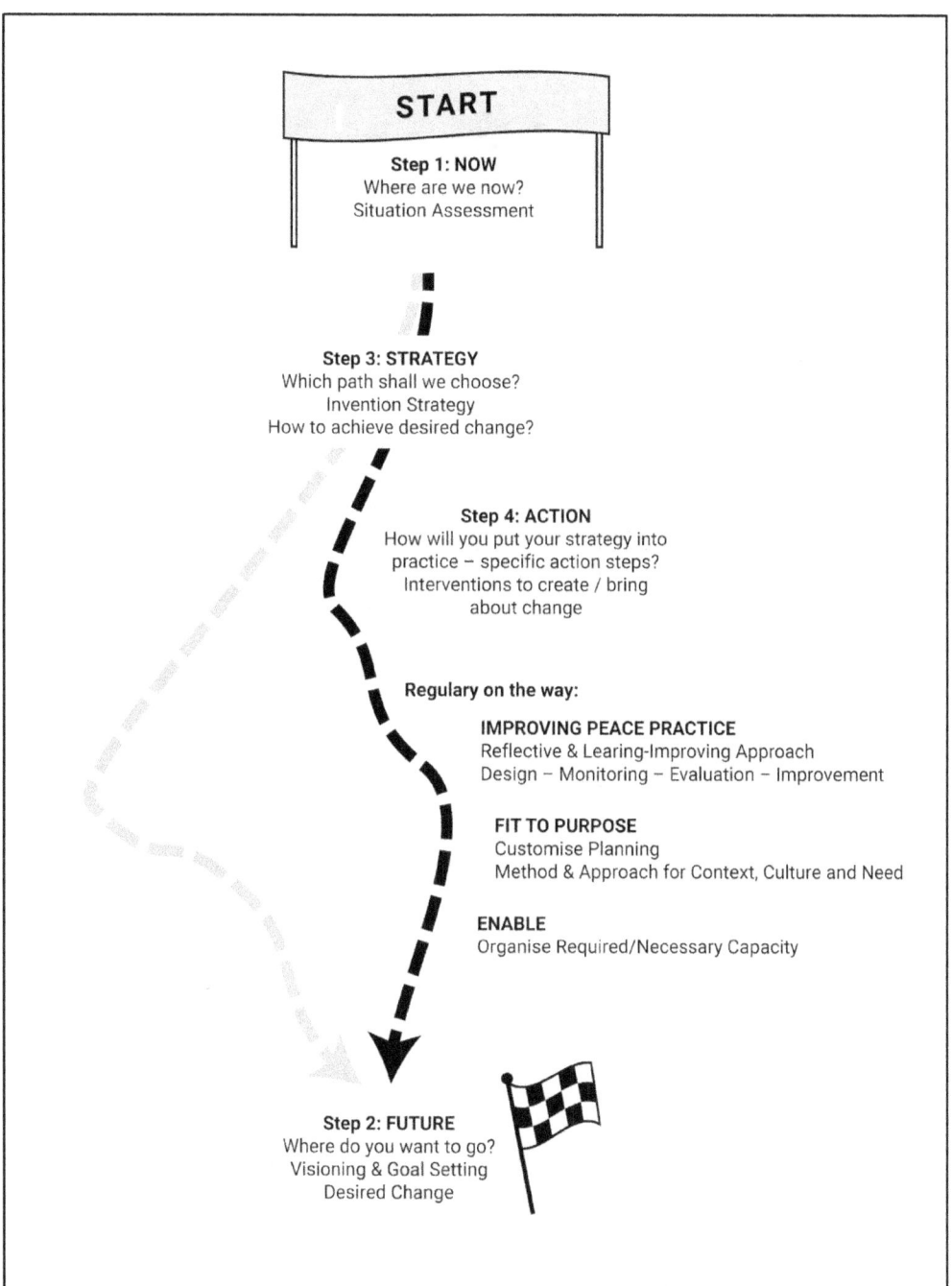

Figure 8.2 *Project cycle.*

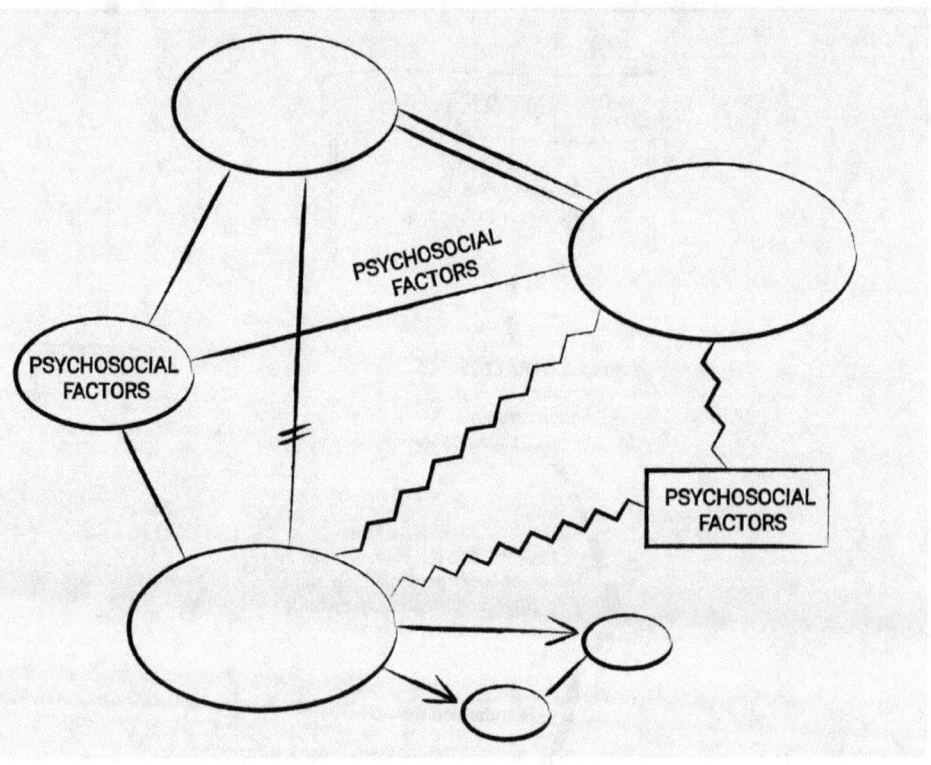

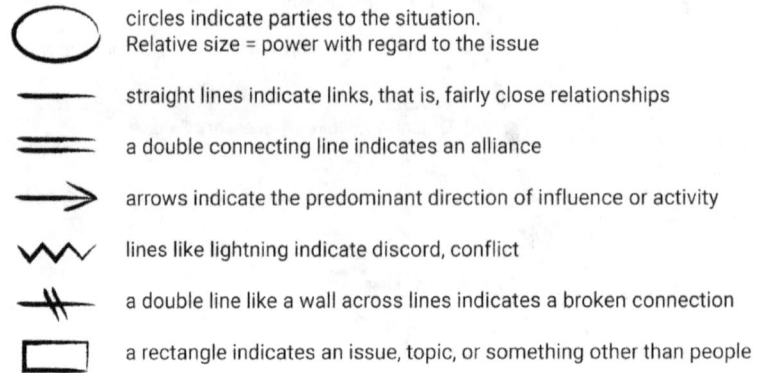

Figure 8.3 *Psychosocial actor mapping.*

Actor or stakeholder mapping is one of the most widely used tools of conflict and peace analysis, providing a visible representation or map of

- The actors involved in a certain conflict context, both directly and indirectly, proximate and remote;
- Their respective power;
- The relationships between them;
- The conflict issues between them.

Integrating a psychosocial perspective into this method of analysis would require the inclusion of the significant psychosocial factors which are influencing and characterizing the actors, their relationships and the conflict issues, and how these are contributing to peace-enhancing and inhibiting dynamics.

> **Exercise 12: Psychosocial actor mapping**
>
> After having done the actor mapping, place yourself in the position of one of the actors in the conflict and impersonate them with all their characteristics (living circumstances, family situation, history, experience, point of view, values, emotions, outlook on life, possible traumas, etc.) and consider: How would this person experience, perceive and interpret the conflict? How would this person want to, and be able to, deal with it? How and which solution would be preferred and possible?

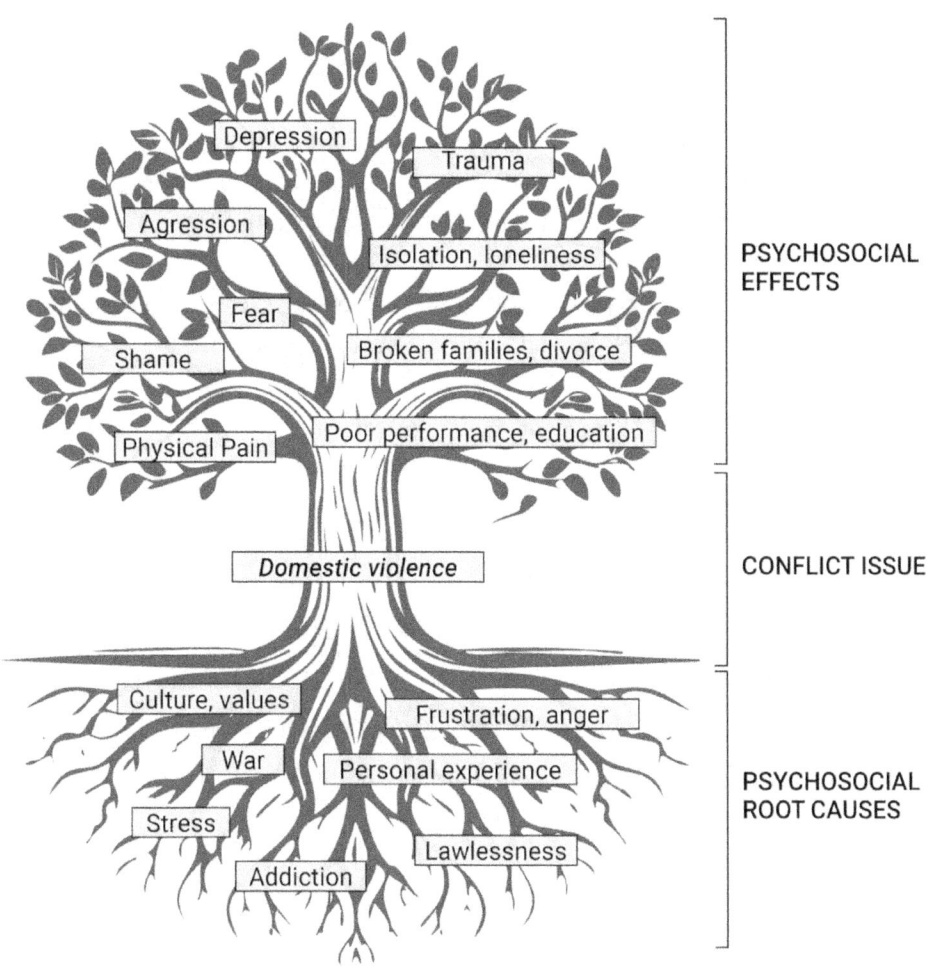

Figure 8.4 *Psychosocial conflict – peace tree: Example of domestic violence.*

An equally widely used tool for conflict and peace analysis is the conflict-peace tree, which provides a visible representation of the root causes of a certain conflict and the consequences of it. While the trunk represents the conflict issue being analysed, the roots represent its causes and the leaves its consequences. During the analysis, it often becomes clear that the consequences of long-term conflicts can become triggers and causes in an ongoing vicious cycle.

It is important to understand that the perception of the person or people undertaking the analysis or assessment is influential towards the outcome of the analysis. Putting it simply, development specialists are more likely to see unequal development as driving conflict, political scientists may focus on political power and dynamics, military personnel are more likely to see a military solution to the problem involving the use of force against specific targets, local people may feel the conflict is instigated by outsiders while outsiders may focus on the local conflict actors. Similarly, someone who is focused on the role of psychosocial factors in conflict and peace dynamics will likely emphasize these in the analysis and assessment.

In a peacebuilding context, the analysis and assessment are ideally conducted in a participatory way. Getting an understanding of the current situation is in itself a process, since different individuals and groups have different information, opinions and interpretations of the reality as they know it. A skilfully conducted participatory analysis as a process in peacebuilding allows people to express themselves, to get the feeling of being heard and to become aware of other, complementary points of view. When conducted in a skilful way, it can create an atmosphere of respectful listening, mutual understanding and empathy, and therefore be considered as a peacebuilding intervention in itself.

As an example, the psychosocial analysis of the IAHV peacebuilding project in Lebanon (Chapter 4) was conducted through various methods, including focus groups, and key informant interviews with representatives of the target groups and other stakeholders; joint participatory analysis processes; baseline surveys; and the consultation of existing primary and secondary sources.

The analysis contained the following elements, among others:

- Types of conflict, violence, distress occurring in Tripoli at the time;
- Mapping of specific actors/target groups involved in or affected by these;
- Psychosocial and other driving forces and consequences of violence/Conflict-Peace Tree;
- The specific context and culture of psychosocial well-being in general, and specific factors;
- Sources of resilience, support systems, coping resources, local practices;
- Other actors/organizations: who, what, where, how, gaps, what works well;
- Groups that need special attention.

Future vision, intended overall impact and project objectives

The next step following the analysis and assessment is to envision the desired situation in the future. Also here, the envisioned state of psychosocial factors and dynamics should be included alongside the other factors and aspects of the future scenario.

When the vision of the future is clear, the intended impact of the specific project needs to be formulated in view of the time available, short- or long-term. The overall impact can then be translated into specific project goals or objectives.

Strategy

How to move from the current situation to the desired situation in the future? Here a strategy needs to be developed that outlines the approach to achieve the desired change. Strategies could include:

- Addressing the consequences of conflict;
- Addressing the causes of conflict in order to prevent / reduce it;
- Strengthening the resilience and support networks of people to cope with conflict and violence and their impact;
- Impacting many people or impacting key people to change the conflict dynamics;
- Transforming specific psychosocial factors that can positively influence peace dynamics;
- Transforming individuals or communities or structures.

As part of the strategy, we need to analyse and define what the most important changes required to achieve the desired change are. Below is a non-exhaustive list of factors, with an emphasis on psychosocial factors, that can be focused on (Table 8.1).

Table 8.1 *Psychosocial Changes in a Peacebuilding Strategy*

Factors	Strategic Conflict Analysis – From What –	*Strategy* – How –	Vision: Desired Future – To What –
Physiological and Mental Well-being & Excellence			
Attitudes, Mindsets & Emotions			
Behaviours & Empowerment			
Relationships, Trust & Interactions			
Identities & Narratives		⇨	
Cultures, Beliefs, Values			
Existential connection, meaning, worldview			
Contradictions, Conflict Issues, Root Causes, Context			
Leadership, Societal and Sectoral Engagement			
Skills & Capabilities			
Structures, institutions and Systems			

Theory of change and checking assumptions

The decision about what to change and how is defined by the underlying theory of change. A theory of change outlines how we believe or know that change will happen. General theories of change include, for example:

a. If basic human needs of people are covered, then there is a foundation for social peace.
b. If we create personal inner transformation, then violence will disappear from society.
c. If underlying root causes of injustice, victimization, oppression and other structural violence are eliminated, then a peaceful society can be created.
d. If we develop institutions that provide stability and effectively address and resolve conflict, then we can effectively prevent violence and maintain peace in society.

In practice, theories of change are more detailed, outlining how one change or intervention leads to a specific outcome, and how this outcome in turn leads to another outcome. There are many theories of change being used in the peacebuilding and development fields. These theories of change are partly based on knowledge and evidence, and partly on assumptions. In order to know that the theories of change work, it is important to check the underlying assumptions and to verify if the logic or beliefs behind them are effectively valid:

- What is the underlying assumption, logic or belief here?
- What is the logic of cause and effect? Why do we think that a certain intervention or activity will lead to this specific outcome or result?
- In the process, have we considered cultural and gender assumptions, for example?

Below we will check some assumptions related to psychosocial factors in theories of change which are commonly used in the peacebuilding field (Table 8.2).

As an example, **IAHV's theory of change for psychosocial peacebuilding** is formulated as follows (as presented in Chapter 3):

- If individuals and communities get access to techniques and tools for the improvement of their own mental, emotional, physical and social well-being, which are self-empowering, accessible, easy to use, cost-effective, and applicable across cultures, a significant proportion of these populations will use these in their lives.
- If individuals and communities use techniques and tools which strengthen their physiology for peace, with evidence-based outcomes such as reduced depression, anxiety, PTSD and stress, along with improved clarity, focus, calm and optimism, then the negative impact of adverse experiences will reduce, overall well-being will improve, and attitudes, behaviour and relationships will be positively affected.

Table 8.2 *Assumptions in Theories of Change Related to Psychosocial Factors*

Examples of Assumptions	Examples of Checking These Assumptions
IF we organize joint football matches, THEN relationships between conflicting groups will improve	Joint matches can increase division and tension without additional measures, such as playing in mixed teams, integrating conflict resolution skills, emphasizing codes of ethics and human values, engaging the broader community.
IF we provide MHPSS to violence-affected people, THEN people's well-being will improve	MHPSS interventions need to be assessed on their quality, accessibility, stigmatizing effect, cultural adaptation, appropriateness and other factors, for them to have a positive effect on people's well-being. In addition, other inhibiting and contributing factors to well-being need to be taken into account and engaged with where necessary, such as direct, structural and cultural violence.
IF we train youth in non-violent communication, THEN they will handle local conflicts non-violently	Communication skills are but one skill and tool to improve conflict management and transformation, and more may be required to manage conflicts non-violently. The choice to use non-violent communication and the capacity to implement it are also defined by the state of mind, inner strength and motivation of the people involved. Participation in a training does not automatically translate into implementation, especially in the face of provocation and conflict escalation.
IF we engage in dialogue, THEN relationships will improve	Dialogue is a mostly cognitive and often rational process, while other, non-cognitive psychosocial factors are often strongly influential in shaping relationships. The way dialogue is organized in terms of participants, process, facilitation, can be conducive or detrimental to improved relationships.

- If individuals and communities process their adverse experiences, wounds and responses to traumas effectively, they are less likely to commit harm to themselves or others. If individuals and communities become resilient, they can withstand and recover more quickly from such negative impacts and better resist violent and divisive tendencies.
- If individuals and communities are non-violently empowered, they can be positive agents for change in society to transform those negative impacts and improve both well-being and peacebuilding objectives.
- Healed, resilient, empowered and trained individuals and communities together constitute a strong psychosocial foundation for any society to prevent or overcome the effects of conflict and violence, to strengthen peacebuilding and development efforts, to address root causes, and to create peace-enhancing systems, thus increasing overall impact and making peace self-sustainable.
- If peacebuilding practitioners improve their personal well-being and develop peacebuilding personalities and qualities, their professional performance is optimized.

> **Exercise 13: Psychosocial theory of change**
>
> What type of theory of change do you ascribe to? Write down your theory of change as it is. Does it have psychosocial factors integrated? If not, reflect and brainstorm on the psychosocial factors permeating your strategy. Check the implicit assumptions of your theory of change and elaborate or modify them further if needed.

Activities

Activities need to be selected, organized and developed in such a way that they will bring about the desired changes as defined earlier. If psychosocial factors are integrated into the strategy and intended changes, they also need to be integrated in a practical way into the activities that are designed to achieve these changes. The activities need to be carefully designed and reviewed to check that the intended psychosocial changes can take place effectively: how to organize the activities, who is participating and who is facilitating, which methods are used, where or in which circumstances are they conducted, is the time appropriate, how do they link up with other activities and so on? The methods to achieve psychosocial changes for peacebuilding are numerous and need to be carefully evaluated for their evidence, effectiveness and appropriateness.

Monitoring and evaluation

In order to monitor and evaluate psychosocial peacebuilding projects, we need methodologies and tools that can effectively and comprehensively capture the bio-psycho-social dimension through appropriate indicators. Bio-psycho-social indicators include changes in psychological, biological/physiological and social indicators, among others.

In addition, the evaluation methodology would aim to capture the interlinks between such changes on the individual and the social level.

One of the most challenging aspects of impact measurement may be the question of attribution to understand which changes on the individual level correlate to changes at the social level and vice versa. This would arguably also be one of the most interesting aspects of M&E for psychosocial peacebuilding, and much more evidence would need to be collected in this regard.

While identifying and developing M&E for integrated approaches, it is important to ensure that the data collection methods are culturally applicable, simple enough and well designed to measure intended changes on both micro- and macro-levels.

Synergies for optimal impact

In cooperation with other actors and organizations, psychosocial interventions could be leveraged for increased impact through specific synergies. Integrating psychosocial interventions strategically with other peacebuilding initiatives in a holistic, systemic way would arguably lead to maximum impact. For example, the added value of psychosocial interventions in partnership and coordination with other organizations could be (Table 8.3):

Table 8.3 *Synergies of Psychosocial Interventions for Increased Peacebuilding Impact*

- To transform the mindsets and attitudes of key stakeholders and agents of change in a certain context.
  For example, gang leaders.
- To remove psychosocial obstacles for peace in a peacebuilding process.
  For example, existential fear due to past genocide.
- To strengthen the psychosocial foundation of the broader population for sustainable peace.
  For example, making peace education part of the school curricula.
- To target specific change or give support to the peacebuilding efforts of other organizations through the integration of a psychosocial component.
  For example, to work with the mindsets, traumas and emotions of conflict parties during negotiation processes.

Conclusion
Way forward

Building capacity for psychosocial peacebuilding and transforming organizations

Building capacity for psychosocial peacebuilding within organizations entails several components, such as:

- Embracing an organizational commitment to psychosocial peacebuilding and making this clearly recognizable internally and externally, for example in official documents, mission statements, values and the philosophy of the organization.

- Designing and implementing working policies and procedures that reflect this commitment.

- Assigning and allocating human and financial resources to support the implementation of PSPB in the internal and external functioning of the organization.

- Promoting leaders and leadership practice that inspire, motivate and exemplify PSPB, 'walk the talk', and specifically adopt PSPB as an approach within everyday working practice and being, rather than including it as a tick-the-box exercise.

- Ensuring the philosophy, values and approach of PSPB are clearly raised and discussed in the staff selection process, and the assessment of the respective individual's qualities forming part of that process.

- Building staff capacity for psychosocial peacebuilding. In our view, comprehensive PSPB training needs to include the three important components of IAHV's psychosocial peacebuilding training 'Towards Integrated Peacebuilding: Psychosocial Well-being, Knowledge and Skills for Increased Peacebuilding Impact':

    - Resilience, Stress Management and Self-Care: Provide staff not just with theoretical insights and information, but with practical tools that are easy to integrate and work effectively to improve their well-being, reducing trauma and depression, managing stress, preventing burnout, improving sleep, increasing energy and focus and strengthening overall well-being and resilience.

    - Developing one's potential as a peacebuilder: Working proactively to cultivate knowledge, skills, reflections and insights to deepen, nurture and fine-tune one's inner resources and qualities for transformative and effective peacebuilding practice, including self-knowledge, self-awareness and self-management.

- Skills Training in Psychosocial Peacebuilding Projects: Providing tools for analysis, design and delivery of psychosocial interventions, offering participants insight and confidence to work in an effective way with crucial psychosocial factors in order to make a meaningful impact on conflict and peace dynamics.

Such training provides professional peacebuilders and peacebuilding organizations with the well-being, knowledge and skills for personal stress management, professional excellence and innovation in psychosocial peacebuilding. It enables them to become healthier, stress-resilient, smart, effective, creative, innovative, connecting, impactful, strategic and empathetic peacebuilders, and to improve and integrate psychosocial peacebuilding into their work and organizations.

- Ensuring staff have access to resources, support and additional training during employment and assignment.
- Ensuring ownership and participation of staff, open discussions and sharing within the organization, feedback loops, support networks.
- Assessing and evaluating internal and external PSPB initiatives and readjusting if and where necessary.

Through some of the non-exhaustive processes mentioned above, we can transform organizations to excel in psychosocial peacebuilding.

Strengthening the knowledge and practice of psychosocial peacebuilding requires

1. A **more developed compendium of psychosocial peacebuilding frameworks, approaches and methodologies**, according to agreed criteria for comprehensive, integrated approaches, in order to develop more understanding and knowledge of psychosocial peacebuilding practice around the world.

2. **Rigorous multidisciplinary research into the impact of existing and new methodologies and approaches for psychosocial peacebuilding and the establishment of a solid evidence base**. How does inner peace really link to outer peace? Which aspects of personal transformation lead to what kind of interpersonal and social changes, and under which conditions? For example, what is really the effect of relieving post-traumatic stress in war-affected populations on the reduction of interpersonal violence? Or do peace negotiations produce more results when accompanied by self-reflective methods for negotiators? How much violence is actually prevented if we lay a psychosocial foundation for non-violence and human values through the school curriculum? We still need a better understanding of the specific way in which intra- and interpersonal psychosocial factors interact with, influence, reinforce or inhibit other essential elements of peacebuilding and vice versa. How do psychosocial peacebuilding interventions link up with the other components required for sustainable peace?

In addition, we need to understand the process and conditions which make these transformations possible, including the parameters of effective implementation related to quality, context, target group, adaptability and trainers. How and why does psychosocial peacebuilding work and which components exactly are most crucial for success? Before psychosocial peacebuilding becomes the next fashionable trend in the peacebuilding field, it would be desirable to develop more detailed theories of change in order to develop more effective interventions.

3. **Increased awareness among policymakers, implementing organizations and donors** to integrate psychosocial peacebuilding into policies and programming, and to allocate funding for integrated psychosocial peacebuilding approaches based on robust evidence.
4. Much more widespread **training of peacebuilding practitioners** and integration of psychosocial peacebuilding modules into student curricula to gain knowledge, well-being, skills and confidence to design and implement psychosocial peacebuilding approaches.

When psychosocial peacebuilding is truly integrated and internalized by peacebuilding practitioners, and integrated in their teams, organizations and programming, as well as in the conflict context, we will truly be able to speak about 'the art and soul of building peace.'

Afterword

The peace that emanates from consciousness: Gurudev Sri Sri Ravi Shankar's mission of integrated peace

Following all the above, an additional, less tangible dimension of peacebuilding still remains to be explored: the peace that emanates from consciousness. This form of peace is to be experienced rather than to be understood. It seems to arise from an infinite source and operates beyond the confines of intellect, logic or even words. Unlike the peacebuilding efforts described above, it is characterized not by deliberate human effort. It cannot be planned, designed, captured, or evaluated.

I have witnessed and experienced this effulgent peace through the presence and teachings of Gurudev Sri Sri Ravi Shankar. The first time I met Gurudev Sri Sri Ravi Shankar, he did not speak, but I felt a deep presence. The space was filled with love and serenity. I had a profound sense of trust and knowing, even though I had not met him before. Even though I "know" him now for over 20 years, he seems to me a bigger enigma the more I meditate, spend time with him, listen to his knowledge or practise his techniques.

Over the course of more than four decades, his role as founder of the Art of Living Foundation and the International Association for Human Values – as well as his recognition as a peace ambassador (with nominations for the Nobel Peace Prize and multiple honorary accolades) – has been well documented. Yet, while his institutional contributions are readily describable, the experiential depth of his spiritual leadership remains more of an enigma beyond my grasp. I have seen how he carries a peace that has provided healing to thousands of people, settled fires of discord, exposed and transformed social distortions, diffused violence before it escalated and reconciled seemingly irreconcilable opposites. This all takes place in different settings around the world, regardless of the backgrounds, beliefs, cultures, nationalities or education of those he is interacting with.

To illustrate this rather unfamiliar dimension, I will share here several case studies and documented accounts. IAHV and Art of Living trainers and volunteers regularly share about mysterious happenings and situations they experience during their projects and endeavours, as if something else is at work.

Resolution of the 450-year-old Hindu-Muslim conflict in Ayodhya

Gurudev is credited with playing a major role in the resolution of the 450-year-old conflict over the Babri mosque and Ram temple in Ayodhya, India. In the sixteenth century, the Mongols built a mosque on the site of an old Hindu temple that was believed to be the birthplace of the Hindu God Ram. Over hundreds of years, dozens of conflicts have been fought over the place, resulting in thousands of deaths, and intercommunal and interreligious strife and animosity. Gurudev was invited to play a mediating role, which he fulfilled successfully in the material realm, though not without many challenges. In another realm, however, something totally different happened as well, which he had reported afterwards.[1]

Back in 2001, Gurudev was asked by the then prime minister of India to find a peaceful resolution of the conflict. He met with the main parties to the conflict, but at that time there was no opening in their well-entrenched positions and no progress could be made. His account is that around that time, he had a vision of a dilapidated Devi temple with a pond that needed to be resurrected. He didn't pay much attention to it at the time though. However, a few days later, an elderly palm leaf reader visited Gurudev's ashram in Bangalore and wanted to meet him. As he read the ancient palm leaves, which outline people's lives, he said with a gentle authority, 'Gurudev, it is written that you will need to play a role in bringing both communities together to resolve the Ram Janmabhoomi (. . .) issue.' He added, 'The nadi leaves also reveal that a temple built for Sri Ram's family deity, Devkali, is languishing in severe neglect. Unless it is restored, the violence and strife surrounding the Ram Temple in Ayodhya will not end.' He repeated with a strong sense of urgency and conviction: 'It has to be done!'

Neither the palm leaf reader nor Gurudev was actually aware of the existence of such a temple. After some enquiry, it turned out that indeed a Devkali temple existed. It was in ruins, with its central pond reduced to a dumping ground. Art of Living volunteers then rejuvenated the pond and renovated the temple, which was reconsecrated in September 2002 by priests from Gurudev's ashram. During the fire offerings, the aged priest of the temple had tears of joy and gratitude in his eyes. According to Gurudev, 'Goddess Devkali was shining in all her glory' at that moment.

Around this time, Gurudev again met with hard-line Hindu leaders, who began to soften their stance and built bridges with Muslim leaders. Gurudev had a premonition that it would take at least another fourteen years for the Ram temple issue to be resolved. There was a need for a resolution of the conflict that would withstand the test of time, since so much blood had already been shed over centuries. Despite this prediction, Gurudev proposed an out-of-court settlement in 2003. His proposal involved the Muslim community transferring the disputed Ram

Janmabhoomi site to the Hindus as a goodwill gesture, and the Hindu community giving a five-acre parcel of land for the construction of a mosque they would help to build.

Years passed. By 2017, Gurudev resumed his efforts to mediate the conflict, asked so by leaders from both communities and the Supreme Court of India. Ultimately, these renewed mediation efforts culminated in a Supreme Court judgement that allocated the ancient temple land for the construction of a Hindu temple and designated five acres for the establishment of a mosque. The conflict that had persisted for nearly 500 years was finally effectively resolved.

> *Gurudev wrote: 'What may often seem like a gross phenomenon, actually has an underlying, subtle aspect. We tend to navigate the cause-and-effect dynamics within the realm of the tangible, seldom extending our perception beyond it. However, if we did, we would realise that the forces of the subtle realm impact what ultimately materializes in the physical world. It is not human effort alone, but Divine will too, that plays a role in the fructification of any action. And for that, we need patience. Another mystery of this enigmatic world that we inhabit.'[2]*

Unusual assistance in the middle of the jungle

In a separate incident from Bihar, volunteer team leader Sanjay Kumar and his colleagues encountered a critical situation while returning from a visit to Maoist-controlled areas in the dense forests of Sahar. Their vehicle experienced a breakdown in a remote location late in the evening when they ran out of petrol. The Maoist leader, who had been holding a stronghold in the jungle amidst enemy forces, had warned them they should at all costs make their way back before nightfall, because anything could happen in the area. Aware that all petrol pumps in the region close at five in the afternoon for fear of being robbed, they switched off the headlights afraid of being discovered, with the moonlight as their only remaining source of light. They got a sense of what local people live through on a daily basis, cut off from facilities, shops and help, hiding in fear.

After a while, they decided to restart the car and see if they could drive a little bit further. If not, they would sleep in the car. Sanjay recounted as follows: 'The car started with a groan and they moved forward. One, two, five, ten . . . Sanjay's eyes kept counting the kilometres as the car kept going. They passed several abandoned and closed petrol pumps, and it became harder for them to conceal their disappointment. The car started groaning again when they had reached sixty kilometres. They were still terrified, unable to acknowledge that it was a miracle that the car was still running at all. Finally, after sixty-eight kilometres, they saw a faint light at a turn of the road. The car slowed down with a couple of jerks but stuttered forward. A few metres further, then noticed the symbol of a petrol pump. Their ecstatic shouts were immediately drowned by a loud groan from the car as it finally spluttered to a halt. The three men jumped down in relief and pushed the car for another hundred metres towards the petrol pump. They didn't say a word to each other as the attendant filled the fuel tank with petrol. Slowly, each of their faces lit up with a smile and a huge sense of relief.'

Sanjay knew it was not just relief but also faith that had dawned, since they slowly started realizing they had witnessed some sort of miracle. Their anxiety calmed down and a smile of wonder appeared: 'They were feeling that something supernatural was aiding them in their quest.'[3]

A high-risk family reunion in Kashmir

Another documented case involves a former Kashmiri militant who, having renounced militancy after participating in an Art of Living course, expressed to Gurudev his earnest desire to meet his mother once again. However, such a reunion was complicated by his political status, which precluded travel to his home village. Gurudev assigned Sanjay Kumar the task of fulfilling the wish of the former militant and facilitating this reunion.

When they travelled into the village, they were immediately handed over by locals to the local police station, where they got interrogated. Sanjay's innocent sharing of the true story was not believed. Instead, suspicion was raised about his motives and possible related security threats. During the nighttime interrogations, he was threatened with death by the next morning and was then left alone. Surprisingly, early in the morning, they were released and allowed to visit the house of the militant's mother. Suspiciously and carefully, they walked through the village where the locals had handed them in, but to their surprise, they found a huge crowd now cheering them, hugging them, kissing their hands and expressing their gratitude for bringing one of their sons back to them. Mother and son cried and hugged when they finally met after thirteen years of separation.

Sanjay did not understand what had happened. Later that morning, the commander who had interrogated Sanjay invited him to his house for breakfast, where the commander's wife shared:

> I am from Dehradun. I usually don't come to the police post, but yesterday, I had come to meet my husband here. When he left without a word last night, I was worried. Later, when he came back, he told me that a teacher from the Art of Living had arrived, bringing along a militant who wanted to meet his mother. My husband said that the teacher was from Bihar. So I immediately asked him if the teacher's name was Sanjay. Last week I did an Art of Living course in Dehradun. The teacher there told us about one of the other teachers who had gone into the jungles of Bihar and brought the CPI(ML) and the Ranvir Sena to meet Gurudev, and of how much good the teacher's bravery had brought about. So, upon learning that it was you who had been detained, I immediately told my husband who you really are and urged him that he should immediately, respectfully, release you.[4]

It did not seem a coincidence that the commander's wife travelled to the faraway police post on exactly the evening that Sanjay would be detained there, and that she would know him because another Art of Living teacher told her about him during the course just the week before. Thus, she saved Sanjay's life.

And so it also did not seem coincidence that, a few weeks earlier, Gurudev had contacted Sanjay and, in an informal manner, suggested that it was time to fulfil the militant's request due to the impending snowfall in the area. Despite having postponed the organization of the trip for several months, Sanjay proceeded promptly after receiving the call.

Emergency intervention in a life-or-death scenario

The moment Prison Programme trainer Jakob found himself between two senior gang members wanting to kill each other, something very unusual happened.

Through his extensive work with gangs, Jakob got to work in the highest security prison in Scandinavia, which specializes in the detention of gang members and other high-risk offenders who constitute a danger to each other. The prison is designed in such a way that offenders who are in active conflict with each other are kept apart in strictly separate buildings and do not have any opportunity for contact. Big was Jakob's surprise as he was walking along a corridor with one senior gang member when another senior member of a rival gang and sworn enemy of the first suddenly came through a door right in front of them. Immediately, they started shouting and readying themselves to fight. Before he knew it, Jakob found himself standing between the two enflamed men, holding a hand on each of their chests. In that critical moment, he was overcome with an overwhelming sensation of tranquillity and a profound experience of absolute non-violence. He reported that it was in fact a very pleasant feeling, despite the unexpected crazy situation in which he found himself. He remembers that he experienced a space where he felt completely safe. The experience felt beyond time. Those few moments of being in that space appeared to change the dynamic between the two men and suspend the immediate threat of violence. The gang members suddenly stopped shouting, turned around and walked away without further incident. This occurrence was later confirmed as extraordinary, given that these individuals had been targeting and threatening each other's lives and were to be kept strictly apart under the security regime.

Jakob wondered what had actually occurred there in that moment. It felt as though something happened through him, which was not him.

Conclusion

In summary, the dimension of peace that flows from consciousness represents a complex, multidimensional aspect of peacebuilding that extends beyond traditional frameworks. The interventions associated with Gurudev Sri Sri Ravi Shankar, as illustrated by these diverse case studies, indicate that transformative outcomes may arise through processes that challenge conventional notions of causality and human agency. Numerous reports from trainers and volunteers associated with the International Association for Human Values and the Art of Living Foundation describe experiences that point to the operation of subtle, transformative forces in critical situations. They have documented instances of inexplicable assistance in critical moments, rapid de-escalation in high-security conflicts, life-changing transformations of people far beyond their interventions and of sensing a gentle, unknown energy through everything they are doing. These accounts invite further inquiry into the interplay between individual agency and broader, less tangible energies.

Gurudev Sri Sri Ravi Shankar's broader work encompasses promoting human values and peace through holding conferences around the world, mediating in conflicts, designing and conducting courses to raise people's happiness and awareness, recording knowledge series to uplift people's understanding and lives, visiting disaster-struck communities, streaming online meditations, initiating innovative projects to support the environment and development, promoting complementary health systems for holistic well-being, setting up schools for first-generation learners, and sharing advice, consolation and wisdom through individual meetings and mass gatherings, all of which are underpinned by efforts to elevate human consciousness.

In addition to this, he has also developed the revival of the ancient Vedic tradition of chanting Sanskrit verses, a practice posited to have positive effects on peace, health and prosperity. At the Art of Living ashram in Bangalore, continuous chanting is maintained to foster global peace, culminating in a few celebrations per year when tens of thousands of people gather together to meditate during several days and nights of intense chanting. Insights from quantum physics and from the Vedic tradition suggest that the vibrational energy associated with such practices and their positive effects may extend well beyond the immediate context and that the transformative potential of these practices operates on levels that are not readily observable in the material world. We can only wonder how and when they impact the material observable world as we know it, since the reality we can perceive through our senses is only a fraction of the Existence. According to Vedic science, the ultimate reality of creation transcends the observed duality of this world, and thus the conventional dualities of good and bad, peace and non-peace. In the space where dualities are transcended and where the knowing, the knower and the known merge, lies an enigmatic yet significant dimension of peace. A Peace which is – in a way – beyond peace.

Notes

1. The below description is based on Gurudev Sri Sri Ravi Shankar's relay as published in the article Ayodhya Ram Temple and Goddess Kali Connection, 11 Jan 2024, https://timesofindia.indiatimes.com/speaking-tree/daily-ecstasy/ayodhya-ram-temple-and-goddess-kali-connection/amp_articleshow/106734415.cms.
2. Ibidem.
3. Duseja, S. 2022. *The Man Who Froze Fire*. Garuda, pp. 36–7.
4. Duseja, S. 2022, pp. 108–9.

Bibliography

This bibliography mainly provides a survey of books, book chapters, scientific articles, papers, and websites which are referred to more than once. References to newspaper and online articles are as a rule mentioned in the footnotes

Abu-Nimer, M. (Ed.). 2001. *Reconciliation, Justice and Coexistence: Theory and Practice*. Oxford: Lexington Books.

Allen, S. 2022. *Interactive Peacemaking: A People-Centered Approach*. New York, NY: Routledge.

Appleby, R. S. 2000. *The Ambivalence of the Sacred: Religion, Violence and Reconciliation*. New York: Rowman & Littlefield Publishers.

Art of Living. 2007. 'Rebuilding war Torn Kosovo: Art of living report'.

Art of Living. 2008. *The Voice of Nonviolence*. Bangalore: Sri Sri Publications Trust

Art of Living. 2013. *The Voice of Non-Violence*. Volume Two. Bangalore: Sri Sri Publications Trust

Art of Living. 2021. *Impact Report 2018–2020*. https://www.artofliving.org/sites/www.artofliving.org/files/wysiwyg_imageupload/India-Impact-Report-2021.pdf.

Bar Tal, D. 2011. *Intergroup Conflicts and Their Resolution: A Social Psychological Perspective*. New York: Psychology Press.

Bar Tal, D. 2013. *Intractable Conflicts: Socio-Psychological Foundations and Dynamics*. Cambridge: Cambridge University Press.

Blumberg, H. H., Hare, A. P., & Costin, A. 2006. *Peace Psychology: A Comprehensive Introduction*. New York: Cambridge University Press.

Bramsen, I., & Poder, P. 2018. 'Emotional dynamics in conflict and conflict transformation'. Berghof Foundation.

Curle, A. 1981. *True Justice: Quaker Peace Makers and Peace Making*. London: Quaker Home Service.

Descillo, T., et al. 2010. 'Effects of a yoga breath intervention alone and in combination with an exposure therapy for post-traumatic stress disorder and depression in survivors of the 2004 South-East Asia tsunami'. *Acta Psychiatrica Scandinavica* 121:4, pp. 289–300.

Deutsch, M. 2012. *The Psychological Components of Sustainable Peace*. New York: Springer.

Deutsch, M., Coleman, P. T., & Marcus, E. C. (Eds.). 2006. *The Handbook of Conflict Resolution: Theory and Practice*. San Francisco: Jossey-Bass.

Duseja, S. 2022. *The Man Who Froze Fire*. Delhi (Central Delhi), India: Garuda Prakashan Pvt. Ltd.

Fitzduff, M. 2021. *Our Brains at War: The Neuroscience of Conflict and Peacebuilding*. New York, NY: Oxford University Press.

Ghahremani, D. G., et al. 2013. 'Effects of the youth empowerment seminar on impulsive behavior in adolescents'. *Journal of Adolescent Health* 53:1, pp. 139–41. doi: 10.1016/j.jadohealth.2013.02.010. PMID: 23601502.

Ginty, R. Mac. 2011. *International Peacebuilding and Local Resistance: Hybrid Forms of Peace*. Basingstoke: Palgrave Macmillan.

Ginty, R. Mac, & Richmond, O. P. 2013. 'The local turn in peace building: A critical agenda for peace'. *Third World Quarterly* 34:5, pp. 763–83. doi:10.1080/01436597.2013.800750.

Goldstein, M. R., Lewin, R. K., & Allen, J. J. B. 2020. 'Improvements in well-being and cardiac metrics of stress following a yogic breathing workshop: Randomized controlled trial with active comparison'. *Journal of American College Health* 70:3, pp. 918–28. https://doi.org/10.1080/07448481.2020.1781867.

Gopin, M. 2000. *Between Eden and Armageddon: Essays on the Future of Religion, Violence and Peacemaking*. New York: Oxford University Press.

Gopin, M. 2004. *Healing the Heart of Conflict: 8 Crucial Steps to Making Peace with Yourself and Others*. s.l.: Rodale.

Hamber, B. 2021. 'The nexus between peacebuilding and mental health and psychosocial support'. Paper presented at the UN Peacebuilding Commission Expert-level Meeting, 3 December 2021.

Hamber, B., & Gallagher, E. 2015. *Psychosocial Perspectives on Peacebuilding*. New York: Springer.

Hertog, K. 2010. *The Complex Reality of Religious Peacebuilding: Conceptual Contributions and Critical Analysis*. Lanham, MD: Rowman & Littlefield.

Hertog, K. 2017. 'The intrinsic interlinkage between peacebuilding and mental health and psychosocial support: The International Association for Human Values model of integrated psychosocial peacebuilding'. *Intervention* 15:3, pp. 278–92.

Hertog, K. 2019. 'Towards integrated peacebuilding: Comprehensively integrating psychosocial factors in peacebuilding trainings and programmes for increased impact'. *Journal of Peacebuilding & Development* 14:3, pp. 333–9. https://doi.org/10.1177/1542316619862766.

Hertog, K. 2024. 'Integrating mental health and psychosocial support (MHPSS) and peacebuilding: A critical and constructive perspective from the integrated field of psychosocial peacebuilding'. *Peace and Conflict: Journal of Peace Psychology*. https://doi.org/10.1037/pac0000773.

Huser, K. s.a. 'Integrating mental health & Psycho-social support in peace-building programming: Conceptual framework for Norwegian Church aid'. s.l.

Institute for Justice and Reconciliation and the War Trauma Foundation. 2017. 'Peacebuilding and mental health and psychosocial support: A review of current theory and practice'.

Inter-Agency Standing Committee (IASC). 2007. 'Guidelines on mental health and psychosocial support in emergency settings'.

Inter-Agency Standing Committee (IASC). 2024. 'IASC guidance integrating MHPSS and peacebuilding: A mapping and recommendations for practitioners'. https://interagencystandingcommittee.org/iasc-reference-group-mental-health-and-psychosocial-support-emergency-settings/iasc-guidance-integrating-mhpss-and-peacebuilding-mapping-and-recommendations-practitioners.

International Association for Human Values (IAHV). 2020. 'Healing, nonviolent empowerment and preventing extremism. Final Project Report'. https://www.iahv-peace.org/jordan_lebanon/about-this-project/.

International Association for Human Values (IAHV). 'Beyond violent extremism'. Presentation Brochure. https://iahv-peace.org/wp-content/uploads/2016/11/IAHV-Beyond-Violent-Extremism-and-Armed-Conflict.pdf.

Jeong, H. W. 2005. *Peacebuilding in Postconflict Societies*. London: Lynne Rienner.

Johnston, D., & Sampson, C. (Eds.). 1994. *Religion: The Missing Dimension of Statecraft*. New York: Oxford University Press.

Kelman, H. C. 1990. 'Interactive problem-solving: A social-psychological approach to conflict resolution'. In Burton, J., & Dukes, F. (Eds.), *Conflict: Readings in Management and Resolution*. The Conflict Series. London: Palgrave Macmillan, pp. 201–45. https://doi.org/10.1007/978-1-349-21003-9_11.

Kelman, H. C. 1997. 'Social-psychological dimensions of international conflict'. In Zartman, W., & Rasmussen, J. L. (Eds.), *Peacemaking in International Conflict: Methods and Techniques*. Washington: USIP Press.

Kelman, H. C. 2008. 'A social-psychological approach to conflict analysis and resolution'. In Sandole, D., Byrne, S., Sandole-Staroste, I., & Senehi, J. (Eds.), *Handbook of Conflict Analysis and Resolution*. London: Routledge [Taylor & Francis], pp. 170–83.

Kjellgren, A., et al. 2007. 'Wellness through a comprehensive yogic breathing program – A controlled pilot trial'. *BMC Complementary & Alternative Medicine* 7, p. 43.

Kumar, S. 2023. *Militancy to Meditation*. Bangalore: Sri Sri Publications Trust.

Lederach, J. P. 1997. *Building Peace: Sustainable Reconciliation in Divided Societies*. Washington: USIP Press.

Lederach, J. P. 2005. *The Moral Imagination: The Art and Soul of Building Peace*. New York: Oxford University Press.

Lederach, J. P., & Sampson, C. (Ed.). 2000. *From the Ground Up: Mennonite Contributions to International Peacebuilding*. New York: Oxford University Press.

Levine, P. A., & Kline, M. 2006. *Trauma Through a Child's Eyes: Awakening the Ordinary Miracle of Healing*. Berkeley, CA: North Atlantic Books.

Lund, J. 2017. 'Survival mechanisms that become life threatening'. In Hviid, S. (Ed.), *Traumebehandling og Resocialisering*. Aarhus: Turbine Akademisk.

McConnell, J. A. 1995. *Mindful Mediation: A Handbook for Buddhist Peacemakers*. Thailand: Buddhist Research Institute & Mahachula Buddhist University.

Neagoe, L. 2023. 'Psycho-sociological aspects of education in the 21st century'. In Soare, E. & Langa, C. (Eds.), 2022. *Education Facing Contemporary World Issues – EDU WORLD 2022, Vol 5. European Proceedings of Educational Sciences*. European Publisher, pp. 387–97. https://doi.org/10.15405/epes.23045.40.

Nestor, J. 2020. *Breath: The New Science of a Lost Art*. New York, NY: Riverhead Books.

Neuroscience and Peacebuilding Initiative. 2015. https://www.neuropeace.org/volumes.

Newman, R. I., Yim, O., & Stewart, M. C. 2024. 'Breathing life into social emotional learning programs: A Bio-Psycho-Social approach to risk reduction and positive youth development'. *Journal of Adolescence* 96, pp. 1065–77. https://doi.org/10.1002/jad.12317.

Njoku, M. G., Jason, L. A., & Johnson, R. B. (Eds.). 2019. *The Psychology of Peace Promotion: Global Perspectives on Personal Peace, Children and Adolescents, and Social Justice*. Cham: Springer.

Porges, S. W. 2001. *The Polyvagal Theory: Neurophysiological Foundations of Emotions, Attachment, Communication, and Self-Regulation*. New York: Norton.

Rausch, C. (Ed.). May 2021. *Neuroscience and Peacebuilding*. Neuropeace Vol. 3. Fairfax, VA: Mary Hoch Center for Reconciliation, Jimmy & Rosalynn Carter School for Peace and Conflict Resolution, George Mason University.

Rausch, C. (Ed.). 2021. *Exploring the Neurobiological Dimensions of Violent Conflict and the Peacebuilding Potential of Neuroscientific Discoveries*. Arlington, VA: Mary Hoch Center for Reconciliation.

Reychler, L., & Langer, A. 2006. *Researching Peace Building Architecture*. Cahiers Internationale Betrekkingen en Vredesonderzoek Vol. 75. Leuven, Belgium: Center for Peace Research and Strategic Studies.

Seppälä, E. M., et al. 2014. 'Breathing-based meditation decreases posttraumatic stress disorder symptoms in US military veterans: A randomized controlled longitudinal study'. *Journal of Traumatic Stress* 27:4, pp. 397–405.

Seppälä, E. M., Bradley, C., Moeller, J., Harouni, L., Nandamudi, D., & Brackett, M. A. 2020. 'Promoting mental health and psychological thriving in university students: A randomized controlled trial of three well-being interventions'. *Front Psychiatry* 11, p. 590. doi: 10.3389/fpsyt.2020.00590.

Sharma, H., et al. 2008. 'Gene expression profiling in practitioners of Sudarshan Kriya'. *Journal of Psychosomatic Research* 64:2, pp. 213–18.

Swami Virupaksha. 2002. *The Tiger's Pause: The Untold Story of Gurudev Sri Sri Ravi Shankar's Peace Efforts in Sri Lanka*. New Delhi, India: Penguin Random House India.

Travouillon, K. 2021. 'Emotions and post-liberal peacebuilding'. In Jeong, H. W. (Ed.), *Transitions to Peace. Between Norms and Practice*. Lanham, MD: Rowman & Littlefield Publishers, pp. 51–70.

UNDP. 2022. 'Integrating mental health and psychosocial support into peacebuilding: Guidance note'. https://www.undp.org/publications/integrating-mental-health-and-psychosocial-support-peacebuilding.

UNDP. 2022. 'Integrating mental health and psychosocial support into peacebuilding: Research findings: Summary report'. NY: UNDP. https://www.undp.org/sites/g/files/zskgke326/files/2022-05/UNDP-Integrating-Mental-Health-and-Psychosocial-Support-into-Peacebuilding-Summary-Report-V2.pdf.

United Religions Initiative. 2004. *Interfaith Peacebuilding Guide*. s.l.

Van der Kolk, B. A. 2014. *The Body Keeps the Score: Brain, Mind, and Body in the Healing of Trauma*. New York, NY: Viking

Vedamurthachar, A., et al. 2006. 'Antidepressant efficacy and hormonal effects of Sudarshana Kriya Yoga (SKY) in alcohol dependent individuals'. *Journal of Affective Disorders* 94:1, pp. 249–53.

Velez, G., & Gavrielides, T. 2022. *Restorative Justice: Promoting Peace and Wellbeing*. Cham: Springer Cham.

Volkan, V. D. 1988. *The Need to Have Enemies and Allies: From Clinical Practice to International Relationships*. Northvale, NJ: Jason Aronson.

Volkan, V. D. 2004. *Blind Trust: Large Groups and Their Leaders in Times of Crisis and Terror*. Charlottesville, VA: Pitchstone Publishing.

Volkan, V. D. 2006. *Killing in the Name of Identity: A Study of Bloody Conflicts*. Charlottesville, VA: Pitchstone Publishing.

Volkan, V. D. 2020. *Large-Group Psychology: Racism, Societal Divisions, Narcissistic Leaders and Who We Are Now*. Oxfordshire (UK): Phoenix Publishing House Ltd.

Wilber, K. 2000. *Integral Psychology: Consciousness, Spirit, Psychology, Therapy*. Boston, MA: Shambhala Publications.

Wilber, K. 2006. *Integral Spirituality: A Startling New Role for Religion in the Modern and Postmodern World*. Boston, MA: Shambhala Publications.

Index

active nonviolence; *see* nonviolence
aggression   79, 84, 186–7, 194
anxiety   83
armed groups   32–6, 77, 80, 252, 259–66
Art of Living; *see also* IAHV
assumptions in project design   306–7

Bar-Tal, Daniel   8, 13, 40–2, 171, 209–10, 214–22, 233
behavioral science   10
Belgium   xxii, xxv, xxviii, 198, 254–5
Brand-Jacobsen, Kai   xvi–xx, 146
breath   159, 162–5, 167, 179, 191; *see also* Nestor, James, Sudarshan Kriya
Buddhist peacebuilding   55–6
bullying   98–9
burn-out   82–3, 151, 284–5; *see also* stress

capacity building for peaceworkers and organizations; *see* PSPB Training
children, war affected/vulnerable/at-risk   97–139
    juvenile institution and orphanage   79, 107–8, 125–6
climate change; *see* environment
Colombia, Farc   32–5, 78, 253–4
consciousness   315, 319–20
conflict   209–37
    definition   17, 210
    ethnic   5
    interpersonal and intergroup   113–14, 174–5, 209–37
    polarization/repertoire/infrastructure   215–26
    styles   210–12
corporate sector, TLEX   273
Culture of War/Culture of Peace   5, 75–6, 218–26, 233–5

Disarmament, Demobilization, and Reintegration (DDR); *see* reintegration of ex-combatants
depression   15, 83, 258, 272
DNA   38, 85
drugs   190, 192, 278

early marriage   99–100
economy and development, psychosocial factors in   270
education   275–82
    peace education   12, 276
    SKY campus   282
    SKY schools   79, 278–81
ego; *see* identity
emotions   10, 145, 167, 178–80, 187–8, 191–4, 216–17, 220–1, 225, 228–9, 286
    emotional regulation   83, 164, 179, 212, 280
empathy; *see* emotions
empowerment   77, 114–16, 181–2
energy   152–3, 172
environment   286–8

FARC; *see* Colombia

gangs   78, 256–7
governance and politics, psychosocial factors in   266–8
Gurudev Sri Sri Ravi Shankar   68, 315, 319–20
    peace interventions   xxvii, 32–5, 76, 178, 260, 262, 269, 316–17
    quotes and wisdom   v, 27, 67, 143, 147, 149, 162, 169, 176–7, 182–4, 213, 222, 224, 226, 228, 250, 277, 279

health/health sector   161–5, 282–5
human values; *see* IAHV universal human values

identity   173–6, 189, 192, 215–17, 220, 224, 228
India
   Assam, UFLA, UPLA   147–8, 259–63
   Ayodhya   316–17
   Bihar, Maoists   264–5, 317
   farmers   272, 286
   Kashmir   42–3, 230, 318
   Naxalites   263–4
   schools   281–2
   village councils   268
Integrated peacebuilding; see Psychosocial peacebuilding
intellect   169–71, 221
Inter–Agency Standing Committee (IASC)   44–5
International Association for Human Values (IAHV)   xxvi, 67–8
   case study PSPB   97–139
   conceptual model integrated peacebuilding   xxvi–xxvii, 69–87
   interpersonal   74–5, 113–14, 209–37
   intrapersonal   70–2, 111–13, 143–203
   structural and systemic change   72–4, 116–17, 241–93
   Healing, Resilience and Empowerment program   104, 131–2, 195–201, 251
   peacebuilding impact   77–80, 135–8
   programs   xxii, 80, 101–5, 123–33, 191, 196, 249–52, 273, 278–82, 311–12
   Theory of Change   69–70, 118, 306–7
   training of trainers   104–5, 115, 133
   universal human values   67, 75–6, 123, 147, 220–2, 244–5
   violent extremism   244–66
   Youth Peace Ambassadors   97–101, 103, 115, 121, 127–31, 231–3, 249–50, 265, 272
Iraq   250, 252–3, 258, 269, 271
Ivory Coast   230–3

Jordan   100–1, 106–8, 126–8, 133
justice, psychosocial factors in   274–5
   restorative justice   12, 227, 274

Kenya, Wajir   223–4
Kosovo   159, 255, 258–9

leadership, peacebuilding   288–9
Lebanon   31–2, 97–139, 198
Lederach, John Paul   5, 6, 18, 57, 222

meditation   167–8
memory   171–3, 190, 219–20, 226
Mennonite peacebuilding   56–7
mental health   15, 48, 80, 83–4, 107, 110, 199, 278, 283–4; see also depression, stress, trauma
Mental Health and Psychosocial Support (MHPSS)   15–16, 44–51
mind
   perception, observation, expression   165–8, 212–13
   self-awareness   168, 179–81, 183, 191–4, 212–13, 277
Mir, Ufra   42–3

Nestor, James   162–5
neuroscience   12, 84–6, 154–60, 185–95, 280
   autonomous nervous system   85–6, 163, 185–95
nonviolence   5, 182–3, 217–18, 247
non–violent communication   213

Palestine/Israel   39, 198, 224
Panama   256–7
pandemic, Covid 19   284–5
peace definition   18
peace, inner   51–3, 176–7, 180
peace studies and theory   3–18, 144–5
   human–centered   4, 7–9, 119
   liberal peacebuilding model   4
   local peacebuilding   10
peacebuilding definition   18
Philippines, Mindanao   265–6
police training   80, 82, 255
politics; see governance

Prison Program Art of Living/IAHV   xxii–xxv, 78, 79, 184, 191–5, 252, 319
professional care; *see* self-care
project cycle and design   299–309
psychology (peace, social)   8, 10
Psychosocial Peacebuilding (PSPB)   xvi–xx, xxv–xxvii, xxix, 9–17, 25–40, 47–51
   case study IAHV   97–138
   definition   18, 25–8
   development   9–17
   IAHV's Integrated Psychosocial Peacebuilding approach   xxvi–xxvii, 69–87
   inner integration   143–203
   interpersonal   209–37
   psychosocial factors in peacebuilding   28–9, 36–7, 118, 143–203, 209–37, 241–93, 300
   structural and systemic change   241–93
   training   95–6, 144–53, 311–13

Quaker peacebuilding   58, 267–8

reconciliation   4, 226–33
rehabilitation of offenders   xxiii–xxv, 79, 184–95, 228
reintegration of ex-combatants (DDR)   77, 80, 248–51, 259–66
religious peacebuilding   xi, 12, 52
resilience   184, 222, 243
river rejuvenation; *see* environment

security sector   12, 242–66
Self   176–8

self-care   xxvii, 104, 110, 132, 144–53, 285
spiritual approaches to peacebuilding   51–9
Sri Lanka, Tamil Tigers   252
stories and testimonials   xxviii, 29–35, 97–101, 108, 110–16, 120–33, 136, 147–9, 152, 159, 173, 175, 177, 180, 184, 186–7, 192–4, 197–201, 231–3, 250–64, 269–72, 281, 317–19
stress   82–3, 101, 149–52, 215, 283
Sudarshan Kriya/SKY technique   xxii, 30, 82–7, 110, 148, 159, 176, 192, 262, 280
   research   79–85, 280–2, 285
Syria   31–2, 97–139
systems and structures   72–4, 241–90

trauma/PTSD   83, 153–60
   Adverse Childhood Experiences (ACE)   184–90
   transgenerational   37–40, 219
   trauma–relief   4, 77, 103, 157–60, 191–5, 195–201, 257–9

Ukraine   199–200, 253
UN Development Goals   15, 68

veterans of war   257–9
violence   14, 17, 36–7, 128, 182, 219; *see also* aggression
violent extremism and its prevention   243–66

women empowerment   271
World Health Organization (WHO)   15, 47, 150, 199, 270, 285

About the author

Katrien Hertog is a peacebuilding researcher, trainer and practitioner with twenty-five years of experience in the academic and non-governmental sector.

In her capacity as Director of Peacebuilding Programmes for IAHV, as well as a researcher, she has been pioneering the practice of psychosocial peacebuilding (PSPB) for more impactful peacebuilding practice and advocating for its integration in international peacebuilding policy and practice. She develops, implements and advocates for PSPB programmes on preventing and transforming violent extremism, trauma-relief to break the cycles of violence, strengthening mediation and reconciliation processes and training peacebuilding personnel.

She has an MA in peace studies from the University of Bradford and a PhD from the Centre for Peace Research at the University of Leuven. As a trainer in peacebuilding, rehabilitation, stress management and capacity development, she has trained 2,500+ individuals, including prisoners, refugees, security forces, frontline workers, NGO staff and personnel from international and public-sector institutions across the Middle East, North Caucasus and Europe.

In addition to leading the Art of Living Prison Programme in Europe – renowned for its innovative approach to rehabilitation – she coordinates IAHV's refugee programmes in Europe and the Middle East, which have reached over 25,000 beneficiaries. She also directs large-scale, EU-funded peacebuilding and resilience initiatives in conflict-affected regions.

Dr Hertog is the author of the internationally recognized volume *The Complex Reality of Religious Peacebuilding: Conceptual Contributions and Critical Analysis*, a foundational text in the field of religious peacebuilding.

www.ingramcontent.com/pod-product-compliance
Lightning Source LLC
Chambersburg PA
CBHW080726300426
44114CB00019B/2497